THE LOOM OF TIME

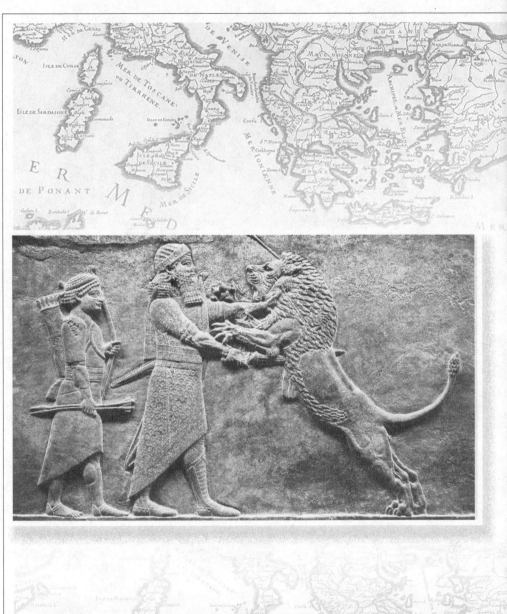

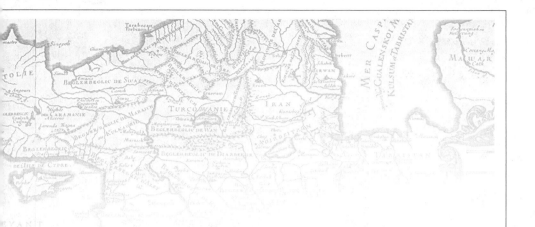

The LOOM of TIME

BETWEEN
EMPIRE AND ANARCHY,
FROM THE
MEDITERRANEAN TO CHINA

ROBERT D. KAPLAN

RANDOM HOUSE

NEW YORK

Published in the United States by Random House,
an imprint and division of
Penguin Random House LLC, New York.

RANDOM HOUSE and the HOUSE colophon are
registered trademarks of Penguin Random House LLC.

LIBRARY OF CONGRESS CATALOGING-IN-PUBLICATION DATA
NAMES: Kaplan, Robert D., author.
TITLE: The loom of time: between empire and anarchy from the
Mediterranean to China / Robert D. Kaplan.
DESCRIPTION: New York: Random House, [2023] |
Includes bibliographical references and index.
IDENTIFIERS: LCCN 2023001473 (print) | LCCN 2023001474 (ebook) |
ISBN 9780593242797 (hardcover) | ISBN 9780593242803 (ebook)
SUBJECTS: LCSH: Imperialism. | Middle East—Politics and government. |
Asia, Central—Politics and government.
CLASSIFICATION: LCC DS62.4 .K28 2023 (print) |
LCC DS62.4 (ebook) | DDC 327.56058—dc23/eng/20230414
LC record available at https://lccn.loc.gov/2023001473
LC ebook record available at https://lccn.loc.gov/2023001474

Printed in Canada on acid-free paper

randomhousebooks.com

2 4 6 8 9 7 5 3 1

FIRST EDITION

Title-page art: Adobe Stock

Book design by Barbara M. Bachman

To Robert L. Freedman

THE FACT IS that we can obtain no more than an impression of a whole from a part, but certainly neither a thorough knowledge nor an accurate understanding. We must conclude then that specialized studies or monographs contribute very little to our grasp of the whole and our conviction of its truth. On the contrary, it is only by combining and comparing the various parts of the whole with one another and noting their resemblances and their differences that we shall arrive at a comprehensive view, and thus encompass both the practical benefits and the pleasures that the reading of history affords.

POLYBIUS, *THE RISE OF THE ROMAN EMPIRE*
TRANSLATION BY IAN SCOTT-KILVERT

RAGE AND PHRENSY will pull down more in half an hour, than prudence, deliberation, and foresight can build up in a hundred years.

EDMUND BURKE, *REFLECTIONS ON*
THE REVOLUTION IN FRANCE (1790)

CONTENTS

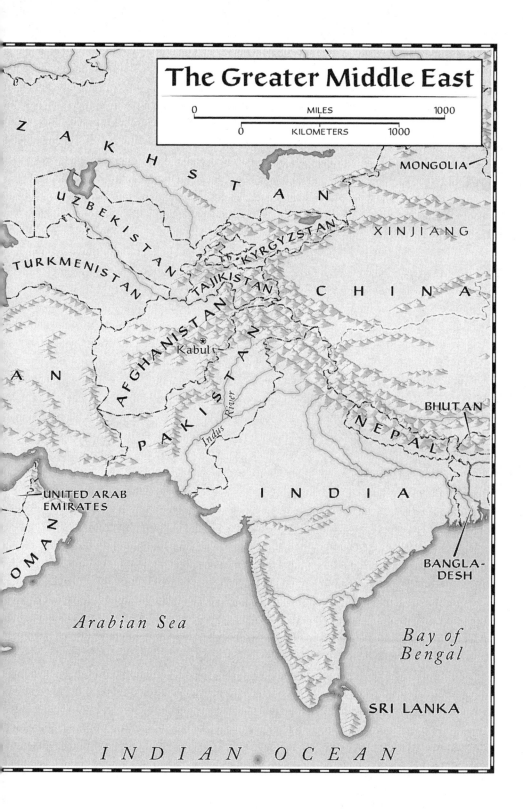

The Greater Middle East

MILES
0   1000

KILOMETERS
0   1000

KAZAKHSTAN

MONGOLIA

UZBEKISTAN

TURKMENISTAN

KYRGYZSTAN

TAJIKISTAN

XINJIANG

CHINA

AFGHANISTAN

Kabul

PAKISTAN

Indus River

NEPAL

BHUTAN

IRAN

UNITED ARAB
EMIRATES

OMAN

INDIA

BANGLA-
DESH

Arabian Sea

Bay of
Bengal

SRI LANKA

INDIAN OCEAN

PROLOGUE

—

CHINA IN THE AFTERLIFE
OF EMPIRE

*I*n the spring of 1994, I first traveled through China's Xinjiang Province, *a region inhabited by 11 million Turkic Uighur Muslims who, as I learned from interview after interview, were even then trapped in a grip of surveillance and brutal repression by the Chinese authorities. To the Uighurs, as well as to geographers and ethnographers, this western outpost of China was historically East Turkestan: the easternmost extension of the deserts and steppe lands of the Greater Middle East. China gained control over East Turkestan only in the mid-eighteenth century, even though a Chinese imperial state has existed for 3,500 years. To the Chinese, these Muslims have always represented a dangerous, inchoate force more numerous and harder to absorb than the Tibetans even.*

In the town of Kashgar, hard up against China's borders with Kyrgyzstan, Tajikistan, Afghanistan, and Pakistan, 90 percent of the population of 300,000 in 1994 were Uighur Turks. Old bicycles, motorized rickshaws, and donkeys laden with produce and firewood crowded the streets. Decaying wooden stalls served up fatty meat and mare's milk. The men wore flat caps and mud-stained sport coats. A greater percentage of women were wearing cloaks and veils than in Iran, from where I had just come. The Uighur Turks had never been influenced by Byzantium or proximity to the Mediterranean like the Turks of Anatolia, and their unique culture was then in the early process of being ground down by the Beijing Communists' relentless threshing machine. Back then, in the mid-1990s, an editor had suggested that my interest in the Uighurs was testing the limits of obscurantism. It would take a quarter century for the Uighurs to make it into world news headlines.

As I learned during another visit to Xinjiang in 2015—still a few years before the region did, in fact, make it into world headlines—the intimate chaos of the Sunday livestock market in Kashgar had been moved to a vast rectangular space miles away, where it was no longer integrated into the life of the town. By then Kashgar had changed beyond recognition into a grid-work of grim apartment blocks, as part of a plan to regiment the daily life of the inhabitants. This cultural sterilization preceded the movement of up to a million Uighurs into penal camps, where they were to be exploited as slave labor. It was the largest incarceration of a religious minority since World War II, according to The Wall Street Journal.[1]

The backdrop for this repression was China's $1 trillion Belt and Road Initiative, featuring a postmodern transportation network of highways, railways, and energy pipelines linking China by land and sea with Europe across the Greater Middle East. Xinjiang, the homeland of the Uighur Turks, had become a key nodal point in this twenty-first-century Silk Route, with roads and pipelines going west to Iran and beyond, and south to the Arabian Sea near the Persian Gulf. The Chinese state could not afford to tolerate even the potential for Muslim separatism inside its own borders at this junction where Belt and Road joins Han China with Muslim Central Asia.

Indeed, all that stands in the way of defining China's relationship with the Uighur Turks as outright colonial is Xinjiang's location: though a frontier province, it still exists within China's legal borders. Yet, in a spiritual sense, China's treatment of its Muslim minority, integrated as it is with the perceived requirements of Belt and Road, is the closest one gets to traditional nineteenth-century imperialism in the twenty-first century. In fact, something worse may have been happening, with its forced assimilation and colonial settlement by ethnic Hans.

Belt and Road, along with the persecution of the Muslim Uighurs, is all about the Greater Middle East, where China has been equally aggressive at sea and on land. In the spring of 2009, I spent a night in jail in Hambantota, Sri Lanka, after trespassing on a construction site in order to observe hundreds of Chinese workers relocating vast amounts of soil in order to lit-erally move the coast inland. This was part of the process of building a state-of-the-art port for the transshipment of Chinese goods to the Arabian Peninsula and beyond. A year before that, I had obtained a permit to visit the new Chinese-built port of Gwadar, located at a point where the south-western tip of Pakistan meets Iran and the Gulf of Oman. I had crossed hundreds of miles of the bleak Baluchistan desert in order to see Gwadar's neat and glittering steel angles, spanking-new gantry cranes, and other cargo-handling equipment. According to the vision of planners in Beijing, oil and gas will be shipped from the Persian Gulf to nearby Gwadar, then be transported overland by pipeline north through Pakistan into Xinjiang Province. With China having built a large military base in Djibouti at the mouth of the Red Sea, and contemplating others further north along the Red Sea at Port Sudan and at Jiwani by the Pakistan-Iran border near Gwa-dar, it is a great age in history to be a Chinese civil engineer.

The Chinese map of the Greater Middle East, which encompasses much more than the Arab world—but includes the vast expanse of the subtropical earth between Europe and China itself—has two critical knots: Pakistan and Iran. The energy corridor from Kashgar in western China south through Pakistan to Gwadar on the Arabian Sea will link the land and maritime Silk Routes, while the China-Iran strategic alliance will make China the leading economic and political partner of a country that—as feared as it has been by almost two generations of Americans on account of terrorism and radical politics—is the geographical organizing principle of both the Middle East and Central Asia.

Empire may be dead, because in a globalized world one culture cannot simply appropriate and subjugate other cultures for its own ends. But the imperial mindset is experiencing a disturbing afterlife, as the example of China in the Greater Middle East demonstrates. Whereas the British East India Company in the early modern era advanced eastward from Europe across the Middle East to China, China is now advancing in the opposite geographical direction westward, though with similar commercial and strategic motives.

And as the Americans have tried unsuccessfully to turn away from the Greater Middle East, it isn't only the Chinese who have been moving in, seeking energy resources, influence over navigational choke points, and local proxies. The Russians have been militarily involved in Syria and Libya, as are the Turks, even as the Iranians run a network of local armies and militias all the way from Iran westward to the Mediterranean, and to the south in Yemen as well. All these countries, it should be said, have long-standing imperial traditions to draw upon, and thus feel themselves to be on a mission. For it isn't only the Chinese, but especially the Iranians and Turks, who look proudly on their imperial pasts. Western imperialism may be looked down upon, but not so the record of indigenous empires.

The Greater Middle East is the fight zone for these ghost empires: the vast puzzle piece that China needs to command, if it can link its budding commercial outposts in Europe with those in East Asia. Here states are often weak and in key places nonexistent, and democracy has generally failed, at least so far. Local autocracies, meanwhile, while vibrant in the Arabian Peninsula, are exhausted elsewhere in the region. Even political Islam is beginning to suffer a distinct loss of enthusiasm, as we know from the case of Iran. Thus, outside powers cannot resist the temptation.

It is time to explore further this harsh geography that will be a register of future great-power struggles across the globe, as it always has been in the past. And like in the past, thousands of years of imperial rule will continue to cast a long shadow on politics as it is practiced today, in a region where stability remains a prized commodity.

THE LOOM OF TIME

TIME AND TERRAIN

═══

Bᴇᴛᴡᴇᴇɴ ᴇᴜʀᴏᴘᴇ ᴀɴᴅ ᴛʜᴇ ɢʀᴇᴀᴛ, ᴍᴀᴛᴜʀᴇ ᴄɪᴠɪʟɪᴢᴀᴛɪᴏɴꜱ of China and India lies a belt of over three thousand miles, dominated by desert and stony tableland, where rainfall is relatively little, frontiers are contested, political unity has rarely existed, and where, as the late Princeton historian Bernard Lewis claimed, there has been no historical pattern of authority.[1] Lewis's generalization is imperfect, to be sure. Egypt and Iran, it could well be argued, were mature civilizations for thousands of years, as were Iraq and Turkey. Nevertheless, there is a point to be made regarding the general aridity, sheer variety, and political tumult in the lands between the Mediterranean and China. It is this austere landscape that constitutes the "Land of Insolence," declared mid-twentieth-century American anthropologist Carleton Coon, referring to the rebellious nature of modern Middle Eastern politics, with its tradition of pride and independence that combines with tribalism and ethnic and sectarian tensions.* Coon's phraseology

---

* Carleton S. Coon, *Caravan: The Story of the Middle East* (New York: Henry Holt and Company, 1954), p. 295. Coon's book, with its antiquated style, reads like something out of Herodotus compared to contemporary books on the Middle East. Moreover, Coon's field of racial anthropology has long been discredited. Nevertheless, *Caravan* is full of keen perceptions about the region. It was a book that State Department Arabists of the late twentieth century cut their teeth on. I profiled Coon and his son, Carleton Coon, Jr., a diplomat and area specialist in his own right, in my book *The Arabists: The Romance of an American Elite* (New York: The Free Press, 1993), pp. 103–07. Regarding the racial theories of Coon senior,

is especially quaint and deterministic, particularly since tribalism has kept the peace within large groups, and in other ways is not the altogether divisive factor the West thinks it is. Nevertheless, Coon's phrase has an undeniable resonance, owing to the indisputably high level of violence and political instability in this yawning region compared to other parts of the globe. For example, a significant part of the population of the Arab world has experienced violent anarchy in recent decades, and according to a U.N. report, though Arabs account for only 5 percent of humanity, they have generated 58 percent of the world's refugees and 68 percent of its "battle-related deaths" in the second decade of the twenty-first century.* Indeed, the maturation from medieval kingdoms to early modern states, and then to modern democratic states, as happened in Europe, or of the successive, millennia-long drumroll of elaborate dynastic empires as in China and the Indian subcontinent—places with lusher, more habitable landscapes—do not obtain to the same degree in the vast and thin-soiled battlefield of different cultures and civilizations that sweeps across the southern rimland of Eurasia, too often disunited by a singular religion rather than united by it. Keep in mind, however, that the tragedy of the Greater Middle East ever since the collapse of the Ottoman Empire has as much to do with the West's dynamic interaction with it as with the region itself, as we shall see later on.

But first, back to the essentials.

THE VERY QUESTION OF political authority—of *who* controls *whom*—has often been unsettled across the Middle East. Islam, re-

---

see Pat Shipman's *The Evolution of Racism: Human Differences and the Use and Abuse of Science* (New York: Simon & Schuster, 1994), pp. 170–221.

* Tim Mackintosh-Smith, *Arabs: A 3,000-Year History of Peoples, Tribes, and Empires* (New Haven, CT: Yale University Press, 2019), pp. xiii and 96. Only some of this can be blamed on the American-led invasion of Iraq in 2003. Yale University historian Samuel Moyn reports that the estimated 200,000 Iraqi fatalities died mainly from civil war and disorder rather than specifically because of American military action. The figures on refugees are before the Russian invasion of Ukraine. *Humane: How the United States Abandoned Peace and Reinvented War* (New York: Farrar, Straus and Giroux, 2021), p. 5.

vealed by the Prophet Muhammad, a trader in the richly cosmopolitan crossroads of Mecca at the beginning of the seventh century A.D., was concerned with ethics and how to live a pure and just life against the demanding limitations of a desert landscape, where the environment was treacherous and travel consequently difficult. Here aridity had created oases that served as "juncture points" across the desert, spurring trade, and thus Islam was a boon to honest-dealing.[2] Though the new religion offered a complete way of existence that spanned civilizations and over the centuries made millions of impoverished people content with their lives,[3] as Coon was one of the first outsiders to observe, it left no sturdy provision for temporal political authority. That is to say, whereas other religions, such as Christianity, did not seek control over politics, but generally limited themselves to private belief, Islam offered a complete way of existence. Olivier Roy, the French academic and political scientist, writes that "Islam was born as a sect and as a society," but without institutions or even a clergy to organize it.[4] Indeed, the great linguist and area specialist of the Sorbonne, the late Maxime Rodinson, called Islam "not only an association of believers," but a "total society."[5] And as a total society—encompassing the heretofore secular world—Islam required but often crucially lacked, as Roy puts it, a philosophy of political organization.

Because Muhammad offered an utterly new and purer interpretation of existence that would replace the previous social contract, he was naturally met with opposition. When he and his followers left Mecca because of its hostility to the new creed and fled northward to Yathrib (Medina, "the city"), they essentially founded a new community. Significantly, the Islamic calendar begins not with Muhammad's birth or even with the beginning of his revelation, but with this migration, or *Hegira*. This new community was for all intents and purposes revolutionary. And in the Arab and Islamic worlds it would consequently breed over the centuries and millennia dynastic upheavals and other revolutions having to do with sect, ambition, legitimacy, and purity. The very rise and fall of dynastic empires across the Middle East, and the political dramas within them, often had to do with the intersection of religion and politics. Sayyid Qutb, the Egyptian intellectual

and Muslim Brotherhood leader, famously used this argument to attack the impure, pagan (*kafir*) system of Gamal Abdel Nasser, who
would have Qutb executed by hanging in 1966.[6]

Ever since the first half century of Islam's founding, authority has
been disputed and struggles have ensued over the leadership of the
faith, with Sunnis, Ibadis, and Shi'ites—and the various offshoots of
Shi'ism such as Zaidis, Isma'ilis, Alawites, Druzes, and so on—all
maintaining different theories of spiritual governance, in a way not so
dissimilar to Christianity.* Political legitimacy was very difficult to
come by.[7] This became true not only at the state level, but at the level
of the town and tribe, and within tribes, so that many a place was divided between "Arabian Montagues and Capulets," in the words of the
Oxford-trained Arabist Tim Mackintosh-Smith.† Particularly after
the collapse following World War I of the Ottoman Empire, which
had led the Islamic world in the Middle East for at least half a millennium, there have been bloody struggles over the inheritance of power,
leading to a contest over which group could claim to be the purest in
doctrine, and sometimes by inference the most extreme, a tendency
that has had its similarities with medieval Christianity. The corollary
was the 1978–79 Iranian Revolution, the various offshoots of Salafism,
and particularly ISIS:‡ making for a Grand Guignol of violence and
breathless headlines with which we have all become depressingly familiar.

This, then, is the Greater Middle East, broadly speaking the Islamic world of the desert and plains (as opposed to the Indian Ocean
world of seafaring Islam), a vast swath of the earth that I have spent

---

* Albert Hourani, *A History of the Arab Peoples*, with a new afterword by Malise Ruthven
(Cambridge, MA: Harvard University Press, 1991), pp. 60–61. The most lucid description of
the divisions of Islam is found in Edward Mortimer's 1982 classic, *Faith and Power* (London:
Faber and Faber, 1982), particularly in the chart on p. 50.

† Mackintosh-Smith, *Arabs*, p. 96. He relies on the account of Abu Muhammad al-Hasan
al-Hamdani, the tenth-century historian-geographer from Yemen.

‡ *Salafi* literally refers to the virtuous ancestors of the first generations of Islam, thus indicating a back-to-basic-roots movement. ISIS is the acronym for the Islamic State in Iraq and
Sham (the "Levant").

the past fifty years traveling and reading about: stretching from Morocco in the western Mediterranean to East Turkestan, abutting the arable cradle of China; or from the Eastern Orthodox Balkans south to the mountainous monsoon land of Yemen; or, by yet another measure, from the violent anarchy of Libya to that of Afghanistan. It is an area that the Greeks referred to as the *oikoumene*, meaning the inhabited part of the globe that the Greeks knew and knew of. The *oikoumene* was an idea more than a geography. A concept much larger than the arid zone of the Arab world, it included Ethiopia, Turkey, Iran, Afghanistan, the Caucasus, and Central Asia, and featured an interconnectedness that constituted an early form of globalization. This is the same map largely traversed by Herodotus and Alexander the Great. It is often the most antique and storied places that have provided the datelines for the worst modern horrors.

For example, witness Palmyra. Lodged in my memory of decades ago are its slender Corinthian columns punctuating the horizontality of the Syrian Desert. Here the "Queen of the East," Zenobia, a far more substantial figure than Cleopatra, was finally subjugated by the Roman emperor Aurelian in A.D. 272.* Aurelian burnt the city down a year later. Palmyra would be subjugated once again and have many of its greatest antiquities mutilated and destroyed by ISIS between 2015 and 2017. It was a seminal crime against sacred objects of the past, confirming the group's nihilistic violence against human beings.

What is the direction of it all? What political dimensions will this vast region located largely in the subtropics between Europe and the Far East ultimately assume? Might it emerge out of decades of instability and bad governance to find a crucial middle ground between tyranny on one hand, and anarchy on the other?

The answers begin with a perspective across the chasm of the decades and centuries.

---

* Under Zenobia, Palmyra, which extended its power over all of Syria, parts of Asia Minor, and northern Arabia, "assumed the proportions of a real empire." Philip K. Hitti, *History of Syria: Including Lebanon and Palestine* (New York: Macmillan, 1951), p. 393.

———

TO EXPLORE THAT DISTANCE so far beyond the scope of human comprehension, as well as other questions, requires the help of not only contemporary experts but also writers long out of fashion. For while the values of those deceased writers may not measure up to our own, their brilliance is undeniable, the reason why their works have been judged as classics in the first place. Thus, we should be humble regarding previous ages of scholarship, which, flawed as they may be, provide the foundation for our own.

So let us begin.

ARNOLD J. TOYNBEE, the prolific British historian and philosopher who recorded twenty-six world civilizations in his twelve-volume *Study of History,* wrote that throughout the human past there has been a "master-tendency" toward "standardization" at work. Over the millennia, we have all become more similar rather than dissimilar. As the protagonists in Paul Bowles's 1949 novel about Algeria observe, "The people of each country get more like the people of every other country. . . . Everything's getting gray, and it'll be grayer."[8]

But though the direction is clear, the path over ten thousand years has been notoriously slow and complicated, with many reversals and twists and turns, and with still such a long way to go. In this tortuous process, while "differentiation" and "diversity" mark the growth stage of civilizations, civilizational decline always proceeds in the same manner. Toynbee compares it to the parable of Penelope's web. In Ithaca, the faithful wife of the absent Odysseus promises her suitors that she will give herself in marriage to one of them, just as soon as she finishes weaving a winding-sheet for old Laertes, Odysseus's father. But she never completes the winding-sheet, since after weaving a pattern on her loom all day, she spends the nights in the monotonous task of unpicking her day's work. That way she will never give herself away in marriage and can stay faithful to her missing husband. The patterns she weaves on her loom each day are different from each other, but the unraveling at night is always the same. In this way, Penelope's labor mirrors the rise and decline of civilizations. But Penelope's labors, according to Toynbee's interpretation, are not "unbearable," since each day she is closer to being reunited with her husband, who eventually does return home.[9]

The same goes for what Toynbee calls the "mightier weaver," who suggests the progress of civilizations themselves.[10]

Inspired by an image from Goethe's *Faust*, Toynbee explains: "The work of the Spirit of the Earth, as he weaves and draws his threads on the Loom of Time," constitutes the "elemental rhythm" of the history of man, as it "manifests itself in the geneses and growths and breakdowns and disintegrations of human societies." But this "perpetual turning of the wheel is not a vain repetition, if, at each revolution, it is carrying the vehicle that much nearer to its goal . . . and signifies the birth of something new."[11] Because the "loom of time" moves so slowly, the individual "breakdowns and disintegrations" that, as it happens, today so obsess the media about the Middle East, do not afford a view of something entirely new being created.

To actually glimpse what is being created requires the scale of Toynbee, focusing as he does on all of human history, as well as the magisterial distance and pacing of historians such as Gibbon and Braudel. Edward Gibbon, the late-eighteenth-century British historian of *The Decline and Fall of the Roman Empire*, registers, among so much else, the grand sweep of rising and falling Mongol and Turkic dynasties, interwoven with the intricacies of Roman and Persian court intrigues, all in just a few paragraphs, with the sedate concision of Tacitus. Emerging from this tapestry is the very process of history itself, in which decline means merely a protracted transformation; so that Western Rome's fall is so gradual and relative that it leads, ultimately, to the rudimentary beginnings of the early modern European state system. Imagine an airplane moving at the speed of 500 miles per hour, which from an altitude of 30,000 feet seems to crawl across the landscape below. One crawls through Gibbon's ironic and stately paragraphs, while quickly passing through decades and centuries. Fernand Braudel, the mid-twentieth-century French geographer and historian of the Mediterranean, calls this phenomenon the *longue durée*—the slow, imperceptible changes, like the sluggish movements of the ocean at its deepest depths, which invisibly determine the fast-moving, transitory ripples at the surface, upon which the media remain focused.

In other words, it becomes a matter of dramatically widening one's vision across time and terrain and in this way rediscovering the deeper past: only then might the future become discernible.

Seeing the future also requires seeing what is directly in front of one's eyes. That is more easily said than done, since what is in front of one's eyes is often unpleasant and has a way of unraveling acceptable ideas about how far-flung societies behave and operate. Seeing clearly also requires encounters not only with the living but with the dead: that is, rereading the work of precisely those great thinkers who have stood the test of time and who make one the most uneasy. In particular, I have in mind three men: the great American anthropologist Clifford Geertz, who identified culture—precisely what many contemporary political scientists often prefer to ignore—as the underlying force behind all politics; the great sociologist Barrington Moore, Jr., who demonstrated that each state and society comes to democracy or dictatorship in its own complex and intricate way that cannot be replicated anywhere else, and certainly cannot be imposed from outside; and the great Arabist and intellectual historian Elie Kedourie, who, in the course of challenging Toynbee's guilt-inspired sympathies for the Arabs (we will get to all that later), mercilessly and meticulously demonstrated how the actual record of modern history in Egypt, Syria, and Iraq imperils the theories of political science and other optimistic programs. Kedourie's was a pessimism rooted in observation, rather than an optimism rooted in willful illusion. Progress is possible, all these men believed, but just not in the way that we in the West imagine it. Such men, who were giants in their day, mark good departure points for my journey across a few selected parts of the Greater Middle East, the goal of which is to meet local historians and other present-day thinkers in order to both challenge and confirm these mid-twentieth-century eminences.

Truly, it is a journey across time as well as terrain. Letting the camera zoom out to encompass the centuries and millennia, contemporary Oxford University archaeologist Barry Cunliffe documents how the story of the Greater Middle East is one of nomads and settled empires, the former usually threatening the latter. And these nomads and empires reappear in different forms and under different labels right up through the present moment, as the battle between insurgencies and entrenched regimes goes on, so that ancient and medieval maps bear startling likenesses to those of our own era. The Berber Tuaregs of the deep Sahara who live tensely under Algerian army occupation, the Islamic war bands of Libya, the various armed factions in Syria, the ethnic and sectarian divisions of Iraq, the warring tribes of Yemen, the perpetual absence of effective governance in the hinterlands of sprawling and tribalized Sudan, and so forth are part of the same old story about the dearth of unity and authority across this vast region. Observe other similarities. The Achaemenid and Seljuk empires, as well as the Han protectorate, all for so long extinct, nevertheless mirror the extent of Iranian, Turkish, and Chinese influence today in the parched terrain between Europe and Asia.[12]

"The past resembles the future more than one drop of water another," wrote the fourteenth-century Arab historian Ibn Khaldun.[13] A considerable exaggeration, no doubt, but one that at least encourages an approach to the present grounded in all that has come before.

Let me pause awhile with Ibn Khaldun, a writer and thinker of the caliber of the Italian Renaissance, who traveled from Fez in the west to Damascus in the east in the course of a storied life. He believed that while the Bedouin aspire to a sedentary existence, those in the towns and cities have no such reverse inclination. Urban life, rather than leading to a longing for a return to the desert, leads instead to political strength and luxury. But inexorably, that same luxury—which goes on increasing—leads to a loss of group solidarity or _asabiyyah,_ and hence to a very fragile sophistication, decadence, senility, and decay: so that new dynasties, built on new _asabiyyah_s, emerge to form yet another grand cycle of history, with new migrants pouring out from the desert to again infiltrate the towns and cities.[14] Think of the mass migration to Tehran and other cities of a new and only partially urbanized proletariat that preceded the 1978–79 Iranian Revolution, and in fact made it possible. Think of the *asabiyyah* of Saddam Hussein's al-Bu Nasr clan from Tikrit, on the Tigris north of Baghdad, which eventually overwhelmed the Iraqi capital in the name of secular Arab nationalism and Ba'ath socialism, but soon broke through the skin of those artificial contrivances, and ruled as peasant thugs and murderers for decades.[15] Muammar Gaddafi was from a poor Bedouin family far from the capital before he took over Libya. He ruled for over four decades, fell into a crazed form of decadence and luxury, and was killed in a general uprising that led to new forms of chaos and disorder. The military officers who took over regimes in Egypt and Syria in the second half of the twentieth century often came from humble, rural backgrounds. Of course, the Al Sauds are an example of a tribal *asabiyyah* from the desert that went on to conquer and give their name to a country.

But what of the Arab Spring? Didn't that register a break from this debilitating past?

No. Alas, it did not.

Rather than a straightforward movement for democracy as commentators from the West self-referentially claimed at the time, the Arab Spring was something more general: a revolt against decadent, luxurious, and discredited central authority. In the spirit of Ibn Khaldun's Bedouin disorder, as the cases of Libya and Yemen make clear, the Arab Spring led to tribal gunmen eventually infiltrating the cities, causing anarchy. As for Syria, which we will explore later in depth, it quickly crumbled into a Hobbesian state of all against all, once decadent and oppressive central authority was challenged. Tunisia bravely hobbled on as a democracy in its capital and major cities for some time, but central control in the provinces weakened and its borderlands became easily violated. Tunisia, in any case, is the most European of Arab countries: fortified by a secular foundation myth provided by its independence leader, Habib Bourguiba (the Atatürk of the Arab world), and constituting an age-old cluster of civilization that originated with ancient Carthage, it was later buttressed by the Roman, Vandal, and Byzantine empires. Thus, despite its problems and backsliding into autocracy, Tunisia represents the most hopeful proving ground for a Western democratic experiment.

With all of the political and economic complexities introduced by rapid urbanization and postmodern technology, an ancient and medieval rhythm still persists underneath the glaze of modernity across the Middle East. This rhythm is not determinative and neither is it often dominant; but neither can it be denied. Hope, thus—at least the kind of hope that is unsentimental—rests in the *longue durée*.

PLUS ÇA CHANGE . . .

Of course, one might argue, the Middle East has been in permanent upheaval against the past since I first stepped foot in the region half a century ago. Turkey went from being a secular military regime to an Islamic-trending one. Iran had a great revolution, and is on the brink of another. Afghanistan has gone from a kingdom nervously at peace to a permanent state of war and semi-chaos. The Muslim Turkic Uighurs of western China have gone from a traditional lifestyle to being under assault by a modernizing Chinese state. Pakistan has gone from a military regime to a partial democracy and perhaps back again. Iran and Iraq fought a war in which many hundreds of thousands died. Iraq and Syria have gone from suffocating Ba'athist dictatorships to war and anarchy, as Islamism has replaced Arab nationalism there. The radical and rejectionist axis of Syria, Iraq, and Libya, so strong and influential for decades during the Cold War and after, has been shattered by state collapse. Within that anarchy, the ethnic Kurds have fought several wars of survival. Lebanon had a long civil war and totters still, barely surviving. Saudi Arabia has gone from a sleepy autocracy to a hyperactive and socially reforming one, whatever its image in the West. The Arabian Gulf sheikhdoms, built on oil wealth and global trade, have been utterly transformed into gleaming, futuristic cities. Yemen, without a royal system, has had by contrast several civil wars. Egypt and Libya have toppled dictators. Algeria had a drawn-out civil war. Israel has moved from center-left politics to hard-right politics, with wars in Lebanon and Gaza in between, and yet has established diplomatic relations with a number of Arab states—something that few predicted would ever happen. Ethiopia, which, as I will later explain, is very much part of the Greater Middle East, has gone from Marxist dictatorship to milder authoritarian rule, to a tumultuous experiment with partial democracy leading to a vast and extremely bloody civil war. There is enough variety here to encompass the entire globe.

PLUS C'EST LA MÊME CHOSE...

But the Middle East, looked at from the ocean depths—or from 30,000 feet—has barely changed in the fifty years I have intimately known it.

Turkey is back where it was before the secular revolution of Mustafa Kemal Atatürk following World War I: having moved too far away from Islam under Atatürk, Turkey has now in historical terms righted itself, though future readjustments are in the offing. The Afghan government, even when it was nominally at peace in the middle decades of the twentieth century, never ruled much beyond the major cities: exactly as now. Afghanistan remains, as it always was, an unstable transition zone of tribes and ethnicities between Russianized Central Asia and the Indian subcontinent. The Muslim Uighurs of Chinese Turkestan have been ferociously repressed for decades, as I learned during several extended visits there starting in the 1990s. It is only lately that the media has paid attention to this most historically unstable part of China's geography. The military always encompassed Pakistan's deep state. Nothing there has changed. The Iran-Iraq War of the 1980s, as immeasurably bloody as it was, changed neither the regimes involved nor the border between them. Iraq and Syria at first constituted a situation of anarchy under the carapace of extreme tyranny. All that has happened is that the carapace of tyranny has been shattered in one place and severely shaken in the other, revealing the absence of civil society beneath. In all my visits to both countries over the decades, I always sensed a terrifying emptiness and extremity, where normal politics have never been practiced since the abolition of any form of constitutionalism in Syria and Iraq in 1958. Lebanon for decades constituted a volatile Levantine urbanity where war and Iranian-backed guerrillas have existed a few miles away from gourmet restaurants serving fine wine: a foreign correspondent's dream. The country's economic collapse is relatively recent. As for the Kurds, they have often been in a state of war or near war. Saudi Arabia is ruled by the Al Sauds as it has been for a century, while Egypt has been ruled by the same line of Nasserite pharaohs since 1952. For a brief period, from 2011 to 2013, Egypt experimented with democracy, an event covered exhaustively by the world media, until military rule merely resumed, under a dictator strikingly similar to the previous ones, only a bit worse in the human rights field. Regarding Yemen, even when it was at peace, to travel the length and breadth of it, as I did in 1986 and 2002, revealed an anarchic void where a traveler required a bodyguard. Since independence in 1962, Algeria has been ruled by shadowy military and security juntas. The vast south of the country has always been more or less under informal army occupation from Algiers, as I learned during a month-long visit to the central Sahara in 2005. The traditional monarchies of Morocco, Jordan, and Oman continue unchallenged. Ethiopia (the subject of my first book), during the Cold War and afterward, has remained a very unstable, often violent mini-empire of different ethnic groups.

Of course, Iran had one of the twentieth century's pivotal revolutions, going in a matter of weeks in 1978 and 1979 from an artificial monarchy of a shah and shahbanu to a radical Islamic state ruled by a Shi'ite clerisy. Yet, underneath the politics, Iran, as I learned traveling throughout the country in the years before the revolution and in the years afterward, is singularly eternal: one of history's oldest and urbanized civilizations, with great pretensions of imperial power, whose people look down on the Arabs as chaotic and tribal. The roots of Iranian influence in the Middle East remain substantially cultural; nor has there been anarchy in Iran, as a bureaucratic hierarchy of clerics quickly replaced that of the shah. The Persian experience, so much more in a sense European compared to that of the Arabs, will continue to surprise as its uprisings against the ayatollahs remind me of the sophistication of the Solidarity movement against the Communist rulers of Poland in the 1980s.

It is true that Israel, again, so much of a cultural outlier in the region, has undergone a singular shift. The Israeli Peace Now movement is dead, the victim of Palestinian *intifada*s. In the eyes of many Israelis, Palestinians have gone from being interlocutors to being enemies. The occupied territories have remained such for over five decades. So in the grand scheme of things, not so much has changed there either. Of course, the establishment of diplomatic relations between Israel and a number of Arab countries, particularly in the Persian Gulf, constitutes an unquestioned historical development. But keep in mind that for decades Israel cooperated on security matters and maintained regular links with those same Gulf Arab states, whose ruthless pragmatism in all matters is evocative of Singapore's. This has been much more of a step-by-step, organic process than the media suggested at the time.

What has most dramatically shifted in the Middle East has been the behavior of outside powers: that is, of empires. Now we come closer to the heart of this story.

"LARGELY UNDER THE RELATIVE peace assured by the great empires that were built following the Axial Age . . . came the beginnings of a series of movements which are spoken of as the great historical religions."[16] So wrote Marshall G. S. Hodgson, the mid-twentieth-century University of Chicago historian of the Middle East. Indeed, the depressing but undeniable fact is that empires have dominated much of political history going back to early antiquity, in the Middle East and elsewhere, because they offered, in relative terms at least, the most practical default means of political and geographical organization. Empires may leave chaos in their wake, but it is also true that they have arisen as solutions to chaos.[17]

Most civilizational advancements occurred under empires. The Golden Age of Islam was an imperial one, primarily under the Abbasids, and in reduced measure under the Fatimids and the Hafsids. The

Mongol empire could be cruel beyond measure, but who did the Mongols subjugate or destroy: other empires—the Abbasid, Khwarazmian, Bulgarian, Song, and so on. The Ottomans in the Middle East (and the Habsburgs in Central Europe and the Balkans) provided conspicuous protection for Jews and other minorities consistent with the most enlightened values of their particular age. The Armenian genocide did not, as is commonly thought, occur under the Ottoman Empire per se, but rather under the influence of Young Turk nationalists who were in the process of superseding it. Monoethnic nationalism, more than multiethnic imperialism with its cosmopolitan quality, has been more lethal toward minorities.

Yet, as Oxford historian John Darwin dryly notes, "Empire is often seen as the original sin of European peoples, who corrupted an innocent world," even as its "real origins are much older," intrinsic to the course of history itself.[18]

In fact, the major reason for the violence in the Middle East in recent years and decades—the fleeting ripples to which the media pay attention—is that for the first time in modern history the region is in a post-imperial phase. There are no longer any world empires to keep order. The Assyrian, Roman, Persian, Byzantine, Ottoman, British, Soviet, and American empires are gone from the region. That is the underlying *longue durée* in the spirit of Braudel, however disturbing it is to postmodern sensibilities. But it is something we simply have to grapple with.

The Ottoman Turkish Empire, which governed the Middle East from Algeria to Iraq for four hundred years, collapsed following World War I. The British and French imperial mandate authorities that governed the states of the Levant and Fertile Crescent, from Lebanon to Iraq, came to an end in the aftermath of World War II. As for the Cold War, the United States and the Soviet Union were empires "in all but name," Darwin observes.[19] The Soviet Union disintegrated in 1991, while the U.S. reputation for power has been steadily diminishing since the 2003 invasion of Iraq. Regrettably, without empire in some form, the Middle East (and the Arab world in particular) has always evinced a "fissile tendency . . . towards division," observes the Arabist Tim Mackintosh-Smith, who has resided in Yemen for decades, refusing to desert that war-torn nation.[20]

Witness Syria, which, after an eight-year-long civil war that killed perhaps half a million people, has temporarily stabilized under the aegis of Russia and Iran, and to a lesser extent Turkey, all three states drawing directly on long-standing imperial traditions. In sum, the Middle East after a hundred years has still not found an adequate solution to the collapse of the Ottoman Empire.*

Of course, this thesis runs counter to much of the wisdom of the academic and journalistic communities at the moment. Understandably, with modern European colonialism still constituting a living history, scholars and reporters remain preoccupied with the crimes of the British and French in the Middle East, Africa, and elsewhere. In time, that preoccupation will dissipate and a calmer view of both European and non-European imperialism over thousands of years of human history will assuredly take root. Because we live in a postcolonial moment-in-time, it is only natural that the misdeeds of European colonialism loom large. The challenge is to move beyond those misdeeds, without minimizing them.†

BY THE STANDARDS OF Gibbon and Toynbee, the big story in the Middle East today is not necessarily the failure of democracy—but the departure of empire. With empire gone, the issue is to stave off anarchy. Though empire represents an extreme form of order and anarchy an extreme form of disorder, it might seem that one is as bad as the

---

* In 1862, the Ottoman foreign minister, Ali Pasha, warned in a letter that if the Ottomans were ever forced to give in to "national aspirations . . . It would need a century and torrents of blood to establish even a fairly stable state of affairs." Lewis, *The Middle East*, p. 315.

† In 2019, Guy Verhofstadt, the former Belgian prime minister and one of the most prominent members of the European Union's parliament, told an audience in the United Kingdom that "The world of tomorrow is not a world order based on nation states or countries. It is a world order based on empires." Thus, he argued, there was no European future outside the imperial-like dimensions of the European Union. Andrew Stuttaford, "'Too Small to Fail' Review: Crawling Between the Giants' Toes," *The Wall Street Journal*, May 3, 2020.

other. But that is simply not true. As the eleventh- and twelfth-century Persian philosopher Abu Hamid al-Ghazali indicated in an obvious exaggeration, "a hundred years" of tyranny causes less damage than "one year's" anarchy, because anarchy is the tyranny of a whole population against each other.[21] I experienced this firsthand, traveling all over Saddam Hussein's Iraq in 1984 and 1986, and thinking nothing could be worse than the pulverizing, prison-yard oppression that I experienced—until I traveled twice throughout Iraq with the U.S. military in the post-Saddam years of chaos of 2004 and 2005, where I experienced an anarchic situation significantly more frightening than even Saddam's tyranny. Had I come to this realization earlier, I would not have supported the Iraq War (more about that to come). One can say the same thing about Syria during the relatively stable rules of the elder and younger Assads between 1970 and 2011, and the anarchic abyss that followed; or about Libya during Muammar Gaddafi's tyrannical rule and afterwards. Little else but the toughest regimes have so far worked in these countries with their artificial geographies and consequent illogical borders; rather, they are vague geographical expressions, whose very artificiality has necessitated, at least in the past, the most extreme forms of compulsion and control. To wit, Egypt and Tunisia have long and sturdy roots as states and societies that predate Islam. Libya, which lies between them, does not. Western Libya, Tripolitania, with its relative cosmopolitanism, has historically gravitated toward Carthage and Greater Tunisia. Eastern Libya, Cyrenaica, much more conservative, has historically gravitated toward cosmopolitan Alexandria in Egypt. In between, including the Fezzan to the south, is a relative desert void except for tribal and subregional identities.[22]

In fact, the least oppressive regimes in the Middle East have been the traditional monarchies of Morocco, Oman, and Jordan. Because of their inherent historical legitimacy, they have been able to govern with the minimum degree of cruelty, despite being authoritarian. The Hobbesian laboratory of the Middle East proves that along with empire, monarchy is the most natural form of government. As Marshall Hodgson patiently explains, for centuries "monarchy seemed the only suitable alternative to a rapacious armed oligarchy."[23] But following the defeat of fascism and then Communism, Western discourse narrow-mindedly assumed that "capitalist democracy—the market and the election"—constituted the final phase of modernity, writes Barnett Rubin, the contemporary New York University area specialist on Afghanistan and Pakistan.[24] This Western logic, as he suggests, falsely assumed that beautiful ideas alone could overcome objective realities, such as illiteracy, ethnic and religious conflict, and the absence of controllable borders.

Democracy, again, according to the long arc of time, remains but a bold experiment. The hue and cry against authoritarianism that one has heard for many years, especially in Washington, is ahistorical. Authoritarianism is merely a category, not a movement. And a very loose category at that. After all, what did the late Sultan Qaboos bin Said of Oman—who governed for fifty years in the twentieth and twenty-first centuries, an absolute dictator who respected civil liberties, and who championed environmentalism, women's rights, and institution-building—have in common with regimes in North Korea, China, or Russia? I could make a similar argument regarding Morocco or Jordan. As a journalist traveling around the world for decades in the Middle East and elsewhere, I have experienced regimes across a wide spectrum of gray shades, with relatively few being either stable and exemplary democracies at one end of the spectrum, or brutal and asphyxiating tyrannies at the other end.

Indeed, the Arab world has too often moved between empire, tyranny, and anarchy, since venerable monarchies are only possible in a few places. The sheikhdoms of the Arabian Gulf are exceptions because they are mere city-states with vast stores of hydrocarbons, so that their rulers can adequately bribe their populations and get foreigners to do the work for them. The Gulf rulers also manifest a hard-headed Machiavellian empiricism that is amoral, rather than immoral.[25] While the majority of Arabs yearn for the ideal of justice, too, few really yearn for democracy and its legalisms as elites in the West understand them. Meanwhile, the vast majority cooperate and collaborate with the strongmen.[26] Thus, to define the Arab world in particular as a contest between democracy and authoritarianism—as so many people do—is to impose simulated categories upon it, specific to America's own historical experience, not to the historical experience of the region in question. A few years ago this was succinctly expressed by *Wall Street Journal* foreign affairs columnist Walter Russell Mead, who wrote in regard to stirrings of democracy in North Africa that neither the autocratic rulers nor the protesters in the streets had "the organization, political experience, ideological clarity and technical knowledge" to constitute a modern, bureaucratic governing elite that is neither oppressive nor anarchic. And Americans, despite all the experts, he said, "have no solutions to offer" because the problems are deeply woven into the history and culture of the region.[27]

Modernity, among other things, is about liberal states with organized bureaucratic systems interacting with each other on a secular basis.[28] That, at least, is the ideal conception of our world. But contrarily, Islamic societies, explains the contemporary political scientist and Middle East area specialist Michael C. Hudson, have "exhibited despotism punctuated by rebellion and chronic succession crises."[29]

Urbanization in the second half of the twentieth century and beyond has only complicated the situation. In Muslim villages, religion was an unconscious element of a traditional existence—whereas in the slums and shantytowns on the outskirts of Middle Eastern cities, religion has had to be reinvented in more austere and uncompromising form, making it an ideological project, in order to maintain traditional values amid the crowds and anonymity of strangers. The Arab Spring uprisings signaled a longing for proper modernity. Yet the region as a whole is still far from achieving it—something that is not only a flaw of its leaders and inhabitants, but also of ourselves, as I shall now explain.

IN FACT, THE ISLAMIC world of the Greater Middle East, demonstrating as it does postcolonial and post–Cold War fragmentation, reveals the dark side of modernism and postmodernism (with all of its uneven aesthetic and cultural juxtapositions) that we prefer to ignore; as states like Syria, Iraq, and Afghanistan monstrously fail to integrate their well-functioning traditional societies operating for so long without hard borders into the tight strictures of the modern state system as constructed by the West. Look at just one obscure and diminutive example: Barnett Rubin reports that "the decline of border controls in a consolidating [1990s] Europe has eased the way for Turkish syndicates to smuggle Afghan heroin from Pakistan in Panamanian-registered ships."[30] In other words, the triumph of European Union expansionism in the early years of the post–Cold War had many aftershocks, due to Europe's own social tensions and disorders, such as increased drug addiction, that distorted society—and thus politics—along the Afghan-Pakistani frontier, so far from Europe.

Ever since the Muslim East in the late medieval period began to encounter the more economically and politically dynamic civilizations of Sung and Ming China and Renaissance Europe, the Islamic world truly entered the grand tapestry of world history (that is, from a Western point of view), and as a result, any reflection we make on Islam and the Greater Middle East is a reflection, however indirect, on our own civilization and on ourselves. As history in the Toynbeean sense brings us *oh*-so-gradually together in this increasingly claustrophobic world, we all become part of the same human family. What the Sung and Ming emperors and particularly the culture of the European Renaissance actually did was to set the stage for a technical flowering that would culminate in the Industrial Revolution at both fringes of Eurasia, with which the Muslim *oikoumene,* stretching from the Mediterranean to China, could not compete. Marshall Hodgson, arguably the greatest modern-day chronicler of the history of the Middle East, who is somewhat forgotten now only because his work is quite academic and he died well over half a century ago, points out that the "rooted discontent and disruption" of the Islamic East, expressed through anti-colonialism, nationalism, and religious extremism, are ultimately reactions to its greater contact with the threatening industrial and post-industrial world on its peripheries, of which Western imperialism was naturally a by-product. And because of the very diversity of the Muslim peoples, they did not react uniformly to this threat. This helped aggravate the deep divisions within their world that would be truly revealed upon the collapse of the Ottoman Empire, and which have never been reconciled.[31]

THUS, THIS BOOK IS not a justification of the West or of imperialism, despite the latter's ability to provide some measure of coherence and order in a challenging zone of the world. The interplay between the West and the Greater Middle East is far more twisted and complicated than that. It is again Arnold Toynbee who provided the signal insight into all of this. Please bear with me.

In 1922 at the age of thirty-three, Toynbee published an early book, *The Western Question: In Greece and Turkey; A Study in the Contact of Civilisations*. It dealt with what was the headline news of the day: the military conflict between two countries straddling the Balkans and the Middle East. Following World War I and the dissolution of the Ottoman Empire, Greece attempted to annex the western edge of Anatolia with its 1.5 million ethnic Greeks concentrated around the great cosmopolitan city of Smyrna. The Greek army, tacitly supported by the Western Allied powers, landed on the Turkish coast in 1919 and advanced inland almost as far east as Ankara, deep in the Anatolian interior. In 1922, a Turkish army under the command of Mustafa Kemal "Atatürk" (Father Turk) counterattacked and literally drove Greek forces backward into the sea. Tens of thousands of ethnic-Greek civilians around Smyrna were killed and 1.2 million—practically the entire population of ethnic Greeks in Turkey—were made refugees in Greece. At least 100,000 ethnic Greeks were marched into the interior of Anatolia, most never to be seen again. Two thousand five hundred years of Greek civilization in Asia Minor abruptly came to an end. The population exchange, which also featured 400,000 Muslims being forced to move from Greece to Turkey, provided a template for ethnic cleansing in the twentieth century. For as the Ottoman Empire collapsed, a multicultural and traditional world—representing the last vestige of early modernism—gave birth to monoethnic modern states.

Toynbee ultimately blames the West for this tragedy.

He begins his argument with this arresting, unforgettable image, which deserves to be quoted at length:

> Savages are distressed at the waning of the moon and attempt to counteract it by magical remedies. They do not realize that the shadow which creeps forward till it blots out all but a fragment of the shining disc, is cast by their [own] world. In much the same way we [supposedly] civilized people of the West glance with pity or contempt at our non-Western contemporaries lying under the shadow of some stronger power, which seems to paralyze their energies by depriving them of light. Generally we are too deeply engrossed in our own business to look closer ... Yet if we paused to examine that dim gigantic overshadowing figure standing, apparently unconscious, with its back to its victims, we should be startled to find that its features are ours.[32]

For the shadow cast over the modern Balkans and Middle East, accounting for many of its horrors, is that cast by our own world. The ferocity of the horrors perpetrated by both the Greeks and the Turks, and which, in fact, had begun in the late nineteenth century with the massacre of Armenians in eastern Anatolia, and with the mutual massacres of Greeks, Bulgarians, Serbs, and Albanians in Macedonia, was ultimately caused by the "fatal" idea of modern nationalism imported from the West, in which religion and ethnicity became linked directly to the modern state itself, forming a toxic and bureaucratically powerful form of identity.[33] Whereas Western imperialism had provided some coherence to the region, the more amorphous political ideals of the West, Toynbee suggests, reacted bloodily with ideas of group identity throughout the Greater Middle East: so that, for example, Orthodox Christians and Muslims living in a somewhat tense harmony under benign, albeit decrepit, Ottoman rule, quickly became nationalistic Greeks and Turks lunging at each other's throats. To wit, the genocidal Young Turks during their exile in Europe had imbibed

Western ideas of nationalism, not realizing its incompatibility with an Anatolian landscape of mixed ethnic groups with different national aspirations: Turk, Kurd, Greek, and Armenian. And within groups, sectarianism, too, which divides Arabs into Sunni and Shi'ite sects, is also partly a problem of Western-influenced development that quickened the fight for equality and spoils.[34] These are less primordial hatreds than divisions wrought by an intensive interaction between the West and the so-called East.

Of course, the West didn't mean to do all of this. But the West's very dynamism in the realm of ideas and technology both overwhelmed and forcibly modernized the former Ottoman Empire, from North Africa and the Balkans all the way to Iraq, amplifying the lethality of the imperial wreckage, made worse by often ineffective Western meddling afterwards. Then there are Marxism, Nazism, and Arab nationalism, all ideas rooted in the modern West, which would influence the minds of Arab intellectuals living in Europe in the 1930s, and thus provide the blueprint for the Ba'athist dictators of Syria and Iraq, culminating in the elder and younger Assads and Saddam Hussein. An autopsy of those shattered countries of the early twenty-first century would reveal not only local but also Western pathogens. And this is to say nothing of the Bush administration's fatal decision in 2003 to invade Iraq.

Paul Bowles, the American novelist living in postwar Morocco—the literary genius of the West's encounter with the Middle East and Africa—put his finger on it. He wrote that only when there was no sign of Western influence at all did a place have "an unexpected quality of being complete which dissipated the feeling of chaos."[35] Chaos, in other words, is a normal circumstance for a traditional, ruralized world lacking in the precision and efficiency required by modern technological civilization. But the assault of the West, from urbanization to imperialism to modern nationalism to weapons technology, created complex and hybrid cultural orders throughout the developing world, where chaos took on a magnified and deadly quality. That is the anarchy about which I speak.

Indeed, as Stanford's Francis Fukuyama and Harvard's Noah Feldman point out, the ferocity and mechanization of Arab dictatorships are a partial result of the Arab world's encounter with the techniques of the West; and thus the demands of Islamists for Shari'a law represent less an extreme philosophy than an understandable rejection of the lawless authoritarianism under which they suffer.[36]

The Greater Middle East certainly presents a challenging canvas, at least according to the dreams and aspirations of Western elites. But this stems not merely from the region's own traditions, but from a culture that is itself a fusion of its encounter with the West. This is something that began in earnest with Napoleon's invasion of Egypt and Greater Syria in 1798, and which, in turn, led to European technology and ideas, mainly French and British, directly infiltrating the traditional cultures of the Levant.

And so the story continues . . .

THE MIDDLE EAST HURTLES forward, but not in a linear direction. Digital technology, including social media, flattens hierarchies and emboldens the masses, who consequently hold the powers-that-be in less and less awe—and more and more to account—so that dictators obsess about public opinion in a way that they never used to. Meanwhile, attrition of the same adds up to big change: even though the seaborne empires of the Portuguese, Dutch, and British swept the Middle East into a world trading system in the early modern and modern eras, the intensity of that interaction increasingly overwhelms the region as time goes on. In fact, streets may erupt with protesters at the hair-trigger of a global economic movement, as happened in Lebanon a few years back. Though good governance always seems to recede just over the horizon, grassroots changes bring us closer to the end of Penelope's labor on her loom. Area specialist Steven A. Cook calls the Arab Spring a "false dawn."[37] Yet that implies a real dawn may still be forthcoming. Thus, this journey upon which I now embark is not an altogether pessimistic one. Rather than expecting an Arab Spring 2.0 or 3.0, my exploration of books and landscapes seeks instead to identify the signals of decay and renewal across the infinity of time.

AT A GREEK CHURCH in Jerusalem, the mid-twentieth-century poet and Nobel laureate from ethnic-Greek Smyrna, George Seferis, once heard the banging on the clapboard summoning the Orthodox faithful to prayer, and immediately imagined the cry of the pagan priestess Cassandra to Apollo.[38] Ancient Greece lived on, he suddenly realized, disguising itself under the cloak of Eastern Christianity. Likewise, the Middle East of antiquity and of the Middle Ages lives on, disguising itself in modern forms even as it is distorted by them, and will adapt itself to the global political and economic evolutions to come.

AEGEAN

T HE MIDDLE EAST WAS FORMERLY CALLED THE NEAR EAST because it bordered Central Europe at the point where the Ottoman Turkish Empire began. "Turkey-in-Europe" was the phrase given to the Balkans in the nineteenth and early twentieth centuries. My first encounter with this world that lay contiguous to the West was in a Greek Orthodox Church in 1971 when I was nineteen years old. I had entered Greece on a train traveling south through Yugoslavia from Central Europe and was conscious of a dramatic atmospheric shift that culminated that first morning in Athens inside the eleventh-century Kapnikarea Church, located at the time in a traffic island on a noisy, crowded street of drapery shops. Athens had already over-whelmed me. I was someone who had never been beyond North America and Western Europe. Therefore, I had never experienced such blinding, shimmering light dousing the crummy and chaotic sprawl of what was essentially a third world city, with little order or central plan-ning. There was no cozy, vertical accumulation of statues and other cultural monuments that defined the Europe I had just left behind. It was as if the entire urban landscape had been stripped naked. It was both ugly and exhilarating.

Dodging automobiles with their loud horns, I entered the church almost breathless. Everything seemed out of focus in the darkness and my mind and senses reeled from the clouds of pine incense and the crackle of beeswax candles. The apse had been painted only in 1950 by

Photis Kontoglou, whose work in those days was creating a renewed interest in Byzantine art—the fusion of ancient Greek and Syrian styles to project the values of the medieval church. The art here revealed the grace and simplicity of classical Greek sculpture superimposed on a background of luxuriant eastern carpets, bordered and highlighted in gold leaf. Western realism was gone. The eyes of all the subjects were painted deliberately large and the parts of their bodies elongated, as if the human form were now a dematerialized abstraction of divine thought, further enhanced by the pallor of the skin. The figures in these icons in the Kapnikarea were "two dimensional, like visions," in the words of Constantine Cavarnos, a Harvard-trained specialist in Byzantine art.[1] Back then, all I knew was that I had entered an utterly magical realm radically different from what in comparison were the sparer Latin cathedrals of Europe.

Claude Lévi-Strauss, the French anthropologist, wrote in 1955 that "Mankind" had "opted for monoculture," and was "in the process of creating a mass civilization."[2] But because I was young and unsophisticated, I lacked Lévi-Strauss's lifetime perspective of how the various parts of the world were (even back then) gradually becoming similar under the force of technology and the consequent collapse of distance. Thus, what I experienced in this church was an ambient sense of how starkly different Greece still was—compared to the western part of Europe. I had entered the Near East but did not yet know it. Islam was not the dividing line. The dividing line was within Christianity itself.

EVERY RELIGION IS IDIOSYNCRATIC, according to the early-twentieth-century Spanish-American philosopher George Santayana, and is more primitively connected to the local landscape than art even. This is something Lévi-Strauss's monoculture cannot take away from it. Greece, as a living embodiment of an idea across the chasm of the centuries, is most intensely felt inside the candlelit darkness of an Orthodox church where there have been no Middle Ages with their kings and nobles advancing a form of political consent, no Renaissance, no Reformation, and no Counter-Reformation as in the West. In fact, everything that actually defined the West was herein absent. The Parthenon speaks only about what ended in Greece over two millennia ago, not about Greece as it evolved through the whole of its history, especially during the medieval centuries, and so cannot really compare with the Kapnikarea and other Orthodox churches as a vital, breathing historical symbol of what constitutes Greece. Early Christianity is key here. Santayana says that whereas the teachings of Jesus constitute "pure Hebraism," the incarnation of God in man is a "pagan conception," made into a universal ideal by the vitality of Greek thought, which combined art and beauty with morality.[3] Christianity, in both the East and the West, truly begins with the ancient Greeks, as Arnold Toynbee noted in his *Study of History*.[4]

Inside the Kapnikarea, for the first time I had come face-to-face with the unparalleled dynamism of Greek culture: a force that combined philosophy and aesthetics in which classical Greece, rather than simply expire, lived on in its brilliance through the art and language of the Orthodox Byzantine Empire, or Rome in the East as Byzantium is properly called. Indeed, Greece has always had a strong Eastern element. Hellenism, furthermore—a fusion of Greek and Semitic culture that arose in the wake of Alexander the Great's conquests in the Middle East—influenced the art and architecture, as well as the thought, of early Islam. Even in our own day, Taha Hussein, the great twentieth-century liberal philosopher of Al-Azhar University in Cairo, could speak of the powerful influence of Greek rationalism on the Egyptian mind.[5] Greece was able to be the birthplace of Western democracy precisely because it was so close to the East. It is where the liberating oxygen of the West began to diffuse the crushing and abstract logic of the Egyptian and Mesopotamian deserts with their antique versions of totalitarianism; and therefore, to breathe humanism into the inhumanity of the pharaonic and Babylonian tyrannies.[6] Because the Parthenon and other ancient ruins are so symbolic of Western ideals, it was in the Kapnikarea Church where I first met Greece as the antechamber of the Near East, a region where ritual, beginning with the crackling beeswax candles, triumphs over pure logic. Truly, a candle bears witness, and thus encourages memory and introspection.

The conquering dynamism of Greek civilization, a matter of its union of orient and occident, was first demonstrated by the way that Alexander's military expedition across the Middle East in the late fourth century B.C., as relatively brief as it was, nevertheless allowed Hellenistic culture to sink stubborn roots in numerous places from the Aegean to the Pamirs (that is, as far away as what is now Afghanistan and Tajikistan), with one Central Asian town after another raising theaters and temples dedicated to the Greek gods. It would not be the last time that Greek civilization would infiltrate the wider Middle East, and make the story of the Middle East inseparable from the Greek influence upon it. The Greek Hellenes would dominate the Near East much as the Persians, Arabs, and Turks have.[7]

The Greek Orthodox Church, which split from the Latin Church in the A.D. 1054 schism between Rome and Constantinople, "opted," in Toynbee's words, "for political submission to the [Muslim] Turk in preference to accepting the Western Christian Pope's ecclesiastical supremacy." To the Greeks, the Latin Franks were parvenu "barbarians"; to the Latins, the Greeks were "Levantines."[8] For the medieval Greeks carried with them the pain and humiliation of all the blood-curdling cruelty of the siege and sack of Constantinople in 1204 during the Fourth Crusade, as well as other Latin depredations upon them following the schism. The Crusades were directed not just against the Muslim Arabs, but against the Orthodox Greeks, too. Western Christianity, as a consequence, had no appeal to the Greeks: they preferred "the turban of the Turk" to "the tiara of the Pope."[9] In fact, the Ottoman Turks, who dominated the Middle East from Algeria to Iraq and from the Balkans to the Hejaz for four hundred years, ruled in places through Greek (as well as Persian) officialdom, and treated the Orthodox Church quite well. Greek communities throughout the Middle East were both assertive and prosperous under Ottoman rule. The Ottoman Empire not only governed from the same imperial capital (Constantinople) as had the Greek Byzantines, but had replaced a weak and decentralized, multilingual Byzantine state with a vigorous and more centralized one;[10] so that the spirit of the medieval Greeks and their Orthodox Church survived, however feebly, until the final embers of Ottomanism in the Middle East were snuffed out after World War I.

It may not be surprising, therefore, that of all the Christian communities in the modern Middle East (during the Ottoman and European mandate periods) the most fervent and active in support of Arab nationalism were the Greek Orthodox. (Alas, this corresponded with the Greeks' communal tradition of periodic anti-Semitism.)[11] George Antonius, the author of the seminal work of Palestinian nationalism, *The Arab Awakening* (1938), had himself been Greek Orthodox.[12] So, too, had been George Habash, the leader of the most radical Palestinian armed group, the Popular Front for the Liberation of Palestine. And so, too, had been Michel Aflaq, one of the key founders of Syrian and Iraqi Ba'athism.[13] Toynbee spoke of an Arab world allied with Greek Orthodox Christendom, and a Turkish-Persian world oriented toward the West.[14] These are odd facts, but together they are significant.

Greece, like Russia, has always been partially Eurasian, with an ambivalent relationship to Europe. Thus, for me, the incense-filled darkness of the Kapnikarea Church offered lessons (to be learned not immediately, but slowly over a lifetime) in both the continuity and intermingling of cultures and civilizations: that is, from ancient Athens through all the historical vicissitudes until the end of the Ottoman Empire, when the faint candle smoke of Hellenistic and Roman traditions is finally extinguished. Too, in this incense-filled cavern I experienced in a very visceral sense the salience of geography: meeting the Near East for the first time at Europe's last landfall on the eastern Mediterranean.

I WOULD RETURN TO Greece to live for seven years from 1982 to 1989, working there as a freelance foreign correspondent. Based in Athens, and living close to the sea, I traveled throughout the Balkans and the Middle East as far as Central Asia. One month I was in Yugoslavia, another month on the Iran-Iraq border: in my mind they both were linked as the western and eastern frontiers of the Ottoman Empire.

There were only a handful of other journalists in Athens who used the city as a base to cover what was, in fact, the old Near East. But my own travel pattern in particular had a venerable tradition, that of Herodotus and Alexander the Great. For Herodotus, the father of history and, in truth, the world's first reporter in the fifth century B.C., the Aegean Sea was his base. From here he organized his far-flung expeditions throughout the Near East[15]—Macedonia, Syria, Palestine, Egypt, and so on—in order to investigate the causes of that first great struggle between West and East: the Greco-Persian Wars. Little more than a hundred years later, between 334 and 323 B.C., Alexander the Great, a veritable geographical force in human form,[16] traveled from his base in Macedonia near the Aegean Sea to conquer the whole Near East: what in antiquity constituted the Persian Empire, just as it would constitute the Ottoman Empire in early modern and modern times.

Thus, without realizing it, I was covering an historically coherent geography, even if it did not fit into the conventional journalistic boundaries of the Cold War, which demanded sharp divisions between the Balkans, Turkey, the Arab world, and beyond. But it is that older geography that forms the contours of this book, not just as a basis for my travels and memories, but for my reading as well.

Yes, I am very much out of date. But there is no understanding of the present without a vivid notion of the past. The travel writer Paul Theroux, defending his old age, rebukes the young with this: "I have been to a place where none of you have ever been, where none of you can ever go. It is the past. I spent decades there and I can say, you don't have the slightest idea."[17]

That is my defense for writing a book of history, travel, reporting, memoir, and geography about parts of the Greater Middle East in my seventies. I have vivid, living memories of being at the front in the Iran-Iraq War in 1984, of experiencing the relative peace and beauty of Hafez al-Assad's Syria in 1976, and of traveling all over the shah's Iran in 1973. I knew Egypt in the relatively hopeful Sadat and early Mubarak years. I knew Tunisia under the enlightened dictatorship of Habib Bourguiba, one of the great minor men of the twentieth century, who gave Tunisia a secular nation-state identity rare in the Arab world, and who was therefore crucial to its peaceful experiment with democracy more than a third of a century after I had first visited there.

I could go on.

The past merging into the present is all we ever have to go on. Age renders me a bit withered and invisible in the crowd, and more inhibited as to where I can venture, but it can have its uses. Like Yeats's protagonist in "Sailing to Byzantium," I will also begin my journey in earnest in Istanbul, not to defeat mortality as in the poem, but to understand what has happened to our world in the course of my own lifetime.[18]

AND WHAT HAS HAPPENED to our world includes the intellectual world as well. For the intellectual and journalistic climate in the 2020s is radically different than it was when I began work in the 1980s as an Athens-based foreign correspondent. How do I explain just how different the intellectual climate was back then? Oddly enough, I can do this most effectively by describing a public duel over the Middle East that took place in 1982 between two brilliant men. Describing that duel, blow by blow, illustrates how my own relationship with the region—and how to think about it—has spanned starkly different eras.

IT WAS TRULY A battle royal fought out in the pages of *The New York Review of Books* between Princeton University historian of the Near East Bernard Lewis and Columbia University professor of literature Edward W. Said. The subject of the duel was Said's book *Orientalism*, published in 1978, which had become an academic sensation. By assaulting what he considered the surreptitious imperialist motivations of Western writers and experts on the Near East, Said with just one book arguably did more than anyone else to invent the field of postcolonial studies. Lewis eviscerated Said's book at great length, criticizing its accuracy and deconstructing its entire postcolonial theme, demonstrating, in the process, his own formidable knowledge in several Near Eastern languages and traditions. This prompted Said to respond with equal venom, again at great length, playing the role of the suave rebel who had invaded the house of the almighty savants. It was a case of the historian-expert armed with the corpus of source material versus the English professor who grasped the literary implications of it all, and thus the effect on people's political imaginations. Both men are now dead. Lewis, a British-born Jew, chose burial in the historic Trumpeldor Cemetery in Tel Aviv. Said, who identified as an exiled Palestinian, elected to have his ashes interred at a Protestant cemetery near Beirut. Clearly, here were two Americans whose deepest sympathies lay elsewhere. Because the Israeli-Palestinian dispute lay deep in their psyches as the bedrock of their disagreement, it allowed for the presentation of two incalculably different scholarly approaches and worldviews. In fact, their duel of four decades ago wears very well. This battle royal radiates a timeless, classical quality.

The drama begins with Said's book itself.

Employing nineteenth-century French painter Jean-Léon Gérôme's glittering orientalist fantasy of a nude snake charmer in the East as the book's cover, Said's work immediately electrifies with both condemnation and exotica even before the reader encounters the first word. Said defines orientalism as nothing less than "the Western approach to the Orient" in its entirety, and because orientalism constituted the systematic study of the Orient, it also involved a province of "dreams, images, and vocabulary" that the West practically inhaled in order to come to terms with this seemingly hostile, "Other" world. Because this "Other" world was so different and outwardly opposite to that of European civilization, Europeans, Said claimed, used the Orient as a vehicle to define themselves by what they were against: a geography close by and yet fantastically threatening. Said circumscribes the branch of orientalism with which he is especially concerned to mean the British and French imperialist encounter with the Near East: that part of the East that is geographically nearest to Europe, and thus the part that exercised the most elaborate effect on Europe's political and intellectual imagination. Because the Near East (more or less interchangeable with the Middle East) is mainly Arab and Islamic, *Orientalism* is a book focused primarily on how Western imperialism succeeded in distorting the study and interpretation of Arab culture and politics.[19]

Europe, Said alleges, is the "genuine creator" of the Near East as it has been imagined by scholars, journalists, and policymakers for centuries. For it was the blunt and violent fact of empire that facilitated the study and travels of generations of British and French scholars, who, whether they admitted it or not—whether they were aware of it or not—were directly or indirectly imperial agents. Said's indictment includes Richard Francis Burton, T. E. Lawrence, D. G. Hogarth, Harry St. John Philby, Gertrude Bell, Hamilton A. R. Gibb, and many others stretching deep into the modern era, as well as novelists and travel writers, to say nothing of the Arabists and national-security experts who have regularly delivered expertise on the Near East from their perches in London, Paris, and Washington. And this expertise, as Said explains, was based on the Middle East of their imaginations, not on what it was in fact.

Because such expertise was based on their imaginations, which in turn were supported by the superior position that imperialism and later American dominance afforded them, these men and women "bandied about" clichés and generalizations concerning Arab Muslims that "no one would risk in talking about blacks or Jews." This is how, for example, the myth of the so-called *Arab mind* took root. From imperialism to determinism and essentialism there was a straight line that poisoned everything from travel writing to scholarship to area studies and finally to foreign policy. In short, military and economic dominance had offered up cultural stereotypes.[20]

Keep in mind that the literary vehicle for this whole argument is an elegant and sumptuous tour de force of well over three hundred pages that takes no prisoners, and takes one's breath away. Bernard Lewis is singled out by Said for especially harsh treatment, as someone respected by the Anglo-American establishment as the "learned Orientalist," and whose writings are "steeped in the 'authority' of the field," yet who, Said charges, became "aggressively ideological" later in life, writing "propaganda *against* his subject material" (against the Arabs, that is).[21]

Lewis's counterattack appeared in the June 24, 1982, edition of *The New York Review of Books,* four years after the publication of *Orientalism.* The fact that he did not reply much sooner was possibly due to the fact that the relentless success of the book at some point simply made it impossible for him to ignore. Lewis's response certainly reads with the tight organization that betrays maturation and slow, meticulous writing.

Lewis begins with an analogy: a rich description of the European classicists who translated and interpreted the work of the ancient Greek tragedians and historians, preserving the origins of the Western tradition in Greece in all its glory and brilliance. Lewis then pivots:

"The time has come to save Greece from the classicists and bring the whole pernicious tradition of classical scholarship to an end. Only Greeks are truly able to teach and write on Greek history and culture from remote antiquity to the present day." The only non-Greeks who should be permitted to join this great endeavor, Lewis continues in jest, would be those who demonstrated pro-Greek sentiments, such as support for the Greek cause in Cyprus or ill will toward the Turks. Lewis thus undermines the whole edifice of Said's *Orientalism* as absurd, since what it amounts to is that only Arabs and other oppressed people are qualified to write about their own cultures. "The implication would seem to be," Lewis argues, "that by learning Arabic, Englishmen and Frenchmen were committing some kind of offense." Said, in Lewis's words, misrepresents "what scholars do and what scholarship is about." In fact, "orientalist," as a professional term, Lewis goes on, was long ago discarded by the very people Edward Said attacks, as modern historians and academically trained specialists have long since taken over the field. Orientalism survives only in Said's mind as a term of "polemical abuse," Lewis writes. As for the crimes of orientalism, Lewis quotes Said on how Western scholars "appropriate" and "ransack" the intellectual and aesthetic riches of the Middle East, as if those things were, Lewis writes, "commodities which exist in finite quantities." In fact, nothing has been stolen or "appropriated" since such intellectual and other riches exist for endless interpretation by whoever wants to undertake it.[22]

Said fired back in the August 12, 1982, issue of *The New York Review of Books.* He rejected Lewis's comparison between orientalism and classical Greek studies, because the latter constitutes true "philology" and thus is much more rigorous as a scholarly field. In any case, Greek classical studies are further removed from the tradition of empire than is orientalism. Said also draws a link between orientalist scholarship and the foggy, romantic writings of European novelists, poets, journalists, and politicians about Islam, noting the migration of prejudice from one field of knowledge to the next. Said's ultimate point is that contemporary orientalism of the kind represented by Lewis "is a discourse of power"—of one civilization dominating another—that thoughtful Arabs and Muslims now reject.[23]

In fact, the core issue of how one culture and civilization should regard another, and how all of us, as individuals, should report on and analyze cultures and civilizations different from our own, is more urgent than ever. Globalization and the defeat of distance through technology have brought us all into thrilling and yet uncomfortable proximity. This renders the disagreement between Bernard Lewis and Edward Said of signal importance. Just consider that the late Harvard professor Samuel P. Huntington's 1993 thesis on *The Clash of Civilizations* actually borrowed the term from Lewis's "The Roots of Muslim Rage," which first appeared in *The Atlantic* in September 1990. Though Lewis used the phrase in a somewhat different context, the connection with Huntington's famous thesis is not incidental, since what Lewis and Said were really arguing about was, to repeat, the ability or inability of one civilization to comprehend another nearby. And that, as Huntington explained, constituted a malady of the last phase of the modern world, before postmodernism with all of its cultural mixings and juxtapositions took over.

The fact that it was a very different world in 1982 only further demonstrates the clairvoyance manifested unintentionally by both Lewis and Said in the course of intellectually assaulting one another. Let me explain. As a young reporter in Greece in the 1980s, the world of journalism that I experienced was one of Americans and Europeans holding forth in print about the Arab world and Israel. The idea that Jews could not be expected to report objectively about Israel still held currency among journalists back then. Arabs could work as stringers in the Middle Eastern bureaus of major publications but, though it was never openly stated, with few exceptions they were thought to lack the emotional distance of staff correspondents. Interpreting the Middle East was the province of Westerners who were neither Jewish nor Muslim. Indeed, the ideal situation was to write, report, and provide analysis about countries and peoples with which one had no emotional or personal links whatsoever. For to have any kind of a stake in any particular place could be professionally disqualifying. Foreign correspondents often had a familiarity with other languages, such as French or German, but rarely with Arabic. Rather than true area expertise, an Olympian degree of distance and objectivity was sought. Of course, the idea that merely being from the West burdened one with a viewpoint and cultural baggage all its own was rarely realized, or even considered.

In this world of Western observers of the Middle East during the Cold War, groups such as the State Department Arabists (about whom I later wrote a book) were truly caught in the middle. Mainly Protestants who spoke Arabic, they were thought of by those like Said as diplomats-cum-imperialists, and by many others, especially the pro-Israel community, as having gone native with the culture that they were supposed to be analyzing and reporting on. Neither the Arabs nor the Washington policy community wholly trusted them.

This entire world was rendered sepia-toned by the globalization that followed the end of the Cold War, which, by dramatically enlarging middle classes nearly everywhere and the air links between them, to say nothing of connecting everyone with digital platforms, has plunged the West and the Arab worlds both into the cross currents of multiple civilizations. Of course, the Arab encounter with the West, following the conquests of Roman lands and the Crusades, began in earnest in the late eighteenth century with Napoleon's invasion of Egypt. But, as I've said before, attrition of the same adds up to big change. Thus, it is the very intensity and magnitude of this intermingling at the higher levels of society that has been so critical, fostered as it has been by technology. The consequence is a whole new generation of Arabs and Africans who are middle class, extremely well educated, and filtering steadily into the ranks of the global elite, and thus into the ranks of journalism and policy studies.

This new generation of experts is more analytically demanding than the old one. In such a professional environment, subjective observations about national cultures, even positive observations, rarely make it through editorial filters without substantial backup. The exception is the work of anthropologists, who build cultural models out of particulars from the ground up.

Truly, we inhabit Edward Said's world now. Though one has to wonder whether postcolonial thinking, with its denunciatory references to imperialism and racism, is but a phase that will dissipate somewhat as the distance between the present and the end of European empires lengthens in the coming decades. Keep in mind that, as I've already explained, empires have been the political rule for humanity for thousands of years, so we are still immediately in the shadow of them. This makes natural the current obsession.

If Edward Said rules the roost, then Bernard Lewis is considered by some a relic, like the old and gracious foreign correspondents of major newspapers I used to know in the 1980s. I say this more as a lament than with pleasure. It is tragic that Lewis had his reputation tarnished by the Iraq War. While his influential support for the war fits nicely with Said's profile of him as the very personification of imperialism, it is also true that Lewis's long and intimate association with the Arab world and its language—rather than make him cynical— gave him hope for liberal change. Saddam Hussein was not merely a dictator. He was a Stalinist tyrant and Lewis may have felt the opportunity to topple him just too good to pass up. And all this transpired in Lewis's ninth decade of life.

To fairly judge Lewis we need to realize that, like postcolonialism itself perhaps, he represents a chapter in the accumulation and interpretation of knowledge that was already ending by the time Said set his sights on him. But that does not make his vast and learned experience of the Arab world—in addition to the Turkish and Persian ones whose languages he also knew—any less valuable. To judge Lewis we need to recognize not only what has come after him but what came before him. For the younger Lewis helped shake up the world of scholarship just as Said would do much later.

Bernard Lewis, it could be argued, was the original modern historian of the Middle East, having evolved indirectly from that original orientalist and Victorian-era traveler in the Near East, Sir Richard Francis Burton, who was also fabulously multilingual. The likes of Burton gave way to the likes of Lewis, who gave way to the likes of Said. It is all part of an evolutionary process. It was Burton in 1885, working at his desk in Trieste, who translated into English from Arabic *The Thousand and One Nights.* Burton along with Lewis was among the principal targets of Said in *Orientalism,* who accused Burton in so many words of determinism and essentialism. And yet *not* to be able to generalize immobilizes discussion and analysis. "When people think seriously, they think abstractly," writes Samuel Huntington; "they conjure up simplified pictures of reality called concepts, theories, paradigms," without which intellectual life simply cannot advance.[24] In particular, Burton's translation of the *Nights* helped bring the genius of Arab-Persian-Indian literature and civilization to Europe, a giant step in constructing the cultural bridge we call cosmopolitanism—thus making Burton's translation, after a fashion, a much earlier phase of Said's own work. Before there can be understandings, there must be misunderstandings, which are the natural outgrowth of first contact.

Indeed, though Said and many others have refused to countenance it, often it was the imperialists themselves who experienced foreign locales firsthand, and who consequently gained a nuanced appreciation of foreign systems unavailable to their untraveled compatriots at home. This is how imperialism, cosmopolitanism, and universalism are all connected. Burton helped lead the way. Said sought to correct his errors, considering any expertise gained by virtue of imperialism, even direct observation, to be tainted. Thus one paradigm replaced another, more or less as Huntington suggested. It is all part of a process that may eventually lead to a common world culture beyond East and West, that offers a grand finale for the Loom of Time.

And Lewis, with his amazingly clear and concise histories of the Middle East, which buttress the literary sweep of events with telling details culled from his research in the Ottoman archives or some such, in terms of style and viewpoint lies midway between Burton and Said.

Nor is Lewis completely out-of-date. The whole business of political forecasting requires generalizations, often about countries and national cultures, since it is not only exceptional individuals who make history but the vast average of populations, which less and less make it into the reports of elite journalism and policy studies, as the victory of Edward Said's mindset has intimidated journalists and others from offering up analyses that might be criticized as orientalist. This partly explains the growth of the geopolitical forecasting industry since the end of the Cold War. As someone who worked for years as a senior analyst for both Stratfor and Eurasia Group, two prominent forecasting firms, I can attest that generalizations of the kind Huntington defends, Lewis employs, and Said condemns help form the heart of the analytical process at those firms.

That is why the complete defeat of orientalism in journalism and policy studies has its ironic side, since it discourages the category of broad observations that, while risking prejudice, can also make readers and practitioners less surprised by the middle-term future in various countries. What is the solution? The late Russian-American poet and Nobel laureate Joseph Brodsky writes that "a semblance of objectivity might be achieved, no doubt, by way of a complete self-awareness at the moment of observation."[25] The whole trick is to be self-aware. Indeed, the more we are honest about ourselves, and who we are in the eyes of others, the surer will be our judgments about those we encounter in foreign places. Edward Said, though he may have overreached in his attack on Bernard Lewis and other orientalists, has certainly encouraged this process of criticism of ourselves and of our own culture as it relates to other cultures. Said's work is thus fundamental to the spirit of globalization and to making the world smaller, as proximity discourages broad civilizational judgments.

Nevertheless, while the world might be smaller, differences between peoples and states—between one region of the earth and another—persist. In my travels I simply could not ignore the contrasts between one society and another, between how things work in one place and work in another. Thus, to repeat, as I visited and revisited discrete parts of the sprawling Greater Middle East—all very different from each other—and developed assumptions and conclusions, it was always a matter of being self-aware.

BEING SELF-AWARE MEANT NOT only realizing I was from one culture implicitly judging other cultures, but realizing what position I occupied within my own profession. On the one hand, I was not among the many Western writers on world affairs, particularly in Washington, whose research consisted merely of googling, rather than visiting the places in question; nor was I a specialist who had lived in each country in question and knew the language. I was somewhere in the middle. In the course of my life I had visited most of the countries of the world, many several times. Thus I was a generalist rather than a globalist: the former is respectful of the nuances and minutiae of each place even if he or she doesn't grasp it all; the latter sees one-size-fits-all solutions to vastly different places with their own ground-level realities. The generalist builds up from the bottom in as many places as he can possibly manage; the globalist always looks down from the top. In a world of more and more specialists, a generalist may still prove useful by providing analytical coherence across an immense geography, without denying each place its uniqueness.

With this in mind I set out to explore some places and my own memories of others. I had no particular road map. I just did what I have been doing my whole life: look at a map and say, *There's where I want to go or think about next.*

And even at my best, all I could ever do was catch a fleeting moment in time. For change and evolution were constant everywhere.

CONSTANTINOPLE

———

MY FIRST MORNING IN ISTANBUL, RATHER THAN TURKISH, it is Greek words that form in my mind. *Stin poli* ("in the city," or "to the city"), of which *Istanbul* is a corruption. *Chrysokeras,* the "Golden Horn," the estuary where the Byzantine Greeks, besieged by the conquering Ottoman Turks in that fateful spring of 1453, supposedly dumped their gold. On the other side of the Golden Horn is the newer part of the city where Europeans originally congregated. It was called Pera until the early twentieth century, meaning "across" or "beyond" in Greek. Until that time, Istanbul was still often referred to as *Konstantinoupolis* or Constantinople ("Constantine's city"). Ernest Hemingway titled a 1922 newspaper dispatch "Old Constan," the name he said old-timers used for Constantinople.[1]

Greek words help explain Turkey's historical logic, and therefore it is at a Greek monument where I begin.

Perched over the Golden Horn in old Istanbul, at the spot where two continents and two seas meet, is the Greek Monastery of the *Pantokrator* ("Christ Almighty"), an imposing Byzantine pile of recessed brick and polygonal domes. I slowly circumambulate this architecturally complex and monumental structure that many of the guidebooks ignore. The street and square are empty except for prowling, emaciated cats. Here and there the pavement is littered with ancient stone blocks and stubbles of late Roman walls. I walk inside of what is now an Islamic prayer hall, and am still alone except for a lone workman with a carpet sweeper. There are religious medallions in Arabic and a *minbar*. The early modern Ottoman-era geometric patterns reaching to the ceiling have wiped out what was once sumptuous medieval art. Here three great Byzantine emperors were laid to rest: John II Comnenus, Manuel I Comnenus, and Manuel II Palaeologus. In the twelfth and fifteenth centuries these men ingeniously applied deceit, diplomacy, the military arts, and strategic patience: balancing one foe against another in Sicily, the Balkans, and the Near East in order to win short-term victories. Thus, they extended the life span of their Eastern Orthodox empire. I think first of John II Comnenus and the mosaic depicting his distinguished visage that graces a wall of Hagia Sophia ("Divine Wisdom"), that great cathedral of Byzantium, built by Justinian, with its own rippling domes appearing like half-planets in the heavens, a little more than a mile away from where I now stand on the same bank of the Golden Horn. As a ruler, John II "combined clever prudence with purposeful energy, while at the same time he was a man of upright, steadfast character . . . never losing sight of the boundaries of possibility," writes the late Russian-born Byzantinist George Ostrogorsky, who also writes of Manuel I: "he was a skilled diplomat, and a statesman with bold and far-reaching ideas." As for Manuel II, Ostrogorsky observes that he was "one of the most sympathetic figures" of Byzantium in its death throes, forced to humiliate himself at the court of a rising Ottoman Empire.[2] Not only have such men and their marathon labors been largely forgotten, but not even their graves are left.[3] Rarely has there been such grandeur in the human spirit as when men struggle against certain oblivion.

The Pantokrator Monastery is now the Zeyrek Mosque, just as Hagia Sophia is now the Grand Mosque of Aya Sofya. You must remove your shoes and if you are a woman don a headscarf in order to view, in the case of Aya Sofya, the ancient mosaics of the Virgin Mary with the infant Jesus. Religion here, ever since Constantine the Great converted to Christianity in A.D. 337, has always constituted the groundwork of imperial identity. And so the passage from church to mosque—from gold-plated icons and beeswax candles to painted geometric tiles and prayer carpets—registers the passage from eleven centuries of Byzantine rule to six centuries of Ottoman rule, each of equal aesthetic abundance as the Ottoman sultans through their multiethnic empire did not so much extinguish Byzantine imperialism as transform and invigorate it. That taut imperial thread, however frayed and often hidden—emanating from where the Golden Horn meets the Bosporus at Seraglio Point—lives on in spirit through the millennia into the twenty-first century. To wit, from Seraglio Point one can almost catch a glimpse of the Çamlica Mosque on the city's Asian side, built by the longtime sultanic ruler of Turkey, Recep Tayyip Erdoğan, which with its mammoth domes and six minarets rivals the proportions of the sixth-century Hagia Sophia and the adjacent seventeenth-century Sultan Ahmet "Blue" Mosque.

History, culture, empire, geography: Istanbul, formerly Constantinople, is the quintessence of it all. The tapestry of human interactions at such a critical point on the earth's surface is what we lazily and conveniently label as *fate*.

It might as well begin with Gibbon, I thought, as I left the empty Pantokrator and walked through the narrow, crumbly streets of old Istanbul to the bank of the Golden Horn. Never, I believe, was there such a city to match an author, each able to join the Mediterranean story with that of Inner Asia: each equally able to evoke the process of history itself.

The multiplicity of broad hills before me are jammed with every manner of habitation, both precise and slapdash—wood, stucco, brick, plexiglass—and crowned by domes and minarets, with water on three sides further dramatizing the prospect. The proud domes and loud, knocking seas of Istanbul conjure up the very spirit of Gibbon's timelines, as one emperor and sultan follows the next in a linear progression marching through the millennia.

Gibbon is justly famous for his early volumes on Rome in the West. But it is the latter volumes on Rome in the East that concern me herein, and which manifest his true geographical and philosophical breadth. Rome in the West does not do him justice to the extent of Rome in the East—more commonly known to modern ears as the

Byzantine Empire, the heart of which constitutes the ground I now stand on.

FOR EDWARD GIBBON, the enlightenment intellectual who wrote the greatest historical work in the English language, geography was the "eye" of history. Thus, he often began his research by looking at maps.[4] But *The Decline and Fall of the Roman Empire,* composed between 1776 and 1788, saw geography less as an exercise in fatalism than as a backdrop for an examination of the equally large forces of culture and human nature. This is what particularly manifests itself in the volumes dealing with the Byzantine Empire.

In addition to an acceleration in time—spanning eight centuries instead of four centuries as in the first part—the second part of *The Decline and Fall* registers a dramatic expansion in geographical and historical breadth, in which Gibbon covers the rise and fall of the Byzantine, Sassanid, Vandal, Arab, Mongol, Timurid, Seljuk, and Ottoman empires. In the process, he expands his story beyond the Mediterranean Basin in order to write a true world history: encompassing everything from the silk caravans of Eurasia to the Coptic Church in Ethiopia, as the cultural unity of the Mediterranean established by the Romans completely evaporates (most obviously with the Arab conquest of North Africa). This is less a story of internal decay, despite the received wisdom about Byzantium, than of the rise of Islam and of non-European peoples who migrated westward from the Near East and Asia. It is, too, the story of Achaemenid and Sassanid Persia, which for a thousand years was the enemy of Greece and of Rome in the East.

The key to both parts of *The Decline and Fall* is Gibbon's theme about how triumph and catastrophe can be one and the same: something that the great Byzantine emperors profiled by George Ostrogorsky knew only too well. As Gibbon suggests, conquest in and of itself brings a great power into the webwork of other people's histories and civilizations, and thus multiplies the opportunities for tragedy and miscalculation.

"Prosperity ripened the principle of decay; the causes of destruction multiplied with the extent of the conquest; and as soon as time or accident had removed the artificial supports, the stupendous [imperial] fabric yielded to the pressure of its own weight."[5]

From these typically magisterial—that is, Gibbonian—statements issue forth more specific lessons, equally uncomfortable to postmodern ears.

Gibbon quotes Tacitus about how empire protects politically immature peoples from themselves and from their neighbors. And empires function most calmly and effectively under the principle of hereditary succession. It is, he says, only fear and shame that mitigate tyranny, just as it is general manners that can be far more important than written constitutions. It is the barbarians, which to Gibbon means those who lived outside Rome's borders, who gave birth to the modern and postmodern worlds, and thus in the long run to progress. As for decline, it can be so gradual and relative that people argue about the very existence of it, though at root it means the inability to "combine military and civic virtue."[6] For as civilian morals become decadent, power subsequently devolves to the uniformed brass. That is, the rise of the political power of a nation's military is a sure sign of that nation's cultural decline.

Through it all there is Gibbon's famously stately and ironic style, in which a single sentence can evince the concision of an argument raised and an argument settled, while with an extra phrase or clause he accommodates a further consideration or nuance.[7] And this is to say nothing of his delicious footnotes: like the one about the younger Gordian and all the children he had by his concubines, to which Gibbon adds, Gordian's "literary productions were [also] by no means contemptible."[8]

GIBBON BEGINS HIS SAGA of Rome in the East, that is, of Constantinople—this great city of empire and geopolitics—with a microcosm that illuminates the macrocosm: a dry but devastating portrait of an illiterate youth, Antony, who at the beginning of the

fourth century A.D. forsakes his home and family and wanders eastward away from the Nile and into the utter desert of Upper Egypt, in
order to become *perfect*. This monastic penance, though "original and
intrepid," nevertheless, according to Gibbon, constituted a "dark and
implacable ... fanaticism," reeking of "superstition." And as thousands of anchorites from as far away as Ethiopia followed Antony's
example, "the same cause which relieved the distress of individuals
impaired the strength and fortitude of the empire."⁹ Rome, in the
twilight of the Western Empire and near the dawn of the Eastern
one, was being demonstrably weakened, rather than fortified, by
Christianity with its extremist offshoots like anchorite monasticism.

Defining Christianity as a victory of radicalism over a more moderate paganism may be the most commonly known of Gibbon's themes.
It is what caused *The Decline and Fall* to be met with attacks and great
controversy in Gibbon's own lifetime.* Though, as Gibbon makes us
aware, the very intense Christian identity of Constantinople's ruling
elite constituted, in psychological terms at least, a strategic benefit,
since it allowed them a singular, moral idea of empire.¹⁰ And yet, as
Gibbon explains it with his understated yet devastating condescen-
sion, it is only a short step from the baleful influence of fundamentalist
monasticism to perverse and doctrinal church controversies, which
lead, in turn, to a weakening through distraction of the political order
in both Western Rome and Constantinople. "In the fever of the times
the sense," Gibbon writes, "or rather the sound of a syllable" in the
course of argumentation, "was sufficient to disturb the peace of an
empire."¹¹ In this way, Antony's story fits well within the decline of
Western Rome and serves as a prologue to the long and drawn-out

---

* Today, *The Decline and Fall* is controversial for a related reason. Gibbon's assault on
Christianity has been challenged by the well-known Princeton professor Peter Brown.
Brown has written voluminously about how the centuries of Gibbon's so-called decline were
really those of great intellectual flowering under the very Christian thinkers Gibbon de-
spises. Brown calls this epoch Late Antiquity, which he believes is every bit as distinctive a
period as antiquity and the Dark Ages. See for example Brown's *The World of Late Antiquity*
(London: Thames and Hudson, 1971). Also see Mark Whittow's "Do Byzantine Historians
Still Read Gibbon?" in *The Cambridge Companion to Edward Gibbon,* ed. Karen O'Brien and
Brian Young (New York: Cambridge University Press, 2018).

decline of Eastern Rome. According to Gibbon, the monks' assault on
the vitality of the East would prove no less significant than the barbarians' assault on the West.

As the narrative tentacles of this extreme form of monasticism enter
the main body of Gibbon's history of the eastern empire, the canvas
dramatically widens. The chief virtue of Gibbon's work, especially as he
relates the crowded events of Justinian's rule in the mid-sixth century
(when Justinian was finishing the construction of Hagia Sophia), with
all of its circuitous asides and descriptions of wanton, murderous factions and lavish building sprees, is a godlike perspective on events that
is the gift of distance and the immense passage of time: the *longue
durée*. As Gibbon recounts Justinian's age, time on the throne, enfeeble-
ment of body, and conquests in Italy and Africa, the tone becomes
biblical. Always emanating from this history is the author's matter-of-
fact realism and objectivity: to wit, Justinian's ministers were rarely pro-
moted or selected for their "virtues" or for their "talents"; the Byzantine
emperors "consulted the dictates of interest, without recollecting the
obligations of oaths and treaties;" the "triumph of Christ [in Hagia
Sophia] was adorned with the last spoils of paganism."[12] Justinian
played the Gepidae off against the Lombards: better to shed the blood
of these Germanic peoples rather than one's own. Dissuade, deter, subvert, and only use your own military power as a last resort.[13] It was, in
part, a curious, unwarlike grand strategy, even as it was supremely cynical and supremely effective. Indeed, Rome in the East lasted over
eleven hundred years. Again, a sign of grandeur in the human spirit.

Amid many obscure calamities across the millennia in this fateful
city creeps in the rise of the Turks, migrating from the east. Very little
that is truly historical happens overnight, or within the strictures of a
news deadline. Indeed, the great battles fought between Byzantium
and Sassanid Persia, conducted against the sandpaper emptiness of the
Euphrates river valley near today's Syria-Iraq border, are in Gibbon's
literary hands a study in compression, since they constitute a story of
almost endless repetition. In the midst of this rich infinity of drama,
Gibbon zooms out to mention the Mohammedan wind that defeats
and renders obscure the seesawing war between the two great imperial

powers of Byzantium and Persia. While Byzantium stumbles on, as its expansion from the Danube to the Nile leads to decay, Sassanid Persia crumbles into anarchy until it falls "under the common yoke of the Arabian caliphs."[14]

What is both amazing and devastating is the degree to which almost everything in history is forgotten. The carnage of the Gothic War, fought for nineteen years in the middle of the sixth century between Byzantium and the Ostrogothic kingdom of Italy, was epic in its repercussions on the development of Europe itself (just as it is painstakingly explained by Gibbon), yet it is barely remembered now except by antiquarians. The *longue durée* offers a frightening and inhuman perspective, in other words, in the way that almost everything that truly matters to us, what men fight and die for—their honor and their ideas even—becomes either lost to memory or infinitely condensed, and usually distorted. Gibbon's work is thus the ultimate salvage effort against complete oblivion. For it is important not to forget. It is forgetting that leads to future mistakes. We cannot remember everything, but it is worth the effort to try, given the policy disasters that have befallen us in this region.

And then there is Gibbon's humanity—with portraits of Belisarius, Muhammad, and Charlemagne that equal Plutarch's in their detail and concentration on the moral legacy of great men. Gibbon is simply without comparison. He makes one think of the artistic effort manifested in the statuary of Praxiteles and Michelangelo, something impossible to duplicate in the digital-video age, which by absolving our minds of any real effort immeasurably cheapens them. Gibbon's vast and complex canvas of Byzantium and the barbarian penumbrae from Central Europe to Central Asia, all emanating from this very city, provides the early modern equivalent in the form of text to what those great sculptors of antiquity and the Renaissance wrought.

JUST AS GIBBON ADMITS to the benefits of empire in terms of relative peace and political stability, he also admits to what an unnatural effort is actually required of empire itself:

"There is nothing perhaps more adverse to nature and reason than to hold in obedience remote countries and foreign nations in opposition to their inclination . . . A torrent of barbarians may pass over the earth, but an extensive empire must be supported by a refined system of policy and oppression," in which there is, nevertheless, "a swift and easy communication with the extreme parts . . ."[15]

Perhaps, the empire more than all the others that Gibbon sees as extraordinary is that of the Arabs, essentially because of geography. While Rome in the East was distracted by its war with Persia, and the imperial and church bureaucracies here in Constantinople were equally distracted by Nestorian and Monophysite sects and heresies, Muhammad, "with the sword in one hand and the Koran in the other, erected his throne on the ruins of Christianity and of Rome." This throne took as its dominion a vast, relatively empty, and seemingly unlivable space between the southern shore of the Mediterranean and Ethiopia, and between Asia Minor and the fecund valleys of Yemen. Gibbon describes this "boundless level of sand . . . intersected by sharp and naked mountains . . . without shade or shelter" as bleak even by the rigorous standards of Tartary. It is precisely because of this inhospitable, practically lunar landscape that, according to Gibbon, the Arabs were unconquerable. The armies, as he says, of Sesostris, Cyrus, Trajan, and Pompey, as well as the legions of Augustus, would have "melted away in disease and lassitude" were they ever to face such a landscape.[16]

Muhammad, though he "breathed among the faithful a spirit of charity and friendship,"[17] did not bequeath a political system, or a hierarchy of power, and thus Muhammad's legacy was utopian in its way, given over in the coming decades and centuries to tyranny and anarchy. Some of the roots of Middle Eastern chaos—and why the Middle East in recent centuries has not quite developed as has Europe or the Far East—go back to the very founding of Islam, and are inextricable from the region's geography. And this is all in Gibbon. For example, Egypt is more stable than its neighbors because it is a river valley civilization that does not lie athwart the historic path of conquest and migration like that other great river valley civilization: that of the Tigris and Euphrates. Because such facts imply a destiny, and destiny interferes with human agency, journalists, academics, and intellectuals often ignore them or play them down. Yet, as for Gibbon's own sweeping cultural and geographical summaries about the Middle East, they are the precursor to those of the great Arabian travelers and explorers, Charles M. Doughty and T. E. Lawrence. His writing, like theirs, is full of subjectivities and generalities, to be sure, but one rejects them outright at one's own analytic peril. He simply makes one less surprised about why things happen as they do. To read him is to realize that not to be able to generalize is to immobilize discussion altogether.

Gibbon's description of the desert Middle East contains details of every Arab conquest from Persia to Africa, and from the Pyrenees to China, replete with the profiles of the military leaders involved, again often rising to the level of Plutarch. He writes about the tax administration of early Muslim Egypt, and of the tensions between the invading Arabs and the Berber tribes in the Maghreb. Yet emanating from all of this is the realization that the various Arab armies, followed by civilian administrators, subdued Christianity and "all memory of the language and religion of Rome" between the Nile (with its durable Coptic civilization) and the Atlantic clean across North Africa.[18] The very utopian and anarchic tendencies of the Arabs (attributes of which the Europeans, too, were not innocent in their history) led to such explosions of conquest, coupled with the complete dissolution of dynasties. The desert Middle East, from the early seventh century onward, was a region of extreme turbulence.

Meanwhile, as Arab dynasties rose and fell, Rome in the East, headquartered here in Constantinople, continued its relative and tortuous decline, marked by an increasing pomposity in the capital (with the profusion of titles and privileges), reinforcing, in turn, distinctions between the elites and the common people: a fate natural to far-flung imperial systems. As Gibbon writes, hostilities at home and in the capital are the most potent cause of decay. Bluntly, he states: "The Greeks, by their . . . divisions, were the authors of their own final ruin."[19] Truly, toward the Byzantine empire's end, in the mid-fourteenth century, during civil wars in the capital under the rules of the elder and younger Andronicus, the Ottoman Turks were able to wrest away the large, nearby region of Bithynia.

IN THE LAST VOLUME of *The Decline and Fall* Gibbon observes how it was various irruptions to the east that both directly and indirectly vanquished the Byzantine Empire: so that in this way Asia determined the fate of Europe, for Europe at the end of the day is but a subcontinent of Eurasia. This is another reason why Gibbon is so refreshing: innocent as he is of the modern tendency to divide up the world into subdivisions of area expertise, he sees the interconnectedness of the world, and would not be surprised by, for example, the inroads being made now by China, Japan, and India into the economies of the Persian Gulf and Africa—to say nothing of the effect of China and Russia upon Europe.

Gibbon, a paragon of the Western Enlightenment, nevertheless registers what he considers the moral superiority of the Mongols under Genghis Khan. "The Catholic inquisitors of Europe, who defended nonsense by cruelty, might have been confounded by the example of a barbarian, who anticipated the lessons of philosophy, and established by his laws a system of pure theism and perfect toleration."[20] The Mongols conquered practically half the longitudes of the globe, and it was only the parched Arabian desert around Mecca and Medina, which lacked grazing ground for the Mongol cavalry, that protected those holy cities from the fate of Aleppo, Damascus, and Baghdad to the north.

In the face of such onslaughts, Byzantium might have fallen sooner than it did. Gibbon, in teleological fashion, credits the rise of Tamerlane in Samarkand and his war against the Ottoman Turks (following Tamerlane's conquest of Tartary and Persia) as delaying for about half a century the final collapse of Rome in the East. Truly, the overrunning of Constantinople in 1453 by the Ottoman Sultan Mehmed II ("the Conqueror") was both a matter of contingent individual actions in the heat of battle as well as the culmination of an historical process spanning centuries and involving peoples from the Mediterranean to the shadow zones of China.

The Ottoman Turkish Empire would constitute, by way of Byzantium, the final reincarnation of ancient Rome, governing in a city and in a manner that recalled the empire of the Caesars. Actually they were preceded by their Turkic relatives, the Seljuk Kingdom of Rum (Rome), which dominated Anatolia between the eleventh and thirteenth centuries. It had been the Byzantine Greeks who invited Turkic tribes into eastern Anatolia to protect Constantinople from the Persians. And in 1071, at Manzikert in eastern Anatolia, the Seljuks defeated the Byzantines themselves, an early death knell for the latter's entire Christian empire.[21] History is a weaving, where the past always lives inside the present.

Turkic culture had been made strong by the harsh living conditions and economic requirements of life on Inner Asia's high steppe. The Seljuks adopted Islam in Khorasan, in northeastern Iran, on their path westward. A strict, top-down warrior hierarchy and a heightened role for women contributed to a cultural dynamism that would help the Turkic peoples dominate the Middle East into the twentieth century.[22] In sum, the Turks were Islamized steppe warriors with a veneer of Persian culture,[23] who, as a show of their dynamism, in quick succession in the early sixteenth century crushed the Persians, Kurds, Syrian Arabs, and Egyptians.

This is all the world of Gibbon, with its emphasis on culture and geography. Gibbon may frequently rise to the level of a philosopher, but he is firmly rooted in the nuts and bolts of history, and in the world of power, so that, for example, he admits that the spread of gunpowder (among the Ottoman Turks, Safavid Persians, and Mughal Indians) was quicker and more decisive than developments in ideas, reason, and the arts of peace. "A philosopher, according to his temper, will laugh or weep at the folly of mankind," he concludes.[24]

Prescience is something that can only be hoped for. But if it is in any way achievable, it must be a matter of merging Gibbon's clarifying realism, wide-screen sensibility, and subjective insights on terrain and ethnography with the stream of current events—which begin with the bustling and dramatic water-born reality now before my eyes. As the Golden Horn empties into the Bosporus, which literally separates Europe from Asia, and indirectly the Mediterranean from the Black Sea, nowhere else on earth is there a city more pregnant with geographical power. You can forgive someone being a determinist here: a place where since antiquity Constantinople—a melodic name I prefer to Istanbul—has been the seat of vast, longitude-spanning empires. There is something very uneasy and historically seismic about where I now stand.

MY INITIAL IMPRESSIONS:

A gargantuan, postmodern airport, vast superhighways, leading to a teeming and sprawling city, utterly intimidating even for a veteran visitor: storied, without being a museum piece. It is equipped with its own quirky form of dynamic efficiency matched to semicontinental scale and a stirring geography. Digitalization has been the great equalizer. In an age of COVID-19 you order your meals electronically at my hotel restaurant because of the fear of touching printed menus. Jazzy video signage is everywhere. For decades when Turkey was comparatively backward, and allowed inside NATO only because of its ultra-strategic geography, this country was an alliance member that simply shut up and followed along. Now it is too powerful in its own right to be a mere follower. When I first visited Turkey in 1973, I had the feeling of stepping into an old movie. This time my impressions confirm a more equal, multipolar world. The haunting, seedy aspect of Istanbul's historical center in the 1970s, preserving, as in a *plein air* painting, the monuments of the Byzantine and Ottoman past, is now a crowded, global tourist trap with glitzy boutiques and theme restaurants. The *gecekondus* ("constructed in the night"), the slum settlements of the old Istanbul, barely exist anymore. They have all been engulfed by new building projects.

THIS IS MY FIRST visit here in over twenty years. Before then, in the 1980s and 1990s, I visited Istanbul regularly, when the city's population was half the size and before the real explosion in coastal development. That was a time when the end of the Cold War was starting to enhance Turkey's geopolitical significance: when artificial divisions between East and West began to crumble and Mustafa Kemal Atatürk's fiercely modernizing, geographically compact, and uniethnic Turkish state—a rebuke to the easygoing cosmopolitanism of the far-flung Byzantine and Ottoman empires—was losing its secular grip. Now, of course, Istanbul has become a city of more headscarves and the latest smartphones: nothing unusual there, as the advance of technology requires the emotional grounding of intensified religion.

Yet the stage set is still recognizable. As with my earlier visits, I have always been conscious of Istanbul being windy and cold, tempestuous in its weather, more of a Black Sea city than a Mediterranean one: a bit gritty, especially by the docks, trapped by geographic destiny rather than unleashed by it, a city still best photographed in black-and-white by the late Ara Güler, an Armenian-Turkish photojournalist I was once privileged to know.

Of course, from the 1970s to the 1990s Istanbul looked seedy only to me, because I was new to the place. Yet even back then, by historical standards, Istanbul was in an advanced state of modernism, which had truly begun at the end of World War I.

Wars put history on fast-forward. In a matter of years or weeks even, decades can advance, as Lenin famously noted. World War I saw the collapse of four early modern empires: Wilhelmine Prussia, Romanov Russia, Habsburg Austria-Hungary, and Ottoman Turkey, the last of which in particular was for many decades an already creaking and moldy imperial machine before it smashed into dust. The First World War marked the ultimate end of early modernism—with its ambiguous, multilingual, and multiethnic identities—and the real beginning of the modern age with its rigid, uniethnic, and ultimately violent nation-state formulas that all detonated in World War II. The world had gone forward, but it had not morally progressed.

Mustafa Kemal "Atatürk" (Father Turk), who single-handedly invented modern republican Turkey out of the ruins of World War I and the Ottoman Empire, was in truth a creature of early modern imperialism. Born and raised in Salonica (now Thessaloniki in Greece) in the 1880s and 1890s, he experienced the fabulous intercommunal cosmopolitanism of an imperial city with its large population of Christians and Jews, as well as of Muslims. Counterintuitively, this played a vital role in Atatürk's avowed secularism, in which all religions could exist since none was advantaged by the state.

But it was a gradual process. Atatürk's military victory over the invading Greeks, who were seeking to carve up the carcass of the Ottoman Empire in Anatolia, was conducted as a Muslim holy war against Orthodox Christianity, in which he relied on a network of local mosques for support. The Turkish population subsequently declared him *Gazi*, the "victor over the infidels."

But once having established a new state over all of Anatolia, Atatürk's true intentions emerged. He abolished the Muslim religious courts. He forbade men from wearing the fez and discouraged women from wearing the veil. Crucially, he adopted the Western calendar, so that events would date from Jesus's birth rather than from Muhammad's *Hegira.* And he replaced the Arabic script with the Latin one, which would in time create a vast mental gulf between Turks and other Muslims in the Middle East.[25] Atatürk was a complicated figure. In 1923 he moved the capital from Istanbul, with its connections to the Ottoman Empire and the Muslim caliphate, to Ankara, deep in the Anatolian interior and rooted in a more pagan Turkic past. Atatürk's definition of Turkishness was racial, and thus he was opposed to the cosmopolitan bonding of different peoples that was a hallmark of Ottoman imperialism.[26] He wanted Turkey to escape from the backwardness of a declining empire, even as it was the multiethnic spirit of that empire that, deny it as he might, contributed to his otherwise broadmindedness and obsession with making Turkey truly Western, and open to ideas in a scientific and technological age.

In the early and mid 1980s, nearly a half century after Atatürk's death, I first started reporting on Turkey in earnest, making frequent trips to Turkey from Greece. It was then that it began to dawn on me that Atatürk had gone too far in his secularization of the country. Of course, the process of a moderated return to religion that I expected to happen had already been under way for some time. In the 1950s, Muslim education had begun reviving with new and expanded curriculums. Small Islamic parties had also emerged on the political fringes as a backlash to secularization. The public calls to prayer were now chanted in Arabic rather than in Turkish. And when Turkey fell into near anarchy in the late 1970s and 1980, there were fears of another Islamic revolution as had just occurred in neighboring Iran. Yet when order was finally restored by a military junta in September 1980, the generals deliberately did not altogether return Turkey to Atatürk's brutal and militant secularism, but allowed religion to coexist with the secularist Kemalist state.

But this was all a matter of degrees. The demonstrable shift back toward religion only occurred in December 1983, when Turgut Özal, a deeply religious Turk who lacked all of Atatürk's graces—the kind of man you met in the shantytowns and in the Anatolian interior—was elected prime minister. Özal would remain prime minister throughout the decade before becoming president. He operated under the guise of the secular military, whose basic directives he did not challenge. The military would just hint and he would get the message. Moreover, Özal was a pronounced believer in the secular republic founded by Atatürk, even as he himself was publicly very religious and subtly advanced a neo-Ottoman foreign policy: stressing Islam as something that both the Turks and the large minority of ethnic Kurds inside Turkey's borders—as well as Turkey's Arab neighbors—could all hold in common. I met Özal on a number of occasions. He was rather uncouth. He chewed while he talked. It was said that he never learned properly how to use a knife and fork. But he was also absolutely magnetic, somewhat short in stature but with real presence. Özal was a man of the up-and-coming urbanized peasantry: brilliant and sly in his way, a man who squared many circles, believing in both Kemalism and religion, in both the Koran and a close alliance with Ronald Reagan's America.

Özal, in fact, was a great transition figure of post-Ottoman Turkey—standing halfway between Atatürk and the present. He came after Atatürk, and after turbulent bouts of democracy and a succession of military rulers, yet before another bout of ineffectual and turbulent democracy, which would culminate dramatically in more than two decades of rule by hardcore Islamists: men who didn't care about squaring circles with the secularists as Özal did, but only in undermining the very modern secular republic that Atatürk had founded. Özal in his very person embodied the perfect synthesis between deeply held religion and a secular state. Özal helped devout Muslims make their peace with Kemalism, as Atatürk's philosophy is called. Alas, the Islamists who ruled Turkey after him took national politics to the opposite extreme of Atatürk.

In 2002, Recep Tayyip Erdoğan's Justice and Development Party (AK Party) won a resounding victory in national elections, bringing those Islamists to power on the back of a conservative and Islamic bourgeoisie that had its beginnings in the Özal era. Globalization played a role in the continued rise of this new Islamic class, as small- and medium-sized firms throughout the conservative Anatolian hinterland took advantage of the new, worldwide economic system to find markets for their products. In fact, in the early years of Erdoğan's rule as prime minister, his government cut a figure of moderation and technical expertise, in keeping with Erdoğan's own record as mayor of Istanbul back in the 1990s, when he measurably improved the water system, garbage collection, and air quality. Erdoğan was the classic and dynamic big-city boss, raised in the poor, rough-and-tumble Istanbul neighborhood of Kasimpasa, with its dockyards and masculine culture, and its resentment of Europeanized elites. His own family was from the remote Black Sea region of northeastern Anatolia, close to the border with former Soviet Georgia. Over time, though, in the course of years and decades in power, featuring purges of more liberal and centrist party members, Erdoğan's autocratic tendencies, first learned as a roughneck in Kasimpasa, truly became evident. It is telling that one of the rulers Erdoğan came to admire most was Russia's Vladimir Putin. Erdoğan was even said to take notes whenever he met with Putin. Both men shared a fate: neither could leave power peaceably because of wide-ranging corruption charges that would be leveled against them—and this was long before the Ukraine war.

As Erdoğan evolved into a democratically elected autocrat, he truly Islamized Turkey: changing school curriculums, clamping down on dissenting journalists and media organs, playing with election laws in order to eventually make himself an executive president, and, most crucially, emasculating the secular military, so that if it ever again attempted a coup it would fail—exactly as happened in July 2016. At one point, Erdoğan had a quarter of the country's generals and admirals imprisoned.

The failed coup of July 15, 2016, was seen inside Turkey as akin to an attempted foreign invasion by a population that, having achieved near-universal literacy,[27] now feels itself beyond the coups d'état of an earlier stage of political development. It was also proof that even after so many years in power Erdoğan still maintained popularity with a Turkish population that is more anti-Western and far more religious than it was during the Cold War, when Turkey's membership in NATO, its friendship with the West, and its close ties with Israel could be taken for granted. Those days when the secular generals held power behind the scenes are long gone. After all, Turkey's attempts to gain entry to the European Union have over the years been regularly rebuffed, humiliating Turkish Muslims. Then there was the abject unpopularity of America's invasion of neighboring Iraq, which both threatened stability on Turkey's southeastern border and raised the specter of an independent (and for Turkey, destabilizing) Kurdish state in northern Iraq. The Europeanized and whiskey-sipping secular elite in Istanbul and Ankara—the true spiritual descendants of Atatürk—could do nothing to help America, whose invasion of Iraq even they themselves opposed. This was all prologue to Erdoğan's Islamicized Turkey gradually moving closer to Russia and radical Arab groups.

The story of the Turkish military is telling. Formerly, time spent at NATO headquarters in Brussels and at military war colleges in the United States was fundamental to the career paths of ambitious Turkish officers. But under Erdoğan, it has been precisely such assignments that have ended promotion prospects within the Turkish armed forces. The failed coup of 2016 led to an even more personalized emergency rule by Erdoğan, who used it to continue remolding the military in the direction of the Iranian one. This led to mass purges of officers, including dozens of generals and admirals, as well as 18,000 officials ousted from the police and judiciary, whose loyalty seemed questionable to the Islamic authorities. Indeed, Erdoğan's purchase of the S-400 missile and air defense system from Putin's Russia, in stark violation of NATO policy, was emblematic of Turkey's drift away from Western alliance structures. In sum, the failed coup attempt of 2016 fostered further regime consolidation and a heightened sense of mission within Erdoğan's inner circle that, in effect, virtually ended the full-bore Kemalist epoch in Turkish history.

In 2017, Erdoğan established an alliance with the far-right National Movement Party (MHP) so that he could govern as a nationalist Islamist, with an aggressive military approach against Kurdish minorities in neighboring Syria, Iraq, and Iran that dovetailed perfectly with his neo-Ottoman imperialism in the Middle East. Whereas Özal's neo-Ottomanism was subtle and organic, Erdoğan's was militaristic. Moreover, in the years following the failed coup, Erdoğan summarily removed roughly 70 percent of the ethnic-Kurdish district leaders in eastern and southeastern Turkey, replacing them with far more compliant figures, so that autocracy within Turkey's official borders went hand in hand with a policy of advancing Turkey's interests beyond those very borders, with Turkish troops in Syria and Iraq. Erdoğan's nationalist Islamist approach to history asserted that once Turks had fully embraced Islam they would be prepared to become the natural leaders of the entire Muslim world, in a sort of return to empire.[28] This was the core of the Ottoman mentality, which for many hundreds of years gave the Muslim world a dependable dynastic direction following the many wars over succession that had typified the early Islamic centuries under Arab leadership.

There were also acts of historical symbolism writ large. Atatürk had converted the great sixth-century Eastern Orthodox cathedral of Byzantium, Hagia Sophia, into the museum of Aya Sofya, in keeping with his secular vision of a modern Turkish republic. Erdoğan, on July 24, 2020, the ninety-seventh anniversary of the signing of the Treaty of Lausanne, which had established Turkey's current borders, held a Muslim prayer service in Aya Sofya, newly converted from a museum back into a mosque, just as it had been during the nearly five centuries of Ottoman rule. The imperial thread was thus reestablished, rendering Atatürk's pro-Western policy of secular modernism and rejection of empire as but an interregnum in the long march of Turkish history.

Just consider: Erdoğan said that the "revival of the Hagia Sophia as a mosque is ushering the news for the liberation of [the] al-Aqsa mosque in Jerusalem."[29] Erdoğan saw Turkey as the pillar of the radical Muslim Brotherhood in the whole Middle East. He provided citizenship and passports to a "dozen" members of Hamas, the radical, Gaza-based Palestinian group.[30] He dispatched five thousand Turkish soldiers to pro-Iranian Qatar to help it protect itself against moderates in the Arab world. Tellingly, when in 2015 he received Mahmoud Abbas in Ankara, the Palestinian president was flanked by an honor guard decked out in the uniform of the Ottoman soldiery.[31]

For decades, throughout much of the twentieth century, Kemalist rule had established the secular military as the guarantor of political stability, with military coups occurring every decade or so whenever democracy risked sliding into anarchy. But now there was no secular and Westernized military capable of staging a so-called corrective movement. This means that better governments and better democratic governance become absolutely essential if Turkey is to remain stable. Also essential is a peaceful solution to the Kurdish problem. And because those things seem natural but are incredibly difficult to implement, the question becomes, Where exactly does an Islamist, post-Atatürk Turkey go from here? Could there be a soft landing to Erdoğan's quasi-dictatorial rule?

Turkey has always been full of contradictions. Whereas Atatürk was a fierce secularist, Erdoğan pulled Turkey back in the direction of the Islamic politics of the Middle East. As the clerical regime in neighboring Iran may begin to crumble, it will be interesting to see if it shifts Turkey back in the direction of secularism.

I CONTINUE WALKING TOWARD the Golden Horn away from the Pantokrator Monastery, past the shops with their sacks of spices out-

doors on the street and their stage-lit interiors filled with more delec-
tables. It occurs to me while walking that Erdoğan has ruled Turkey
longer than Atatürk, who established the Turkish republic in 1923 and
died in 1938. Whereas Atatürk had oriented Turkey toward Europe
and away from Islam, Erdoğan oriented Turkey toward Islam and
away from Europe. Or rather, Erdoğan and particularly his former
foreign minister and prime minister, Ahmet Davutoğlu, turned Turkey
back toward the world of the former Ottoman Empire: that is, toward
the Balkans, the Middle East, and North Africa. "Understanding the
importance of Turkey's imperial past is essential to understanding
modern Turkey," writes Soner Cagaptay of the Washington Institute
for Near East Policy, adding that Erdoğan, like the last effective Ottoman sultan, Abdul Hamid II, and the Young Turks who opposed
Abdul Hamid at the beginning of the twentieth century, all had a
"common goal, reviving Ottoman greatness."[32]

The Ottoman Empire, like other early modern empires, is not coming back. But it may still be a better compass point than any other for
discerning where Turkey is headed. For empire and imperialism are
concepts denounced only in a guilt-ridden West. Here people take
pride in such legacies.

MY HOTEL, THE PERA Palace, practically drips with neoclassical and
art nouveau surfaces, positively oriental with its gaudy, overabundant
decoration. At the height of the Belle Epoque, when it was built, the
Pera Palace announced itself as the last outpost of Europe on the brink
of Asia. Now my somewhat shabby and picturesque-yet-impractical
room is a tourist's cliché in a city of other residences that are postmodern masterpieces. In the café I met a fashionably dressed man with a
Lacoste sweater who, with his degrees from the most prestigious international universities, was a full-fledged member of the global elite. I
might have met him at any number of high-level gatherings around
the world, or had the same discussion with him over Zoom. My insis-
tence on meeting him, as well as others like him, here in Turkey was an
indulgence. I feel that even in an age of global communications, meet-

ing someone *in situ* intensifies the interaction and allows one to concentrate especially hard on the place under discussion.

We decided to leave the hotel café and walk outside on the terrace, away from other people. Then he just started talking, gently correcting some of my preconceptions, and in the process downplaying and adding nuance to what is known about Turkey's Islamic rulers. The political changes I had noticed were less changes than evolutions, he said. For example, Turkey, long before Erdoğan, had never actually been a normal member of NATO. As a hybrid European–Middle Eastern country it always had its differences with the West. For example, during the first Gulf War in 1991, when the U.S. military's ejection of Saddam Hussein's army from Kuwait was backed by dozens of countries in Europe, the Turkish public beyond the ruling elites roundly rejected it. The big difference is not that Turkey had changed, but more crucially that the international situation had. "In terms of global leadership, we are in a transition period," he explained, "between outright American dominance and whatever lies beyond. That means it's a Hobbesian world, where the strong do what they want and the weak must adjust. And this guy," continuing, with a reference to Erdoğan, "saw power voids and kept pushing into them. And guess what, there was often no response." As for the Erdoğan government's religiosity, it was the end result of the 1980 military coup, which "Sunnified" Turkey out of fear of the Shi'ite revolution next door in Iran the year before. "It was in 1980, two decades before Erdoğan came to power, that the Islamic genie was let out of the bottle here in Turkey."

"You see," he went on, "these guys in power are really provincials. Turgut Özal may have been uncouth and from the provinces. But he was educated. His wife was a liberal, who smoked and drank in public. And Özal was very much influenced by his wife. You cannot compare Özal with Tayyip Erdoğan."

Nevertheless, by the 2020s Erdoğan was already boxed in. As long as there existed at least the possibility of an historic reconciliation with the ethnic Kurds, who demographically dominated southeastern Turkey and had large communities throughout all the major cities, the political parties to the left and center retained the possibility for regaining power. But the across-the-board political refusal in the elections of 2015 to allow the Kurds the right as a distinct group to political representation meant that the ethnic-Turkish nationalists now had Erdoğan's Islamic clique "by the balls," since it was the nationalists' hardline view about the Kurds that had prevailed. Erdoğan could no longer stay in power without the far-right Nationalist Movement Party (MHP), especially after breaking with his erstwhile religious allies, the Gülenists, a Sunni Islamic social service movement established by the religious scholar Fethullah Gülen in the 1970s.* In other words, Erdoğan was already a weakened dictator at the time of my visit. And I wondered how long he would stay in power.

The upshot of the Islamic-nationalist alliance meant, according to a local contact, that the Turkish political system had finally become "unbearable." Political legitimacy had been "totally destroyed." For decades, even during the hair-raisingly thin electoral victories of competing political parties in the 1970s, in which one minority government replaced another, everyone still accepted the results of elections, and understood them to be generally fair and untainted. The system had held. Now it was, he repeated, "destroyed." Beyond Erdoğan's base of supporters, which accounted for roughly one-third of the electorate, election results were no longer understood to be automatically fair and governments were no longer considered to be legitimate.

Meanwhile, as my friend continued his narrative, Erdoğan and his regime have become ever more radicalized. "Whatever you write, never underestimate the effect on Erdoğan of the silence of the entire West in the wake of the July 15, 2016, coup attempt against him. That silence changed Erdoğan. It made him hateful," and pushed him toward Russia's Vladimir Putin, who immediately reached out to him with a personal phone call, and according to some reports even alerted him hours in advance of the coup attempt.†

---

* Gülen, a charismatic scholar and cleric-like figure, has been living in exile in the United States.

† Subsequently, Erdoğan decided to purchase the Russian-made S-400 missile defense system, enraging NATO and the U.S. Congress.

My friend concluded:

"Even if Erdoğan wanted to leave office, he can't anymore. After years of consolidating power, the layers of people surrounding him depend on him for their very lives."

Thus, the question of political legitimacy in Turkey was not completely answered. And this was after decades of predominantly democratic rule.

I VISITED THE LEAFY, tony suburb of Etiler, full of malls, cafés, and gyms, with winding residential streets packed with late-model cars and spectacular views of the Bosporus, reminding me of the suburb of Glyfada in Athens, where I used to live by the sea in the 1980s, another indication of the vast wealth created here in recent decades. Asli Aydıntaşbaş, a local journalist with international degrees, welcomed me into her apartment. We sat outside on her balcony. Her fingers moving as she talked, she led me through the labyrinth of Turkish attitudes toward empire.

"The Turkey I grew up in had no imperial pride, except for the specific fact of the many Ottoman conquests. We were all at that time spiritual children of Atatürk, who had thought of the Ottoman past as backward and hindering our march to catch up with the West. The ultimate mission of Atatürk's republic was to arrive at contemporary civilization, which was defined as European and American. After all, Kemalist doctrine taught us that the Ottoman Empire had collapsed under its own weight. Atatürk himself had spent his youth with the Young Turks trying to topple the bankrupt Ottoman system led by Abdul Hamid II," the last sultan exercising full control over the empire, who was an embattled, complex, and fascinating figure: a symbol of both repression and ultimately failed attempts at reform and institution-building.

"That was then," she said. "Under the Islamists, a wave of nostalgia for the Ottoman Empire emerged. Rather than the Young Turks, it is Abdul Hamid who demands our sympathy in public discussions, the sultan who tried to save the empire. Atatürk's modern republic is now seen as a mistake.* His nation-state is viewed as reductionist, robbing us of our real geography" in the Balkans and the Middle East beyond Anatolia. "The nation-state, we are told, means selling ourselves short. According to this new imperial mindset, as the Islamists explain it, 'Turks need to close the hundred-year parenthesis' that was Atatürk's Turkey."

"As for Erdoğan's Turkey," she went on, "it wants to be a stand-alone . . . non-aligned power on the periphery of Europe," in a way like Tito's Yugoslavia during the Cold War. "The conservative rulers of modern Turkey want to constantly remind the nation of its glorified past, whether in new television dramas or in theme parks . . . In this way, Turkey's military adventures in Syria, Libya, Qatar, and Somalia are part of an 'imperial destiny,' and 'certainly not a liability.'"

Encouraging Erdoğan's regional aggressiveness were the changes in the region itself. The political vacuums created in Syria, Iraq, and Libya had created temptations for Erdoğan. For example, the Syrian civil war had thrown up independent Kurdish forces right on Turkey's border, arguably aligned with guerrillas inside Turkey. Erdoğan's motive for action was not, therefore, illegitimate. Meanwhile, Russia, despite Vladimir Putin's machinations, was still weaker than the old Soviet Union—even before the Ukraine war—so that Turkey now had less reason to be closely allied with the United States as it had been during the Cold War.

But this is where the Gibbonian storyline, in which empire is the default system of order, gets undermined, she suggested. While Tito, with his half-Croat, half-Slovene background, was a creature of Central Europe, who ruled Yugoslavia in the manner of a Habsburg emperor, and who during the Cold War deftly helped create the non-aligned movement as a hedge against the two superpowers, Turkey's Islamist rulers had no such aptitude. Unlike Ottoman-era diplo-

---

*   Erdoğan's regime sees not only Atatürk as problematic, but also the Westernized Ottoman Empire of the 1800s. Cagaptay, p. 294.

mats whom the Islamists professed to admire, they didn't ingratiate themselves with their neighbors, or know how to play one adversary off against the other, while calming them at the same time, in the manner of both the Ottoman and Byzantine empires: rather, they made enemies all around. To wit, the Greeks and the Israelis, who had been quiet adversaries for decades, were at the time closely allied with the Egyptians, French, and others against Turkey over gas-drilling rights in the eastern Mediterranean. True, Turkey moved closer to Russia, an historical enemy in the Crimean War and World War I in the Caucasus. Indeed, the Ottoman Empire fought fifteen major wars with the Russian Empire between the fifteenth and early twentieth centuries.[33] But rather than two states that have assuaged their differences, what emerged was merely an alliance between two individuals, Erdoğan and Putin, both of whom were in the process of trying to rebuild their respective empires. "It is a weird dance involving just two men," Aydintaşbaş said, with no bureaucracies beneath them to help whenever there is a crisis, since the bureaucracies on both sides have deeper memories of the enmity between the two states. And, she emphasized, "Erdoğan stands a real chance of losing a future election."

Catching her breath, Aydintaşbaş observed that the Ottoman Empire stood for cosmopolitanism and the protection of minorities, since it was more decentralized and tolerant than its British and French imperial counterparts. "It may have been the sick man of Europe, but it wasn't the sick man of Asia. Mehmed II 'the Conqueror,' who captured Constantinople from the Byzantines in 1453, was fabulously multilingual. He was close to the Greeks and Armenians. He had his portrait painted by the Venetian artist [Gentile] Bellini. But this narrow, provincial crew is not going to build or rebuild an empire like Mehmed's. Instead, what you have now is lumpen-Ottomanism. Turgut Özal was much closer to being a true descendant of the Ottomans." As for Erdoğan, "he represents Ottomanism as a cover for authoritarianism," building layers of militias and security apparatchiks around him.

Later she happened to mention the pedestrian thoroughfare, Istiklal Caddesi, near my hotel. "It used to have a real Left Bank aura," she said, "with art galleries and many little handicraft bazaars. Now it is sterile."

"Yes," I said. "I found it disappointing, not at all like I remember it from the 1990s. I even recall going to a gallery opening there in 1998. What happened?"

She shrugged. "They," meaning the regime, "shut down the whole arts scene there. Now it's just bland cafés and kebab joints. This is what gradually happens with revolutions. They all end with sterility."

I thought of the Russian Revolution, which began with a tumultuous and euphoric upheaval toppling the tsar, painstakingly captured by Aleksandr Solzhenitsyn in his Red Wheel series, and ended with the graveyard silence and absolute repression of the Bolsheviks. The Iranian Revolution, too, began with the mass euphoria of toppling the shah and ended with the deadening lumpen silence and undermining of Persian culture by the ayatollahs, as if the whole country had gone from Technicolor to black-and-white. Turkey under the Islamists was experiencing a diluted version of this phenomenon.

"What lies beyond Erdoğan?" I asked.

"There is no soft landing for Erdoğan. But there can be a soft landing for Turkey." Turkey, she intimated, still had a European structure that would prevent the chaos of the 1970s, when it was far less developed.

"Might there be a coup sometime in the future?"

"It's an unknown unknown," she replied. The 2016 coup attempt was widely unpopular for two reasons. First, simply because it failed, nobody wanted to stick their head out by voicing support for it. Second, there was the fear that it might have only brought the Gülenists, another Sunni Islamic movement, to power—as they were thought to be behind the coup attempt.

As I prepared to leave, she looked out over the Bosporus and started talking about all the myriad restrictions imposed by Erdoğan's regime and previous Turkish governments on the small Greek Orthodox Patriarchate in Istanbul, which in theory leads the Orthodox Christian world, but in practice represents a dying community in the city. The Greeks must send their children out of Turkey for proper religious training and hope that they come back, despite all the temptations of Europe and America, so passing on their legacy is problematic. Nor could they select a new patriarch from abroad, since all church officials had to be Turkish citizens. It was all part of the effort to weaken and eventually extinguish Greek life here. The Greek Patriarchate was the last true breath of Rome and Constantinople here, and therefore, at least officially, of Gibbon's world. I suddenly yearned to meet the patriarch, but he was in Rome at the time of my visit, seeking assistance for his general situation from the Catholic pope.

MURAT ONGUN, THE SPOKESMAN for the opposition mayor of Istanbul, Ekrem İmamoğlu, met me in his private club, the Soho House, formerly the U. S. consulate in the city. He had just come from a smoke outside, and as we sat down with glasses of wine, he picked up where Asli Aydintaşbaş had left off.

Like his boss, the mayor, Ongun was a man of the Republican People's Party, founded in 1923 and the oldest party in Turkey. The party was staunchly democratic and Kemalist. Thus, Ongun was a young man of the old Turkey.

"Erdoğan's government has been in power for two decades," he said, so it has institutionally entrenched itself. "But what I call the common sense of the state, its underlying structure, prevents us from becoming like Russia." He mentioned the Istanbul election as an example.

It was Erdoğan who had said that whoever wins Istanbul wins Turkey. Erdoğan himself had been a mayor of Istanbul and had used it as a power base to become prime minister. Well, İmamoğlu of the Republican People's Party defeated Erdoğan's candidate of the Islamic Justice and Development (AK) Party in the March 19, 2019, mayoral election. Erdoğan then got the result annulled and a second election was held in June 2019, which İmamoğlu again won by an even bigger majority, making him the mayor. "This will lead eventually to a change in power for all of Turkey," Ongun said.

He went on:

"Atatürk is still widely popular. Erdoğan has tried to have it both ways with Atatürk, undermining Atatürk's legacy yet celebrating him at the same time. Kemalism is just too deeply rooted to be overturned and Erdoğan knows it. Erdoğan uses neo-Ottomanism for domestic consumption only. He has a caliph mentality."* Turkish military involvement in Libya, Syria, Qatar, even if unsuccessful, appeals to people's pride.

Ongun told me he was an optimist about Turkey, and it had to do with the trajectory of Islam.

"We have 5.5 million refugees from the Syrian war here in Turkey, 1.5 million of them in Istanbul. They all want to go to Europe or the United States. It isn't just that they want to escape from conflict. It's that the secular West appeals to them. Because of technology and the ease of access to information, you have a new generation of Muslims integrated into the world. Religion is perishing from their lives, since they are able to seek answers online without going to local authority figures. Then there is the alienation from faith-based Islam precisely because of the politicization of it."

While it was true that ISIS, for example, had a technological component with its videos of beheadings transmitted over the internet, and the spread of its message to Muslims in the West, this merely represented the exceptions; whereas the vast average of young Muslims were using technology to discover the wider world and its values. As for the alienation from faith-based Islam, that had already happened in Iran, whose population had turned cynical and secular on account of how religion had been hijacked by the ruling mullahs, thus tainting true devotion with politics. The mullahs were no longer a refuge from an oppressive state: they *were* the oppressive state.

But Iran was different from Turkey, Ongun tried to explain.

"At the end of the day we will go back to Anatolianism," that is, to the geography of Atatürk, of the Turkic tribes who moved westward across the Anatolian land bridge from Central Asia, where they had for millennia lived a pagan existence. The Sunni Islam adopted by

---

* The Ottoman sultan was also the caliph who led the entire House of Islam.

those Turkic tribes (both Seljuk and Ottoman) in Anatolia was different from the Shi'ism of the Iranian plateau," which had been radicalized by the obsession with defeat experienced in the early days of Islam, when the Shi'ites had lost a monumental power struggle for the leadership of the Muslim faith.* The Sunni Muslim faith of Anatolia, or Asia Minor, Ongun observed, is leavened by the open-minded mysticism of the Mevlevis, a Sufi order founded by the Persian mystic Jalaluddin Rumi in Konya in the thirteenth century. Indeed, Anatolia and the Iranian plateau are both heirs to an eclectic Turco-Persianate tradition, but the Islam that evolved in Anatolia had, by the modern era, turned into a more tolerant and easygoing version of what existed in Iran.

"Anatolia's somewhat elusive tradition of tolerance will ultimately triumph over Erdoğan's bleak Islamism," Ongun said, and in that way lead Turkey to an identity that blends Atatürk's republicanism with the riches of the Ottoman imperial past.

I WENT TO TESHVIKYE, another smart suburb, closer to the city center than Etiler, full of thin and stylish people and shops with captivating signage. Again, I was reminded of the better parts of Athens and also of Tel Aviv. In many ways the world—including the Near East—is becoming similar, as Claude Lévi-Strauss had detected back in 1955. Nuray Mert greeted me in her apartment full of books, old photographs, and artwork. She had a simple, lithe, and elegant appearance. Mert is a cancer survivor who lost her positions in both journalism and the university on account of her political views. Istanbul was full of established writers suddenly having trouble in mid or late career finding outlets for their work, because of regime oppression. A number of them told me that they were "horrified" by the "cancel culture" in the United States, because it vaguely reminded them of what was going on

---

* The Shi'ites were literally the *Shiat Ali,* the "Party of Ali," the rightful successor to the Prophet, who was assassinated in A.D. 661.

in Turkey, even though it was a bottom-up phenomenon in America, emanating from social media, rather than top-down as here.

"Though the nationalists and the Islamists are proud of their own imperial tradition," Mert began almost in midsentence, "nevertheless, they think of imperialism in the hands of Westerners as an outright evil, and it is at the heart of many of their conspiracy theories. Their conspiracy theories about Jews merge with those about Western imperialism. Such theories are really about resentment. This is how the Islamists and nationalists console themselves and strip themselves of any responsibility for what has happened."

Under Turgut Özal, she explained, "neo-Ottomanism was relatively harmless and nonthreatening. But it was always at heart an antidemocratic, irredentist force," a force interested in other people's territories. "And in the 1990s, after the Cold War ended, it was encouraged by the U.S., which appreciated [NATO member] Turkey's outreach to the Turkic-speaking states of former Soviet Central Asia. Islamism and nationalism had two underlying tendencies in Turkey," she went on, "the first was *empire,* and the second was *authoritarianism,* and the two work together. Even Kemalism," which confined itself to building a republic in Anatolia only, "was imperfect. Remember, it was a revolution that had come after the destruction of a great war, and which built a one-party state." Atatürk, after all, she said, may have been a Westernizer, but he was no democrat.

"At root, democracy is not about religion and it is not about empire. Democracy means secularism and individual freedom." Democracy, in this definition, should be inseparable from classical liberalism. That is its guiding spirit. "Unfortunately, that has not been fashionable in Turkey since the 1990s."

Mert's short gray hair and thin features intensified her abstract and cerebral manner. She was like a formidable old-world intellectual. "The issue is really modernism," she said, raising her head, "and how religion is being redefined by it." Her explanation took time to establish. First, she agreed that the 1980 military coup here had led to Sunnification and had also let the religious genie out of the bottle. But the

Turkish generals allowed that to happen not only because of the Shi'ite revolution next door in Iran, but also because of the proximate threat of communism nearby. The Soviet Union was actively trying to undermine Turkey, and thus religion and nationalism combined well as a counterforce. Necmettin Erbakan, the longtime Islamist leader in the Turkish parliament before Tayyip Erdoğan, was emblematic of this tendency. Though a religious militant, "Erbakan was also a patriotic man of his time," Mert explained, an engineer and academic who worked well within the confines of Atatürk's republic and of the democratic system that had fitfully emerged in the decades after Atatürk's death in 1938.* "Erbakan always had a national focus. He believed that the Turks deserved to rule the Islamic world," which they had done for nearly a millennium following the Seljuks' defeat of the Byzantines in 1071 at Manzikert in eastern Anatolia. "Of course, it was a patronizing, neo-Ottoman view."

But whereas Erbakan embodied the natural certainties of a more rural society, Erdoğan spoke for the movement of religious Turks into the cities of Anatolia, where Islam had to become more ideological because of the need for it to survive in the impersonal, modernizing environment of urban life.

"Erdoğan," she said, "spoke for a new, lumpen-Islamist and nationalist generation": an Islamic working class liberated from the fatalism of the village and consequently more angry and demanding. The Marxists used the term *lumpen* to denote an unshaped proletariat uninterested in revolutionary advancement, which therefore required direction from above. But as Asli Aydintaşbaş and Nuray Mert, as well as others, employed the term, it had a more pointed emphasis: a badly urbanized and angry class that constituted perfect fodder for revolutionaries. Mert explained that Erdoğan was leading a drawn-out, neo-Ottoman "counter-revolution" against Atatürk's republican revolution.

"And after Erdoğan there might only be left a wasteland of destroyed institutions," with perhaps even paramilitary forces that he has

---

* I interviewed Erbakan in the spring of 1993 on assignment for *National Geographic* and that was also the impression I got from him.

gradually raised up following two decades in power. "This was no longer a state of laws."

She spoke of Trabzon, the Black Sea city in the east not far from
the Georgian border where she had grown up. As a girl, she remembered there were only three or four restaurants in the entire city. It had
been a traditional world where people ate only at home. "But today
there are dozens of restaurants and the religious all go out to eat. No
wine is served at these restaurants, though. The city has become ruralized as religious peasants have flocked into it, bringing their own traditions, but also being changed in the process. This is modernization."
It was not pretty or aesthetic. But it was progress: a world of newly
urbanized peasants, who had left their fatalism back in the countryside, and had given the world nationalist and hardcore religious leaders
who had come to power through elections, like Tayyip Erdoğan and
Narendra Modi in India.

Economic, social, and technological progress did not necessarily
lead to a more sensitive or a more stable world, she suggested. The
modern age was about the demographic movement to the cities, which
led to ideologies, intransigent nationalisms, and wars. Postmodernism
was about trying to extend a rules-based order to the domains of chaos.
We were living in the interregnum between the two ages.

THE ÇAMLICA MOSQUE IN the area of Üsküdar, on the Asian side of
the city, was Erdoğan's great monument to his rule. Though the project
originated just before he came to power, it was under his leadership
that all of the construction happened. The Çamlica Mosque was based
on the plan of the Suleymaniye Mosque on the European side of Istanbul, which had been commissioned by Sultan Suleiman "the Magnificent" in 1550, and was designed by the great classical Ottoman
architect Mimar Sinan. The Suleymaniye, with its constellation of half
domes, was itself derivative of Byzantine emperor Justinian's Hagia
Sophia. The Suleymaniye had been among the largest mosques in Turkey until it was surpassed in size by this one, which opened in 2019.

All the Ottoman details were here in this mosque: the constellation of domes; the *ablaq* archways, in which black basalt alternated with white limestone; the stalactite carvings above the doors; and the fan-like fountain-dome for ablutions in the inner courtyard. The problem was with the proportions. Rather than feel exhilarated, as I had been at Sinan's masterpiece, the Selimiye Mosque at Edirne ("Adrianople"), decades back, here I felt crushed. The Selimiye Mosque, built in 1568, was integrated into the city, whereas this one was built on a hill virtually surrounded by expressways with only two greasy kebab joints in sight. The Ottoman details here were mere decorations, swallowed by a concrete immensity. For this was a grand mosque, auditorium, museum, and underground parking garage encased in one boxlike structure. It had the dimensions of not just one, but several American football stadiums. The Communists loved concrete and the true spirit of the Çamlica Mosque is Stalinist. It is at once gargantuan and tacky, made worse by a remote geodesic-like structure in the outer courtyard, the sum of which pulverized the individual with its inhuman proportions.

Erdoğan's personality was captured by this architectural behemoth; just as Atatürk's was by his Great Tomb (*Anit Kabir*) in Ankara, with its pagan motifs of mother goddesses and wolf tracks set in marble and stone to announce secularism writ large. Here it was all about hard power. Unlike the last true Ottoman sultan, Abdul Hamid, there was no subtlety in Erdoğan's approach. It was always confrontational. Even when outwardly calm, Erdoğan's eyes often betrayed anger. He had dismantled the meritocracy and thus, after a fashion, dismantled the governing institutions. The media, the judiciary, the parliament—it was all his, despite the appearance of democracy. "The effect is chilling," one Turkish columnist told me. "You must now think two and three times before you write anything, and that's if you weren't already forcibly retired."

I thought of the Çamlica Mosque's opposite: the Grand Mosque in Muscat, Oman, which despite its large proportions felt manageable and intimate with its Indian sandstone, graceful courtyards and arcades, and exquisite examples of art from throughout the Islamic world. That mosque was built in the 1990s by the late Sultan Qaboos

not how it declined and failed. Ottoman greatness is implanted deep
in our subconscious, therefore. Not even Atatürk's republican revolution dared to challenge this notion of imperial pride, though it did
impress us with the idea that it was the Ottoman Empire's failure to
modernize that led to its destruction."

My Turkish colleague mentioned a speech that Erdoğan had given
in October 2020, in which the Turkish leader, despite his neo-
Ottomanism, distanced himself from the entire imperial tradition
after 1839, when Sultan Mahmud II instituted several Western-style
reforms dealing with individual freedom and the rule of law, known as
the Decree of *Tanzimat* (Organizing Concepts). "By rejecting the Ottoman Empire all the way back to 1839," my colleague explained,
"Erdoğan in this speech not only distanced himself from Atatürk's
republican revolution, but also from Western civilization and influence
on Turkey altogether." Erdoğan, who had then been in high office for
two decades, had acquired near-total bureaucratic power. And he was
now attempting to dominate the symbolic intellectual ground in Turkey with his references to "our civilization," which harked all the way
back to the Turco-Persian Seljuks, who had migrated to Anatolia from
Central Asia and fought the European Crusaders. That, in turn, meant
dislodging Atatürk's revolution as the mere culmination of a failed
Western relationship with Turkey, which in the modern era had begun
with the period of Ottoman reforms in the 1800s.

"But Atatürk," my colleague said, "was presenting Erdoğan with a
dilemma, since it had been Atatürk who ejected foreign armies from
Anatolia in the aftermath of World War I, preventing the Turkish
heartland itself from being dismembered. It was Atatürk who had
united the country. And so, even Erdoğan had to pay lip service to
him, while also working to undo everything that Atatürk had built."
Erdoğan could praise Atatürk as *Gazi Pasha*, the late-Ottoman military officer who had defeated the Western Allies in World War I at
Gallipoli and went on to defeat the Greeks on sacred Turkish soil,
while also preventing the European powers from establishing an independent Kurdistan upon it. But Atatürk the fierce Westernizer and
creator of Republican Turkey could not be mentioned. "Yet Atatürk,"

bin Said, a wise traditionalist who worshipped aesthetics and loved classical music. And I thought of the Çamlica Mosque's equal: the House of the Republic in Bucharest, Romania, built by the Stalinist tyrant Nicolae Ceauşescu and his mad wife Elena in the years before their overthrow and execution. That was another architectural monster of pulverizing proportions, on the scale of the Pentagon, that was at once expensive and utterly tasteless.* The Ceauşescus were vindictive peasants who worshipped *bigness,* and modeled their country after North Korea. Erdoğan was an urban peasant, a man of the ruralized city: not remotely as cruel as Ceauşescu, but there were certain similarities. Erdoğan wanted to impress his own kind, people who were ambitious for themselves and for their families, but who lacked refinement. This mosque was for them, for those who had migrated to the city from the villages, and who needed proof that their values were conquering Istanbul. "I am one of you," the Turkish president, who had risen from the rough neighborhood of Kasimpaşa, seemed to be saying with this building, in his populist, man-in-the-street rhetoric. As Nuray Mert had hinted to me, it was about the ugly side of modernism.

From the mosque I could see the various other skylines of Istanbul: those on the Asian side. This is truly a megacity. For an instant I thought of São Paulo. There were no sidewalks anywhere beyond the mosque, so I stepped out into the expressway and eventually hailed a taxi that screeched to a halt.

BACK AT THE PERA Palace, I met an old colleague who agreed to be identified only as a Turkish expert. This is what he said:

"The Turkish education system indoctrinated all of us in the belief that we are heirs to one of the great world-empires, that spanned three continents: from the Balkans and from North Africa to Asia. What was emphasized in school was the origins and rise of this great empire;

---

*   In fact, Erdoğan's presidential palace complex in Ankara, completed in 2014 and housing over a thousand rooms, has been compared to Ceauşescu's House of the Republic.

he said, "continues to communicate with us from the grave. Therefore, the only way that Erdoğan can ultimately erase Atatürk is to re-create the Ottoman Empire in postmodern form. But as we see from Erdoğan's quagmires and mistakes in Syria and Libya, Turkey simply lacks the capacity to do that."

THE TRAIN SLID OUT of the station heading east. The calm, whispering waters of the Sea of Marmara were on my right outside the window, where soon appeared a port with rows of gantry cranes and hundreds of shipping containers, and the world's fourth-longest suspension bridge. On my left Istanbul never seemed to end: suburbs, office parks, malls, grain elevators, a cement plant, and more housing complexes. Only after ninety minutes did the development thin out. But then came a spooky-looking power plant with lights blinking. Turkey had undergone vast modernization even as it had become increasingly authoritarian. It was a story similar to China's.

We reached İzmit, the Nicomedia of antiquity, which Diocletian in A.D. 286 had made his easternmost capital when he divided the Roman Empire into four governing parts. It appeared charmless and suffocated in concrete, with massive housing projects. Finally, I saw steeply wooded hills and the first line of mountains as darkness began to swallow the landscape. But there was never quite an end to habitation.

The journey to the capital of Ankara on the fast train took nearly five hours, and Ankara was only a third of the way across Anatolia. Anatolia was, in fact, a mini-continent in its own right: one that I had crossed and recrossed over the decades in buses and much slower trains. It was a mini-continent in which the term "rugged" didn't quite do it justice, crammed as it is with high mountains, baked yellow hillsides, and spectacular, broken plateaus. Few terrains anywhere are as dramatic. Anatolia, a bleak and rural environment when I first encountered it in the early 1970s, had become a landscape of expanding towns and cities, at once deeply religious and economically dynamic. Cities had grown up and the ruralized culture of the village had overtaken them, making them appear to our eyes at least ugly, working class, and rustic in the process: again, such was the underside of modernization. Notably, such urban centers as Konya, Kayseri, and Malatya in central Anatolia were known as the "Koran belt," vaguely akin to our "Bible belt," and were a key to the political power of both Özal in the late twentieth century and Erdoğan in the early twenty-first. The explosion of Turkish trade with the Middle East that occurred especially under Erdoğan, going from 10 to 20 percent of exports from 2002 to 2010, heavily benefitted these dynamic and burgeoning cities of the interior. It was such cities that were crucial to Turkey's economy of scale, dwarfing the economies of its neighbors. Though Turkey's population was roughly the size of Iran's, despite being energy-poor Turkey's economy was nearly 20 percent larger than that of its oil-and-gas-rich eastern neighbor.[34] And Turkey had an abundance of the twenty-first century's most crucial commodity: water. The headwaters of both the Tigris and the Euphrates were located in Anatolia. As night engulfed the landscape on this fall evening, what lay outside my window was not a dark emptiness but a landscape whose significance was palpable to me.

My first visit to Ankara was in January 1983. Then it had the aura of the Communist capitals in the Balkans: dark, intimate, and redolent of lignite fumes. I returned year after year until the end of the twentieth century. By 1999 there were some small, upscale shopping malls on the edges of downtown. I used to stay at the Bulvar Palace, a lively and somewhat seedy haunt for journalists with small or nonexistent expense accounts, whose restaurant specialized in kebab and yoghurt dishes. In mild weather the restaurant had tables set out on the main boulevard. I was in my early thirties then, and I remember an old and grizzled British foreign correspondent who actually lived there alone in one of the rooms, his knowledge of and fascination with Turkey having reached such an extreme. Sadly I can't remember his name. Now that whole section of the boulevard has been redeveloped with high-end boutiques, cafés, and gourmet sandwich shops. There was no sign of the past that had meant so much to me.

Whereas Istanbul, an ancient and eternal city with historic landmarks, was a place where, despite the passage of years, I could find my way around, upon my return to Ankara I was disoriented entirely. The new railway station was an immense expanse of stone that glittered like marble. And in the city itself rows of the most expensive boutiques went on for miles, with new traffic and pedestrian underpasses. Now every upscale hotel chain had a massive presence, complete with over-the-top dining and conference centers: all glitz and no intimacy.

MY FIRST MEETING IN Ankara was with two staffers at the German Marshall Fund, its director Özgür Ünlühisarcikli and his colleague Şaban Kardaş. They explained how Erdoğan's Islamic-nationalist rule had its origins partially in European Union policy.

"Before Erdoğan," Ünlühisarcikli said, "Turkey was a weak democracy under military tutelage, like a man with one leg walking with a cane. By pressuring the military to the sidelines of Turkish politics, the Europeans took away the cane without giving Turkey a new leg." The military had stabilized Turkish politics in two ways: first, by its broad institutional support; and second, by its ideological loyalty to Kemalism. The two elements kept Turkey on a path that was both stable and pro-Western. Of course, the military wasn't perfect. It weakened core civilian institutions and had itself a colonial mindset toward them. But as military influence weakened, domestic politics became more corrupt and directionless, with one ineffectual political leader succeeding and confronting the next. It was in such a climate that Erdoğan rose to power. When Erdoğan's party achieved control in the elections of 2002, Turkey was three years into the accession process toward joining the European Union. Erdoğan took advantage of European pressure on the Turkish military to further weaken its power and thus to weaken Kemalism as an ideology. Both the Islamic Gülenists and the secular liberals were allies of his when it came to undermining the Turkish generals. Later, when Erdoğan had sufficiently weakened the generals, he would be able to cast off the Gülenists and the liberals, since they had already achieved their purpose for him. And when it became devastatingly clear that the European Union had had no intention all along of admitting Turkey as a member, Erdoğan could further unleash his neo-Ottoman policy, which moved Turkey away from the West and toward the Middle East and Russia.

Erdoğan was well on his way to attaining political power in Turkey. As mayor of Istanbul in the 1990s, understanding the hatred of working-class religious migrants toward the secular elites, he established a house-to-house "Hezbollah-like network" inside the semi-slum *gecekondus*, Ünlühisarcikli explained. Erdoğan, in this manner, was an early proponent of Muslim identity politics. His outreach to the Arab world, Şaban Kardaş added, flowed from this. "Erdoğan did not have a pragmatic approach to the Arab world. Instead, he approached the Middle East through his own identity politics," employing foreign crises for domestic purposes, which is why Turkey sided with the Palestinians and the Muslim Brotherhood against a slew of conservative Arab regimes.

Again, I asked the question:

Could there ever be another coup in Turkey?

The answer I got from the two men was that with pro-Western Kemalism weakened and the strongest political networks now Islamic—themselves aided by new security forces—any future military or security force intervention would not necessarily be Kemalist. Ünlühisarcikli observed that "given the damage to institutions, in the future beyond Erdoğan we could also have very divided and very weak governments," with an out-of-power Erdoğan possibly still influential as a grand old man or figurehead. "A political vacuum. A Turkish Weimar Republic."

"ERDOĞAN WOULD NOT BE the person he was had the European Union not stabbed Turkey in the back," said Faruk Kaymakci, a senior Turkish diplomat. He explained that the European Union had all along refused Turkish membership because Turkey was—as EU officials put it—"'too big, too poor, and Muslim.'" Despite the breakneck economic development, the agricultural sector still employed a significant part of the Turkish workforce. That meant Turkey would have

cost the European Union many billions of dollars in agricultural sub-
sidies.

"Had the European Union accepted Turkey as a member in the
early 2000s," Kaymakci told me, not only would Turkey be richer and
with better governing institutions, "but Europe today would be better
integrated into the Middle East, with much more influence there." In
fact, the whole region would have been more stable, with positive repercussions for Syria and Iraq. Kaymakci was ever hopeful: "Turkish
accession to the EU has been the most complicated, most questioned,
and most challenging accession of all. But if it ever happens, it will be
the most meaningful accession of all."

It had been the Greeks, Greek Cypriots, and in particular the
French president at the time, Nicolas Sarkozy, who prevented Turkey's
accession. In 2004, the European Union, in effect, chose Cyprus over
Turkey, admitting the Greek part of the island to full EU membership.
As for France, because of its own large population of Muslims of Algerian background, it has always been especially sensitive to the whole
issue of Islam in Europe and of a Muslim nation joining the EU.

Between the two world wars, Atatürk had put Turkey on the path
to becoming European. When that option was finally closed by the
European Union three-quarters of a century later, Turkey rediscovered
the post-Ottoman Middle East in full force. Erdoğan's neo-
authoritarian rule and the consequent weakening of Turkish democracy was not only a matter of Turkey's own historical and political
development, but of outside forces acting upon it.

OF COURSE, NOT EVEN the actions of the European Union can equal
the effect of sheer geography upon Turkey's historic challenge of
achieving a middle ground of enlightened governance. For Anatolia is
home to two peoples, not one: the Turks and the Kurds, the latter of
whom are Indo-Europeans speaking a language related to Persian. In
the immediate aftermath of World War I, the European powers in the
1920 Treaty of Sèvres attempted to carve out a separate Kurdish state

in southeastern Anatolia and northern Iraq.[35] Such efforts to divide Anatolia have to this day fed Turkey's "collective paranoia and its xenophobia," helping to enable authoritarianism, writes the American scholar Michael Rubin.[36]

Kurdish rebellions in Anatolia were crushed by Atatürk's new republican army in the 1920s and 1930s. The Kurds had fought with Atatürk against the Greeks and other Christian invaders, believing that they were defending Islam. Yet the new nationalist regime betrayed them.[37] Henceforth Kurdish identity was officially denied and Kurds were designated by Ankara as "mountain Turks." During the Cold War the United States supported Turkey's efforts to destroy the Marxist Kurdistan Workers Party, or PKK, led by Abdullah Öcalan. In the 1980s and 1990s, Turkey fielded as many as 130,000 troops in the southeast of the country against the PKK insurgency.[38] In the early twenty-first century, the collapse of Iraq due to the American invasion and the Syrian civil war only quickened Turkey's fears, as it led to self-governing Kurdish regions on Turkey's borders. The fact that Kurdish fighters were indispensable in defeating Al-Qaeda and the Islamic State in Syria and Iraq, raising their international prestige, only frustrated Turkey more.

Because the Iraq and Syrian wars led to chaos on Turkey's ethnic-Kurdish border areas, the Kurdish issue was now bigger than Turkey itself and thus harder to solve than ever—as it involved three nations, two of which were in varying phases of anarchy.

"The Kurdish question, like others in the Middle East, emerged from the collapse of the Ottoman Empire," explained Mithat Sancar, a Turkish politician and academic who grew up speaking Arabic and Kurdish in southeastern Turkey. "The Ottoman Empire, like the Habsburg Empire, was decentralized and protected minorities. What followed, however, were nation-states dominated by a single ethnic group. In fact, the nation-state model only deepened the problem of the Kurds," since they don't fit in easily anywhere. The only long-term solution, he told me, was a "decentralized," federalist-like millet system throughout Turkey, Syria, and Iraq, governed "in the spirit of the European Union," but with a vague similarity to the Byzantine and

Ottoman empires. Sancar envisioned a sort of neo-Ottoman peace among the various ethnic groups and Muslim sects, with no single sultan at the top. Of course, he admitted, this ran completely counter to Erdoğan's authoritarian and nationalist-Islamist agenda.

HOWEVER, IN FOREIGN POLICY Erdoğan did not start out as a hardliner. When his Justice and Development Party came to power in 2002, he and Ahmet Davutoğlu, his brilliant foreign minister, believed that in order to transform their inward-looking Kemalist state into a regional force, they had to look beyond the confines of Europe and engage the former Ottoman imperial space.

Davutoğlu's strategy became known as "zero problems with neighbors." Thus, Turkey engaged with Syria's Bashar al-Assad; with Iraq's Nouri al-Maliki, despite Maliki's anti-Sunni sectarian worldview; with Turkey's historical adversaries the Greeks and the Armenians; and so on. It was an outreach that implicitly "accepted the regional status quo" and sought to better integrate Turkey within it, explained Burhanettin Duran, the head of the Erdoğan government's own think tank, the Foundation for Political, Economic and Social Research. The turning point was the Arab Spring in 2011, when Erdoğan and Davutoğlu adopted a more assertive policy in the Middle East, believing they could help shape an emerging new order more friendly to radical and democratic forces, which they thought would eventually benefit from the regional uprising. Turkey, as a stable Muslim democracy, was well placed to offer advice in this regard, they felt. They specifically counted on an alliance between Turkey and Egypt's newly elected leader, Mohamed Morsi, a member of the Muslim Brotherhood, to counterbalance the Saudi-Iranian regional rivalry. "But we misjudged Morsi's capacity as a leader, because we lacked sufficient intelligence and subtle knowledge about Egypt and the Arab world," Duran admitted to me. Morsi was toppled by Egypt's pro-Western strongman, former General Abdel Fattah al-Sisi. What emerged was not a new order in the Arab world as Erdoğan and Davutoğlu had hoped, but the reassertion of old conservative and authoritarian forces, so that as time marched on, Turkey was left allied with only the Muslim Brotherhood, radical Qatar, and the Palestinians.

Making matters worse was the fact that neither the Americans nor the Europeans would intervene in war-torn Syria, so that NATO proved useless there. This left Turkey with little choice but to intervene because of the Kurdish threat and the cross-border refugee crisis. And because the Russians intervened in Syria as well, Erdoğan has had little choice but to more closely engage Putin. "Erdoğan," Duran summarized, "learned over time, especially in Syria, that soft power alone is not enough. But within the realm of hard power calculations, Erdoğan is prepared to be pragmatic and back down when necessary."

IT WAS TIME FOR me to meet Ahmet Davutoğlu, who by Turkish standards is a Kissingerian force of nature—once an ally of Erdoğan but by the time of my visit his bitter enemy. Because he's uninterruptible, I just let Davutoğlu talk for ninety minutes in Ankara, in his yawning office at the new political party he leads.

In the beginning, as Davutoğlu explained to me, the idea wasn't specifically imperial: it was only about bringing Turkey's experience of forging a secure and democratic nation-state to the wider region. After all, for too long Turkey had been psychologically estranged from its neighbors, which in Turkish eyes were Greek and Armenian enemies, once-traitorous Arabs, rival Iranians, and so forth. Why not make friends with everybody, and thereby construct a regional order emanating from Turkey's strength and stability? "If the region could experience more freedom, there would be more security and fewer problems," Davutoğlu observed. In this spirit, Davutoğlu spearheaded various mediation efforts: in the former war-torn Yugoslavia, between Sunnis and Shi'ites in Iraq, and even between Israel and Syria in the time before Benjamin Netanyahu returned to power. It was all familiar historical terrain for Turkey, since from the Balkans to Mesopotamia, the Ottomans had ruled through a millet system of self-governing communities, which had provided for intercommunal peace under an imperial umbrella. But particularly in the Balkans, where the Ottoman experience had often been harsh and bloody, Turkey's enemies accused Davutoğlu of "neo-Ottomanism." It was a term used in this case to discredit his efforts, downplaying the cosmopolitan and decentralized aspects of Ottoman rule.

Davutoğlu's essentially liberal vision suffered from one, pivotal flaw, though. He underestimated the fragile nature of Arab states and their institutions, which, as it turned out in the Arab Spring, could not remain stable or even intact once their dictators were severely weakened or dislodged. Erdoğan and Davutoğlu would be devastated by Morsi's and the Muslim Brotherhood's inability to properly govern Egypt. But for Davutoğlu, it was his experience with Syria's Bashar al-Assad that constituted a real reckoning.

Davutoğlu originally saw Assad as "a young modernizer and potential progressive: not like the old corrupt dictators [Hosni] Mubarak in Egypt and [Zine El Abidine] Ben Ali in Tunisia." And Assad, for his part, "saw Turkey as a good model." Moreover, largely for geographical reasons, "Syria was essential as an entry point for Turkey into the Arab world," Davutoğlu explained. Thus, when the Arab Spring first ignited in early 2011, "we urged Assad to loosen up, to allow other parties besides the Ba'ath to form, to liberalize the economy, to lead Syria towards a semi-democracy. I advised Assad to hold an election. 'You'll win,' I told him. 'You're not Mubarak or Ben Ali who were overthrown. You have real credentials as someone whose family dynasty never compromised on the question of the Palestinians.'"

But then Assad, upon whom Davutoğlu had invested so much hope, gave his devastating reply: "But what would happen to my people if I lose the election?" the Syrian dictator said. By "my people" he meant his fellow Alawites. "At the end of the day," Davutoğlu recounted, "Assad saw himself as a communal leader only," not as a leader of a whole nation-state. Alas, both Syria and Iraq were riven by sectarianism, worsened by the French, who had favored the Alawites in Syria, and the British, who had favored the Sunnis in Iraq.

"Assad's dilemma," Davutoğlu observed with the wisdom of hindsight, "was that he needed Turkey in peace, but he needed Iran in war." And it was war that Assad was heading into. Thus, he leaned on his father Hafez Assad's old Iranian allies, thereby strengthening the Shi'ite-Alawite alliance.

Erdoğan, who intimidates everyone around him, listened for some years to Davutoğlu's advice, because Davutoğlu was not seen by Erdoğan as political; rather, Davutoğlu was seen as an intellectual and an academic who could instruct his boss. Erdoğan's increasing authoritarianism resulted in a general rupture between the two men, and to a foreign policy that was neo-Ottoman only in the worst sense, creating enemies instead of friends. This led eventually to Davutoğlu forming his own political party, composed of all groups in the country, including Kurds and members of the various Christian communities.

"There is only one solution to the Kurdish question," Davutoğlu told me before I left. "Full democratization, that is, empowering local governments in the southeast, making Kurdish a language of the country like Turkish, and establishing excellent relations with the Kurds of Syria and Iraq."

Leaving Davutoğlu's office I thought of the concept of Tufts University professor Malik Mufti, who writes that Turkish strategic culture has oscillated between Atatürk's Republican paradigm that "seeks security by turning inward in pursuit of a homogeneous and harmonious polity insulated from foreign threats" and an imperial paradigm that "views Turkey's external environment as capable of yielding great rewards if only one is open to engaging with and trying to reshape it."[39] Özal's unleashing of the Turkish business community generated Republican Turkey's first truly active engagement with the former Ottoman near-abroad, something which Davutoğlu built upon before Erdoğan, having left Davutoğlu behind, undermined neo-Ottomanism with Muslim identity politics.

THE PRESIDENTIAL PALACE COMPLEX in Ankara was completed in 2014, after Erdoğan had been in power for over a decade. Unlike the Çamlica Mosque in Istanbul, it is not reminiscent of Ceauşescu's House of the Republic. The Palace Complex appears bigger than that—bigger than the Kremlin or Versailles, fifty-eight times the size of the White House.⁴⁰ Combining Seljuk and Ottoman architectural motifs, its size is truly otherworldly; with over a thousand rooms, marble atriums, fountains, a great mosque, and a price tag—with additions and renovations—of close to a billion dollars: an enormous sum given the much cheaper cost of labor in Turkey than in the West. The level of pretension and ambition that the complex exudes is frightening. Here Erdoğan reputedly worked eighteen-hour days, including one or two rousing speeches daily, making key decisions near midnight. Following almost two decades in power, he was surrounded by a "swirling courtier system," with perhaps no one to challenge him. This was especially the case after the failed 2016 coup against him, after which he purged the military "and really took power," according to Burhanettin Duran.

Erdoğan had always pushed into voids: intervening in Syria to protect his borders; intervening in Libya to obtain energy concessions and help an ideologically sympathetic regime; helping his Turkish brothers, the Azeris, against the Armenians; and challenging the Greeks, the Cypriots, and the French in the Aegean, because he could not countenance their interpretation of maritime rights that violated Turkey's economic and geopolitical interests. There were good reasons to intervene in all these cases. Yet a more cautious leader would not have done so, or would not have done so as often. But the longer Erdoğan remained in power, the more he learned what he could get away with— despite the caviling of the policy communities in Ankara, Istanbul, Brussels, and Washington. The 2016 coup attempt made him at once more self-confident and more paranoid. And the more that economic problems mounted at home, the more he shook his fist in populist style at the world, in order to impress his political base at home. But don't confuse Erdoğan with someone like Donald Trump. Erdoğan was methodical, self-disciplined, and always thinking several steps ahead in a system without the venerable and sturdy democratic institutions of the United States. True authoritarians crave power and the consolidation of it more than they crave attention. How lonely it must be at the top, I thought, staring at this colossal building. I also thought of what the Greek writer Nikos Kazantzakis had observed upon meeting Mussolini in 1926: "He feels a power constantly pushing him. He cannot stop; if he does he knows he is lost. It is the most characteristic and most tragic agony of Dictators. It is necessary that they do battle incessantly, and win. They are lost . . . if they are overcome by indecision . . ."⁴¹

Could a normal democratic process dislodge Erdoğan from this Palace Complex, whose proportions were such that only someone with his amount of ambition could feel at ease inside of it? Actually, Turkey's second president, İsmet İnönü, a virtual dictator, surprised the world by stepping down from office in 1950 after losing an election that he didn't even have to hold, paving the way for the birth of Turkish democracy.⁴² Thus, I tried to imagine a post-Erdoğan Turkish Weimar Republic against the backdrop of this architectural monster, or some such other scenario that will surely play out in the months and years to come. Actually, I could imagine it, after a fashion. The fantastically grand buildings designed as the administrative heart of British India by Sir Edwin Lutyens in New Delhi were constructed mainly in the interwar years, with the assumption of eternal colonial rule. Yet the British empire came crashing down some years later. And an act of God, namely an earthquake, may undo Erdoğan. There was irony aplenty in history, as Gibbon knew.

LOWER NILE

═══

MY LIFETIME HAS SEEN THE CONTINUED ADVANCE OF PO-
litical science at the expense of the study of geography. I refer to geography in the nineteenth-century sense of the term: in which the relief
map constitutes the starting point for the study of people, culture,
trade routes, natural resources, and so on. More problematic has been
a burgeoning in the ranks of experts drawn mainly from the most cosmopolitan and economically privileged backgrounds—people who
have never known financial or physical insecurity—which can make it
harder rather than easier for them to understand the ground-level reality of distant countries. As expertise becomes narrower, rarefied, and
compartmentalized, reality itself becomes obscured. There is the illusion of knowledge where little may actually exist. Too few of the categories experts use to judge and define countries can really tell you
how honest the taxi drivers are, if you need a fixer to make it through
customs at the airport, if people stand in organized lines at shops and
government offices, if the streets of major cities are safe to walk at
night, what the level of infighting and corruption in government is,
and what is the ability of bureaucratic institutions to service citizens.
The pages of leading foreign policy journals don't help much in this
regard. But the accounts of travelers, foreign correspondents, and ex-
patriates will. And what they will immediately begin talking about is
the *culture* of the country in question. Yet "culture" is the very word
that makes political scientists and other professional social scientists

To raise the issue of culture as a factor in geopolitical analysis is to risk being accused of determinism and essentialism, fancy academic terms for fatalism and stereotyping. Of course, I myself am generalizing about all of this. But not to be able to generalize is to immobilize argument.

Indeed, not to consider culture as a factor in the fate of nations is a contradiction in terms. Nations, if they are anything, are cultural entities. For culture is the sum total of a people's "collective" experience inhabiting a particular landscape for hundreds and thousands of years.[1] To dismiss the relevance of culture in politics is, in essence, to dismiss the whole field of anthropology, which is the study of the cultures of peoples and ethnic groups, and their social meaning. The policy elite is uncomfortable with all of this because in many cases it does not concur with their own life experience: that of having grown up in international settings among a global class that has transcended national and ethnic culture. But because most of the world has still not transcended it, culture must remain a vital element of political analysis.

Nevertheless, the elite do have a crucial point to make. For it isn't really culture that is a problem for them. Rather, what they really mean to say is, *Culture is so subjective a thing, that because you can't measure it or even analyze it properly, it may be safer just to ignore it.* Among policy and bureaucratic types, whatever cannot be objectively quantified, or categorized, or tested should be virtually ignored in one's analysis, or treated with extreme skepticism.

Is there a way out of this dilemma?

Yes. It begins with one man.

CLIFFORD GEERTZ WAS ARGUABLY the greatest American anthropologist of the twentieth century. In his otherwise savage attack on Western orientalists dealing in stereotypes of the Islamic world, the late Columbia University professor Edward W. Said singles out Clifford Geertz as among the handful of exceptions. Geertz's "interest in Islam," Said writes, "is discrete and concrete enough to be animated by the specific societies and problems he studies and not by the rituals, preconceptions, and doctrines of Orientalism."*

Like many an anthropologist, Geertz's worldview was built out of particulars: from the ground up. He did his pathbreaking fieldwork in Indonesia and Morocco, the two ends of the Islamic world. Living for years in remote villages in these countries, he developed a theory of humanity best summarized in his essay collection *The Interpretation of Cultures,* published in 1973. It is the opposite of the many tracts on globalization, which explain the world from the top down. Geertz is seeing the world whole, from the vantage point of a wooden shack on a dusty road.

"Culture," Geertz begins, is an "acted document," a public utterance of a kind, even though it may be but a wink and a nod, or an impolite suck of the tongue when a Greek taxi driver refuses a rider. Culture is "not an occult" thing that exists only in someone's mind. It is not a prejudice. It is real, Geertz says. Being real, "men unmodified by the customs of particular places do not in fact exist . . ." Men are "unfinished animals," who only complete themselves through a specific culture. Quoting Santayana, Geertz says that no man can speak without speaking a particular language, which itself is full of cultural implications. All men, therefore, are "cultural artifacts." The only generalization that one can make about humankind is that man is "a most various animal." And any notion of the unity of humankind must begin with that.[2]

Culture, Geertz goes on, must be interpreted, because it cannot be added up or measured. That is the task of the anthropologist, who becomes, in effect, an ethnographer, someone who studies ethnic groups and by inference their characteristics. Quoting the British philosopher Gilbert Ryle, Geertz says that such interpretation requires "thick description." Establishing rapport, interviewing subjects, keeping a diary,

---

* Geertz and Said later got into a nasty fight over Said's book *Orientalism,* which Geertz was critical of, despite the praise given to him by Said. Edward W. Said, *Orientalism* (New York: Random House, 1978), p. 326.

and so on all add up to what thick description means.[3] This has more in common with what the great British travel writers of the Near East—Charles M. Doughty, Wilfred Thesiger, and Patrick Leigh Fermor—have done rather than what most political scientists have. This is also why the area specialists—the Cold War–era Arabists, China hands, and so on—have usually had the profoundest wisdom to offer in Washington. And what all of these travelers and experts have shown in their writings—and what Geertz, the anthropologist, makes especially clear—is that culture, above all, consists of what it takes for an individual to acceptably operate in a given society.*

Culture is context. "Understanding a people's culture exposes their normalness without reducing their particularity," writes Geertz, adding that during his fieldwork in Morocco, the more he figured out what Moroccans were up to in their daily lives, "the more logical, and the more singular," they seemed. "Culture . . . is the ultimate source for what we think constitutes common sense," writes Charles King, a Georgetown University professor who has chronicled the lives of anthropologists. This is why cultural relativism—that is, making allowances for different behavior patterns—something which conservatives decry, is actually a good and true thing, since it makes us aware that all cultures, not just those in the West, are efficient and rational in their own particular way. Thus, the different cultural patterns of the earth's peoples express an underlying unity of the human species.[4]

That is, provided we look closely at culture. For it is from concentrating on the mundane, on the minutiae of ground-level existence, that the most crucial insights about such things as violence, individual identity, political legitimacy, and revolution are revealed. "The aim," says Geertz, "is to draw large conclusions from small, but very densely textured facts." Evidence is not theory alone, it is something built up from "directly observable" cultural modes of thought. Thus, Geertz's pièce de résistance as an anthropologist is not a grand theory or set of perceptions; rather, it is his famous study of the traditional Balinese

---

* Here Geertz is leaning somewhat on the work of fellow anthropologist Ward Goode- nough, also a giant in his field in the twentieth century.

cockfight, which reveals "social order, abstract hatred, masculinity, demonic power," and much more. It is all about a descent into detail, in order to get beneath the bland clichés, labels, and nostrums that define conventional thinking about places.[5]

Such a descent into detail and closely observable facts led Geertz to warn as far back as 1963 about the future of new states of Africa and elsewhere in the third world. Because their governing institutions and history of civil politics were so weak and underdeveloped, he explained, they would be prone to "primordial" sentiments, namely "tribalism" and ethnic hatreds. Self-rule would exacerbate these tendencies rather than alleviate them, since it would lead to a fight over spoils now that the "aloof and unresponsive" colonial regimes had departed. Mind you, Geertz's argument was more complex than essentialist. "Tribalism," for instance, can be a form of political order emerging from group solidarity, even as competing tribes that are forced to coexist within the artificial boundaries drawn by colonialists can be a force of dissolution.

Drawing on his years of living experience in third world villages, Geertz observes: "The power of the 'givens' of place, tongue, blood, looks, and way-of-life to shape an individual's notion of who, at bottom, he is and with whom, indissolubly, he belongs is rooted in the nonrational foundations of personality."[6]

And that, in turn, is a foundation stone of a place's politics.

Geertz says that the rise of independent states in the third world "does not do away with ethnocentrism; it merely modernizes it."[7] The late Harvard professor Samuel P. Huntington would come to a similar conclusion three decades later, arguing that the *clash of civilizations* would signal the final phase of modernism, as the weakness of states gives rise to group consciousness. Moreover, those various ethnic, sectarian, and civilizational disputes would not be alleviated by the growth and expansion of cities, since having fled the age-old ways of the village and inhabiting badly urbanized shantytowns, people's primordial identities would merely be reinvented in more abstract and extreme forms in order to cope with impersonal urban settings.[8]

Geertz knows that "a country's politics reflect the design of its culture." But it does so in "obscure" ways. Moreover, awareness of this does not help much in forecasting, since, to take the example of Indonesia (where Geertz had so much experience), it has seen revolution, parliamentary democracy, autocracy, mass murder, and military rule. So, as he asks, "Where is the design in that?"[9]

Yet we must still try to grapple with political and geopolitical reality in countries. And that is more completely done by Geertz's and Ryle's example of thick description, however much we fail at it, and however inadequate are our efforts. For the attempt itself will improve the value of our analysis.

THICK DESCRIPTION GOES ALONG with a close reading of history, since a people's experience, upon which their behavior is based, does not begin the moment a journalist lands at the airport, or the moment a political scientist begins his study of them. Human behavior, of the kind that anthropologists observe, is influenced by everything that has happened in a village, city, or country right up until the moment we begin observing it. Every moment is the culmination of ages of history before it. Therefore, the most satisfying political science is the kind with a deep historical sensibility behind it.

Of the great political scientists of the twentieth century, the one who fits hand in glove with Clifford Geertz's anthropology is the American Barrington Moore, Jr., who received a grounding in Greek, Latin, and history at Williams College in Massachusetts. Moore's work emphasizes the historical particularity of countries and places, and how each one is unique from the others. Perhaps his most significant book is *Social Origins of Dictatorship and Democracy: Lord and Peasant in the Making of the Modern World,* published in 1966. In it he tells how England, France, the United States, China, Japan, and India each arrived at its system of government, with all of its strengths and weaknesses, through the most original, complex, and convoluted of ways—ways that could not be replicated anywhere else. If Geertz does thick description, Moore does thick history, with a strong analytical bent.

Moore begins with England, where the growth of commerce in the towns adjacent to agricultural areas in the sixteenth and seventeenth centuries created different economic groups, which gradually elbowed aside titled local aristocrats, leading to the destruction of the ancien régime. This was symbolized by the beheading of Charles I in 1649. Henceforth, no English king dared to take royal absolutism seriously. By the eighteenth century, following the civil war of 1642–51, Parliament had evolved into a "committee of landlords," breaking the power of the king. Nevertheless, the aristocratic order survived: but mainly because of its money, not its birth. As Moore states, warming to his theme, "Revolutionary violence may contribute as much as peaceful reform to the establishment of a relatively free society . . ."

Yet the path of progress was never straight forward. The brutal enclosure laws that further strengthened the landlords eliminated the English peasantry. But it did so over time within a framework of law and order. Once the peasantry was eliminated, there was no need of deeply conservative and reactionary forces to uphold the values of such a peasantry, as would develop in Germany and Japan, and which would lead to fascist regimes there. Nor was there the possibility of large-scale peasant revolutions as would occur in Russia and China in the twentieth century. And because imperialism developed early in England, rather than late as in Germany, it was for a long time integrated into the system, and thus not an impediment to the ripening of democracy.[10]

Meanwhile, in France, as the forces of modernization cleaved ancient village society that had peacefully governed the division of labor, the rural poor became desperate and blamed the wealthier peasants or small landowners, whom Moore roughly compares with the kulaks in Russia. That's why, he says, "At the height of the Revolution, radicalism in the cities and the countryside could join hands, a fact that helps to explain the depth and violence of the French Revolution in comparison with its English precursor." For deep and complex reasons of culture and geography, "the underlying social structure of France was fundamentally different" from England, Moore explains, hence ruling out the more peaceful transformation that England had and would be experiencing. There was just no way for France "to enter the modern world through the democratic door" except by violent revolution, which sanctioned private property and equality before the law, and did away with seigneurial rights. Without such a decisive break with the reactionary past, France might have been carried forward "into a form of conservative modernization from above," similar to Bismarckian Germany and Meiji Japan.[11]

America was a totally different story. It was advantaged by a late start. "The United States did not face the problem of dismounting a complex and well-established agrarian society" composed of a feudal peasantry. Yet, the southern plantation system did constitute a latifundia economy, encouraging an "antidemocratic aristocracy" and a "weak and dependent commercial and industrial class." Thus, a civil war was required to usher America into the democratic and industrial age; the Constitution alone wasn't enough, Moore suggests.[12]

A theme that emerges in Moore's work is that the survival of semi-feudal peasantries deep into the modern age is very problematic, since it inhibits the development of a robust and cosmopolitan-trending middle class, and leads instead to fascism and totalitarianism in order to deal with the crisis of industrial development. Neither Japan nor Germany had successful bourgeois revolutions. In Japan, for example, the "patriotic exaltation" of peasant virtues and consequent fear of a rising commercial class paved the way for militarism and fascism. While Japan was more backward than Germany, right-wing radicalism emerged in both countries because of the plight of peasants and a new and insecure bourgeoisie under advancing capitalism. The price for avoiding an earlier civil war or revolution—as happened in England, France, and America—was for Japan and Germany a very high one. The Communist revolution in China, of course, would have been impossible without the survival of a vast peasantry into the twentieth century. As for India, it experienced neither a bourgeois revolution nor a conservative revolution from above, so rather than some appalling upheaval as in the Axis and Communist countries, it has merely wallowed in slow growth and underperformance.[13]

But all this constitutes only Moore's broad themes, even as he constantly underlines that "human beings individually and collectively do not react to an 'objective' situation in the same way as one chemical reacts to another . . . There is always an intervening variable, a filter, one might say, between people and an 'objective' situation, made up," he goes on, "from all sorts of wants, expectations, and other ideas derived from the past." Culture, in other words, is the key. But though culture can be stated as an overriding fact, explaining its effects is problematic.¹⁴ And because cultural influences are by their very nature obscure and ambiguous, observes the late University of Chicago sociologist Donald N. Levine, whose own work on Ethiopia was heavily influenced by Clifford Geertz, culture is easily dismissed by an elite policy class, which, itself influenced by the communications revolution, rewards only clarity and concision.

Thus, peoples and places remain more of a mystery than ever, since what is required to explain them is increasingly further out of reach. Globalization, by diluting national and ethnic cultures, makes their effects even more obscure and ambiguous. Walking the streets of countries, experiencing scenes and smells, and watching closely how people behave, will provide no definite answers. But it will help. The aim is to touch solid ground, so that real places don't dissolve into abstraction.

I'LL NEVER FORGET MY first moments in Cairo in the spring of 1976. Cratered roads, rolling layers of dust and black soot, redistributed by the occasional breeze. Monumental congestion with the constant, ear-piercing bleating of car horns. Schoolchildren riding on the backs of trams, whose wires were lit with electric sparks a few feet over their heads. Kiosks packed together with winking overhead light bulbs because of the unsteady current. Ancient rickety tables and chairs set out on the street, daring the traffic almost, where men in kaftans and cloth turbans around their heads sipped tea, inhaled tobacco with hookahs, and played *shesh besh*. Everywhere there was the crushing presence of what seemed to be too many males. The noise, the heat, the pollution, the glaring sunlight, the crowds were just so overwhelming. It was like returning to India, where I had been a few years earlier, except that here the colors had been drained out of the tableau, owing to the pollution and the nearby desert. It was a grainy, black-and-white cityscape, oily with human sweat. Cairo in the second half of the twentieth century registered the most densely packed large urban population in the world, in some central districts reaching 300,000 people per square mile.[15] Istanbul, 11 degrees latitude to the north, with its cooler temperatures and, by comparison, its quiet and more dynamic European-like organization, was a radically distant memory. Modern Cairo was always an environmental-demographic nightmare, rooted in both antiquity and an uncontrollable, nerve-racking present.

There were the Muqattam Hills, the same hills where the stones for the Pyramids had been quarried 4,500 years ago. In the 1970s and 1980s, they were a world of mountains and valleys of stinking refuse that went on for miles, sorted and resold by thousands of *zabaleen*, "people of the garbage": a caste unto themselves, more efficient at their task than the municipal authorities. The mortality rate for *zabaleen* children, who died of malnutrition, disease, and pollution before adulthood, was 50 percent, I would learn on later visits with them.[16] The Muqattam Hills and the *zabaleen* were emblematic of Cairo's assault on the senses.

"Today, the cry of the laborer—hoarse from drink, smoke, and hatred—is the cry of the Earth. And this heartrending cry accompanied me throughout my journey, from one end of Egypt to the other, and guided me," writes Nikos Kazantzakis, whose 1920s travel diary on the Levant had been the first work I consulted upon arriving in Cairo.[17]

But within a few days in Cairo the abnormal became normal to me, as Geertz would have understood. The city had its own inner logic. The fact that I was shocked did not make the city shocking. And there were places of escape within the most crowded parts of the city. As I explored Cairo's great medieval mosques and Koranic schools, built between the thirteenth and sixteenth centuries by the Mamluks, a dynasty of slaves-turned-sultans, I took refuge in silent empty courtyards of pharaonic grandeur fitted to Muslim specifications, with walls rising as much as six stories and adjacent to minarets of skyscraper proportions. The architectural keys here were volume and space arrangement, amplified by stone and dust, akin to the strength of Rodin's sculpture and without any glittering surfaces like the mosques of Iran with their blue faience. Just as there was, at least to me, seeming chaos in the streets, these medieval sanctums of purity and quietude echoed absolute authority. Cairo has always been a city of steep, vertical power.

Max Rodenbeck, a journalist for *The Economist,* writes, "After 5,000 years of civilization, Egypt's political system remains pyramid-shaped. Cairo sits indomitably at the pinnacle." Its irrigation ministry decides how much water farmers get for their crops. Its religious affairs ministry decides who is to deliver sermons and what they can say. Its interior ministry chooses the mayors for thousands of villages. On top of them all is the president.[18]

And as always, it begins with the Nile.

"The Nile not only begets the land, the trees, the animals and the people, it also begets the laws and the first sciences," writes Kazantzakis. Because the Nile's overflow was not always benevolent, people needed to organize themselves into communities. "And because one province is dependent on the other and its prosperity depends upon the properly regulated distribution of water, the Nile compelled people to accept an austere hierarchy."[19]

From antiquity to now, from the pharaohs to the dictator of the moment, President and Field Marshal Abdel Fattah al-Sisi, Egypt has constituted a steep, crushing tyranny for thousands of years. Though modernism wrought stirrings for more representative rule, it is a tortured legacy. And it always, ultimately, foundered on the struggle to maintain order over a densely packed and miserably poor population living along the Nile, a population which in 1976, the year of my first arrival in Egypt, had a literacy rate of 38 percent.[20]

Unlike in India, which in the 1970s was equally poor and illiterate, autocracy has always been particularly convenient to Egypt: for rather than a sprawling subcontinent of different groups and languages like India—disunited by river valleys rather than united by them—Egypt is much more linguistically and ethnically uniform, with everyone living along a narrow, easily controllable corridor of life and commerce. Cairo may appear unmanageable, but Egypt is a categorically coherent state utterly defined by geography, and thus governable. Governable, that is, if history is any guide, by a remote autocracy. And whenever it wasn't, anarchy loomed at the edges. Cairo, in and of itself—so overwhelming to the senses—presents a challenge that, thus far, only autocracy has been able to master.

The past is instructive.

BETWEEN THE SECOND CENTURY B.C., when the Greek Ptolemies defeated the last pharaoh, until the middle of the twentieth century, when the Free Officers Movement led by Major General Mohammed Naguib and Lieutenant Colonel Gamal Abdel Nasser toppled the last Turco-Circassian king, Farouk I, Egypt was generally ruled by foreigners. Greeks, Romans, Byzantines, Persians, Hejazi Arabs, and Ottomans tyrannized the Nile for thousands of years. The modern era had its beginnings, Kazantzakis notes correctly, with Muhammed Ali, an Albanian who was born in the now-Greek city of Kavala, and who became the Ottoman Pasha in 1805, in the wake of Napoleon's conquest and subsequent withdrawal from Egypt.[21] Muhammed Ali gradually wrested de facto control of Egypt from the Ottoman Empire, and ruled until 1848, near his death, establishing a dynasty that would not be toppled until 1952. He designed much of downtown Cairo, built schools and palaces, restructured the army, initiated industrialization, and developed the cotton monoculture. Muhammed Ali's successors governed as khedives, or Ottoman viceroys. In 1882 the British invaded khedivial Egypt in order to collect on the vast debt that had accumulated, as well as to protect both their own investments and the Suez Canal, the lifeline of British India. The British would grant Egypt a fair measure of independence in 1922, henceforth restricting their interests to protecting both the canal and the rights of the minority communities.

For thirty years thereafter, until the 1952 coup, a rivalry ensued between an elected Egyptian government, a British-supported Turco-Circassian king, and the British themselves, who continued to yield significant authority. The Egyptian-American scholar Afaf Lutfi Al-Sayyid Marsot calls this period "the liberal experiment."[22] It was a highly imperfect arrangement, to be sure, given imperial Britain's interference: plus the fact that because of the unexpected carnage and expense of World War I, Britain transferred some of those financial hardships to Egypt. But the three-decade period was nonetheless telling, since it is the only modern, long-term example of any kind that we have of the Egyptians' efforts to govern themselves without resorting to outright dictatorship. During the Arab Spring of 2011, when many of the world's leading journalists flooded Cairo's Tahrir Square, feverishly interviewing young Egyptians pining for democracy, there was insufficient mention of this critical period in the early and mid twentieth century. An assumption in 2011 was that the world was new, that history would now begin from scratch, uncompromised by what had happened before. Tahrir Square back then "was like touching something holy," reported the Egyptian scholar M. Cherif Bassiouni.[23] But the abject disappointments of the Arab Spring in Egypt have their echo in what transpired between 1922 and 1952, when the British, for all their faults, truly gave Egypt a chance at democratic self-rule, and tried in vain to locate a stable Egyptian government with which to conclude a final treaty. Though the British certainly threw their weight around back then, there was real debate and pluralism, so that Egypt in those years achieved a degree of multiparty democracy previously unknown in the Arab world.[24]

The signature personality of this period, a time that was originally so full of promise, was Saad Zaghlul, a lawyer and politician whose brilliance at debating, combined with an earthy upbringing in the rural Nile Delta, made him a formidable populist-style leader, and thus a daunting challenge to the British. Zaghlul was a disciple of the late nineteenth-century Islamic modernizer Mohammed Abduh, an Egyptian scholar who believed that Muslims had to use reason in order to adapt the Koran to the changes wrought by industrial life. Zaghlul, inspired by Abduh, believed that it was possible to construe the need for constitutional government directly from the writings of Islam; and that it was only a matter of finding a balance between the two.

Alas, personality matters as much as intellect, and by many accounts Zaghlul was marked by a "complete want of tact" that made him difficult to work with.[25] He had an "authoritarian style" and almost always could not hide the fact that he was the smartest person in the room. Naturally, such a spellbinding manner made him the premier politician in early-twentieth-century Egypt, garnering him a political party, the Wafd, and many supporters, not to mention a secret terrorist apparatus. Zaghlul, a true leader and at times a rabble-rouser, was Egypt's first democratically elected prime minister, and each time the British exiled him (to Malta, to the Seychelles, Gibraltar) Cairo erupted in riots. After all, while the morality of the issue was that Zaghlul and his delegation should have been able to appeal for Egyptian independence to the international community at the post–World War I Paris Peace Conference, the realities of power dictated that this was an imperial question which Zaghlul would just have to settle with the British.[26]

Keep in mind, however, that Zaghlul's Wafd was somewhat less of a party centered around specific ideas or ideology than a movement designed for Zaghlul himself to achieve power. And whereas the Wafd was a movement, the other parties were really factions made up of clusters of individuals, replete with animosities and jealousies, utilizing their connections with the palace and the British.[27] This unfortunate phenomenon was not exclusive to Egypt, but was common in newly modernizing and underdeveloped societies the world over, where institutions were weak and personalities perforce dominated. I even observed it in Greece in the middle and late twentieth century. But democracy has to start somewhere. And as Barrington Moore's thesis makes clear, each country has to find its own way to stable and liberal governance, a process that can take centuries, even in the West. For the moment, however, what that meant in Egypt in the years immediately following World War I was domination by a charismatic political chieftain who would sadly achieve little beyond his own survival.

The result was increased public disorder, featuring assassinations, street violence, and anarchy, sometimes instigated by the paramilitary wings of the various political parties, including the Wafd. Parliaments were dissolved and governance occurred by decree, as the British looked on from the sidelines. This all became a desultory element of political life in Egypt at a time when the population was growing dramatically and the cities kept expanding, making the country in any case more difficult to rule. Arguably, the unrest was inflamed by Great Britain's failure to let go of Egypt altogether, so that the politicians and the king were able to play the British off against each other, making solutions and agreements even harder to come by. And yet without the British security presence the situation might well have deteriorated further. One could claim, as the Iraqi-born British Middle East scholar Elie Kedourie does, that Britain's policy was too soft, as it abandoned the country to unsavory local politicians, Zaghlul among them, "to milk and misgovern."[28] Though Zaghlul died in 1927, he had "inaugurated" three decades of parliamentary turmoil "under the specious title of free institutions," as Lord Cromer, the former British colonial administrator of Egypt, had cynically put it.[29] Unstable minority governments were the order of the day. In fact, the original British sin might have been to help impose an essentially foreign political system on Egypt rather than let one organically and gradually arise from local traditions, even as the British colluded with one local politician after another for their own purposes. Imperialism, often born in chaos, often ends in chaos.

In any case, the Free Officers coup of July 23, 1952, deposed and exiled the king, obliterated the governing institutions, and broke up the political parties, consigning the whole thirty-year experiment in democratic self-rule and all of its many little dramas to oblivion.[30]

And as we know, the process would be repeated in 2013 following the Arab Spring, when the Egyptian military extinguished two years of rapturous liberal hopes and incipient anarchy, amid the incompetent, democratic rule of the Muslim Brotherhood, and in effect merely resurrected the tyranny of the Nasserite pharaohs. As *New Yorker* writer Peter Hessler observed, the Free Officers coup in 1952 and the

Tahrir Square movement in 2011 "were narrowly political events in a country that needed deep social, cultural, and economic reform."[31] Truly, Tahrir Square, as intense and intoxicating as it was for those who were there in 2011, was still more of an "outburst" than a program for developing an alternative power structure.[32]

Of course, at the root of all these failures lay the matter of Islam. "Islam always has an answer for us," an Egyptian journalist in Cairo told me almost forty years ago, in a discussion about the country's modern history.[33]

It was the frequent appeals to religious passions that had in the period between the two world wars pivotally undermined Egypt's first democratic experiment—just as it would undermine the second experiment. Zaghlul and others, despite their professed belief in constitutionalism and reform (as inspired by the example of Mohammed Abduh), could not avoid mixing Islam and politics. There is, as it happens, no secularity in the Arab world, as an American diplomat in Cairo told me in the mid-1990s, since religion plays a role in daily life to a degree that the West has not known since the days when it was called Christendom.

Islam as a religion was born in the Arabian peninsula, but Islam as a modern and organized political movement was born in Egypt in the late 1920s with the formation of the Muslim Brotherhood, under the leadership of the young Hassan al-Banna. Raised like Saad Zaghlul in the rural Nile Delta, al-Banna was also intellectually formed by the teachings of Mohammed Abduh. But rather than engage in the political process like Zaghlul in order to merge it with Koranic precepts, al-Banna, the rural migrant to the city, worked outside of the system, alienated as he was by the decreasing respect for tradition and morals in a rapidly modernizing country that was being undermined by a noxious attraction to Western secular culture. The Muslim Brotherhood (*al-Ikhwan al-Muslimun*) actually was more innovative as a class-based, bureaucratic organization than as a theological and philosophical one. Its urban, middle-class origins engendered an economically based hostility to the Coptic Christian and Jewish business communities in Cairo and Alexandria, even as it built a very hierarchical and ultimately effective political structure through a system of five-man cells, similar to early communist and fascist organizations.[34] Again, as in Turkey, we have the phenomenon of modernism—in part, the letting go of rural traditions—as Islam became angrier and more austere as a reaction to urbanization and the mass society it engendered. The networks formed around mosques in poor urban neighborhoods were crucial to this development. This is a detail that Barrington Moore would have rated highly.

It was this bureaucratic structure that made the Muslim Brotherhood a rising force during the country's first democratic experiment, so that when Nasser and his fellow officers took power in 1952 and wiped out the entire multiparty apparatus, they nevertheless were forced to remain tolerant of the Ikhwan. But the relationship quickly soured because of an Ikhwan assassination attempt on the Egyptian leader in 1954, and as it became obvious that Nasser was unwilling to share power with anybody: for Egypt had returned to its age-old pharaonic system of remote central authority.

Events helped Nasser in this endeavor. After the Suez Crisis of 1956–57, in which he nationalized the Suez Canal and survived an invasion by Israeli, British, and French forces, Nasser—abetted by his down-to-earth, emotional appeal—became the towering face of Arab nationalism and the most popular pan-Arab leader in modern history. Nasser's tragedy was that driven forward by his own overwhelming charisma, he was compelled to act the part of the Arab savior who would soon liberate Palestine, even as he manifestly lacked the military means to do so. This contradiction in Nasser's strategy allowed the Israelis to lure him into a war in 1967, in which Egypt lost much of its air force and the entire Sinai Peninsula. Nasser died of a broken heart in 1970, and was replaced by his fellow officer and vice president, Anwar Sadat. Sadat loosened up Nasser's police state, releasing from prison many of the Muslim Brothers, who then went on to profit from Sadat's economic liberalization as the new Egyptian leader moved away from the military and ideological reliance on the Soviet Union. Sadat came into his own as a leader worthy of Nasser when he launched a surprise military attack on Israel in 1973 and regained the Suez Canal

and part of the Sinai Peninsula. But it was Sadat's 1977 trip to Jerusalem, followed by his 1979 peace treaty with Israel, that fated him to
become an enemy of the Ikhwan. In 1981, a group of radical Muslims
assassinated Sadat while he stood on the reviewing stand of a military
parade celebrating the 1973 war. Sadat's replacement, Vice President
and Air Force Commander Hosni Mubarak, had the perpetrators ar-
rested and executed, and afterward followed a policy of brutally crushing Islamic radicals. But Mubarak later gave the more moderate
elements of the Muslim Brotherhood the freedom to organize and
take part in Egypt's politics—to the degree, that is, that politics existed
under Mubarak's police state.

Nasser with all of his charisma governed Egypt for almost two
decades, dying as a failure. Sadat with all of his bold moves—attacking
Israel in 1973, making peace with it in 1979—governed for eleven years,
before being assassinated. Mubarak with neither Nasser's charisma,
nor Sadat's imagination and bold moves, nor any charm or political
creativity whatsoever, governed for thirty years. Under Mubarak,
Egypt discovered a deadening, praetorian stability that eventually
shaded into political and economic calcification. Mubarak's supreme
goal and accomplishment was to die peacefully in his bed, without
being assassinated. And survival left little room for innovation. When
Mubarak was forced to resign in the course of the Arab Spring, the
demonstrators at Tahrir Square roared in celebration, as if a great
weight had been lifted off their backs and they and their country could
breathe again.

But all the while, precisely because it was so well organized and
disciplined compared to the spontaneous demonstrators in Tahrir
Square, the Muslim Brotherhood was planning how to take advantage
of the leadership vacuum that had emerged with Mubarak's removal.

The Tahrir Square demonstrators got their wish. Democracy returned to Egypt after a hiatus of sixty years. In June 2012, eighteen
months after the start of the Arab Spring uprising, Mohamed Morsi
of the Muslim Brotherhood was elected president of Egypt. But the
Ikhwan, though better prepared to wield power than the young ideal-
ists in Tahrir Square, was still not ready to govern a country of 86 mil-

lion people at the time. As the Turkish foreign minister Ahmet Davutoğlu would discover to his horror upon holding discussions with Morsi, the new Egyptian president was barely qualified and in way over his head. Morsi was stubborn, uninterested in the economy, and gave himself extrajudicial powers. Anarchy started to erode what used to be a completely controlled country, some of it arguably stoked by opponents of the Ikhwan, including the military, who wanted the Ikhwan to fail. There were shortages of water, electricity, and gasoline, even at the airport. Demonstrations now featured broken windows and tear gas. There were gunfights and looting. Vehicles were set afire. Coptic churches were burned. The word *azma,* "crisis," became commonly used. "It was hard to believe that two years out of five thousand [in Egypt's history] could feel so long," wrote Hessler of *The New Yorker.*[35] From 2011 to 2013, between Mubarak's rule and that of his fellow military man al-Sisi, the world media covered Egypt obsessively, believing until near the end that Egypt, despite all the chaos of a political transition, despite the violence, had finally turned a decisive page in its history, bringing a good part of the Arab world along with it. Yet, as we know, Egypt, which lay obscured beyond the media spotlight for decades before 2011, was destined to return to obscurity again. The two years that seemed so exciting and pivotal for close observers of Egypt were merely an interregnum between one pharaonic tyranny and another.

Alas, the exhausted Egyptian public had begun to yearn for a hard man to replace the weak and indecisive Morsi. And like the demonstrators of a year or two before, the public got its wish. Abdel Fattah al-Sisi, the commander in chief of the armed forces, assumed control, and after he had killed many hundreds in the streets, calm gradually became the norm in the political space.* Though al-Sisi would soon prove to be a harsher, more murderous tyrant than Mubarak, few at least at the very beginning of his rule were complaining.

For the masses, anarchy had proved more frightening than tyranny.

---

* "Calm" was a relative word, as an insurgency spread in the Sinai desert and occasional terrorist attacks continued to plague the main population centers of the Nile Valley.

The world media remembers the stirrings of democracy; many Egyptians whom I interviewed remember the chaos, the looting, the sound of gunshots at night, homes vandalized by mobs, the gangs of young men in the streets and at the airport. The middle class especially feared for its well-being. The trick was to find a middle ground of political space between tyranny on one hand and anarchy on the other. And now for the second time in modern history Egypt had failed to do so: 2013 was sort of a replay of 1952, with the military again taking absolute control.

At roughly the same time that foreign journalists were being enthralled by the sense of hope and possibility in Tahrir Square, and as the wave of protests comprising the Arab Spring moved on to Libya and Syria, on March 16, 2011, I participated in a meeting of the Pentagon's Defense Policy Board, of which I was then a member. Secretary of Defense Robert Gates went around the room, asking each of us about our reactions to the events in the Middle East. I told the secretary that while Tunisia and Egypt were geographically coherent, age-old clusters of civilization, which therefore had a fair chance of surviving the unrest in one piece and restoring some sort of order, Libya and Syria were mere vague geographical expressions, riven by sect, ethnicity, and tribe, that would in future months and years utterly disintegrate into violence because of the protest movement. Gates looked at me for a long second, and then grimly agreed. He subsequently voiced deep misgivings about the military adventure that the Obama administration was about to launch three days later, in order to topple Libyan leader Muammar Gaddafi.

As a journalist for decades around the world, I empathized with the optimism bleeding through the news reports in those early, heady days of the Arab Spring, especially in Tahrir Square. I knew how journalists were children of the moment, consumed with the intensity of what people were telling them and what was happening right before their eyes. But in that room in the Pentagon that early afternoon, I was thinking of the seventeenth-century English philosopher Thomas Hobbes, who believed that order was more important than freedom because without order there could be no freedom for anyone; and that therefore the role of government was to monopolize the use of violence in order to protect man from the state of nature, in which every man was the enemy of every other man. Anarchy was the ultimate enemy of politics, Hobbes knew. And the opposite of anarchy was hierarchy, from which order emanated.[36] Indeed, order was the first priority. Only then could you go about making order less and less coercive.

Libya and Syria have experienced the utter extremities of tyranny and anarchy. Egypt has achieved order, but only of a coercive and compulsive sort. Robert F. Worth, after years of deep reporting in the Arab world for *The New York Times*, writes that what the Arabs wanted was less democracy than *karama*, "dignity": that is, a state—democratic or not—"that shielded its subjects from humiliation and despair."[37] It didn't seem like too much to ask.

Was there any hope for Egypt? Could it evolve from a regime of arbitrary rule to one of consultative rule, somewhat analogous to the traditional Arab monarchies?[38]

I BEGAN MY MOST recent journey to Egypt raising the study of geography above that of political science. I would end it hearing the voice of a political scientist. Francis Fukuyama of Stanford writes (channeling Samuel Huntington) that upheavals happen when social change outpaces existing institutions. Like the revolutions of 1848 in Europe, the Arab Spring in Egypt (and Tunisia) demonstrated the impatience of an ascending middle class with an existing authoritarian regime. But as in the failed revolutions of 1848, the middle classes of nineteenth-century Europe—like that of early-twenty-first-century Egypt—were just not quite large enough and just not quite established enough to carry the day. Thus, Egypt lumbered forward, possessing a strong state, but not the "rule of law" or "democratic accountability," upon which modern political systems are based.[39]

THE POPULATION OF EGYPT was 40 million in 1976, when I had first been overwhelmed by the dirt and density of the country. It was now, in 2021, 105 million. Yet downtown Cairo was still recognizable, still familiar. Despite the population doubling and almost tripling, despite the chasm of the decades, there was still the surging stampede of automobiles converging on squares and traffic circles that required a bullfighter's bravado for someone on foot to negotiate—for the streetlights, much like forty-five years ago, often didn't work. On the other hand, the pollution has been mitigated by the many late-model cars with their more efficient exhaust systems. Women and men still walked in packs, sometimes arm in arm, but now in Western clothes rather than in faded striped kaftans and turbans as in the 1970s. Quite a few young women wore both hijabs (tight black kerchiefs) and tight black leotards, their arms bare in a few cases, revealing themselves and covering up at the same time, a style that was a cross between traditional and modern that I had first noticed in Muslim Southeast Asia in the early 2000s, and which had henceforth become a sort of de rigueur expression of modernist global Islam. (I even noticed a woman with a baseball cap atop her hijab.) Whereas the hijabs spoke of tradition in the 1970s, now, as I was told, they had become a symbol of Muslim identity politics. Nevertheless, unlike forty-five years ago and even unlike twenty-five years ago, I saw individual women sitting by themselves in cafés, sometimes nursing a bottle of Stella beer while engaged in tense conversation on their smartphones; if not listening to music on Bluetooth devices. There was even a café or two where men and women held hands, and while some women inside wore hijabs, others looked straight out of southern California. Such cafés served exotic coffees and had a security guard and X-ray machine at the door.

Yes, despite the continuation of the line of Nasserite pharaohs, despite the many immemorially dim interiors with their scent of dust and cobwebs, globalization had seeped its way into Cairo's decayed downtown streets. Tahrir ("Liberation") Square had gone from being a windy expanse too vast to encompass a theme or focal point to a seething, joyous, constructively chaotic carnival of democratic yearning in 2011; to a sterile geometry of military-style, parade ground landscaping conspicuously lacking shade and therefore difficult to congregate in, except under the watchful eyes of the regime police. People were now reduced to their private spaces, jabbering alone on mobile phones. Yet, any chance encounter was suffused with demonstrable warmth and talk. I remembered the old cliché: Egyptians were the Italians of the Arab world and the Iraqis the Germans. But I wondered. The Iraqis, after decades under a totalitarian jackboot, had become boisterous in their own way; whereas Tahrir Square as seen from my hotel room was now a tableau of droning, nonstop traffic braiding around an empty, soulless space, as if repeatedly drowning out the cries for freedom from 2011. Here, by way of urban planning, the regime was discernibly making its point. Every few minutes I witnessed a lone pedestrian making his or her way across the landscaped emptiness.

Of course, it was more complicated than that.

Centralized autocracy had wrought a plethora of new highways and overpasses, underground parking garages, bridges, and satellite cities to relieve the stress on the downtown. The state had certainly not stood still. It was dynamic in its own way, now seeing twenty-first-century China and late-twentieth-century East Asia as models of development without freedom that henceforth could be copied.

And many Egyptians were grateful for this.

As I would learn in the course of dozens of conversations over the next few weeks, most Egyptians did not have the wistful disappointment about the Arab Spring that intellectuals and members of the media had. They remembered more the extreme disorder and were traumatized still by their experience of living under the Muslim Brotherhood. The dread had not been dispelled. The overwhelming majority of Egyptians wanted only quiet and economic security. The last thing they wanted was another ideologically driven regime. What had happened in Iraq, Syria, Libya, and even Lebanon in the first two decades of the twenty-first century absolutely terrified them. They had had a taste of it between 2011 and 2013. As for President al-Sisi, he had no ideology and was obsessively focused on the economy. An impressive percentage of his cabinet and judicial bench appointees, as mediocre as these institutions were, was nevertheless composed of women. And he was treating the Coptic Christian minority better than any ruler since before Nasser and the Free Officers. Al-Sisi attended the Christmas mass of this ancient community every year: under Mubarak, I was told, you couldn't build or restore a church. This was part of al-Sisi's efforts to consciously emphasize Egypt's pre-Islamic past and its pharaonic grandeur. In the minds of ordinary Egyptians, al-Sisi represented historical continuity and thus a surer guide to a better future. "By toppling the Muslim Brotherhood regime, he saved us from a creeping, Iranian-style revolution," a prominent Coptic businessman, Karim Sami Saad, told me. *If only the Iranian military had had an al-Sisi back in 1979!* went this way of thinking.

Still, the media was completely muzzled. Journalists were in jail. Hideous, systematic torture was state policy in the country's prisons.

It was arguably the worst human rights record in Egypt's history, I was told by humanitarian aid workers. The president did all this knowingly. The rule of the Ikhwan had brought Egypt to near anarchy. And in his mind, no chances could be taken. It was a self-defeating policy since it brought an avalanche of bad publicity and international condemnation, even as it obscured any good that he was doing. For even human rights advocates with whom I met admitted that "at least there isn't the stagnation of the Mubarak regime." Yet, despite the stability and small, steady economic growth—the white elephant projects notwithstanding—in the final analysis the Egyptian regime was one of compulsion, not modernity. It was this paradox that echoed throughout my journey in Egypt, and one that I listened for in the many conversations I had.

"THERE IS A STELE more than five thousand years old, declaring the unity of Egypt, north and south. Thus, for over five millennia we have had a central government over the same territory along the Nile, from the first cataract near Sudan all the way north to the Mediterranean, and including the desert from Libya [Cyrenaica] in the west to Sinai in the east. China only achieved a form of unity in the third century B.C. By then, Egypt was almost three thousand years old. When Alexander the Great conquered Egypt in the fourth century B.C., the time back from him to the building of the Great Pyramid of Cheops was as great as the time from Alexander to us. As far as the instrument of central governance is concerned, if not the type, Egypt has remained unchanged since the beginning of recorded history."

Ismail Serageldin, who delivered this lecture to me, was an old-world intellectual living deep into the twenty-first century: the opposite of a global technocrat. He talked to me about ancient Egypt, Shakespeare, and democracy in the same breath. Wearing a white shirt, gray suit, and tie, he was an elderly gentleman of the now passing traditional establishment, the distant nephew of the great Fuad Serageldin, who led Egypt's Wafd ("Delegation") party that had been established by Saad Zaghlul himself. It was Ismail Serageldin who was the founding director in 2002 of the Bibliotheca Alexandrina, the conscious postmodern reincarnation of the ancient Library of Alexandria, a meeting place of some of the great minds of middle antiquity, accidentally burned by Julius Caesar in 48 B.C. "Cleopatra," Serageldin explained, "was charismatic, but not necessarily beautiful-looking. Men like Caesar and Marc Antony could have had any beautiful slave girl they desired. It was Cleopatra's mind that lured the two men to her. The proof: Marc Antony gave Cleopatra as a love gift thousands of books from the library of Pergamum in Asia Minor. That was the kind of gesture that impressed her."

In the view of Serageldin, the great leader of modern Egypt had been Saad Zaghlul, who stood up to the British when they tried to thwart him from speaking directly to Woodrow Wilson at the Paris Peace Conference. "The British said, 'who was this Zaghlul to represent Egypt.' So Zaghlul went into the streets of Cairo to gather thousands of signatures, impressing upon the British that it was he, not they, who spoke for Egypt."

As a magnetic man of the people, the only Egyptian comparable to Zaghlul was Nasser, Serageldin explained to me. "But whereas Zaghlul represented the spirit of liberal democracy, Nasser spoke for the lower middle class at a time when single-party states, socialism, and non-alignment hypnotized the third world." As for Sadat, he was brilliant but was assassinated by the Muslim Brotherhood which he thought he had under control. Mubarak was not brilliant, "but he had street smarts and for a long time presented himself as an ordinary man of the people." Crucially, Nassar, Sadat, and Mubarak were all men of the Egyptian military establishment through and through. According to Serageldin and others, it was the likelihood that Mubarak intended to hand power over to his son, Gamal, who had never worn a uniform, that finally influenced the military to consent to Mubarak's removal during the Arab Spring. This went along with the medieval Mamluk tradition in Cairo of a nonhereditary dynasty, whereby a select body of changeable military chiefs always kept power within the group, pointedly not allowing any of their sons to inherit the leadership.[40] "But I also think that the example of [Turkish leader Recep Tayyip] Erdoğan upon [President Barack] Obama and [Secretary of State] Hillary Clinton had a lot to do with Mubarak's removal. The Egyptian military were scared of Erdoğan. Erdoğan had sold the Americans on the notion that the Muslim world would follow Turkey: becoming democratic, capitalist, and moderately Islamist. Remember Erdoğan had a much more positive reputation in 2011 than he has now."

What about President al-Sisi? I asked.

"Another military man. He's decisive and exercised good judgment when he toppled Morsi and the Muslim Brotherhood. He also refused Saudi Arabia's request to send the Egyptian army to hopeless wars in Syria and Yemen. But because he knows he has made good decisions on his own, he doesn't value a diversity of views." That, Serageldin said, was his fatal shortcoming.

To show that he has not given up hope in Egypt and the Muslim world, Serageldin handed me a copy of a seventh-century legal document in Arabic with an English translation. It was written by the Caliph Omar affirming the presumption of innocence regarding the accused, that justice delayed is justice denied, equality before the law, and the willingness to reconsider a judgment. "A thousand years later almost exactly, Galileo was brought before the Inquisition because of his claim that the Earth revolved around the Sun. Think of that! Think of where we have been compared to Europe." The implication, of course, was that history could once again reverse itself at a time of dynamic global transition.

———

DR. HOSSAM BADRAWI, a prominent physician, had less hope than Serageldin. Badrawi had been both a polite opponent and a reformist from within Mubarak's ruling National Democratic party. "We have had a vast increase in population, but have produced a less educated people," he began. Though I had seen educated women sitting alone and working in cafés, like in the West, the larger picture was more telling, Badrawi said.

"Starting in the 1980s, Egyptians had been going to oil-rich Saudi Arabia and the Gulf for work, and had brought back extremist Wahabi Islam from there."* The *niqab*, which covered women in black from head to toe, is an example of Saudi Wahhabi influence. "Ninety percent of the nurses in my hospital prefer to wear veils. Yes, the educated elite here in Egypt are very global and impressive but they represent only three or four percent of the population." He mentioned that despite al-Sisi's efforts, there were growing tensions between religious Muslims and the indigenous Copts, one of the oldest Christian communities in the world who accounted for 10 percent of Egypt's population. The freedom brought by the Arab Spring had in a negative way not completely dissipated: in fact, it had only increased the extremist sway of Muslim institutions like the Al Azhar mosque and university in Egyptian mass culture. "The army, police, and the teachers have all become more and more conservative. Because of the internet and social media we live in an age of postmodern crowd psychology, which again is religious and conservative here. Our political leaders use the language of religion to control the population. The Arab Spring led to black holes of extremism throughout much of the Arab world. Now the al-Sisi regime is more closed than any regime in the past, in order to prevent future Arab Springs. The situation is not sustainable."

---

* Egyptian novelist Alaa Al Aswany also said that the 1970s oil boom drew millions of Egyptians to the Gulf, from where they brought back home a stricter version of Islam. Emily Bobrow, "Weekend Confidential: In a New Novel, Egypt's Celebrated Dissident Assesses the Complicated Aftermath of Revolution," New York: *The Wall Street Journal*, August 7–8, 2021.

Badrawi, who had been personally close to Mubarak, once told the late Egyptian president that for the sake of the country's progress, he had to step down. Mubarak replied: "If I leave, either the Muslim Brotherhood or the military will take power," since they were the only organized forces in the society.

I told Badrawi that this was the eternal dilemma of the dictator, who creates a bad situation that can only get worse if he leaves office.

"It's always like that," Badrawi replied. "We need three things over the long run to escape from this situation: the rule of law, mass education, and sustainable economic policies."

This led Badrawi to talk about Nasser, the first in the line of Egypt's secular military dictators, hence Nasserite pharaohs. "Nasser had a chance that nobody else had: to gradually transform Egypt into a democracy that would be the largest market in the Middle East." But, to repeat, Nasser's tragedy was his own charisma, which in a country with top-heavy but essentially weak bureaucratic institutions led to dictatorship, especially in the 1950s and 1960s, when the third world was in thrall to one-party socialism under the influence of the Soviet Union, Mao Zedong's China, and the non-aligned movement, of which Nasser's Egypt was a leading element. So Nasser, as Badrawi reminded me, "killed the private sector and created monsters" out of public institutions. "I remember my mother hiding her jewelry when the authorities confiscated our property."

Badrawi continued: "Mubarak started gradual reform, so that the economy was actually growing at seven percent annually at the time of his overthrow." It is often like that: political upheavals happen not when things are getting worse but when things are getting a little better, and the population is filled with frustrations that are the fruit of rising expectations. The breakneck economic development under the shah that preceded the Iranian Revolution is the most famous and starkest example of this.

Just as Mubarak had predicted, chaos and rule by the Islamists came in his wake. Now the army was back in power with a vengeance. At every major meeting, no matter the subject, the chief of the army or one of his subordinates was present. Al-Sisi saw threats everywhere.

After all, there was chaos in neighboring Libya, Islamist guerrilla terrorism in the Sinai Peninsula, the construction of a new dam on the Blue Nile in Ethiopia that threatened Egypt's water supply. It had been a conspiracy of outside powers, notably the Obama administration, so went al-Sisi's thinking, that led to the anarchy and extremism of the Arab Spring in Egypt. As for civil society, it was a lax, sagging element as al-Sisi had put it to his advisers, which would lead nowhere. And thus he saw himself as the savior who had gotten rid of the Muslim Brotherhood.

Badrawi repeated: "Rule of law, education, sustainable economic policies that can enlarge the private sector. Only such things will save us."

ANIS SALEM, A FORMER ambassador and high official in the United Nations, was, unlike Ismail Serageldin, a global technocrat whose English was suffused with the buzzwords of the international elite. "What *black swans* lie in Egypt's future?" he asked rhetorically about the possibility of unforeseen events. The subject on his mind was the Egyptian military, the state within the state that had ruled Egypt since 1952, except for when the Islamists were in power following the Arab Spring.

"The military has always been Egypt's premier modern institution that took in vast hordes of lower-middle-class kids, raised them, and educated them. Modernizing militaries take power in weak states where civilian institutions are relatively undeveloped." This was not a new idea. It had first been propagated by the late Harvard professor Samuel Huntington in his classic 1968 book, *Political Order and Changing Societies*. But Ambassador Salem had come to this conclusion on his own, by observing Egypt over the decades.

President al-Sisi, in Salem's opinion, was the summation of this tendency. The Egyptian president saw the military as the only reliable mobilizing force for developing infrastructure, logistics, irrigation systems, desalinization plants, nuclear power, and so on. This made him more dynamic than Mubarak, who according to a widely held view here moved by inches for thirty years while Turkey, South Korea, Taiwan, Malaysia, and other countries were developing by leaps and bounds.

The problem, however, according to Salem, was that the military was an extremely inflexible, hierarchical force in a world where flattened hierarchies were best positioned to take advantage of the new digital age. Al-Sisi was only a finite thinker, more at ease with engineers and others who build things than he was with intellectuals and all manner of political types, quite a few of whom snobbishly looked down at the officer corps as the kids not smart enough to get into university. Nasser tragically had had the opportunity to rein in the military and didn't take it. Nasser ran a country of 25 million whereas al-Sisi had a harder task: to govern over 100 million people, the majority of whom were poor and uneducated. So what to do? For al-Sisi, the answer was wasteful and grandiose infrastructure to unleash development. Build a new capital in the desert. Think of a better superhighway between Cairo and Alexandria, and so on. There was a certain nostalgia in this tendency, a throwback to the nineteenth-century construction of the Suez Canal and the urban planning of downtown Cairo under Mohammed Ali and the khedives. The problem was that the first decades of the twenty-first century were an age of complexity, where a state could only go so far without an educated population and a free media in order to debate and test ideas. Decentralization required efficiency, which Egypt lacked. Salem concluded that in this historical moment, when new technologies were revolutionizing politics worldwide, Egypt had seen the return of the hard, top-down state, with the equivalent of listening devices all through society, willing to go to extremes of repression, unable to enforce even minimum standards of human rights.

I thought of the heavily mobilized military regimes in Iraq and Syria in the early days of Ba'athist rule. All the differences between those countries and Egypt notwithstanding, it seemed that in the 2020s Egypt was hurtling back into the 1960s and 1970s, but without a political program, and governed less by hope than by fears of an Islamic insurrection. The Arab world, with the extremely tenuous democratic exception of Tunisia for a number of years, had only two types of states, those run by the military and those run by a family.

One opinion that all the people I met held, despite their differences, was that the most positive development in the Middle East at the moment was the dramatic secularization of society ongoing in Saudi Arabia under the auspices of Crown Prince Mohammed bin Salman, which they believed would dramatically dilute the regional menace of extremist political Islam. That is, the educated elite in Egypt saw a hero in a man whom the educated elite in the United States saw as a villain, on account of the barbaric murder of *Washington Post* journalist Jamal Khashoggi at the hands of the Saudi crown prince. As one prominent Egyptian warned me, Mohammed bin Salman was liberating Saudi society with one hand while closing it down with the other, adding whole new layers of repressive control. The suffocating national security state was indeed alive and well in the Arab Middle East.

MY INTERLOCUTORS HAD BEEN in the main talking of vast impersonal forces reshaping history: technology, demography, hierarchical military orders, confident dictators, and so on. But just as often there is the critical Shakespearean element that shapes history, revolving around the most intimate of family dramas. So it was with Hosni Mubarak.

A longtime Egyptian friend with the best of connections to the Mubarak regime told me this story:

"Every afternoon, Mubarak had set aside an hour to play with, and be with, his beloved grandson, Mohammed. The boy was the light of the Egyptian leader's life, who was allowed to call Mubarak on his private cell phone. Being with the boy relieved the stress and tension of ruling Egypt for decades on end. The boy returned from school one day with a splitting headache. Then he started to vomit. He was rushed to the military hospital in the suburb of Maadi, south of Cairo. He stayed there only a few hours before being taken to Paris for medical treatment. But he died two days after getting sick, at age twelve, from a brain aneurysm, on May 18, 2009. Mubarak was absolutely devastated. He retreated into himself, utterly distracted, losing interest in his job, as different factions of aides and high officials began to run the country from day to day, while Mubarak spent more time alone at his vacation home in Sharm el-Sheikh. It was as if Egypt suddenly had no president. Thus, the country was drifting. It went on like this until the Arab Spring, nearly two years later."

THROUGHOUT MY STAY IN Egypt, I deliberately sought out older people because they had visited the past and thus had memories with which to put the current moment of history in perspective. Each encounter was a surprise. I expected to hear one thing and heard another. I expected the conversation to go in one direction and it went in another. Reading before my journey, then layering one conversation atop another was the way that I had always learned. The repetitions were as revealing as the differences in what people said. The combination of books read and voices heard constituted my intellectual adventure. I listened and occasionally argued. But I tried not to judge anyone.

I HADN'T PLANNED ON meeting Ahmed Aboul Gheit, the secretary-general of the Arab League, whose headquarters were in Cairo. But a friend recommended I see him and a meeting was quickly arranged. He was seventy-eight at the time of our encounter, but his voice was crisp and booming, dominating a vast and palatial office, in which several of his aides sat beside him. Aboul Gheit constituted a challenging and formidable life force that put you on your guard. He had seen it all: Nasser's War of Attrition following the 1967 Arab-Israeli war, the 1973 Arab-Israeli War, Sadat's negotiations with Henry Kissinger, Sadat's visit to Jerusalem in 1977, the Camp David Accords, and everything afterwards in which he had had a diplomatic front-row seat.

"Never before in my life have I seen such regional chaos as now," Aboul Gheit began. "It all started on August 2, 1990, when Saddam Hussein invaded Kuwait. Then we had a holding action for thirteen years [with the American no-fly zones over Iraq]. But in 2003 came that very, very unwise American military intervention in Iraq, which handed Iraq to Iran on a silver platter. The U.S. is partly responsible for everything bad in the Middle East since then. The Mashriq [Levant]—Syria and Iraq—has been destroyed, the Arab world shattered."

He went on:

"The Arab Gulf states are what is left. They have money. But they are scared. They need an insurance policy." His point was that with Syria and Iraq (as well as Libya and Yemen) finished as states, with the Americans less reliable than in the past, with oil diminishing in value because of new energy technologies, and with the future of war concentrated on the cyber-digital realm, the Gulf sheikhdoms discovered an alliance with Israel, a cyber-digital powerhouse, as a partial solution.

But he also asserted with a voice that cut through the room, "It is not true that the Palestinian issue has been sidelined." I thought momentarily that as Arab League secretary-general he represented all the member states of the Arab world, which still demanded a solution to the Israeli-Palestinian problem, and thus he was a prisoner of his bureaucratic position. But it was more than that, I realized, as he continued to lecture me passionately. He just could not foresee a stable region while millions of Muslim Palestinian Arabs remained under Jewish army occupation. It was that simple.

Aboul Gheit returned to the destruction of the Mashriq, which had opened the door to Iranian and Turkish imperialism. He grabbed a Koran and held it in front of my face. "The Koran is not Marxism. This is why there will be no counterrevolution in Iran as there was in the Soviet Union." Iran, as he saw it, was the danger far into the future, and this spokesman for all the Arab states blamed the United States for allowing Iran into the Mashriq in the first place. (This was before the mass uprising, secular in nature, against the Iranian regime in the autumn of 2022.) As for Turkey, it was the conscious twenty-first-century embodiment of the Ottoman and Eastern Roman empires in his eyes.

Then there was the Arab Spring, which had hit the secular republics of North Africa, Yemen, and Syria harder than the traditional monarchies, because, as he explained, the traditional monarchies had inherent legitimacy so could afford to be less repressive with their populations.

Finally, there were the great powers. "The Chinese and Russian leaders and their delegations come regularly to visit the Arab League, the Americans almost never."

And the Chinese, he implied, were now helping Egypt return to influence by way of infrastructure development. "We have been weakened, but with the strong hand of [al-Sisi's] leadership we will return." Nobody here wanted to hear American lectures about democracy.

DESPITE THE PRESENCE OF President al-Sisi on billboards all over Cairo, despite the rules of Mubarak and Sadat that had preceded al-Sisi, many of the people with whom I spoke still had an obsession with talking about Nasser. They couldn't get Nasser out of their heads. Nasser, though he had died over a half century ago, was *present* in Egypt in a way that his successors were not. Dr. Ahmed Sameh Farid, a physician and former health minister who had grown up under Nasser, explained the phenomenon to me.

Nasser, he said, offered a fully developed ideology and interpretation of history in a pre-internet age when the Egyptian population was closed off from other political values. In psychological terms, Nasser's Egypt was near to constituting an East European, Cold War Communist experience. Today, contrarily, there was merely the military in power without an ideology and with other values available online. Nasser's political ideals, rather than strictly Egyptian, were pan-Arab and anticolonial. Thus, the country was psychologically reoriented from Europe and the West to the Arab world and the East. People had lined the streets to get glimpses of this magnetic leader, "like children waving little flags at Communist Chinese and North Korean rallies." Nasser truly was the pharaoh. He had given his countrymen dignity. He was rather tall, had a very powerful handshake and absolutely mesmerizing eyes. Crucially, though he first came to power at thirty-four and was dead at fifty-two, he always looked older and more experienced than his years. When the Egyptian masses cried at his funeral in 1970, they were mourning the end of Nasser's dream of Arab and third world liberation, following the disastrous Six-Day War with Israel three years earlier.

ABOUT A THIRD OF all Egyptians lived in poverty and were functionally illiterate, with another 40 percent or so existing in grim, working-class conditions. Thus, al-Sisi felt he had no choice but to drive modest change, partly through taxation, helped by digitalization. Because of the digital revolution, the government had more of an ability to track you, and tax evasion would become more difficult. With the rich and superrich beginning to pay more taxes as they should, al-Sisi was trying to engineer a wealth transfer with slums being eradicated and infrastructure at all levels being improved. This approach was inspired by the Chinese model, which had originally been the Singaporean model. Surveillance was about making internal threats minimal, even as the horrific experience with the anarchic rule by the Muslim Brotherhood inoculated the population against attempting further revolts as in 2011. As one former foreign minister angrily told me, explaining the population's tolerance for authoritarianism:

"America caused anarchy in Iraq in 2003. America caused anarchy in Egypt in 2011 by supporting the removal of Mubarak and the election of the Muslim Brotherhood. In the name of what? Democracy? We will not risk anarchy again!" More than a decade after the Arab Spring, he and many other Egyptians with whom I spoke still blamed Obama for "naivete toward political Islam" and for treating the 2011–13 period "as just another political crisis that Egyptians would have to work out," whereas for a large, moderate element of the population, as another diplomat told me, "the crisis was existential and a matter of survival."

"Egypt today, still in the wake of the semi-anarchy of 2011–2013, is becoming modernized, systematized, more controlled," a leading businessman described to me. "Al-Sisi is in fight mode, conscious of a race against time; as if he knows that to relax would make him another turgid Mubarak. He is more confrontational and more of a risk-taker than Mubarak. Mubarak committed the fatal error of letting his circle of advisers age alongside him, rather than gradually replace them with younger people and discover new talent. With al-Sisi if you don't produce, if you're not sharp, you're out of his circle. He has no qualms about replacing people close to him. He wants results."

The American media divides leaders in the developing world into two simplistic categories: dictators and democrats. That misses the point, for there are vast differences between one military strongman and another, as Egypt demonstrates. For much of Washington, Egypt was simply an autocracy going nowhere and of fading relevance. But perhaps that wasn't altogether true.

I INTERVIEWED A PERSON in al-Sisi's inner circle for almost two hours, who had an office in the presidential palace. This is some of what that person said:

"The U.S. view of the world is mind-boggling. It says it wants human rights. But in 2011 it supported a fascist organization—guilty of the assassinations of two prime ministers in the late 1940s—that saw women only in terms of reproduction and told schoolchildren to have nothing to do with Coptic Christians. Every notion of cosmopolitanism in Egypt was undone by the Muslim Brotherhood. But the U.S. is driven by a 'name-and-shame' so-called human rights mentality towards its friends . . .

"Egypt is threatened at every corner of its borders. Our border in the west with Libya is almost seven hundred miles long. And Libya has been in chaos [thanks to U.S.-led intervention against the dictator, Muammar Gaddafi]. To the south for many years there was the Islamic Front in Sudan, which tried to assassinate President Mubarak in 1995 in Addis Ababa [the capital of Ethiopia]. To the south of Sudan there is even more chaos in South Sudan . . ."

This person then went on to talk about challenges to the east in the Suez Canal and the Sinai Peninsula. But it was Ethiopia that animated the discussion the most. "Water is *life*. It's *life* and *death*!" said my source emphatically. Egypt depended on the Nile for 97 percent of its water. And about 86 percent of Nile water during the rainy season comes from the Blue Nile, which rises in the Ethiopian highlands.⁴¹ Now the Grand Ethiopian Renaissance Dam on the Blue Nile, completed in 2018 in northern Ethiopia, threatened Egypt's water supply, by locking up a good portion of that 97 percent of water inside Ethiopia while it was filling the dam. Whereas Egypt needed Nile water for basic existence, Ethiopia needed it to generate electricity in order to light up the country and establish Ethiopia as a modern state. The issue was especially fraught because even the High Dam at Aswan in Upper Egypt, built during Nasser's time, has proved insufficient to satisfy Egypt's water needs—especially as Egypt's population has increased more than fourfold since the 1960s. The Ethiopians began construction of the Renaissance Dam in 2011, when the regime in Addis Ababa sensed weakness in Egypt on account of the Arab Spring and the rise of the Muslim Brotherhood. Egypt presently required a guarantee from Ethiopia that once the new dam filled up, Egypt would still receive enough water flowing north through Sudan during periods of drought. "It was a red line," my source said, and consequently al-Sisi was "upping" the rhetoric. "The Ethiopian dam is now the top national security priority for Egypt," I was told.

Al-Sisi's team felt besieged and unappreciated at the same time. Its military and security relationship with Israel was extremely active and intense. You couldn't ask for a better bilateral situation, Western diplomats told me. Yet as my source in the presidential palace complained, the U.S. media continued to treat Egyptian-Israeli relations as a "cold peace," compared to the normalized relations between Israel and the Arab Gulf states. My source in the palace said: "Egypt offers American ships priority passage through the Suez Canal. Our airspace is open. We have proved for over forty years that peace with Israel is sustainable. We are at the forefront with Israel on cooperation regarding natural gas in the Mediterranean. Without the Egyptian-Israeli peace treaty, the Abraham Accords between Israel and the Gulf states would have less effectiveness and meaning. We are at the core of geopolitics in the Middle East, even though we are taken for granted."

Furthermore, what Americans did not appreciate was that whereas the Arabian Gulf had always had little to do with Israel, Egypt had fought four major wars with Israel between 1948 and 1973, and was still connected with it through the never-ending crisis in Gaza. It was an emotionally complicated historical relationship, in which significant numbers of Egyptians had been killed over the question of land and security. You couldn't expect Egyptians to simply, cold-bloodedly, in the way of the corporate-style United Arab Emirates, orchestrate what amounted to an intimate security merger with the Jewish state.

IN ALL THE TALK I heard about the various Egyptian regimes, the name Saad Zaghlul was rarely mentioned. Yet, as the historian and liberal party activist Mohammed Aboulghar told me, the Saad Zaghlul period and its aftermath between the two world wars, with all of Zaghlul's personal faults, "represented the brightest period in modern Egypt, characterized by a free press and optimism about the future." The Egyptian film industry—the third largest in the world after Hollywood's and Bombay's—the great writings of the Nobel laureate Naguib Mahfouz, the singing of Umm Kulthum, and the singing and acting of Farid al-Atrash, which together constituted the golden age of Egyptian letters and popular entertainment, had its roots in the pre-Nasser era of which Saad Zaghlul had been a principal figure. But not only did Nasser and the Free Officers significantly erase Zaghlul's memory, it was the very overwhelming charisma of Nasser himself that made all that had come before him politically largely irrelevant.

Egypt, therefore, suffered a discontinuity in its own understanding of its modern history, Aboulghar explained. Rather than a steady march from the early twentieth century to a more rooted and stable liberal democracy, there had been a sustained period of fragile democracy, followed by iron-fisted military rule mixed with socialist ideology, itself followed by more sterile military dictatorship. That, in turn, gave way to a tumultuous experiment with democracy between 2011 and 2013, influenced by global trends, and which consequently owed little to the earlier period of democratic experimentation, and which ultimately gave way to military rule once more. The key ingredient, according to Aboulghar, for this discontinuity was the Muslim Brotherhood, which arose in the wake of Zaghlul's death in 1927. The Ikhwan drew its strength from Egypt's semi-literate and devout peasantry and urban lower-middle classes, and became a force of such power that only the military could control it: thus, the harsh military disruption of democratic progress. As in Turkey, modernism had wrought working classes in the cities that reinvented Islam in more ideological form to meet the challenge posed by mass societies and the anonymity they threatened. Given such tumultuous forces of historical change, of which one must add the odd and decisive Shakespearean element involving individual personalities, how could progress be in a straight line?

ABDEL MONEIM SAEED WAS a leading publisher as well as a director of a Cairo think tank. When I gave him the opportunity to speak on background he told me he preferred to speak on the record. "In this system, you can talk and criticize, as long as you don't incite." Whereas Turkey was formally a democracy, I had found that many people there were afraid to talk on the record out of fear of Erdoğan's authoritarian methods. Contrarily, Egypt was formally an authoritarian state, where many people I encountered were less afraid.

"It's hard to be a dictator in the twenty-first century," Saeed observed. "Because of satellite television, the internet, social media, and the flood of statistics coming from all over about poverty, per capita income, and so on, someone like al-Sisi is constantly under a microscope. Al-Sisi has seen Mubarak and Morsi removed by *the street,* so he knows it can also happen to him." Saeed explained that al-Sisi actually operates under several informal checks and balances. "The street, the army underneath him, the immovable bureaucracy, and the rules of international markets all exert pressure on him or limit what he can do. His dictatorship, as you call it, is therefore constrained."

Saeed was not the first person who told me that al-Sisi was being forced to become a "modernizer." The Egyptian ruler's activist style, compared to Mubarak, coupled with the advances of the digital world in the 2020s, was leading him to follow a similar aspirational path as the great Asian modernizers such as Park Chung-hee in South Korea, Lee Kuan Yew in Singapore, and Mahathir bin Mohammed in Malaysia, all of whom either preceded democracy or at least set a foundation for it by building middle classes and industrial bases. Such men were enlightened or at least dynamic dictators, in other words. Thus, it was not true that Egypt was headed nowhere, as the Washington conventional wisdom had it. To be sure, its path was convoluted, but it was also forward. A more dynamic dictator had followed a less dynamic one, after a democratic false start. And that more dynamic dictator might, in the final analysis, set the stage for a more successful experiment in consultative government. The American elite wanted direct, measurable political progress. But history was far messier, even if it could lead in half circles and zigs and zags toward a better future. "Real change happens in between the big events that the media is obsessed with," a human rights worker told me. "For example, progress may someday come about from within the military, as a lighter form of autocracy arises out of splits in the ranks." Such is the indirect way of progress embodied by the Loom of Time.

HISHAM KASSEM WAS A longtime journalist and publisher who did not necessarily contradict Saeed, but did have his own unique perspective. He had been through so much that he was both cynical and passionately committed. He had seen it all. He provided me with a colorful overview of the state of journalism in Egypt over the past century. And he, too, insisted on speaking on the record. Listening to him I realized that even the indirect way of progress is itself particularly convoluted and not so easily accomplished. Indeed, putting Saeed and Kassem together, I realized that the Loom of Time, while not an especially optimistic approach in the minds of Washington's pro-democracy crowd, might actually be too optimistic for the real world of the Greater Middle East.

"Prior to 1952 there was an independent media," Kassem began. "It suffered variations in quality and there was always the problem of raising money to start new ventures. It was a mixed bag. But it was free. Nasser, during his first years in power, gradually nationalized the media and disciplined it with intimidation. This was a factor in Egypt's disastrous counterinsurgency war in Yemen in the 1960s and especially in the 1967 war against Israel. Because there had been no criticism from outside, the military was ruined by a climate of no critical thinking. The military went from constantly claiming great mythical victories and then suddenly being forced to admit abject defeat in the real world.

"Sadat was different," said Kassem, warming to his subject. "In 1972, by expelling the Soviet advisers, Sadat effected the biggest defection of the Cold War, with Egypt switching sides from the Soviet Union to the United States. But now aligned with the West, Sadat felt he had to open up the society a bit so he abolished censorship. There were now political parties and each party had a publication. It was something like the pre-Nasser era of the early twentieth century.

"Sadat's assassination in 1981 handed the country over to Mubarak. Mubarak was the caretaker, the chargé d'affaires. He promised himself to hand the country over to the next guy exactly as he had found it. That was his understanding of duty. By the mid-1990s, he had allowed his cronies to publish weeklies. There was also a satellite television channel here, a newspaper there. It was all garbage. Nothing really substantial had happened in the Egyptian media since the decades before the 1952 revolution.

"Then came George W. Bush. In 2004–05, Bush, to his credit, put real pressure on Mubarak for democratic reforms. But the problem was still financing. Influential people still wanted to control media organs." An enlightened, objective mass media was still far away, Kassem observed.

Kassem explained that the Muslim Brotherhood, which rose to power in the 2011–13 Arab Spring, was just as hostile to a free press as its authoritarian predecessors. "The Muslim Brothers had a short fuse and they were unsophisticated.

"In 2013, in the midst of total chaos, a new and ambitious ruler entered. This guy [al-Sisi] was like a drill sergeant. A critical, undisciplined media was bad for morale, he thought." Kassem compared the early years of al-Sisi, before al-Sisi became a bit more sophisticated in a public relations sense, to the style of Latin American dictators, "Galtieri, Pinochet," with his dark sunglasses and uniform.* As for the media, al-Sisi offered media publications a choice. If you didn't let the intelligence services buy you out or take control, they crushed you.

"Very little of our media now is outside the hands of the various intelligence services," another source told me. "Worse, there is no criteria for how a journalist can get into trouble or not with the authorities. No rules. So you live in fear. The media, the human rights situation, it's all disastrous: disappearances, torture, prison sentences. Al-Sisi is reverse engineering the Arab Spring uprisings. He has no ideology, but is a hard worker." *Nobody sleeps at night until we dig that ditch.*

The economy was the weak link in this scenario. Nasser stayed in power by controlling the economy. Sadat had the Americans and Saudis to prop him up with money. And for a long time, the Americans propped up Mubarak, too, because Mubarak was loyal to the Egyptian-Israeli peace treaty. But al-Sisi has less and less of that level of support, since for the Americans he is simplistically designated as a human rights embarrassment and little more. As for Egypt's 5 percent-or-so annual GDP growth, it is artificially induced by government spending rather than by the private sector, and in any case is partially offset by the 2 percent annual population growth. Kassem explained that the real culprit is just how low Egypt rates in international surveys about the ease of doing business in a given country. Only the giant firms that can get meetings with the president or prime minister are able to operate in Egypt with relatively little hassle, because the bureaucracy at the lower and middle levels "is awful"—another aspect of the inadequate educational system.

---

* Dictator-generals Leopoldo Galtieri of Argentina and Augusto Pinochet of Chile in the 1970s and 1980s.

"The only way out," Kassem concluded, "is to liberate the economy from top-down military control," which of course is the last thing al-Sisi would be expected to do.

SAAD EDDIN IBRAHIM WAS eighty-two when I met him at his house in a distant suburb of Cairo. Even with a cane, he walked with severe difficulty, and clearly had other health problems, most of which began during his several years in prison in the early 2000s. Ibrahim was the grand old man of democracy and human rights in Egypt: a prolific author and longtime professor at the American University in Cairo; a famous dissident intellectual against the stagnation and brutality of the Mubarak regime. Meeting him and listening to him talk about his country with piercing insight for several hours recalled to me my talks in the 1980s in Belgrade, Yugoslavia, with the great anti-Communist dissident Milovan Djilas, who had predicted the collapse of his own country years in advance of it happening.

Mubarak himself had orchestrated Ibrahim's imprisonment and exile, as well as the frivolous court cases and smear campaign against him. Mubarak's hatred of Ibrahim was hot-blooded and personal, since Ibrahim had once been a friend of the Egyptian leader's family, who had taught Mubarak's wife, Suzanne, and his son Gamal, at the American University in Cairo. To Mubarak, Ibrahim had betrayed his family. It was that simple. "That stupid man," Mubarak reportedly said in reference to Ibrahim's persecution, "he could have had anything he wanted." That is, if Ibrahim had only been loyal. It was the same situation with Djilas, who had been Yugoslav leader Josip Broz Tito's World War II comrade in arms and postwar heir apparent, yet broke with his boss over moral and political issues. Tito, a brilliant Communist leader, at least understood Djilas's decision, even as he imprisoned and otherwise tried to crush him for it. But Mubarak, a dull and narrow, long-term caretaker of a ruler, had no understanding of why Ibrahim wanted to give up his position and comfortable life situation merely for the sake of principles. And it wasn't as if Ibrahim in the early 2000s was advocating for Mubarak's overthrow. Back then, Ibrahim only wanted Egypt to liberalize and become a place of enlightened authoritarianism, like Oman for example.

What had specifically got Ibrahim in trouble was an essay he had published in a Saudi weekly on June 30, 2000, in which he speculated that Mubarak was quietly grooming his son Gamal to succeed him. Syrian dictator Hafez al-Assad had died only three weeks earlier, and had been succeeded by his son Bashar. In a way like Syria, Ibrahim argued, Egypt would become half a republic (*jumhuria*) and half a monarchy (*almalakia*), that is, in an Arabic word Ibrahim invented, a *jumlukia*. The regime quickly dispatched Ibrahim to prison.

Ibrahim coolly assessed Mubarak's rule for me. "Mubarak did a great service to the country during his first decade in power [1981–91]. He calmed a nation that was on the brink of conflict after Sadat's assassination, and got the economy back on track. His second ten years there were lots of promises but no delivery, and his last ten years were a disaster, when Egyptians became humiliated on account of the stagnation."

It was a typical story. A dictator at first contemplates liberal change. In the early period of his rule, Mubarak had even dispatched Ibrahim to Mexico to study how that country was transitioning to democracy. But as the dictator realizes just how much risk such liberalization entails, he retreats back into his authoritarian shell. As he ages, it dawns on him that there is no trustworthy mechanism for a succession—one that would protect his family and their wealth—so he decides eventually on a pseudo-monarchy. "Any president of Egypt does well at the beginning—Nasser, Sadat, Mubarak, al-Sisi. But given enough time, no ruler does well," Ibrahim said.

The Arab Spring that eventually toppled Mubarak would itself prove a disappointment, a betrayal even. Ibrahim explained that it is actually quite common for revolutions to be hijacked. The Russian Revolution was hijacked by the Bolsheviks and the Iranian Revolution by the Islamic clergy. The French Revolution had its reign of terror and later military rule by Napoleon. The American Revolution was really an evolution that owed much to British constitutional practices of the century before, thus it was spared this fate.⁴² So it did not come as a great surprise to Ibrahim that the Arab Spring in Egypt would be hijacked, too.

It was the Arab Spring that brought Ibrahim back to Egypt from exile in the United States. On the plane from New York to Cairo the pilot announced that Mubarak had just stepped down. The Egyptian passengers surrounded the dissident hero Ibrahim and erupted in cheers. But as he later surveyed Tahrir Square in person he became worried. "There were no leaders, no platform. Enthusiasm is no substitute for rule." Hence, he wrote a column about the danger of the revolution being hijacked. A decade after the Arab Spring, with the Islamists followed by the dictator al-Sisi in power, Ibrahim told me:

"The Muslim Brotherhood never dissolves. It is always in reserve, a civilian army with the same disciplined hierarchy as the military. What keeps the military in power now is not so much the memory of Ikhwan rule, but the memory of the anarchy that accompanied it."

What about al-Sisi's prospects? Ibrahim intimated that a leader's claim to legitimacy, particularly in the wake of a revolution, is sheer ambition: ambition to build and develop a country. That was Mohammed Ali's claim to legitimacy following Napoleon's departure from Egypt. It was the Khedive Ismail Pasha's claim in the second half of the nineteenth century. And it has been al-Sisi's in the wake of the failed Arab Spring. But Ibrahim worried that now as al-Sisi had entered his second decade in power, he would be prone to the same forces of decline as his military predecessors in power here.

FIFTY YEARS AGO I traveled through the Nile Delta, the agricultural heartland of Egypt, where the Nile splits into a wide fan of channels before emerging at the Mediterranean. Now as I looked out the train window the great green has been eaten away by rashes of partially finished apartment blocks, decked with drying laundry: these were whole new blockhouse developments, only half whitewashed and thus exposing the red brick. These places weren't on the map when I had first traveled this route north by train. Truly, the delta had become a blurry, indistinct landscape of ruralized small cities packed with humanity.

The train approached Alexandria. Now there were masses of new and towering apartment blocks tightly stacked against each other that went on for miles: a new geography of anonymity that seemingly wiped out the past. The train station, under reconstruction, emptied the passengers into a vast and dusty soot-strewn chaos with few landmarks—a veritable war zone of honking cars and belching exhaust fumes. Squatting on the ground amid this sea of humanity were men and women, the latter often covered from head to toe in black *niqab*s, hawking household necessities and other merchandise. I threaded my way between the moving cars when a minivan crawling at a few miles per hour suddenly hit my shoulder. Nobody paid attention. The wide boulevard that I expected to lead me to the sea was narrowed by cars, unending construction, and stores selling low-end global brands. There was no place to walk except between the moving cars. I kept threading my way carefully. The Italian-designed Jewish synagogue, built in the fourteenth century and first renovated in the nineteenth, with its magnificent and fleshy neoclassical columns constituted an oasis of calm. It restored me, but only because it was removed from the life of the city. To enter I had to answer questions, pass through a security barricade, and show my passport. Nearby was the second-floor apartment, preserved as a museum, where the great demotic Greek poet of Alexandria, Constantine Cavafy, had lived in the first decades of the twentieth century. Finding it was an exhausting challenge. Without street signs it was hard to locate the narrow alley with its mess of both dereliction and construction. Cavafy's books and manuscripts lay inside old glass and wooden cases. My eyes fixated on the fine wooden floor and window looking out on the city with its chalky mass of anonymous modernity. There would have been a sea view or at least the breath of the Mediterranean when the poet had lived here. Nobody has ever captured the process of memory and remembered history like Cavafy, who wrote interchangeably about vivid and unforgettable lovers' trysts and "the greatness of our old Byzantine days."[43] Perhaps the view had helped his thoughts.

I resumed my walk. Sweaty and weak in the legs from the oily heat and crowds, I drifted into a cavernous café near the sea filled with groups of men in ball caps and women wearing hijabs sitting separately at round marble tables, engrossed in noisy conversation. Though the conversations were private, the café lacked any intimacy. I thought of the café life when the Greeks, Italians, Jews, and others had dominated Alexandria: the world of Cavafy and Lawrence Durrell's purplish *Alexandria Quartet*. Now it was a middle- and working-class Muslim city. Café life still continued, except not as I had imagined it.

I found another café, not tied to the city's past like the previous one, but with a hipper crowd of men and women sitting at tables together, with fewer hijabs in evidence. It was bursting with cigarette smoke and loud talk. There was no place to move or sit. Though Alexandria was smaller and situated on the Mediterranean, oriented around a harbor with a striking breakwater, it seemed more overwhelming than Cairo.

It was all so ugly. The village had come to the city and was now, in turn, being cheaply urbanized. But these people were making their own history, I told myself, liberated from the second-class status of their grandparents and great grandparents. Durrell had consigned their forebears to extras in his magical canvas of Greek, Jewish, British, and other cosmopolitans. Yet ever since Nasser's revolution and virtual expulsion of the foreign merchant class, the film extras had moved to the forefront of the Alexandrian stage. Egypt, like other countries, now had its own global elite in its capital of Cairo, even as the regime was an expression of the devout and struggling Muslim masses, who, precisely because they were susceptible to the lure of political Islam, had the heavy hand of a modernizing and more secular military forced upon them. The early modern world of Cavafy and Durrell, with its effete lodestones of empire and cosmopolitanism, had been bulldozed by the Nasserite modern state and its tyranny of the Muslim majority. But eyeing all the construction, I thought it possible that a new local elite would soon establish itself here, and continue the cycle of the rise and fall of dynasties and civilization once again.

———

QUIETLY, METHODICALLY, IN A strange way too little discussed, a momentous geopolitical shift was occurring in Egypt. Despite receiving roughly $1.6 billion annually in military and economic aid from the United States—a bribe that is the legacy of Egypt's 1979 peace treaty with Israel—the Egyptians were moving closer to the Chinese orbit. Exhibit A was the Suez Canal, which handles 12 percent of global trade, 10 percent of world oil, and 8 percent of global liquefied natural gas—and is vital to shipping between the Indo-Pacific and Europe. Beijing was the largest investor in Cairo's Suez Canal Corridor Area Project, a massive logistical and industrial hub.[44] The Chinese recognized that domination of maritime Eurasia was a matter of several choke points: the Strait of Malacca, the Strait of Bab el-Mandeb, the Strait of Hormuz, *and* the Suez Canal. Relatedly, in the desert east of Greater Cairo, the Chinese State Construction and Engineering Company had been heavily involved in building Egypt's New Administrative Capital, a grandiose megacity housing twenty-nine ministries and 5 million residents. Chinese banks had financed 85 percent of the $3 billion project. This was in addition to other satellite cities in Egypt that China was involved in building. A Chinese port company had won contracts to manage both harbors of Greater Alexandria on the Mediterranean. China was Egypt's largest trading partner. The Chinese were making Egypt, where the Mediterranean meets the Arab world and Africa, the core of the Middle Eastern component of their Belt and Road Initiative. Consequently, Egyptians had little interest in protesting China's persecution of the fellow Muslim Turkic Uighurs in western China. Egypt's population was slated to grow by 30 million people by 2030, totaling 135 million. With close to a million new jobs required each year for a growing labor force, the Egyptian government was betting that China could help more in this regard than any individual country in the West.[45]

And it wasn't only China. Egypt was also receiving roughly $25 billion in cheap, project-specific loans that didn't have to be paid back for twenty to thirty years, the minister for international cooperation,

Rania Al-Mashat, told me. The loans, for such projects as fisheries, waste water management, and new cities like Al Alamein and Marsa Metruh on the Mediterranean were being financed by Japan, Europe, and other donors. U.S. aid counted for less and less in this climate. The very process of completing these projects on time and up to international standards, she implied, would help to make the Egyptian economy more efficient.

Al-Mashat, the foreign-educated technocrat, offered an impressive vision of progress. But to channel Barrington Moore, Egypt was still a land that contained a reactionary peasantry or semi-literate class that had to be assuaged by millions upon millions of new jobs and better conditions. Nasser and the Free Officers movement notwithstanding, there had never been a true revolution to eliminate or liberate this peasantry. In that sense, there had never been a break from the reactionary past. Thus, the population remained prone to a group like the Muslim Brotherhood, which successive military regimes have tried to control or destroy. It was the fear of the Ikhwan that still constituted the raison d'être of the current regime and its many iniquities. Rather than solve that problem, the Arab Spring had only intensified it, owing to Morsi's and the Ikhwan's short, disastrous rule. Thus, like India, Egypt had so far wallowed in relatively slow growth and underperformance. "The heartrending cry of the laborer," as Nikos Kazantzakis had observed exactly a century earlier, was still the voice of Egypt. But now that an advanced stage of trade, development, and technology was merging countries into an authentic global system, could Egypt finally be liberated without a violent upheaval or revolution? For without a measure of political freedom, if only to generate policy options and decentralize decision-making, even the loans and engineering knowhow of the Chinese and others would not be enough to generate true economic dynamism at the necessary scale. Egypt, despite the abject failure of the Arab Spring, still required a stage of political development beyond the Nasserite pharaohs.

UPPER NILE

———

"THE MOTIVE WHICH LIES BEHIND ANY SCHOLAR'S EFFORT to characterize an exotic culture is ultimately aesthetic," writes the late University of Chicago sociologist Donald N. Levine at the beginning of his classic study of Ethiopian Amhara culture, *Wax and Gold*. It is a book in keeping with Levine's idea of love of subject, for Ethiopia and its peoples enraptured him for five decades of his life. The book's title refers to the Amhara expression *sam-enna warq* ("wax and gold"), the wax being the deceptive veneer and the gold the glowing inner core of meaning. It is a metaphor that Levine uses to explore the Amhara tendency for concealment and ambiguity, as a means to preserve social peace in a traditional society (though these are precisely the traits that are harmful to a modernizing and technological one).[1] In a companion volume, *Greater Ethiopia*, Levine would go on to draw on his unparalleled understanding of Amhara culture in order to explore the Amhara proclivity for empire-building. Levine's lifework constitutes a definitive example of Clifford Geertz's "thick description." In the right hands, cultural explanations gain a deeper truth than do purely historical or political science ones.

As Levine first explained in 1974, cultural consciousness is enhanced rather than submerged by modernization, because of the ability of modern states and societies to offer jobs, status, and other spoils for which individuals of different ethnic, religious, and sectarian identities compete. Through education, modernization also makes people more aware of their collective pasts and their differences with other peoples.[2] Such phenomena have been the forerunners to the identity politics of the postmodern era. Not surprisingly, because of heightened group consciousness, criticism of ethnic cultures is a minefield, opening up the critic to all kinds of attacks, centered around his or her motives and level of expertise. Yet these cultural observations are absolutely necessary in order to understand the dynamics of domestic and international politics. Levine's work on the Amhara and the other ethnic groups of Ethiopia meets the highest standard of this pursuit, because of his years of study and the rigor of his academic mind.

As Levine wrote, aesthetics are at the heart of his passion for Ethiopia and its peoples. The word *exotic*, which has long since become a cliché, is actually appropriate for Ethiopia: a land at the confluence of Africa, Asia, and the Middle East, which glamorously conjures up both sub-Saharan Africa and the classical world of ancient Greece and Rome. To wit, Ethiopia's Miaphysite Christianity is redolent of both indigenous cults and Greek Orthodoxy. Ethiopian Orthodoxy represents the second-oldest official Christian Church in the world after Armenia's, even as it has links with Judaism. Circumcision, for example, is widely practiced in Ethiopia, and the star of David is a symbol used by Ethiopian kings. Here is an ancient civilization, shrouded in myth, seemingly at the very edge of the known world, with storied associations to the Bible, the queen of Sheba, and the Greek classics. There is as well its particular geographical potency, a product of its pitiless and mountainous *Lord of the Rings* and *Game of Thrones* landscapes, fragmented by gorges and bluffs, which enfold the headwaters of the Blue Nile. Its historic coastline (including Eritrea), moreover, provided access to the Red Sea and Indian Ocean. Ethiopia is also, to some extent, an outpost of Middle Eastern and Semitic civilization on the continent of Africa, as historically involved in the affairs of Yemen and Arabia as with those of some of its African neighbors, and with its languages of the northern highlands related to Hebrew and Arabic. The age-old Ethiopian kingdom of Aksum, its Orthodox Christianity influenced by Greek Hellenism, twice sent its troops across the Red Sea to become masters of Yemen. The Tigrayans of northern Ethiopia, who have traditionally exerted far more political and economic power than their numbers suggest, are the direct descendants of the Aksumites of late antiquity, who gave the country its national script.

In addition, Ethiopia attracted Levine's attention because it was a fortress of independence and hope at a time when other states on the continent were being subjugated by European imperialists. Ethiopia was the only traditional society to survive the European scramble for Africa. Its Amhara king, Menelik II, who notionally claimed descent from the Hebrew king Solomon and the south Arabian queen of Sheba, defeated the Italians at the pivotal battle of Adwa in 1896 in Tigray, allowing Ethiopia to negotiate its borders with Europeans as virtually an equal. In 1935 there was Mussolini's invasion of Ethiopia— the world's first large-scale fascist aggression—which came to naught as Emperor Haile Selassie, supported by the bold and innovative British irregular warrior Major Orde Wingate, regained complete control of his empire by 1941.[3] Indeed, there is a triumphal, magical quality to Ethiopian history lacking to the same degree elsewhere in the developing world. Ethiopia was never formally colonized by Europeans. In that sense at least, it is not postcolonial.

ETHIOPIA HAS BEEN AT once a loose and sprawling empire and a deeply institutionalized state. Levine writes, "After they had separated into different tribes with distinct cultures, the peoples of Greater Ethiopia did not live as discrete isolated units. For the last two millennia, at least, they have been in more or less constant interaction through trade, warfare, religious activities, migration, intermarriage." All Ethiopians venerate the lion as a symbol of royalty, many build their homes in a round shape, and share other common cultural traits.[4] As diverse as it is, as prone to internal strife as it has been, Ethiopia, nevertheless, constitutes a singular civilizational and bureaucratic system: it is sort of like what humanity itself might one day become if globalization progresses further. We would then approximate a world still in simmering conflict, but similar enough in its constituent parts to be an

authentic planetary civilization, loosely united by common governance. Ethiopia, exotic and somewhat obscure, carries universal lessons.

For just as the world has had bipolar and great power divides, so
has Ethiopia. The Semitic-speaking Amharas of the mountainous
north and the more African Oromos of the southeastern lowlands
have confronted one another for centuries. As Levine explains it, their
cultural and sociological traditions have also radically contrasted, the
Amhara traditions being closer to the Western world (even as they
and the Oromos have joined forces to expel invaders like the Italians).
"Where the Amhara system is hierarchical, the Oromo is egalitarian.
Where the Amhara is individualistic, the Oromo is solidaristic. Where
religious and political functions are segregated in Amhara institutions,
for the Oromo they are fused. Where the Amhara historical project is
to build an empire, that of the Oromo is to maintain a parochial tradition."[5]

Amhara empire-building, Levine goes on, emerges from within the
social dynamics of the society itself, as each individual seeks to acquire
power over others in daily life: imperialism in this case becomes "the
externalization of an overarching passion to rule."[6] In fact, the life of
an Amhara peasant is dominated by a "low estimate" of man. "Positive
moral obligations ... are thus kept to a minimum." Altruism is unknown unless it serves a functional purpose for the ordering of a peasant's life. Life, in other words, is lived "within a minimal, Hobbesian
order." The reality of "hostility in human relations" is accepted.[7] Indeed, while Ethiopia is not postcolonial in a European sense, Oromos
have long considered the Amhara attitude toward them as colonial in
its own right.

The Ethiopian Miaphysite Church is no exception to this practical
view of existence. Like Orthodox churches in the Balkans and Russia,
the Ethiopian church is a national one, according to Levine, serving as
a standard-bearer in warfare against Muslim, Jewish, and pagan peoples. Its social teachings, Levine says, are couched in terms "of practical
justice, not universal love." As with a Greek church, being inside an

Ethiopian church makes us aware that we are, quite simply, no longer in the West. Nevertheless, there are profound differences between Greek and Ethiopian Christianity. For example, Ethiopian monks, even more than Greek monks, share a predilection toward living alone, in the wilderness, as anchorites, following the example of St. Antony in the utter desert of fourth-century A.D. Egypt. People often live scattered on hillsides, distrustful of those outside the immediate family circle. Levine wrote of a defining penchant for secrecy and intrigue among the Amhara. This was prescient, because nine years after he published *Wax and Gold*, a Marxist coup in 1974 toppled Emperor Haile Selassie, creating a shadowy and extremely secretive ruling "committee," translated as the Dergue, which proceeded to carry out massive human rights crimes for many years, and killed tens of thousands, in the course of fostering revolutionary upheaval.[8]

While Levine's insights may seem quite subjective, remember that it represents the research of a trained outsider with decades of experience living with the culture, looking and listening and asking the same questions for days, weeks, and months at a time in the field.

Yet one piece of thick description can appear to contradict another, in the search for some defining objective truth, if such a truth even exists. Levine, in observing how suspicious the Amharas can be of one another, nevertheless also notes a "sensuous camaraderie" demonstrated by an enjoyment of bodily contact, such as members of the same sex holding hands for long periods.[9]

Thick description at its best leaves one in awe, and yet with more questions than answers, since, as both Geertz and Levine emphasize, the truth is about making room for subtlety and ambiguity, and in the process accepting contradictions.[10] Indeed, the truth is often impossibly complex, and it therefore tests the clarity of the modern social sciences.

I FIRST TRAVELED THROUGHOUT Ethiopia and its borderlands in Eritrea, Somalia, and eastern Sudan in the mid-1980s, in preparation for my first book, *Surrender or Starve* (1988). The precipitating event for my project was the great Ethiopian famine of 1984–85. The major media ascribed the famine wholly to drought—to an act of God, that is, in which human beings were blameless in the days when climate change was not yet an issue or coined as a phrase. My ground-level research revealed something quite different, though: a violent ethnic war, aggravated by drought, in which the dominant Amharas and the Marxist dictator, Mengistu Haile Mariam, were using the denial of food as a weapon against the opposition Tigrayans and Eritreans, even as the Marxist regime was forcing the Muslim Oromo population into collective farm communities that further reduced the food supply. It was in the course of this research that Ethiopia, categorized by both the U.S. government and the media as African, was revealed to me as, at least in part, an outpost of the Middle East.

The degree of precision involved in the prosecution of military battles and the collectivization effort, as well as in the denial of food to certain groups, was significantly greater than what I had experienced in other African countries. The conventional army and guerrilla campaigns of the mid-1980s in Greater Ethiopia, with their tanks and fighter aircraft, were more akin to the Arab-Israeli wars of the 1950s through 1970s than to violent struggles in West and Central Africa. And the ideological rigor of the Mengistu regime was of a much more precise caliber than that exhibited by leftist regimes in southern Africa, and more like that of the Soviet Union itself. Mengistu was turning Ethiopia into an African version of a Soviet East European satellite state. In my book I compared the Ethiopian regime's campaign of food denial and collectivization to that of Stalin's terror famine in the Ukraine in the 1930s. More generally, I wrote that the Ethiopia of the 1980s was like a scene out of Boris Pasternak's novel *Doctor Zhivago* about the Russian Revolution, in which "millions were displaced, often caught between rival armies, and on the move."*

The spectacle of a quasi-empire of nationalities threatened with

---

* Robert D. Kaplan, *Surrender or Starve: Travels in Ethiopia, Sudan, Somalia, and Eritrea* (New York: Vintage Books, 1988 and 2003), pp. 5 and 11–12. Pasternak first published *Doctor Zhivago* in an Italian translation in 1957, to evade Soviet censors.

dissolution, and consequently dragging down the larger region, that I had witnessed in the 1980s was very much evocative of the situation in the early 2020s, when Ethiopia's internal conflicts raged across the face of the land in the country's north. For Ethiopia was qualitatively different than many failed Middle Eastern states, in that instead of being less than a country, it was more than a country. It was an unwieldy empire rather than a flimsy geographical expression like Libya or Iraq. This continued to be Ethiopia's dilemma. For ruling an empire, like ruling an institutionally flimsy state, required a hard hand at the top that, in turn, made democracy problematic. This was partly because, as the scholar and journalist Walter Russell Mead writes, the rules were few and the stakes for those vying for power existential.[11]

In 2018, Ethiopia and its former northern Red Sea province of Eritrea signed a peace treaty ending a decades-long frozen conflict, for which Ethiopian prime minister Abiy Ahmed was awarded a Nobel Peace Prize in 2019. But that peace treaty was merely a necessary prelude to Abiy's military assault in 2020 on the rebellious northern province of Tigray, which lay sandwiched between the Ethiopian heartland and Eritrea itself. What Western elites had seen as altruism in 2019 was really preparation for a war the following year. The new war between Ethiopia and Tigray ignited a refugee exodus in the hundreds of thousands from Tigray to neighboring Sudan. Abiy, as he is known, whose publicly stated goal was to liberalize Ethiopia—allowing elections and more free expression, all the while ejecting its overrepresented Tigrayan economic elite from the halls of government—was, nevertheless, above all about preserving the unity of Ethiopia at whatever cost. And he was using his assault on Tigray as a demonstration of what could happen to any province if it sought independence from the regime in Addis Ababa.

The war between the temporary Oromo-Amhara alliance presently ruling the country and the Tigrayans in the north, following many years of dramatic economic growth, was also an indication of how the development of literacy and nascent middle classes, rather than dampen the tendency for ethnic conflict, could also quicken it, by intensifying the contest for status and spoils within an increasingly wealthy and developing political system. After all, if economic growth and technological advancement were all there was to preventing violent conflict, World War I, which had occurred at the climax of the Industrial Age, never would have happened. The record is clear: economic and political development can feed nationalism and tribalism. This is especially true where there are difficult-to-gratify expectations, with European and Ottoman history offering prominent examples.[12]

The whole region trembled at this latest ethnic war in Ethiopia. Eritrea was hit by bombs dropped by Tigrayan forces. Sudan's fragile regime was threatened by the large influx of refugees. Also on edge was Somalia, which depended on Ethiopian troops to keep the peace there. Egypt, on the other hand, vulnerable because of Ethiopia's new dam on the Blue Nile that could disrupt Egypt's water supply, wanted only for the conflict begun in Tigray to continue, in order to weaken the Ethiopian state generally. The conflict also reverberated geopolitically beyond the Horn of Africa. After all, the Horn of Africa lay astride the Red Sea, which linked the Indian Ocean with the Mediterranean, and along which a number of states, including the United States, China, and Russia, had military bases. Ethiopia, part of the Greater Middle East, truly mattered.

IN AN ADDRESS BEFORE the parliament in Addis Ababa on November 30, 2020, Prime Minister Abiy Ahmed formally thanked Eritrea, which had provided arms and logistical support for Ethiopia's military takeover of the Tigrayan capital of Mekelle two days earlier. Indeed, there had been much bad blood between Isaias Afwerki's Eritrean regime and the one next door in Tigray, ruled by the Tigray People's Liberation Front (TPLF). Between 1998 and 2000, Eritrea and Ethiopia—which was then led by the ethnic-Tigrayan and former TPLF leader, Meles Zenawi—had fought a major war. As far back as 1985, from my perch in Sudan and inside Eritrea and Tigray, I had personally witnessed the tensions between the Tigrayan People's Liberation Front and the Eritrean People's Liberation Front (EPLF), in the course of their joint struggle to oust Mengistu's Marxist Amhara regime in Addis Ababa. This was a battle over ethnicity and territory, as the participants on all sides were professed Marxists. The Tigrayans, especially, had historically enjoyed regional autonomy as well as key positions inside the Ethiopian state. But that all changed when Mengistu's highly centralized Amhara-run regime consolidated power in the mid and late 1970s. Now in the late spring of 2021, the initial, short-lived success of the Ethiopian-Eritrean offensive against many towns in Tigray, including the capital of Mekelle, marked an historic setback for the TPLF, which had run Tigray for decades as the most stable and efficient part of Ethiopia.

Though Prime Minister Abiy Ahmed was himself a Pentecostal, from the largely Muslim and Africanized Oromo population, his forces were mainly Amhara, thus hostile to Tigray. Indeed, the Amhara and Tigrayan elites, though sharing the same Semitic background and Christian Orthodox origins, have always competed for dominance. "Seen from an historical perspective, the conflict of the 2020s had little to do with the process of democratization, but rather with the return to power of the Amharas, who under Abiy Ahmed, a part Oromo, nevertheless controlled the key positions of the Ethiopian state," explained Umberto Tavolato, a leading Italian analyst of the Horn of Africa.

The struggle of the early 2020s was epic in the sense that Tigray "served as a standard-bearer for other regions increasingly opposed to Abiy's centralizing agenda," Tavolato told me.[13]

Abiy Ahmed, like Mengistu, was a centralizer who wanted to do away with the system of federalism that had allowed a large degree of self-government for Ethiopia's varied ethnicities. Though Abiy, unlike Mengistu, was theoretically a democrat rather than a Marxist, the result of his efforts might still be the same: a stronger state in the capital of Addis Ababa and weakened power for the provinces. But whereas Mengistu's Stalinist approach had led to abject tyranny, Abiy's approach of military offensives combined with national elections threatened anarchy for a country of 110 million people speaking eighty languages and dialects. (In fact, Ethiopia's population included 40 million Muslims, more than in Saudi Arabia across the Red Sea.)

———

BUT HERE WAS ANOTHER way to look at the situation:

Tigray was becoming like the war in Afghanistan, a military adventure gone bad, eating away at Ethiopia's resources. Abiy Ahmed's desire to uproot the Tigray People's Liberation Front from its home ground also meant removing Tigrayans from the intelligence services and other bureaucracies in Addis Ababa—from where this ethnic Tigrayan elite had been administering the country's national security for many years. The Tigrayans had a sort of informal historical alliance with the numerically dominant Oromos (35 percent of the population), who also believed in ethnic federalism and for centuries were implicitly critical of Amhara nationalism. This Amhara nationalism was fed, in turn, by an aggrieved sense of lost territories. The Amharas wanted to centralize Ethiopia under their rule. In fact, the war in Tigray was a boon to the Amharas, who saw it as a chance to regain some of those lost territories. Thus, the war in Tigray was a prelude to the collision course that the Oromos and Amharas seemed to be on.

ETHIOPIA, OWING TO ITS very political complexity and intrinsically fascinating geography and culture, has produced a plethora of area specialists. Quite a few, such as the late Maxime Rodinson of the Sorbonne, typically combined an expertise in both Middle Eastern and Ethiopian studies, on account of the rich connections between the two areas (Ethiopia being founded by South Arabians who had crossed the Red Sea).[14] Two of the greatest living area specialists on Ethiopia briefed me just before my trip. They spoke off the record because of their active involvement in Ethiopian affairs. They vented; letting off steam, that is. Their words and thoughts, which often dovetailed, continued to ring in my ears:

"How do you categorize the Ethiopian regime?" I started out. I did not need to ask a second question, as the two of them wouldn't stop talking.

"The regime is a figment of one person's imagination. Abiy Ahmed is a mad prophet. Abiy is like a figure skater doing pirouettes while the ice melts beneath him. He rejects ethnic federalism and wants a centralized government, which is impossible. Remember that Ethiopia is an empire, not an artificial state like Libya or Syria. To repeat, it is more than a state rather than less of one. And the empire is now in the midst of self-decolonization. Get ready for five new countries in the Horn of Africa. . . .

"The West is complicit in what is occurring, since by giving Abiy the Nobel Peace Prize in 2019 it reinforced his own sense of destiny. Abiy is a Pentecostal, which means he is like a Marxist, with a utopian idea of progress that is a challenge to the Orthodox divine and mysterious way. The Ethiopian Church, like the Orthodox churches of Russia and the Balkans, is a nationalistic church in which universal values are not necessarily emphasized. . . .

"Eritrean operatives are all over Ethiopia. Isaias [Afwerki, the ruler of Eritrea] is now the boss behind the scenes. Isaias is a totalitarian genius. Isaias and Abiy want to re-create a Horn of Africa that in terms of power and organization is closer to the Arabian Gulf than to sub-Saharan Africa. . . .

"It is Yugoslavia all over again, and it is happening now: a sprawling Christian Orthodox–led federation that is also an empire. Tito's Yugoslavia was the last remnant of the Habsburg empire. Ethiopia's Tito was Meles Zenawi, who ruled Ethiopia from 1991 until his death in 2012. In difficult situations, Ethiopian politicians still ask themselves, 'What would Meles have done in this case?' Meles was a minority Tigrayan just as Tito was a minority Croat and Slovene. The historically dominant Serbs in Ethiopia's case are the Amharas, who will use Abiy, born to an Oromo father, to take back Ethiopia. Both the Serbs and the Amharas feel themselves to be aggrieved parties entitled to even more power. Yugoslavia descended into half a dozen or more pieces. Ethiopia could be much more of a mess. . . ."

The Yugoslavia comparison was especially poignant for me, as I spent the 1980s, in part, covering the slow-motion dissolution of that country that the media in general only became aware of in the 1990s.

"Abiy has unwittingly unleashed irredentism all over the country.

Whereas before there were pockets of insecurity, now there is general insecurity with banditry profuse and only pockets of security. There are constant small pogroms and extrajudicial killings. The national army is a pale shadow of itself. There are regional and special forces all over the countryside, with fighting between Oromo and Amhara militias. The Oromo Liberation Army is a few dozen miles from Addis. . . .

"Meanwhile, in the midst of all this, the Grand Ethiopian Renaissance Dam, located in northwestern Ethiopia, the building of which was begun by Meles in 2011, has turned thousands of years of history on its head. Ethiopia has now acquired strategic control of the headwaters of the Blue Nile. Egypt, which going back to the pharaohs was the stronger power along the Nile, must henceforth be dependent on Ethiopia. . . ."

POWER, CHAOS, AND ABSOLUTELY no firm direction, I thought, keeping in mind that 70 percent of the Ethiopian population was under twenty-five, with no living memory of Mengistu's Dergue even. What did the young population of Ethiopia want? What did they believe? And what was Ethiopia, by the way? Was it Yugoslavia on the brink of its demise? Was it a version of China from previous dynasties: that is, a vast landscape of interrelated ethnic and linguistic groups not yet united into a single state? Or was Ethiopia, as I alluded to earlier, the globalized world of the future, where we are all increasingly similar and experimenting with common governance, yet periodically at violent odds? All countries are fascinating in their own right, but Ethiopia is just more so.

FITSUM AREGAWI AND RESHID Abdi were aid and development experts who traveled constantly throughout Ethiopia, and therefore had no illusions about the lack of security in a countryside where, for example, local militias often ruled, looking for people to kidnap. They were the first people I met after my arrival in Addis Ababa. They, too, interrupted each other and finished each other's sentences. Reshid especially agreed with the comparison of Ethiopia to the former Yugoslavia. As Reshid explained, the constitutional and political changes of 1991 that immediately followed Mengistu's seventeen-year-long Marxist tyranny diffused power into the hands of the country's many ethnic groups, especially the Tigrayans, so that the Eastern Orthodox Amharas had become aggrieved in the manner of the Orthodox Serbs. The key variable in Ethiopia, both Reshid and Fitsum noted, was interethnic relations, not the mere holding of elections. Fitsum told me: "Everyone now wants political rights. That is what's new here. Because of the battle against illiteracy, begun ironically by Mengistu, people know more about the history of their own ethnic group and are consequently conscious of having been marginalized. It is this empowerment—no longer are Ethiopians merely passive peasants—that is at the root of the current turmoil." The population of 110 million was up in arms, it appeared. Again, this being a case of modernization and education leading to more instability, not less, at least in its initial phases. For on the other side of this disruption may lie more humane and technological societies.

What did everyone yearn for? According to Fitsum and Reshid, "they yearned for a strong leader: a Mengistu but without the oppressive military machine; an emperor like Haile Selassie, but without the feudalism." In fact, some taxi drivers had pictures of Mengistu and Haile Selassie together, even though the former had murdered the latter. That is because many Ethiopians wanted a highly centralized state that was, nevertheless, democratic. And that seemed impossible, Fitsum and Reshid both stressed, given the ethnic divisions and the sprawling size of this mountainous and teeming country that pointed toward a looser, federalized structure. I had heard all this before. But when you hear the same analysis repeated, you give it credence. The national elections that took place at the time of my visit in June 2021 could settle nothing in this regard, since rather than a contest between two visions of Ethiopia, a loosely federalized one and a highly centralized one, only the highly centralized one was represented by the candidates, assuring a victory for Abiy Ahmed's Prosperity Party.

"There is no going back to the old Ethiopia," Fitsum and Reshid went on, "since this war of Abiy's government against Tigray is a transformational war." The Amharas, in their analysis, tied to Abiy, had shattered any hope of working in the future with the Tigrayans. The sheer bloodshed, the government-induced famine, and the massive human rights violations that had been occurring in 2020 and 2021 in Tigray had made that prospect impossible. If there were ever to be a true reconciliation with the Tigrayans, it would have to happen under a new Ethiopian leader, not under Abiy. Abiy had burned his bridges. He could have had an alliance with the Tigrayans, but now he had alienated them and made his government hostage to the whims of that mad Eritrean genius, Isaias Afwerki—with his absolutism and delusions of grandeur.

In fact, I had interviewed Afwerki twice: in 1986 in a cave during his guerrilla fighting days, and in 2002 in his presidential office in Asmara. But he had never stopped being a guerrilla fighter, a remote ascetic obsessed with conflict and domination.[15] Now he was the driving military force behind Abiy. Indeed, Isaias was a curse, the foreign enemy brought by Abiy who unified the Tigrayans against him.

The military alliance with Eritrea notwithstanding, the central Ethiopian government in Addis Ababa would never wholly defeat the Tigrayans, I was told. "The Tigrayans, more than any other group in Ethiopia," Fitsum and Reshid emphasized, "were superior at forging a consensus that cascaded down to the lowest level of society." The Tigrayan elite of the TPLF was literally one with its peasantry. This was a level of intensive social and political cohesion that had similarities only with the Viet Cong fighting the French and the Americans; with the Chinese Communists under then guerrilla leader Mao Zedong in the 1930s and 1940s; and with the early Israelis of the 1940s and 1950s— essentially the Israelis of the Palmach and Haganah days. "The TPLF has reinvented itself in this war. It has gone from Marxism to early Zionism. The Tigrayans no longer feel themselves to be Ethiopian." Alas, Tigray, the key puzzle piece of the complex Ethiopian imperial jigsaw, had just been removed, threatening all of Ethiopia and by extension the Horn of Africa. Among the many extraneous, interconnected, and disintegrative forces at play that the two mentioned, by the way, were the radicalized Muslim lowlanders of Eritrea who now wanted to unite with Sudan, and the Amhara militias, taking advantage of the war in Tigray in order to recover lost territory all over western Ethiopia, hard up against the Sudanese and South Sudanese borders. If it all seems confusing, just keep in mind that every ethnic and religious dispute in Ethiopia is interlocked, albeit indirectly, with every other one, imperiling governance at the top.

I met with Fitsum and Reshid in the garden of the historic Hilton Hotel in Addis Ababa, where I had stayed for several weeks thirty-six years earlier, while covering the Mengistu regime and the great famine of the 1980s in northern Ethiopia. Of course, the internal situation had greatly evolved since then, but in essence it was the same story as in the 1980s: an imperial-minded, repressive regime that was prosecuting a war in Tigray, and using the restriction of food supplies as a weapon. Ethiopia, then and now, was too large and diverse to be governed from a central point. Yet, at the same time, it was culturally and historically distinct from both the Arabs and the Africans on its borderlands.

Did hope reside with a new generation—with the tens of millions of Ethiopians born in the 1990s and the beginning of the twenty-first century? I asked.

"No" came the definitive reply. The young might even be worse. "The young were being socialized and politicized by various ethnic and linguistic forces, mainly at odds with Addis Ababa, through the spread of local media all around the country." Here modernism and postmodernism featured electronic social media that led to eruptions of localized military empowerment, which made it harder than ever to resolve political tensions at the top of the governmental pyramid in the capital city. But it was complicated. The young wanted jobs, and somewhat contradictorily, aspired to a mythical past. For example, among the attributes now being bestowed on Mengistu by those who had never experienced his pulverizing ideological state was that of a "unifier." Ethiopia longed for unity, even though the individual actions of millions of Ethiopians argued for disintegration.

———

IN ALL OF THIS, the West, especially the Americans, had grown disillusioned with Abiy Ahmed, that seemingly idealistic visionary, winner of the Nobel Peace Prize, who spoke constantly about human rights and democratic emancipation, but was now embroiled in a war in Tigray where his forces were committing human rights atrocities including rape and mass killings, and precipitating a famine. Abiy, it appeared, had gone downhill so far and so fast that the Americans felt momentarily betrayed. A foreigner in Addis Ababa with decades of experience in Africa, someone particularly well read in old diplomatic cables, explained it this way:

"It is amazing how often Americans become enamored with one African ruler after another, only to become disillusioned soon afterwards. When a new African ruler talks, preferably in English, about human rights, democracy, anti-corruption, and holding elections, the Americans are immediately lovestruck and taken in at first, whether it is with someone like [Robert] Mugabe in Zimbabwe, [Paul] Kagame in Rwanda, Salva Kiir in South Sudan, or now Abiy Ahmed in Ethiopia. But initial hopes soon give way to bitter recriminations between Washington and those regimes. While all those men, in their own mind, are fighting for political survival amid the most complex ethnic, tribal, and regional forces, the Americans in almost an ideological manner reduce it all to issues of voting, human rights, and anti-corruption. What is 'corruption,' by the way? It is an alternative pathway to getting business done in a place where official institutions and bureaucracy are enfeebled and ineffective. Politicians and others in Africa have no 401(k) or other retirement plans. They have no cushy sinecures or consultancies or speaking tours awaiting them if they leave office. They have no safety net of any kind, physical or financial. They are reduced to cynical calculation, stealing, and using every angle, no matter how ruthless, to provide themselves and their families with security. What we label cynicism is for them pragmatism and survival."

———

THERE IS ANOTHER WAY to look at it, though. Hallelujah Lulie, an Ethiopian intellectual and former member of Abiy's team, who was en route to Oxford for his postgraduate degrees when I met him, observed that the West initially praised Abiy Ahmed not out of naivete, but because of Abiy's very real accomplishments in 2018 and 2019. "It was the most ambitious liberalization process in decades of Ethiopian history, featuring the release of many political prisoners, legal reforms, and dialogue with opposition leaders. The government has allowed itself to be rebuked by human rights commissions and other groups. The very fact of holding elections, as flawed as they are, is an achievement. Progress in history is often crooked, not straightforward." Addis Ababa University professor Kassahun Berhanu concurred. "In a more ideal situation, without ethnic and national threats from Tigray, Eritrea, and other regions, Abiy would be an 'exemplary democrat,'" adding that Ethiopians "don't like weak leaders" in the midst of an ethnic maelstrom.

YUGOSLAVIA WASN'T THE ONLY historical model for Ethiopia that I kept hearing about in Addis Ababa. I also heard about Russia, from the late tsarist period through the Bolshevik Revolution to the present. In this model, the Shoan king Menelik's conquest of Ethiopia in the late nineteenth century and the subsequent expansion of royal territory throughout large parts of the Horn of Africa, in addition to Africanizing this hitherto Middle Eastern imperial kingdom, bore similarities to the tsarist conquests throughout far-flung parts of the ethnically varied Caucasus and Central Asia. The overthrow and murder of Ethiopia's last emperor, Haile Selassie, by Mengistu bore similarities to the overthrow and murder of the Russian royal family by Lenin. The famine of the mid-1980s, as I've noted, bore similarities to the famine inflicted on Ukraine by Stalin. Following the strong rules of Mengistu and Meles Zenawi, Hailemariam Desalegn's tenure as leader of Ethiopia from 2012 to 2018 proved to be short-lived, weak, and chaotic in the mold of Boris Yeltsin; while Abiy Ahmed, the erst-while darling of the West, was in a very rough sense like the early Vladimir Putin, a strong ruler with his hands on an imperial state, wielding information and disinformation coupled with the use of the security services as a means of postmodern control. Abiy was also obsessed with his image and the rebranding of his party, making him the first real politician to ever rule Ethiopia. In Abiy's first years in power, there were elements of Mikhail Gorbachev's glasnost and perestroika. Whatever one might think of those historical comparisons, Yugoslavia or Russia, the fact that people I spoke with constantly used them was an indication that Ethiopia constituted a polity distinct from all others in sub-Saharan Africa, where the written languages usually don't go as far back in time, where governance often did not extend beyond the major cities, where the desert and forested hinterlands were in too many cases ruled by local militias, and where the political comparisons are usually with each other. Ethiopia, on the other hand, was emblematic of the Greater Middle East, an imperial world forever in a state of crumbling further.

THE IMPERIAL PALACE COMPOUND, the spiritual headquarters, as it were, of the Ethiopian state, sits on a vast, meticulously landscaped hill overlooking Addis Ababa: a series of whitewashed pavilions with high wooden arches conjuring up African, Indian, and Greek motifs. The confection of styles, all flowing together, expresses the rich cultural residue that marks this historic kingdom. The compound was built by Emperor Menelik II in 1897, following his defeat of the Italians and his elevation from king of Shoa to ruler of all Ethiopia. There is the throne room, where Emperor Haile Selassie received Queen Elizabeth II, French president Charles de Gaulle, Yugoslav leader Josip Broz Tito, and many others. I also visited the cellars, where amid the low, white-painted archways, members of the royal family and palace officials were murdered by Mengistu and his soldiers. As for Haile Selassie himself, he was strangled in his bed. In these cellars, my mind drifted to Haile Selassie's timeless, eloquent appeal to the League of

Nations in 1936, protesting the Italian fascist occupation of his country. As a boy, I remember watching Haile Selassie on television walking solemnly beside Charles de Gaulle in John F. Kennedy's funeral procession, so much shorter in height compared to the French leader but equally grand in stature. Killing royalty is a bad business, I thought. It often brings to power far more vulgar and brutal forces. The murder of the Russian and Iraqi royal families led to decades of Stalinist and Ba'athist rule. The palace complex, a half century removed from that nightmare, is now a place of peace and national pride. It is crowded with newly married Ethiopian couples, in white wedding gowns and tuxedos, having their pictures taken.

From the palace I took a taxi to the Holy Trinity Church, where outside in the rain I took off my shoes before a guard unlocked the door and ushered me into a darkness suffused with incense. Approaching the altar with its paintings of saints and apostles, I felt close to Greece, the Balkans, and Russia. To the left of the altar is an enclosure with two massive tombs of roseate granite, in ancient Aksumite style: the resting places of Emperor Haile Selassie and Empress Menen Asfaw. Here church and state were fused. Ethiopia, I thought, was built on firm and mystical foundations: a bit like Russia and the historical Balkan nations, where Orthodoxy and nationalism worked together. The state here had a substantial quality. It should not be underestimated. For a moment I distrusted the analogy with the former Yugoslavia, a sprawling federation that had been held together by Marxist theory and Tito's earthly charisma, which vanished after he died. Haile Selassie's influence might be longer-lasting.

ADDIS ABABA ITSELF ILLUSTRATED the struggle to maintain a semblance of tradition and sense of place amid roiling urban and postmodern forces that threatened disintegration. Loud Orthodox chants still echoed from microphones outside the churches into the streets. Otherwise, the rambling city of hutments and greenery, the big village actually, that I remembered from the 1980s was gone, unrecognizable. An immense number of trees had been cut down to make room for new buildings that were now already worn and mildewed. Rambling, corrugated iron slums and working-class neighborhoods edged up against concrete pillars holding up an elevated commuter rail system. Street children and destitute families huddled alongside highway underpasses, signs of a grim urban poverty. Beggars were relatively few, but street hawkers were many. There were whole squatter communities. But everywhere there was juxtaposition and an odd sense of what some scholars called Brazilianization—the clash of wealth and poverty, order and semi-anarchy. Yet the streets were clean and the roads well paved, much better than in New York City, in fact. People waited patiently in long lines, single file, for public transport: there was no pushing or shoving. The traffic was not intimidating and crazy like in Cairo. Streetlights operated and people waited to cross. The United Arab Emirates had supplied Abiy Ahmed with a few billion dollars in cash to make many urban improvements, including the planting of new trees and the creation of new parks to undo the damage of the unplanned urbanization of the previous decades. It can be the passage from dictatorship to quasi-democracy that leads to street crime, in this case threatening the city's reputation as the safest in sub-Saharan Africa. It was all a mixture, with ATMs near ratty market stalls. The new gleaming skyscrapers—gated communities, banks, and office buildings—were often constructed with investment from either the UAE or China, which in a visual sense were the two most significant outside powers here. I passed Revolution Square, a vast semicircle now filled with cars, buses, and shops, where Mengistu had held mass rallies to welcome Cuba's Fidel Castro, Libya's Muammar Gaddafi, and other East Bloc luminaries. A small, futuristic glass enclosure contained an elevator that took you down to the large underground parking garage built by the Chinese. The Chinese had built the commuter rail, the gleaming skyscrapers of new banks, and the most beautiful of the new parks. While I sipped a macchiato with an Ethiopian friend at a patisserie on Revolution Square, my friend said that everywhere you look in Addis Ababa there are signs of the Chinese, as there were of the Soviets during the days of the Dergue and the Cold War. From the café table I people-watched. Muslim men and women in skullcaps and wraparound garments evoked the creeping Islamization that many here talked about. Addis Ababa, which used to be distinct, was much less so. It was one with cities throughout the developing and recently developed world. It was no longer pretty by any means. It was ugly, in fact. But it was full of action and vitality, with restaurants and café tables crowded with people, crammed between building spaces. This was no longer a traditional society, despite the headscarves and Orthodox chants, and it was, therefore, harder to rule and satisfy.

Brazilian-style urbanization, with its wealth and stark poverty and crazy energy, with its cutting-edge technology, rupture of tradition, and in some cases reinvention of religion in more ideological form, constituted the dramatic background noise to the challenge of civilized governance that formed the core of my inquiries in Ethiopia and elsewhere. Being either a dictator or a democrat was just harder than ever in the twenty-first century. Urbanized settings were more complex to organize than rural ones, their inhabitants easy to anger and more likely to complain. Social media benefited the extremes. The drift toward anarchy or the tendency to overcompensate through tyranny remained real possibilities in many places.

I ALTERNATED MEETING PEOPLE with long walks and drives in Addis Ababa. Ethiopian politics offered layers of fascination. Rather than summarize it, or even distill it by way of a single plotline, I preferred to let each person I met approach it from his own point of view, so that I could communicate the whole story through a process of exploring different angles.

ABDETA BEYENE, A FORMER chief of staff for the Ethiopian foreign minister, runs the Center for Dialogue, Research and Cooperation in Addis Ababa, an American-style think tank that does periodic work for the Ethiopian government. Abdeta offered me what was as close as possible to a bottom-line synthesis of the local political situation.

The real break in Ethiopian history, he explained, was not the cinematic rolling revolution of 1974 and 1975 when the military Dergue overthrew the emperor, but in 1991 when, in less exciting fashion, the Tigrayan-led new government crafted a modern federalized state, as opposed to the strong and arbitrary centralized regimes that had existed under both Haile Selassie and Mengistu. Meles Zenawi, the TPLF leader who led the new government here in Addis Ababa, had been brave in the sense that he put an end to Ethiopia's 1998–2000 war with Eritrea, even though he had the upper hand and could therefore have fought on to outright victory. In this new system, crafted by the adaptable Meles, the various nationalities of Ethiopia maintained their historical identities, partly by their controlling everything from farmland to the local security apparatus in the various respective provinces. It was this system that Abiy Ahmed inherited when he came to power as prime minister in 2018 and proceeded to give Ethiopia a more centrally controlled character, helped by the building of roads and airports around the country in the time of Meles. The problem, however, Abdeta said, is that "Ethiopia cannot be a centralized state like China," which represents a far more bureaucratically organized society. It was China, in fact, where bureaucracy as such first began in world history in early antiquity. Nevertheless, Abiy thought differently and, among other things, initiated a war with Tigray in order to bring the economically and militarily powerful province to heel. At this point, a government defeat in Tigray "has the capacity to ignite a general uprising" throughout the country. This is because Tigray and the Tigrayans represent not only a province but a powerful ethnic faction in Addis Ababa, so that the latest war has been in fact "a war over control of the central government itself."

"How do the seven million Tigrayans themselves feel?" Abdeta asked me rhetorically. "They feel humiliated. After all it was they and the TPLF who defeated the Dergue in 1991, and in the 1998–2000 war defeated Isaias Afwerki's Eritrean army. But now Tigray is decimated, and Isaias's Eritrean army has tried to dominate Tigray, as an ally of Abiy Ahmed's Ethiopia." The factories, the universities, health systems, and so forth in Tigray have ceased functioning, he told me. "But the Tigrayans, with their tradition of guerrilla war, will never accept subjugation."

Thus, Ethiopia was at an impasse.

"My fear," Abdeta told me, "is that if Ethiopia collapses there will be no constituent parts to build back upon, since the individual provinces here are more numerous and not as ethnically well delineated as were the various states of Yugoslavia."

History often turns on a hinge, I thought, and it is interesting to speculate how differently Ethiopia might have developed had Meles Zenawi not died at the relatively young age of fifty-seven. Meles, unlike Isaias Afwerki, made the transition from a guerrilla leader into a statesman, organizing Ethiopia's politics into a system of ethnic federalism while making himself useful to the West. He thus set the context for the country's many years of sustained, double-digit economic growth rates. It was under Meles that Ethiopia achieved a sensible fusion of security and economic development, even if the human rights situation left much to be desired. But even in that respect, some say he was about to liberalize at about the time he passed away. Meles bested Isaias on the battlefield in Eritrea and yet didn't get into a ruinous war in Tigray like Abiy, a war that threatened the country's very stability.

Not only Meles Zenawi but Haile Selassie, too, was not an unreasonable leader for his time and situation: the situation being that Ethiopia constitutes a vast trail of languages and ethnic groups, riven by high mountains, forests, and rugged deserts, overlaying both Africa and the Middle East. Given these facts, it has been extraordinary how well Ethiopia has held together over a century that has seen foreign occupation and destabilizing technological development. Girmachew Alemu, another Addis Ababa University professor, told me that of all the Ethiopian leaders in the modern era, only Mengistu Haile Mariam, between 1974 and 1991, could fairly be characterized as an extremist. And that was partly dictated by the Cold War, as the Soviets, Cubans, and East Germans propped up his regime of famine, collectivization, and mass murder. Girmachew, as a little boy in the Mengistu era, remembers teenage bodies lined up in the streets of the capital with placards hung around their necks, identifying them all as traitors and counterrevolutionaries. Striking a middle path of governance—halfway between the demons of tyranny and anarchy—is hard in any case, and particularly in light of Ethiopia's geographical and cultural challenges. But except for Mengistu, this country has thus far produced no monsters.

GETACHEW DIRIBA, AN ECONOMIST and development expert, insisted on talking to me about Ethiopian history, the "millennia-long confluence of Arab and African, and feudalism and religious Orthodoxy." Ethiopian history "paralleled the Roman Empire and the rise of Islam, with close ties between the Horn of Africa and the Red Sea, Yemen, and Jerusalem." It was Menelik II who unified the Horn of Africa and ended the period of the warring princes by moving Ethiopia bodily south, to encompass the Oromos as part of his great kingdom. Warming to his point, Getachew said, "Ethiopia may all along have been feudal, but feudalism, with its formal social and political relationships, did indeed constitute an institutional basis and was therefore a defense of Ethiopian identity against Portuguese, Italian, and other invasions and incursions." It was feudalism, however disparaged it may have been, that allowed Ethiopia to be more organized than its African neighbors.

Feudalism did not really end in Ethiopia until the fall of Haile Selassie and the coming to power of the military under Mengistu Haile Mariam in 1974 and 1975. It was a broad social upheaval, led by students and workers, that had undermined Haile Selassie's feudal kingdom of nobles and vassals. But Mengistu and the military were able to take advantage of the semi-chaos since they were the only ones in the society who were truly well organized—in the same way that the Egyptian military had returned to power in the aftermath of the Arab Spring because it had remained the only organized force in Egypt.

Of course, what has afflicted Ethiopia and the entire African Horn, then and now, Getachew explained, has been the various ethnically based liberation movements: Tigrayan, Eritrean, Oromo, and so on. Yet all these movements, he went on, were heavily influenced by Marxism and the radical politics of Western universities beginning in the 1960s. And now these same movements were mixed up with Western-style identity politics. In other words, and this was Getachew's principal theme, it has partly been ideas and ideologies filtering in from the West and the Soviet Union (in the cases of both Mengistu and the TPLF) that has helped sunder a former feudal society for the past fifty years. Ethiopia, like much of the Middle East, has historically been a victim and playing field of ideas and ideologies ultimately rooted in the West. We truly live in a global world, in other words, Getachew suggested, where the West and the Greater Middle East cannot wholly be separated from each other. We in the West think we have helped these societies with our development aid, when in fact it has been our insidious cultural and political influence that has helped undermine previously stable orders. Decades of African coups have roots in the process of modernization itself, whose origins lay in the West.

LENCHO LETTA, IN HIS seventies, was a founding member of the Oromo Liberation Front, who split with that rebel group years back to form the Oromo Democratic Front. The latter group is dedicated to working within the Ethiopian federal system to solve the problems of the Oromos, the heavily Muslim and Protestant evangelical Africans that demographically dominate southern Ethiopia.

"The Oromo question is a colonial one," Lencho told me. "That's because Ethiopia has been an empire. When I traveled to the United States as a student in the 1960s, my passport said, 'Empire of Ethiopia.' But already in the 1960s, the various Ethiopian student movements, strongly influenced by Marxism," an implant ultimately from the West, "were declaring that the issues dividing the country were neither ethnic nor racial, but were only issues of class, and would be solved as such."

The student Marxists had a point. The Oromos were landless peasants, since all of the land in Ethiopia in the last years of the emperor

had been going to the crown, to the Amhara armies, and to the Orthodox church. Lencho emphasized that one cannot exaggerate how
much ideological influence the student and labor movements had in
Ethiopia in the 1960s and 1970s. "When Mengistu came to power he
hadn't a clue! All he wanted was power, simple." He and the military
provided the organizational element that the students lacked, adopted
the students' ideologies, and then in turn crushed the students. "The
Ethiopian revolution of the mid-1970s was like the French Revolution," as well as like the Russian Revolution, one might say. "It posed
individual identity in class terms only, and completely crushed the aristocracy associated with the emperor. Ethiopia went directly from
imperial rule to the dictatorship of the proletariat, from one form of
dictatorship to another." It was very much a European-style experience, with echoes of the guillotine and Lenin's phrase "all power to the
soviets."

"What about Ethiopia now?" I asked Lencho.

He was silent for a moment, then said, "I am not optimistic. I am
worried."

After another silence, with a reference to Abiy Ahmed's centralizing regime, Lencho said, "Whoever wants to end the multinational
federation will undo Ethiopia." Ethiopia, in other words, had long
been an empire for a specific reason: because of its geographically vast
and multiethnic character, which has not gone away. And accepting
this variety of peoples was key to solving the Oromo problem of poverty and underrepresentation.

Echoing Donald Levine, Lencho said, "The Amharas and Tigrayans believe in their civilizational supremacy and in their thousands of
years of written history, so neither will ultimately accept Oromo leadership. That is still the dilemma."

SOLOMON AYELE DERSSO HEADED the African Commission on
Human and Peoples' Rights. Thus, he looked at Ethiopian history
from a humanitarian perspective. "The emperor granted people a degree of freedom," he began. "But it was a matter of benevolence on the

emperor's part. In his mind, human rights were something that were only his to give. They were not inalienable." It was only in the latter years of Haile Selassie's reign, with the growing strength of trade unions and youth organizations and their demands, that human rights came to be seen as God-given, not the ruler's to give or take away, Solomon explained. "There was such great hope in 1974 with the end of the feudal and land tenure system. The military hijacked it all and suspended the emperor's constitution, ruling by decree." In 1991, with the Tigrayans under Meles Zenawi driving Mengistu into exile in Zimbabwe, "a certain blossoming of civil society followed in the next decade, before a reversal in the 2000s." Solomon said that a lot had to do with the influence of the West. The West had won the Cold War and the Soviet Union collapsed in 1991. No longer were African leaders like Mengistu propped up by the East Bloc. Democracy and globalization were in the air in the 1990s and Ethiopia benefited. But the attacks of September 11, 2001, initiated the War on Terror, which was easily abused by regimes such as Ethiopia's in order to please the Americans. The next big surge in terms of expanding freedoms did not really come until the beginning of Abiy Ahmed's regime in 2018 and 2019. But international praise destabilized him. "Abiy Ahmed was awarded a Nobel Peace Prize for what was in reality a war pact," Solomon said, exasperated. Only the most naïve of people could think that the 2018 Ethiopian accord with Eritrea was anything but a war pact, given Isaias Afwerki's reputation and aims regarding Tigray.

Solomon said that Ethiopia was still in a post-1991 situation. The political settlement of that year has come to an end with nothing definite and comprehensive yet to replace it. Abiy Ahmed's transition to democracy was still uncertain since the ethno-national issues had yet to be settled. Elections weren't enough.

JUST BEFORE I LEFT Addis Ababa at the end of June 2021, Tigrayan forces recaptured the provincial capital of Mekelle on the heels of retreating government forces. It was a grave setback for Abiy Ahmed, who the previous November had confidently predicted that he would bring Tigray under state control within a matter of weeks. The war now threatened to move from the north of the country to the west and northwest, with Amhara militias taking on the Tigrayan rebels themselves. Would Abiy's Prosperity Party, which had relatively little historical tradition or pedigree, begin to unravel? Would Isaias Afwerki, whose Eritrean forces were rampaging in Tigray, accept defeat? To maintain a semblance of control in the north, would Abiy have to draw government forces away from their fight against the Oromo insurgency in the south and from guarding the western frontier against Sudanese incursions? These were just some of the questions swirling around the Ethiopian capital when I met one of the country's leading political scientists, who preferred to remain anonymous.

At this moment of defeat for the government, it was a good time for him to reflect on Abiy himself. What and who, in the end, was the Ethiopian leader in 2021?

"Abiy, a Pentecostal, is at root a Christian idealist. He thinks that he was appointed by God to save Ethiopia. Like liberal internationalists in the West, he believes in human agency. As a consequence, he underestimated geography, culture, geopolitics, and all of the other deterministic forces of fate. In this sense he is a mirror of global elites themselves. Like them, he fails to comprehend the intractable nature of many wars and conflicts—the reason why he has failed in Tigray. Abiy is a product of his time, just as Mengistu was a product of his." The political scientist suggested that just as the internationalist Davos mindset had helped produce Abiy, the Cold War had helped produce Mengistu, a tyrant backed by the East Bloc.

Never has there been such a moment when "Ethiopia, as an idea, was being so contested," he said. He explained that the government collapse in Tigray came amid other deepening cleavages in the society.

"Since 1991, there has been a creeping Islamization here, a mushrooming of the Ikhwan sensibility among the 34 percent of the population that is Muslim. There is still little sense of a Muslim *Umma* or political community, owing to the centuries of feudal Christian domination. But it has been growing. At the same time, the Orthodox Christians have become more religious. Religious identity has been reinforcing the existing ethnic divisions."

In the midst of upheaval, power usually devolves to the most organized force in politics. But what if there was no powerful and organized force? I thought to myself. For example, the Ethiopian military was weak. It lacked the ideology and corporate identity of the Egyptian and Turkish militaries. The military here did not constitute a *class* like those other militaries, the political scientist said. When Ethiopian officers went off duty, they didn't socialize with their fellow officers and their families, but with their own ethnic compatriots. Societal divisions, rather than being alleviated, were reproduced inside the military itself. Thus, Abiy's sudden, perceived weakness in the wake of the Tigray collapse potentially opened an abyss that no one was sure how to fill. In fact, many of the people who had voted for Abiy in the recent elections did so out of fear of what might come next, without him.

IN ALL THEIR FERVENCY and subtle variations, the myriad voices I had heard in Addis Ababa did have a common theme, though. Ethiopia, more than a state rather than less of one, with strong echoes of revolutionary and evolutionary political processes that bore similarities to France, Russia, and Yugoslavia, had over the span of the decades been struggling with the question of what, exactly, it was—an empire, a multinational federation, or a centrally controlled state. Yet, in this crooked and complex history, the possibility of avoiding abject tyranny on one hand and sheer anarchy on the other seemed, nevertheless, promising. The political scientist's analysis that raised the possibility of anarchy here did not in the end make me a pessimist. For my impressions of the capital after a thirty-six-year absence were not altogether negative. The very first-world efficiency of the airport and national airline, the well-functioning infrastructure, and the rigor of the bureaucracy in general testified to the accumulation of centuries and millennia of a state identity, built originally on a sturdy multiethnic feudalism. Ethiopia, as viewed from the grandeur of Menelik's palace;

or as viewed from the institutions that kept Addis Ababa an efficiently running city, lacking the chaos of some other parts of Africa; or as viewed from the Ethiopian diaspora in the West that was pouring money into real estate in Addis Ababa, seemed too substantial to fall apart at the center.

But simply because I could not *imagine* it falling apart did not mean that it wouldn't, or couldn't, happen. Indeed, barely weeks following my visit to Ethiopia, the Tigrayan rebels had advanced far south, capturing towns along the way, which brought them almost within range of Addis Ababa. The specter of state collapse suddenly arose in people's minds, before the government, employing drones provided by Turkey, the United Arab Emirates, and Iran, finally beat back the rebels. It was a signal lesson for me. Mistakes occur in analysis often not by a failure of reason, but by a failure of imagination. You can know something is possible without actually believing it. I knew it was possible for Ethiopia to slide into anarchy but I did not really believe it. Had it not been for the drones, what I couldn't believe might actually have happened. In geopolitics and the understanding of our world, the most powerful tool is imagination. It was an idea that would recur at the end of my journey through parts of the Greater Middle East, a region that, as Ethiopia portended, could become more unified by technology and yet at the same time be at war with itself.

And the factor of imagination was tied to time itself. I had captured Ethiopia during a specific moment in time only. For example, a tenuous peace agreement between Ethiopia and Tigray, negotiated in late 2022 in South Africa, caught me by surprise. Who knows where it might lead?

ARABIA DESERTA

═══

IN THE AUTUMN OF 1916, A TWENTY-SEVEN-YEAR-OLD ARABIC scholar and graduate of Jesus College, Oxford, Thomas Edward Lawrence, assigned to British military intelligence in Cairo, sailed down the Red Sea to the Meccan port of Jeddah in order to sound out Sherif Hussein and his sons about a wartime alliance, the aim of which was to drive the pro-German Ottoman Turks from the Middle East.

Among the items in Lawrence's traveling gear was a two-volume set of *Travels in Arabia Deserta* by Charles Montagu Doughty, the only Briton ever to have penetrated the entire interior of northwestern Arabia where Lawrence was now headed. Lawrence had recently purchased the books from Samuel Zwemer, a Dutch Reformed missionary, who was in Cairo for a rest from his own Arabian wanderings when he happened to bump into Lawrence. Later it was reported that Lawrence had learned the two volumes of Doughty by heart. That was obviously a wild exaggeration. Still, Lawrence himself referred to the books as his bible for dealing with the Arabs.[1]

Travels in Arabia Deserta is a 1,200-page account of a two-year odyssey made between 1876 and 1878. The twin volumes took Doughty a decade to write, and their effect on Lawrence and British Arabist thought in general cannot be exaggerated. Whereas the great Arabian explorer Sir Richard Francis Burton was sui generis, like a star exploding brilliantly to leave only a dark space in its wake, Doughty's book started a literary and psychological movement among Britons drawn to the Middle East, which Burton's incognito journey in 1853 to Mecca and Medina and his later translation of *The Thousand and One Nights* did not. Burton had come along a bit too early. When Burton died in 1890, the Ottoman Empire in the Middle East still had another twenty-six years to run. But Doughty's masterwork was perfectly timed for Lawrence, who was about to become a kind of deus ex machina that helped enable the British military victory over the Ottomans in Arabia. The consequences of that victory for Great Britain were to be an epic and complicated relationship with the Arabs who lived north of Arabia proper in Syria and Mesopotamia: a relationship that would be at once romantic, tragic, and politically tortured, igniting intellectual arguments to this day. Doughty was a literary instigator of this whole drama.

Doughty's Arabia was the anvil and crucible through which the character of an Englishman might be tested and forged. It is a land of "cloud-like strange wasted ranges," "horrid sandstone desolation," "rhomboid masses," and repetitive "ghastly grinning" geological shapes.[2] It is a universe of Old Testament cruelty, where thieves are slowly beaten to death, where dying men are stripped bare on the road before they expend their last breath, where men march forth "in a purgatory of aching fatigue," where there is often nothing to eat but locusts and nothing to drink but water "full of swimming vermin."[3] In the course of two years of wandering amid these vast lava fields and slag heaps offering barely an inch of shade, Doughty is periodically robbed, left stranded without food or water, and threatened with death on a regular basis because of his refusal to deny his Christian religion and submit to Islam. Upon reaching the Turkish garrison town of Taif at the end of his ordeal, Doughty describes himself thus:

"The tunic was rent on my back . . . the beard fallen and unkempt; I had bloodshot eyes, half blinded, and the scorched skin was cracked to the quick upon my face. A barber was sent for, and the bath made ready: and after a cup of tea, it cost the good colonel some pains to reduce me to the likeness of the civil multitude."[4]

Doughty had certainly not gone native. Rather, the reverse. His journey reveals what to postmodern sensibilities is an utter lack of humanity and comprehension, revealing in turn a categorical clash of cultural differences. Lawrence notes that the book's strength lies in Doughty's briar-root English character, which was unyielding and un-influenceable, depicting as it does a complete description of the people he encountered in his journey, in which the good stands out only be-cause it is located among all the bad. It is about as heartfelt a descrip-tion of harrowing circumstances as one could expect, even if it does not meet the postmodern standards of the late Columbia University critic Edward W. Said, who accuses Doughty, along with Lawrence and an assortment of other Western observers, of filling out the empty spaces of their personalities through highly individualistic encounters with the Orient, which they all viewed with "hostility" and "fear."[5]

Yet Doughty describes his journey with scientific detachment. Armed with a notebook and aneroid barometer, he re-creates an entire environment: geological, linguistic, cultural, and psychological. He de-scribes, for example, the practicalities of the moon over the desert, how young camels are named according to the number of their teeth, the various kinds of pumice, basalt, and other desert rock formations, and why the humanity of men's greetings in the wilderness loses some of its authenticity once these salutations are imported into the towns. The romance consists in the way that the desert, in all its beauty, horror, and sameness, is meticulously conveyed. Furthermore, it is conveyed in a sonorous voice that has recalled for many the cadences of the sixteenth-century Tyndale Bible.* What reader of Doughty, for ex-ample, can forget his likening of the desert Semites "to a man sitting in cloaca to the eyes, and whose brow touches heaven," a very mean and yet poetic way of indicating the ability to hold in their minds starkly different attitudes about things.[6]

Yet, as it happened, the abstract and dehumanizing landscape that had such an effect upon men's characters was turned for the first time ever by Doughty into a literary landscape, making it, therefore, per-versely appealing.

---

*   William Tyndale, the translator, was an English religious reformer during the Protestant Reformation, executed for heresy.

Lawrence himself suggested that the very difficulty of the terrain caused Doughty's Arabia to become a masochistic measure of manhood. Doughty, writes Lawrence, "had experienced it himself, the test of nomadism, that most deeply biting of all social disciplines, and for our sakes he strained all the more to paint it in its true colours, as too hard, too empty, too denying for all but the strongest and most determined men."* Lawrence, in fact, as he sailed down the Red Sea from Egypt, was determined to prove himself in Doughty country. And because of the nature of British imperialism in the Middle East at that very moment, this private libidinal desire did not conflict with—rather it abetted—Lawrence's own professional responsibilities; so that it contributed to making Lawrence into a myth of vaster proportions than Lawrence had ever made of Doughty.

"Lawrence of Arabia," Britain's only romantic hero of the otherwise grim and dreary struggle of the trenches that emblemized the First World War, could never have emerged without Doughty's *Travels in Arabia Deserta* as an antecedent.

LAWRENCE'S ABILITY TO FORGE the desert Arabs of the Hejaz into an irregular force that assisted the British victory over the Ottoman Turks was merely a sideshow within a sideshow of World War I. To be sure, it was principally Lawrence's own literary endeavors that created a myth: specifically his massive and magisterial account of World War I in the desert, *Seven Pillars of Wisdom*, one of the great travel and military works of the twentieth century, however questionable some of it may be as accurate history.[†]

In all of the nearly seven hundred pages of the Penguin paperback

---

* This is taken from Lawrence's introduction to a later edition of Doughty's book in 1921. The introduction offers a work in progress, inspired by Doughty, for the famous chapter 3 of Lawrence's own *Seven Pillars of Wisdom* (1926 and 1935).

† To wit, Lawrence's Arabs never really liberated Damascus in October 1918 as he claims. The Allied regular armies, who did the real liberating, permitted the Arabs to march victoriously into the city as a sop to their pride. Elie Kedourie, *The Chatham House Version and Other Middle-Eastern Studies* (London: Weidenfeld and Nicolson, 1970), chapter 3.

edition of *Seven Pillars of Wisdom,* it is the six pages of chapter 3 that account for the most memorable intellectual argument. These six pages were inspired by perceptions first realized by Doughty, but translated by Lawrence into language more popular for its time than Doughty's, derivative as the latter's was of a sixteenth-century bible. Doughty's image of a desert Semite "sitting in cloaca to the eyes, and whose brow touches heaven" was greatly elaborated on by Lawrence into these memorable passages:

> . . . In the very outset, at the first meeting with them, was found a universal clearness or hardness of belief, almost mathematical in its limitation, and repellent in its unsympathetic form. . . . They were a people of primary colours, or rather of black and white, who saw the world always in contour. They were a dogmatic people, despising doubt, our modern crown of thorns. They did not understand our metaphysical difficulties, our introspective questionings. . . . Their thoughts were at ease only in extremes. They inhabited superlatives by choice. . . . they never compromised: they pursued the logic of several incompatible opinions to absurd ends, without perceiving the incongruity.[7]

A postmodern intellectual or political scientist gasps at the essentialism of such a description. Though Lawrence is talking not about all Semites, and not even about most of them, but only about premodern tribesmen in the utter desert of the Arabian interior whose ethos is primarily that of the group. As a fluent Arabic-speaker, who lived for years as the only Westerner among these tribesmen in vexing, war-torn circumstances—the kind that only intensifies one's perception of reality—Lawrence's analysis and prose are actually examples of Clifford Geertz's and Gilbert Ryle's "thick description."[8] But such unalloyed group identities as Lawrence directly experienced, untouched by the outside world, simply do not exist as they used to. Indeed, because of the increasing separation of individuals from the bonds of the group, a Shakespearean reality has little by little gained purchase over an anthropological one in our world. And the earth is less interesting as a consequence, even as it is much fairer and more humane.

As we know from Toynbee's description of "the loom of time," history never simply keeps repeating itself, nor does it simply rhyme as the tired cliché of today's global elite suggests; rather, it moves forward, however imperceptibly, as Lawrence himself realizes. This means that people don't stay the same. Lawrence closes his brief chapter 3 of *Seven Pillars of Wisdom*, noting that the Arabs, as he had found them, "were as unstable as water, and like water would perhaps finally prevail," which one might interpret as outlasting their adversaries and finding their way to a better place in the postmodern world.[9]

ACTUALLY, THE TRADITIONAL ARABIA that Lawrence describes existed in part right up through the early 1970s. In fact, I knew three American foreign service officers, Wat Cluverius IV, Graham Fuller, and Ernest H. Latham, Jr., who together, just before the 1973 Middle East war, toured northern Saudi Arabia with a Wahhabi bodyguard armed with a .38-caliber revolver and a gold-hilted sword. The threesome encountered tribesmen with fiery looks and henna in their beards, and malarial oases identified by the dark skins of the inhabitants, who had apparently built up an immunity to the disease. "This was raw Arabia, the Arabia of Charles Doughty," Latham told me.*

It was a high point of their youths and the end of an epoch.

To explain why this was so, it is necessary to move back in time to the origins of the current Saudi state. Abdulaziz Ibn Saud ("Slave of the Almighty, Son of Saud") was a towering and gangly warrior, literally oozing charisma, who, by attaching himself to Wahhabism, central Arabia's harsh, purifying, back-to-basics version of Islam, vanquished and united the Arabian tribes in the first quarter of the twentieth century, thus bringing order to a sprawling and lawless desert realm. It was Ibn Saud's Wahhabi legions that, by destroying all material signs of

---

* Latham was a close friend; the other two I knew briefly. Kaplan, *The Arabists*, pp. 135–36.

Ottoman culture, such as hookahs and stringed instruments, helped provide the groundwork for Arab nationalism, as well as for the anti-Persian and anti-Shi'ite sentiment that partially defines the Arabian Peninsula to this day.[10]

Ibn Saud's military aggressions were an astounding feat, as they fused three vital and far-flung sections of Arabia, each with a different culture and geographical prospect: the Muslim holy cities of Mecca and Medina in the Hejaz, close to the Red Sea, whose pilgrim trade and proximity to ports had given them a relatively cosmopolitan outlook; the bleak, choking, and dusty plateau region of Nejd in the very center of Arabia, whose Wahhabi faith was fiercely combative and conservative; and the heavily Shi'ite east, where vast quantities of oil were about to be discovered. A geopolitical behemoth was thus born: unmatched in oil reserves and with an expansive geography that dominated the vast Arabian Peninsula.

Had Abdulaziz Ibn Saud not existed, the Middle East today would be a radically different place, with the Hejaz perhaps still governed by the Hashemites as part of a greater Jordan, and without a single power dominating the oil market since the 1970s as Saudi Arabia has. The great Arabist of the Sorbonne, Maxime Rodinson, in roundly attacking fatalism, explains how world history itself has turned on a pivot because of the life of just one man and his characteristics, the Prophet Muhammad. Without Muhammad, or if Muhammad had arrived a generation or two later, Rodinson speculates, Islam might not exist, the Byzantine and Sassanid Persian empires might not have dramatically weakened as they did, and North Africa would still be part of the Latin West.[11] Thus, the ultimate significance of Saudi Arabia is that history is a matter of contingencies as much as it is a matter of large impersonal forces, like geography and culture.

IT WOULD TAKE A while for the geographical advantages of the new state bequeathed by Ibn Saud's military genius to play out. Oil wasn't struck by American engineers in the eastern part of Saudi Arabia until 1938. And it wasn't until near the end of World War II—with Saudi oil now looming as a critical geo-economic prize—that U.S. president Franklin Delano Roosevelt, shortly before his death, concluded a basic understanding with Ibn Saud.

While oil initially made Ibn Saud wealthy, providing his country with development options and removing the need of the Meccan pilgrim trade to supply his budgetary requirements, life did not dramatically change for many people in the towns and in the remote tribal encampments: this is what allowed the three Americans to have a nineteenth-century traveler's experience near the beginning of the last quarter of the twentieth century. King Faisal in the early 1970s was still in the midst of creating a modern bureaucratic state out of his father's unwieldy dominion, a state whose identity was Islamic rather than specifically nationalistic, and which conceived, in Faisal's own words, of the Koran as its constitution.[12]

Then came the October 1973 Arab-Israeli War.

In an attempt to regain the dignity that they had lost in their crushing defeat in 1967 at the hands of Israeli forces—which had captured Egypt's Sinai Peninsula and Syria's Golan Heights—Egyptian and Syrian soldiers launched a coordinated surprise attack on Israel. This attack famously allowed the Egyptians to consolidate their military position on the east bank of the Suez Canal. Though the Israelis would eventually dislodge both the Egyptians and the Syrians from their new positions, capturing even more territory in the process—and though President Sadat would decouple Egypt's postwar strategy from Syria's—nevertheless, the surprise attack and the comparatively high Israeli losses constituted a moral victory for the Arabs. In the midst of this high military drama, the Saudis, whose country now represented the world swing producer of petroleum—able to affect the world price by their own production quotas—helped institute an oil embargo against the United States, to force it to stop supporting Israel. By the time the embargo ended in March 1974, the price of oil had risen 400 percent.

The avalanche of petrodollars tumbling into the kingdom caused an upheaval. What had been slow and gradual social change over the decades now became a steep ascent.

"Foreign money brought foreign ways," writes the preeminent British historian of Saudi Arabia, Robert Lacey.[13] Women started appearing on television and in bathing suits by hotel swimming pools. Saudi cities became vast building sites, with antlike armies of workers in hard hats scurrying in the heat. Schools, universities, palaces, hospitals, masses of office buildings, highways, mosques, and yawning shopping malls suddenly rose out of the previously empty landscape. Once familiar and traditional neighborhoods became unrecognizable. This lurch toward Westernization, ignited by the oil weapon, would soon unleash something else: a militant and fiery religious backlash in the spirit of the back-to-basics Wahhabis—the ones who had established the Saudi kingdom in the first place. It was a movement that gathered force right before the eyes of the country's leaders and intelligence services, yet it was still able to achieve total surprise through a seminal event.

In the predawn hours of November 20, 1979, the symbolic first day of the new Islamic century of 1400, hundreds of young men who had stealthily gathered inside the Grand Mosque of Mecca pulled firearms and ammunition magazines out from under their robes and killed the policemen on duty, taking over the holiest mosque in Islam. These young men thought of themselves as a movement of the *pure*, attempting to topple the godless royals of Saudi Arabia, who, they believed, had led the country into a materialistic world of filth and corruption. It would take two weeks for government security forces to very messily and brutally regain control of the Grand Mosque, at a cost of well over a hundred dead on each side, and hundreds more wounded. It was a seismic shock to the kingdom, especially to its rulers, who had imagined their enemies as Zionists, communists, socialists, and other Western-influenced godless revolutionaries, not those on their right from their own pious Islamic quarters, whom they themselves had reared.

At the same time that this was happening, the Shi'ites of oil-rich eastern Saudi Arabia were becoming restive. Though it was the hard work and industriousness of these same Shi'ites who kept the oil pumping in the otherwise Sunni Saudi kingdom, the Iranian Revolution, barely a year old, constituted a spectacular assertion of Shi'ite power and identity just across the narrow Arabian Gulf. This made the royal authorities in Riyadh all the more nervous. The House of Saud also knew that the shah of Iran had just been toppled because he had gotten on the wrong side of the Islamic clerics. Therefore, "the solution to the religious upheaval [represented by the Grand Mosque takeover] was simple—more religion," Lacey writes.[14] Saudi king Khalid essentially gave in to the philosophy of those who had struck at the heart of his kingdom, and whom he subsequently had beheaded en masse.

Now the austere, conservative streak forged on the plateau heartland of Nejd, from where the Saudi royal family had originally emerged, reasserted itself. Movie theaters and other forms of entertainment were shut down. Courses such as geology, history, and science disappeared from school curriculums, and all that was henceforth taught was Islam and the story of the Saudi ruling family. The rulers also welcomed back into the kingdom Salafists and other Islamic ideologues, exposing Saudi youth to the very religious radicalism that had given rise to the Grand Mosque terrorists in the first place. Later on, in the 1990s, King Fahd, who followed King Khalid after the latter died, gave backing to the fundamentalist Taliban in Afghanistan, in order for the Saudi regime to demonstrate its Salafi credentials. The kingdom that Ibn Saud's galloping, ruthless genius had cobbled together from three disparate regions was now oscillating between extremes: from harsh religious orthodoxy to uncontrolled materialistic development accompanied by Westernization and back again to old-time religion.

It was this latest lurch to the religious right, begun in the aftermath of the 1979 assault on the Grand Mosque, that reached culmination in the September 11, 2001, terrorist attacks in the United States, in which fifteen of the nineteen plane hijackers were citizens of Saudi Arabia. Following a brief period of denial mixed with conspiracy theories, the Saudi government finally came to its senses. The kingdom's rulers stopped appeasing the religious clerics, who would no longer dictate the cultural and moral agenda. While domestic terror attacks and consequent raids and crackdowns by the security forces would go on, the question of who was ultimately in charge had finally been settled (at least from the regime's point of view), even if the resolution had taken decades to achieve. The regime had won and the religious ideologues had lost.

The resolution of who was in control was only relative, however. How could tensions not persist in a society undergoing rapid-fire modernization and postmodernization, kindling demands for more liberalization on one hand, and more fundamentalism on the other?

The stability of the ruling Al Sauds, in the face of all the upheavals in the Middle East in the twentieth and twenty-first centuries, including the Arab Spring, has always rested on the sheer survival skills of a large and diverse royal family with princely tentacles reaching out to all corners of the society, making for an informal domestic intelligence network all its own. This was buttressed by immense oil wealth, and the fatalism and obedience of a still deeply traditional people. Karen Elliott House, who has reported on Saudi Arabia for decades for *The Wall Street Journal*, writes that the kingdom, rather than a unified nation-state, remained still a "collection of tribes, regions, and Islamic factions that coexist in mutual suspicion and fear," in which the Hejaz (the Red Sea region including the holy cities), Nejd, and the oil-rich east still eye each other warily. Meanwhile, an astoundingly large population of unemployed youth remain unqualified for jobs that often go to foreigners. What these young people and, in fact, all Saudis yearn for is dignity: a rule of law as opposed to arbitrary fiat, and a government that provides basic services with a semblance of transparency and efficiency. Yet, as House observes, "With seventy thousand mosques spread across the kingdom, only the religious are an organized force; moderates fear that power inevitably would be seized by the most radical. Whatever lies in Saudi Arabia's future, it is not democracy."[15] David Rundell, an Oxford-educated Arabist who spent his professional life as an American diplomat in the Arabian Peninsula, goes one better: "If a successor government [to the Al Sauds] came to power by the ballot, it would almost certainly be an Islamist populist regime."[16]

It has often been said that regimes face their most dangerous period not when they remain rigid but when they undertake serious reforms, since such a process releases rising expectations that cannot wholly be met. Revolutions often happen when life starts getting better. This is precisely the period in which Saudi Arabia now finds itself under the reformist Crown Prince Mohammed bin Salman.

The potential for instability was driven by several factors. Ibn Saud had left no institutions except himself, and thus regime stability rested on managing the succession. Rather than a father-to-son-to-his-son system, the Al Sauds preserved stability for many decades by a lateral or horizontal succession, whereby the sons of Ibn Saud passed the kingship from one brother to the next, giving all the brothers of roughly the same generation a stake in the system, forming a veritable business-like partnership, in other words. But when Salman bin Abdulaziz came to power in 2015, he shortly removed his younger brother from the line of succession and eventually made his untested son, Mohammed bin Salman, the crown prince and heir to the throne, elevating him above more experienced rivals. Though such a change in the system had to occur eventually—after all, the sons of Ibn Saud could not go on living forever—there is no guarantee that the new line of succession will be as successful as the previous one in preserving stability, especially as hundreds of grandsons of Ibn Saud will be technically eligible for future status as crown prince and deputy crown prince.

Meanwhile, because Mohammed bin Salman, or MBS as he is known, is both autocratic and reformist, so much depends on his own person that were anything to happen to him the succession itself could be in doubt—unlike in March 1975 when King Faisal bin Abdulaziz was assassinated by an emotionally troubled nephew, and the crown passed smoothly and swiftly to his younger brother Khalid bin Abdulaziz.

Under MBS's effective leadership as crown prince, Saudi Arabia has become a police state, where the sophisticated tools of repression, trained originally on Al-Qaeda in the 2000s, were now directed at perceived enemies of the system. At the same time, cinemas, theme parks, rock concerts, and satellite dishes are no longer banned, even as music is no longer forbidden and men and women can dine together. Saudi Arabia under MBS is both more autocratic and freer than ever before.

But despite the impatience with which outsiders viewed the royal family, it is likely that any regime that might replace the Al Sauds would be worse—and that's if the kingdom did not crumble into chaos altogether, much as its northern neighbors Syria and Iraq have crumbled, on account of still-simmering separatist and regional sentiments. Indeed, both the West and the Saudis are stuck with the Al Sauds, who to their credit have never tried to destroy an existing class of merchants, capitalists, and landowners the way that postcolonial revolutionary regimes in the Middle East had. Those Westerners who yearn for a better system of government in Saudi Arabia should heed the late scholar of the Middle East J. B. Kelly's fundamental law: every modernizing dictatorship is worse than its traditional monarchical predecessor.[17] Just look at Russia, where the Bolsheviks replaced the Romanovs, and Iraq, where the Ba'athists replaced the Hashemites. Saudi Arabia could be much worse than it is, given that for long stretches there was little to unite its diverse and rambling regions except for the Al Saud dynasty, whose roots go back to the early 1700s. Indeed, ruling through informal consensus rather than through institutions—with no robust parliament, no trade unions, and an apolitical military—the Al Saud family has been the "glue" holding Saudi Arabia together, somewhat in imperial style, writes the scholar-journalist Thomas W. Lippman.[18]

TRAVELING TO SAUDI ARABIA I had a fundamental question in mind that all my reading had made me especially curious about: how had urban life affected the Saudi mentality, and what were its implications for governance? For whereas the desert was key to the kingdom's early decades, and had totally defined the experiences of storied personages such as Doughty and Lawrence, the cities were now where 84.3 percent of the 36 million Saudis actually lived, an increase from 50 percent in 1971. And as new city dwellers, the Saudis' values and cultural characteristics just had to be in flux, at least to some extent. I thought of the Brazilianization that I had witnessed in Addis Ababa, and therefore wondered what cities like Riyadh and Jeddah would be like. Identifiable cultures and civilizations—and the Arabs constituted one such—begin in the desert and countrysides and end, according to the German historian and philosopher Oswald Spengler, "with a finale of materialism in the world-cities."[19] Cosmopolitanism, which is inseparable from urbanism, is the essence of being landless and rootless, Spengler further implies. Could it be that the pure desert culture that Doughty and Lawrence experienced was even back then on its way to becoming a museum piece, and thus their observations were not only dated, but becoming wholly irrelevant? Or was it far more complicated than that: that desert culture with all of its traditions still existed in the cities, only in more diluted form? And if so, then to what extent?

COUNTRIES USUALLY SURPRISE AND delight upon the first immediate contact. Saudi Arabia does not. And that is its fascination. It is a *hard* country, at least I had initially thought, to be taken on its own terms; certainly not on the terms of a Westerner with his or her own cultural and historical baggage. Whereas Oman presents a forgiving and fragrant seafaring feast of Indian Ocean cultures, with essences of East Africa, Indonesia, and the Indian subcontinent layered atop its Arabian desert topography; and whereas Yemen is breathtakingly mountainous and beset by an almost pre-Islamic warlike tribalism, an upshot of its prison valleys; and whereas Egypt and Iran are complete, urban civilizations in their own rights, where Islam is not the whole story, Saudi Arabia is Arab and Islamic and nothing but. In opposition to the Gulf Arab sheikhdoms whose very wealth and smallness offer up visions of a glittering city-state cosmopolitanism, Saudi Arabia is just plain big, a universe unto itself, occupying most of the Arabian Peninsula, with several climatic zones. (There is actually snow in the mountains near Tabuk in the northwest during winter, while it is stiflingly hot in Asir by the Red Sea.) You can go days on end in Dubai, or even Abu Dhabi, without seeing an Arab, since the guest workers from the Indian subcontinent and East Africa essentially run all the hotels and many other facilities. There are many guest workers, too, in Saudi Arabia, but somewhat less noticeable, and thus you encounter

Saudi Arabs much more. The outside world seems to matter less here because of such an infinite geographic reality. The signage, as in many countries throughout the world, is always in the local language and English, but unlike in the Gulf sheikhdoms the English translations in Saudi Arabia are not dominant to quite the same degree, and one's ability to at least read the Arabic script is just more expected here. Saudi Arabia, at first contact in its inland plateau region, does not admit as much as, say, Dubai or Abu Dhabi to obvious outside influences.

The cityscape of Riyadh, the Saudi capital smack in the center of the country—and thus far from any sea—is pure and sterile: something bizarrely enhanced by the mathematical abstractions of its gleaming, glinting-in-the-sun skyscrapers. It is a quiet city, with very little street life in daytime and drivers who generally obey the rules and don't use their horns. Speed bumps are everywhere: the opposite of the traffic chaos of Cairo. The long rows of global, upmarket stores are constructed of cement and concrete, and sit on dusty streets lacking sidewalks. The automobile is everything in Riyadh, as the dimensions of the roads and highways are simply too vast for walking. There is little hint of any atmosphere or aesthetic. There is only a drab bleakness, despite the flashy signage, vaguely reminding me here and there of parts of West Texas. Of course, the plethora of palaces and tinted Plexiglass hotel complexes scream money. There are, too, the occasional rows of cutting-edge restaurants reminiscent of Austin, Texas, augmented by a vibrant coffee culture in place of a bar scene. The relatively featureless plateau of Nejd, upon which Riyadh rests and which dominates the Saudi interior, is, in the way of other vast and featureless inland geographies the world over, essentially conservative, but it is a conservatism that I found under siege as Saudi society dramatically evolves.

The malls, too, are vast, with space clearly not at a premium, unlike in coastal cities hemmed in by water and mountains. I see women completely covered in burkas, laden with designer shopping bags on each arm. Women here, if not in burkas, wear hijabs and abayas, which cover their hair and bodies. The men usually wear thobes and cover their heads with white or red-checkered ghutras, topped by black ropelike agals.

I stay at an efficient but traditional hotel in the business district, with a somewhat cozy brown and chrome ambience. Women leave their rooms in the morning in black burkas. In such an environment, the fact that alcohol is forbidden throughout the kingdom is but an insignificant detail, since it appears as wholly natural, and thus easy to adjust to: even if one is a wine-drinking Westerner like myself. As another Westerner who lives here explained to me: "When you are in Italy ordering pasta and veal, you expect to drink red wine. Here, amid the desert and Middle Eastern food, having a unique cultural experience, a visitor just does not expect it. Context is everything. And that's why Saudi Arabia, though a dry country, has a future as an international tourist destination."

These were all the quick impressions of a first-time visitor, mind you. A visitor who has been here before would have noticed striking changes. For example, one gets used to seeing women driving cars and walking alone in public. The women in full burkas flowing by me with their designer purchases at the mall were not signs of extremism or conservatism, but of liberal change, as men were not accompanying them. Both travel and reporting, among much else, constitute the art of getting beyond first impressions. And that happened quickly for me in Saudi Arabia.

I DROVE TO THE northwestern edge of Riyadh and visited a large exhibition of contemporary art called *Feeling the Stones,* which was a dead ringer for contemporary art exhibitions I had seen in Austin, Texas; Santa Fe, New Mexico; and Palm Springs, California. Adjacent to the exhibition hall was a slick coffee shop and fine dining. Here and there I saw Saudi women wandering around without hijabs even, their long black hair flowing. The artists had come from Saudi Arabia and from around the world. Their work was of a world-class standard, and was full of statements about political freedom, the struggle against racism, and the need for introspection and individual self-expression. This was an example of a cosmopolitan urban civilization implanting itself in what was once the desert of Doughty and Lawrence. Such exhibitions were unimaginable before the de facto reign of Crown Prince Mohammed bin Salman, which began in 2017. It was of a piece with a recent four-day festival of electronic music here that had featured hundreds of international performances amid the new mingling of the sexes, designed to appeal to a Saudi population in which 70 percent were under thirty-five years old.[20]

The moral message of the art exhibition had come courtesy of a socially modernizing authoritarian state—a state that was still a far cry from the altogether brutal repression of Iraq's Saddam Hussein and the al-Assad family in Syria, but, nevertheless, it fell within the same category, and also at the very top lacked the formal, consultative basis common to all former Saudi rulers. (MBS consulted experts more than he did tribal and religious elements within his society.) Yet, would such exhibitions eventually be part of a process to open up Saudi Arabia at large politically, despite MBS's virtual one-man rule? I was skeptical. Clearly, the country's relatively small cultural elite was increasingly open to universal values. But while journalists have an affinity for the exceptional among us, societies are dominated by the vast average. The few are not indicative of the many. There is also the irony that tight political control at the top, which guaranteed security and public order, allowed for a safe space in order for a cultural elite to entertain its beliefs and even its illusions. Contemporary art especially, with its need for infrastructure and vast exhibition halls, required lots of money and security. Even in the United States, such exhibitions and the museums that housed them were often located in wealthy, crime-free areas. Thus, ugly as it may sound, there was not necessarily a contradiction between a hard authoritarian regime and a large exhibition proclaiming individual liberty. *Feeling the Stones* was interesting, but I was not wholly convinced.

ON THE OTHER HAND, one might argue, what exactly was freedom?

A young Saudi, Mutrik Alajmi, told me: "I can renew my passport within minutes online without waiting in a long queue for hours at some inefficient government office. That's a human right. Women, even after a long maternity leave, can still leave work early until their child is two years old. That's a human right. Reducing corruption, even if it means arresting hundreds of princes and imprisoning them in the Ritz Carlton to set an example, that, too, is a human right."

Sarah Al Tamimi, the young deputy president of a human rights commission, told me: "I was abroad for years and never thought I would move back to Saudi Arabia with all of its restrictions. But now I can go out with male colleagues and attend music festivals and go on camping trips in the desert. So why stay away?"

A middle-aged Saudi minister, Mohammed Al Ash-Shaikh, told me: "The government no longer imposes on you how to dress in public. That is an accommodation to global urban civilization. Isn't the spirit of democracy giving the vast majority of the people what they want?"

He added: "The government has handled the COVID-19 emergency extremely well. It proved that it can deal effectively with a crisis. Everyone has a document on their smartphone showing their vaccination status. Isn't that a human right?"

Salma Alrashid, who works for a human rights organization, said: "Now fathers must have talks with their daughters regarding proper behavior, since their daughters are free to go out and socialize alone. The state, by restricting women's behavior for so long, made such discussions unnecessary. But now the state has put such decisions in the hands of the family where they belong. That is a human right."

All these conversations made me aware of a chilling fact—something I knew in the abstract but had not actually experienced, or at least properly concentrated on: that the widespread torture, floggings, executions, and so on, because they happen here in the dark, in the prisons, away from the public eye, simply do not register in the consciousness of Saudis, even the younger generation, since the face of government that they see is not only more benign, but increasingly efficient and reformist. Saudi Arabia proves that brutality is not necessarily self-destructive or destabilizing for a regime, as long as the regime delivers an ever-improving quality of life for the overwhelming majority of its citizens. But if that improving quality of life ever stalls out, if people's demands begin to seriously outpace the capacity of the regime to deliver, my interlocutors might start interpreting the meaning of human rights differently—more like people in the West. I was seeing Saudi Arabia, as I was seeing every country that I visited, during a moment in time: a time of peak reforms here. Would it last? For how long?

"MBS HAS LEE KUAN Yew imprinted on both sides of his brain," a foreigner who has met Crown Prince Mohammed bin Salman many times told me. "Like Lee in Singapore, MBS has a fanatic attention to both detail and especially to aesthetics. Lee became famous for making it a crime to spit chewing gum on sidewalks. Well, MBS saw a scale model of a large development area and noticed that on a small building at the model's far end there was a dome. 'That's a Turkish-style dome,' MBS said. 'It does not belong in a pre-Turkish historical heritage district.' If you show MBS a plan for planting a tract of palm trees, he wants to know where the water will come from, and if it can be recycled."

My acquaintance continued. "MBS wants to accomplish in fifteen years in a country the size of a continent what it took Lee Kuan Yew decades to accomplish in a small city-state, that for long stretches occupied a more benign geopolitical environment than Saudi Arabia does. So he knows time is his enemy. He is impatient, like the increasingly hyper-connected cohort of Saudi youth he has to govern."

My acquaintance spoke about state dinners that the crown prince has held for various world leaders. They are not large banquets with glittering silverware as these dreadful events tend to be. Instead, the crown prince hosts a small dinner of about a dozen persons in the preserved mud-brick fortress complex of the first full-fledged Saudi state in the eighteenth century, located in the west of Riyadh. After dinner he usually invites the foreign ruler for a walk alone with him around the fort area, a floodlit UNESCO world heritage site.

While the West condemns Mohammed bin Salman for grave human rights violations, especially the 2018 murder and dismemberment of Jamal Khashoggi, a Saudi citizen and *Washington Post* opinion writer, that took place inside the Saudi consulate in Istanbul, it would be an equally grave error to categorize the crown prince by such acts alone. For the crown prince is giving the youthful Saudi population exactly what it wants: technocratic competence joined to societal liberalization. Saudi Arabia is a meritocracy where many officials in the upper reaches of government have been educated in the United States, often at the best schools. When MBS has an idea, his standard instruction, as many who work with him told me, is "to put it through the process," what in Washington lingo translates as "staff it out": that is, MBS wants to know what the experts think before he puts his idea into practice. People who brief him told me they walk into his office intimidated by his mind and attention to detail, which is something different from outright fear of the kind that secular dictators in the mold of Saddam Hussein or Muammar Gaddafi projected. (And this makes his support for the grisly murder of Khashoggi even harder to understand and tolerate.)

While the Western journalistic elite, especially the group that came of age during the post–Cold War 1990s, remain obsessed with the freedom-fighting examples of the Czech Václav Havel and the South African Nelson Mandela, the avatar of governing types such as MBS throughout the developing world, as I have learned in over forty years as a foreign correspondent, has always been Lee Kuan Yew. It was Lee who established a philosophy of governance that was light on representative democracy, but heavy on technocratic competence, meritocracy, and fair dealing. The result was that Singapore went from being a poor, malarial hellhole in the 1960s to one of the wealthiest real estates in the world, and one of the easiest places to do business by the 1990s, all without oil. I will say this for MBS: at least he has the right role model, especially given shambolic experiments with democracy elsewhere in the Middle East. To an extent, the Arab Spring was occurring in Saudi Arabia, except not at all in the manner that self-absorbed Western elites have ever conceived of, and notwithstanding the human rights abuses, as counterintuitive as that may seem. And it was all the more impressive because Saudi Arabia, with its immense desert landscape, was not a natural replica of Singapore in the way of the smaller Gulf city-states.

REHAB MASSOUD SPENT MANY years in Washington as the right-hand man to the brilliant and legendary Saudi ambassador to the United States, Bandar bin Sultan. Massoud has also held security positions in the Saudi government. One evening in Riyadh he talked to me over dinner.

"We are different from other Arabs," he began. "We were never a colony of the West. Even the Ottomans only ruled here through local sheikhs, and only in certain places.* When oil was finally discovered, making us an attractive target of the West, colonialism was no longer fashionable. Hence, we have had no rallying cause against the West like other Arabs, such as the Algerians and the Iraqis, for example. When the West finally did send its people here beginning in the 1930s, it sent businessmen and petroleum engineers, not the 82nd Airborne. Consequently, we never held a grudge against you. So now do not make us choose between you and the Chinese." His implication was that by our moral lectures regarding Saudi behavior, we were only succeeding in making the Chinese option even more attractive for Riyadh.

"We are not the same," Massoud explained. "Do not assume that we are the same. We are not a democracy and probably never will be. You went through your own development for 250 years. Women did not get the right to vote in America and Blacks did not gain their civil rights until much later in your history as a democracy. But nobody in the outside world ever really questioned you about those things. Foreign governments recognized your constraints, since your internal political reality prevented those reforms from happening sooner. In Saudi Arabia," he went on, "the situation has often been the opposite: rather than the people demanding more freedom from their own govern-

---

* It was often Egyptians, deputized by the Ottomans, who partially controlled what is now Saudi Arabia.

ment, generally it was always the government that initiated liberal change, even though conservative elements in the hinterland were against it."

Massoud told me the story about how King Faisal in the 1960s opened girls' schools in the desert, telling the sheikhs that they were not obliged to send their own daughters to these schools, but that the government, in the fashion of rendering unto Caesar what was Caesar's, was determined to provide the tribesmen-at-large at least the option of educating their daughters. "The system here has often been progressive, avant-garde even," that is, compared to the desert hinterland it governs. "But we in the cities never got too far ahead. We were aware of historical cycles regarding the danger of the hinterland overrunning the rulers in the towns, as Ibn Khaldun had warned about. But even in the cities we remain a tribal desert people. We don't jump when we see a water well in the distance. We calculate, in case it is only a mirage. We know we must always bring the majority of the people along with us."

Massoud argued that Saudi Arabia was a self-correcting meritocracy in its own way, as when the royal family, observing the incompetence of King Saud, gathered together in 1964 and had him formally removed in favor of Faisal, who would prove to be a wise statesman. Massoud's argument invited an obvious question: Was King Salman's decision to change the line of succession from a horizontal one to a vertical one—in favor of his son Mohammed bin Salman—another example of the royal family self-correcting, this time for a more dynamic and technological age where a younger leader was required?

THE MIDDLE EAST IS and always has been a dangerous mess, one Saudi after another told me, with many of the major wars the avoidable upshot of missed signals. The Egyptian leader Gamal Abdel Nasser misread the trap the Israelis were setting for him prior to the 1967 war. Israeli leader Golda Meir missed the genuine peace signals that the Egyptian leader Anwar Sadat was sending her after he had come to power, resulting in the 1973 war. Iraqi leader Saddam Hussein misread the American commitment to Kuwait prior to the 1991 Gulf War, as well as the American intention to topple him if he did not open up his country to U.N. weapons inspectors, prior to the second Gulf War in 2003. As for the current situation, the Arab Spring, at least as far as the West has interpreted it, not only proved to be an unmitigated disaster, but so, too, have later, less publicized attempts at democracy-building. For example, Kuwait was a hybrid system of democracy and monarchy, and the result has been deadlock where little comparatively was getting done. Sudan's new civilian leaders were characterized by incoherent infighting. Tunisia had slid back toward autocracy. Thus, where was there any alternative to competent monarchical or authoritarian rule, the Saudis asked me, that could both govern and read signals reasonably well?

Cognizant of this history, as well as of the current regional morass, Saudi foreign minister Faisal bin Farhan Al Saud was trying to steer a diplomatic course for his country. As he explained it to me in a long conversation, foreign policy for Saudi Arabia was all about enabling the kingdom's drive toward sustainable domestic development and reform, while attracting investment from outside. "It is not about competing with Iran for the sake of regional influence, but about countering Iran's specific threats to our security." Iran, in his mind, had a regime that put its national prestige above the needs of its own population, whereas the Saudi regime put the needs and happiness of its own population first. It was this fear of Iran that helps explain the Saudis' difficult decision to intervene militarily in Yemen in 2015, Prince Faisal told me. The de facto Iranian victory in Iraq, Tehran's dominant influence in Lebanon, Iran's support of the opposition in Bahrain, and much else had created a "cacophony of risk," said the foreign minister, forcing Saudi Arabia into a country to its southwest where there were several times more assault rifles than there were people, and probably one rocket-propelled grenade per person. The intervention in Yemen was, Prince Faisal explained, about trying to prevent the Houthis from capturing the Yemeni port of Aden and becoming another Hezbollah.

In the little spare time he had, the prince told me, he had been

reading Thucydides's history of the Peloponnesian War. "Human nature hasn't changed much since ancient Greece," he said. "Governance
and decision-making has always been complex. The difference is that
everything today happens so quickly. You have half an hour—or a few
minutes—to come to a determination instead of a week or more as in
the past."

I asked what regime provided the best model for governance and
decision-making in today's fast-paced world. "Singapore," the foreign
minister said firmly, echoing MBS. "It is one of the most just and well-
governed societies on earth," despite its current problems. That is why
the Saudis were to a man mystified as to why the Biden administration
failed to invite Singapore to its Summit for Democracy in 2021, while
inviting an unstable and crime-plagued country like the Democratic
Republic of the Congo. It was an indication of how the Americans
placed legalistic formalities like the holding of elections ahead of eternal philosophy and plain common sense. Between acts such as placing
the Congo on a pedestal on top of Singapore and the televised spectacle of the January 6, 2021, riot at the U.S. Capitol, I found the Saudis
were in no mood to listen to lectures from Washington about democracy and good governance. Seen from Riyadh, not only had democracy
failed around the Middle East, but it was now in danger inside the
United States itself. The Saudis, like so many others in the Middle
East, were obviously less concerned with the debate of democracy versus autocracy than they were with the stark fear of anarchy.

Prince Faisal, as a member of the Al Saud family, has a personal
connection to a form of tribal government ruled by an emir that goes
back to the fifteenth century, when the mud-brick site of At-Turaif
was founded in Diriyah, west of Riyadh. "We have an historic responsibility to our own political heritage to make reforms happen, to do
things: not to make excuses not to do things."

EIMAN AL-MUTAIRI WAS THE vice minister of commerce and the
head of the National Competitiveness Center. She had done a post-
doctorate at Harvard in genetics. A Bedouin from the Eastern Prov-

ince, she wore a black abaya and hijab when I met her in her office. "The word *reform* doesn't do justice to what is happening here," she told me. "We are breaking taboos, one after the other. The percentage of women in the workforce is up to 33 percent in 2022, from 12 percent in 2015. It will go higher. It took us only three months, a few years back, to review and change all the laws regarding women's participation in society and in the workforce. Our system is characterized by a flat hierarchy, but one with a lot of consultation among experts. So things move fast, and at the same time are well thought through.

"I don't like your Western terms like 'women's empowerment,'" she continued. "It's just that Saudi women are not going to take it anymore. Your system has worked well for you, and ours works well for us. The royal family is part of our society and social relations. You can't just cut and paste from one society to the other." One of her female colleagues added: "We have nice buildings, we're high-tech. But we're tribal, we need a strong leader."

Her point was that particularly in an era of social reforms, a strong central authority is required, otherwise anarchy threatens. The most famous example of getting this wrong was Mikhail Gorbachev's decision to loosen the reins of central authority during a time of ongoing reforms, leading to the collapse of the Soviet Union. The many Saudis I spoke with were not in denial about the oppressive policies of their security services and the ghastly mistakes of MBS, notably the murder of journalist Jamal Khashoggi. But to a man, and to a woman, they were realists, to the degree they understood that successful liberal change in a conservative society required stabilizing rule.

The vice minister's point about the dramatic changes in Saudi society regarding women was really about the vitality of the Saudi system itself, and how that system was positioning itself for the rigors of a postmodern, post-petroleum world. "Despite all the Middle East wars, despite the destruction wrought by the Arab Spring in one country after another, the Kingdom of Saudi Arabia is still standing," she said. "Ever since Abdulaziz Ibn Saud united the tribes in the early part of the twentieth century, we have been stable. So watch us. We will be leading the region. After all, we are Bedouin, and therefore determined." To be sure, amid the shoals of Marxism, Arab nationalism, and Islamic fundamentalism over the span of the decades, Saudi Arabia has managed half a dozen leadership successions without a crisis, including one after the assassination of King Faisal in 1975.[21]

She shook her head in frustration regarding Western ignorance of the Saudi domestic reality. "'There is no freedom here,' you say. But people are shouting and screaming over Twitter all the time about the bureaucracy and all manner of its imperfections. There is real passion in every meeting I attend."

Thoraya Obaid, in her mid-seventies, also wore a black abaya and hijab. She was a generation older than Eiman al-Mutairi, and had been a U.N. undersecretary-general for population in the early 2000s. But what she told me was an echo of her younger compatriot in the women's struggle here. Obaid's education had started in a Christian girls' school in Cairo in 1951, where her middle-class father, who had studied in the holy mosque in Medina, had sent her to learn to read, as there was no girls' education in Saudi Arabia at the time. "He wanted me to know the Koran. For him it was all about religion, not human rights." She told me that before MBS's "shock treatment," there had been earlier stirrings in Saudi Arabia about creating a proper role for women. "I was one of the first blossoms."

After getting her bachelor's and master's degrees in the United States, Obaid married and followed her husband and his development work to south Lebanon in 1982, just as the Israelis invaded. She described the bombings, the occupation, and the roundups of young men. "You can't realize how bad war is until you experience it firsthand. I hate all war." She and her husband left Lebanon for Iraq soon after, experiencing the Iran-Iraq War in the 1980s and the U.S. war with Iraq over Kuwait in 1991. "Nevertheless, as bad as Saddam Hussein was," she said, "we had food, electricity, and water. Then the Americans came in 2003, talking about democracy and human rights, and there was nothing: no food, no electricity, and no water; just chaos."

"The Americans have turned human rights into an ideology," she went on. "How can you talk about free speech if people do not have enough to eat? The most urgent thing is to improve people's material lives." This was straight out of the great British humanist philosopher Isaiah Berlin, who had written: "Men who live in conditions where there is not sufficient food, warmth, shelter, and the minimum degree of security can scarcely be expected to concern themselves with freedom of contract or of the press."[22]

Because political forces in the United States and Europe seem to have lost Berlin's sense of nuance, Obaid believes that "the power of the West as a source of values is diminishing. Human rights should only be institutionalized through national and communal dialogue. It cannot be universally applied from the outside."

It is important at this juncture to emphasize that Eiman al-Mutairi and Thoraya Obaid are far from typical of many Saudi women who have not truly been liberated. While MBS has removed the guardian system and dramatically weakened the notorious religious police, the reforms have worked in favor of women from understanding families rather than in favor of women still suffering under domineering males who have a myriad of ways to oppress the female members of the family.[23] But here we are talking about the culture at large, which governments throughout history have rarely been able to dramatically and quickly change. Indeed, changing outright the culture of a place is not what governments do. The times in modern history when governments were actually able to change a culture from within are few enough to be remembered: for example, the Meiji Restoration in Japan, Kemal Atatürk's revolution in Turkey, and the Zionist revolution in Israel. Lee Kuan Yew's changes in Singapore are another case. Again, the fact that MBS has Lee as a role model is a good thing, even if he is still far from achieving the level of change in Saudi Arabia that Lee achieved in Singapore.

I WAS NOW STANDING inside Al Masmak, the fort stormed by Abdulaziz Ibn Saud in January 1902, heralding his capture of Riyadh. It was from this fort that Saudi Arabia came into being and was originally ruled. Al Masmak (literally "the thickness," a reference to its ramparts) is a spare, geometric, mud-walled affair, lacking any ostentation or much of a design element. What is breathtaking about the fort is its very smallness. Indeed, Riyadh, up through my own birth in 1952, was little more than an overgrown mud-brick village built around Al Masmak—which today is merely part of the southern edge of the city. Since the mid-twentieth century, humanity and Saudi Arabia in particular have had a revolution in scale, as the Saudi capital is now a vast metropolis of 7.4 million people sprawling over dozens of miles in each direction. With scale comes societal complexity, so that leadership becomes more and more of an art form. Technology has defeated and also intensified the effect of that scale, and thus the burden of leadership has become overwhelming. Consequently, tribal tradition must be employed in order to anchor technocratic rule. Saudi Arabia will continue to evolve out of its own past, ever mindful of Abdulaziz breaking down the door of Al Masmak. It will not evolve out of someone else's past imposed upon it, as both Eiman Al-Mutairi and Thoraya Obaid had pointed out.

FROM AL MASMAK I drove to the other end of town to have dinner at the Boulevard, a vast theme park of international restaurants, coffee bars, magic shows, hip-hop music festivals, and mega-malls, with live performances by a lake filled with dancing fountains. At night the labyrinth of wide pedestrian thoroughfares is jammed with people: men and women walking together, sometimes holding hands. You could almost be anywhere. The Boulevard is straight out of Orlando, Florida. It opened in 2021, and as Saudis told me, it is the essence of what for them constitutes freedom. Such freedoms are new and may eventually be taken for granted, though, with calls for more and different freedoms to replace them. I don't know if that will happen. I do know that my first impressions of Riyadh were being transformed before my eyes, as the drab desert capital was being superseded by a global, urban hub in my mind. The acting minister of media, Majid bin Abdullah Al Qasabi, told me: "Because of technology we import culture now the way we have always imported goods and services. There are no barriers. For instance, there is no way to censor what books Saudis buy on Amazon." Moreover, technology was not destabilizing society because that society was anchored in a traditional culture. The family, not the individual, still ruled. Shame was still a powerful force, unlike in the West where celebrities were too often shameless. Despite the hip-hop music, men generally still wore ghutras and agals, and women wore abayas and hijabs.

Saudi Arabia truly represented the Loom of Time: progress here was inexorably taking place outside the boundaries of newspaper opinion pages and political science theory.

ONE NIGHT I HAD dinner at a private home with over a dozen Saudi notables, men all wearing traditional ghutras and agals who were either former government ministers or leading experts in their fields. Such cross-cultural encounters can be awkward at first, but the conversation flowed easily for hours in different directions. Nevertheless, there was a singular thread to everything I heard. It was that the United States was both misunderstanding the kingdom and thus, perhaps, forcing Saudi Arabia to make choices that would not be in America's interest.

The liberal reforms going on in Saudi Arabia, I was told, did not constitute secularization, as the society here by very definition was Islamic to the core. To the contrary, the partial liberation of Saudi women under the de facto rule of Mohammed bin Salman was an element of Vision 2030, which was less a specific plan by the government—with the usual mistakes and vanities that the Western media obsessed about—but a grand strategy to be adjusted constantly and was subject to backtracking if necessary. The most important aspect of Vision 2030, as with China's Belt and Road Initiative, was that at least it provided the country with a direction, however imperfect. And Vision 2030 and Belt and Road were operating in sync, as they both emphasized infrastructure. The United States, by contrast, had little direction because it had no consensus. Liberating many women here had been a necessity in order to facilitate entrepreneurship and competitiveness, without which Saudi society will not be able to navigate the post-petroleum age: the object of Vision 2030 in the first place. "Vision 2030 is a process, not a finish line, since if you fail to plan you're planning for failure," one Saudi minister explained to me. While the demographic explosion that created young societies across the Middle East has produced chaos elsewhere, here because of Vision 2030 it is producing reform. Reform was helped by the social contract between ruler and ruled that existed in the Arabian Gulf countries to a degree it did not exist in North Africa and in the Levant. Political questions at the top here "were only for the royal family to sort out," as one guest at dinner put it, as long as the regime delivered peace and a modicum of justice. And that, in turn, explained the inherent stability characterizing all the monarchical regimes of desert Arabia.

As another dinner guest told me, "one must make a distinction between democracy and liberty." Saudis had acquired personal freedoms in recent years that they never had before and which would have been endangered by democracy, since in any imaginable free and fair national election the Islamists would constitute the only organized force aside from the royal family. Just look at how the Muslim Brotherhood had destroyed Egypt between 2011 and 2013. Instead, democracy here has been forsworn in return for personal freedoms, which have been the consequence of good governance, in turn facilitated by the constant surveys and evaluations that the royal court was conducting on the various government ministries.

Not only did Americans insufficiently appreciate all of this, but as one person at the dinner gathering told me, "We are caught between Iran exporting its revolution and America exporting its values." Another guest told me in reference to the Biden administration's demands that Saudi Arabia respect gay and lesbian rights: "The United States is applying the latest revolutionary conditions—absent even in the West until a short time ago—as a way to judge everyone else." The result, I was told, could be a turn toward China, which, to repeat, not only had no moral lectures to deliver, but was buying more Saudi oil than any other country and offered an "up by the bootstraps" story of development that emotionally appealed to the Saudis and other Arabs. There has already been upwards of $100 billion in Chinese investment in Saudi Arabia. China was a major stakeholder in Vision 2030. Saudi Arabia was becoming a key junction point of the Belt and Road Initiative.[24] Along with English, Chinese was now the major foreign language taught at Saudi schools. Indeed, as the guests at the dinner indicated, China *was just there.* It was the world's second-largest economy and had an insatiable demand for oil and gas. How could energy-rich Saudi Arabia not account it status, especially given Saudi Arabia's frustrations with the United States?

HERE WAS THE DILEMMA. The ongoing reforms in Saudi Arabia were remarkable when encountered close-up. Moreover, they were reforms that in their very origins harked back to the cultural influence of the West via globalization, though the Saudis may never admit this. Yet, these same reforms may only have been possible because of a political condition with which the West, and particularly liberal internationalists and neoconservatives in the United States, could not approve: severe repression directed downwards from the top of the political hierarchy. But had Mohammed bin Salman been any less of an autocrat, had he consulted and listened more to other factions in the royal family and to more conservative religious elements within his society, he might never have attempted those reforms in such depth in the first place. Remember it had been autocrats who tolerated no internal dissent—Anwar Sadat of Egypt, King Hussein of Jordan, Sheikh Mohammed bin Zayed of the United Arab Emirates—who made peace treaties with Israel. Democrats in any Middle Eastern society would have been unable to do it. They would have been too weak. But whereas America demanded not only specific outcomes, it also wanted to dictate the specific means of achieving them.

While I was in Saudi Arabia, *The Economist* ran a story indicating that elements within both the Sunni religious community and the al Saud family were strongly opposed to Mohammed bin Salman's reforms, but out of fear could only whisper about it.[25] The Americans, though they might barely admit it even to themselves, had better hope that such fear persisted and such opposition to MBS's autocracy failed and always would.

In fact, Prince Turki Al Faisal, the youngest son of the late King Faisal and the longtime head of Saudi Arabia's intelligence service, the Mukhabarat Al A'amah, told me in an interview that "anyone who attempts to reverse the reforms undertaken by Mohammed bin Salman will have to take on the majority of the population," and would therefore have to be particularly repressive. Prince Turki said that the population, which included hundreds of thousands of Saudis educated in the West, and was almost to a man influenced by global culture through technology, was now ready for the reforms: the reason why they had gone off so smoothly.

DR. MOHAMMED AL ISSA was the general secretary of the Muslim World League. When I met him in his Riyadh office he wore a skullcap and ghutra, but no agal, an indication of his deep religiosity, since the agal is like a crown and only God wears a crown.

"The holy places of Islam, Mecca and Medina, are here. All the important events regarding the founding of Islam are in Saudi Arabia." Therefore, he explained that as "guardian of the holy places," the Saudi religious establishment was required to be moderate and consensus-driven, and not to swing in any extreme direction, since it spoke for Muslims from North Africa to the Far East.

This also meant reaching out to other religions.

Dr. Mohammed went on at length about the Saudi religious establishment's outreach to Judaism, which included a visit he had made as the head of a Muslim delegation to Auschwitz, the Nazi concentration camp in occupied Poland. "Whatever you read about Auschwitz and the Holocaust," he told me, "is not equal to the emotional experience of actually being there. I saw the slippers of Jewish children, rugs made from the hair of Jewish women, the nearby ovens. . . . The experience of coming face-to-face with the Nazi bestiality and brutality cannot be imagined. These are things the normal human mind cannot conceive of. The world has a responsibility that such things do not happen again."

Keep in mind that Dr. Mohammed's leadership of the World Muslim League coincides with Mohammed bin Salman's de facto rule. Saudi Arabia is an autocracy, and someone with the beliefs about Judaism of Dr. Mohammed could never be in his position without the approval of the crown prince himself. Dr. Mohammed's words conveyed not only a moral message, but also an expression of the crown prince's sheer power, since many people in Saudi Arabia were now speaking from the same page.

As far as reaching out to Judaism and Israel, Mohammed bin Salman was the contemporary equivalent of the late Anwar Sadat of Egypt. Whereas Sadat journeyed to Jerusalem to meet Israeli leaders face-to-face and made peace between Egypt and Israel, MBS made Saudi Arabia the Arab power behind the Abraham Accords, which established diplomatic relations between the Gulf sheikhdoms and Israel. Saudi Arabia was now publicly committed to diplomatically integrating Israel into the Middle East, I was repeatedly told.

But MBS was a human rights violator, he condoned torture,[26] he had sanctioned the murder of the journalist Jamal Khashoggi! you might say. All true, but there may be no contradiction in MBS's behavior since there is no unity of goodness in the amoral world of men and politics. Dramatic social reforms, because of their potential to destabilize society, required strong central authority that by its very nature periodically crossed over into brutality. To repeat, the United States could not demand both ends and the means to achieve them. For the world was not merely an extension of the American historical experience and the values it has produced.

"WE HAVE BEEN LUCKY. We have almost always had good leaders: Faisal, Khalid, Fahd, Abdullah," said Hassan Youssef Yassin, rattling off the names of successive Saudi kings. For decades Yassin had worked at the height of the Saudi establishment and knew Abdulaziz Ibn Saud personally. "Almost all our kings were astute and conservative. And now a new leader, Mohammed bin Salman, [who is much less conservative] has brought us into a new age of tolerance. Oil wealth is often a curse. Look at Venezuela, Nigeria, Iraq, Libya, and Kazakhstan. Not here. It is traditional monarchy, an ancient system, mind you, that has provided stability," which those other countries, which featured either weak democracy or modernizing dictatorship, could never really achieve.

Indeed, in Saudi eyes, their rulers have been more in the spirit of traditional sheikhs rather than outright dictators. Sheikhs have many qualities: wisdom, charisma, force of personality, understanding, and in particular the willingness to consult with tribal elders and many other influential men before taking a decision.[27] It is not democracy, but it is a corollary of it. And it has worked for millennia in its own way.

PALM TREES SWING IN the breeze against a broad panel of silver-blue sea. Egypt and Sudan seem to peek over the western horizon, while Mecca is just behind me. The pilgrim trade, the storied spice highways of the Greater Indian Ocean reaching all the way back to the subcontinent and the Muslim parts of Indochina, all beckon from Jeddah. The Red Sea, from the Strait of Bab el-Mandeb north to the Suez Canal, is pregnant with thoughts of strategy, choke points, and empire. Having come from the baking desert bleakness of the Nejd around Riyadh to the humid embrace of this seaboard, and again thinking about the oil fields of the Eastern Province on the Arabian Gulf, one can palpably appreciate Abdulaziz Ibn Saud's continental vision of uniting Arabia.

Though, as different as the Hejaz was from the Nejd, and as different as both were from the oil-rich Eastern Province, ever since Abdulaziz formally created Saudi Arabia, the more educated and cosmopolitan Hejazis have taken up positions throughout the country, just as Nejdis to a lesser extent have done in the Hejaz and the Eastern Province. There was constant mixing and melding of the population. The imposition of shari'a law, however much hated it is in the West, has further unified Saudi Arabia, I was told again and again.

Since the late nineteenth century this port city, so close to Mecca, has been a cosmopolitan hub and melting pot of the different races constituting the Muslim religion. Because it is more fast-paced than Riyadh, Jeddah is also more informal. To wit, a half dozen middle-aged professionals sat around a café table at a slick mall one evening, without bothering to wear ghutras and agals. That was normal in Jeddah.

"There is a sense of *weight* here," one said, beginning the conversation. "KSA [the Kingdom of Saudi Arabia] has an innate religious legitimacy that no other Muslim state can match. But that legitimacy is going to rely less and less on the two Muslim holy cities and more and more on dramatic social and economic development. For the Saudi state, this is a complete restructuring of its business model."

Another continued the thread: "You want services to work. You want to be able to start a small business without encountering government bureaucracy. You want convenience and a lifestyle that compares favorably with any other Muslim state, and with Israel. Such things matter much more to the average Saudi than simply being given the freedom to argue about politics, and to do so endlessly with no result."

A third: "In the midst of all this social change, women's rights have been normalized, as if it was always like this," eyeing the women sitting alone at the café, and other women mixing with men. "When all this happened," again, looking around, "there were no political upheavals, no terrorist attacks, despite all the dire warnings of an extremist religious reaction. The truth is, the most devout Muslims in Saudi Arabia are being marginalized. They are becoming folkloric, like the Amish." To a greater extent than the dramatic policy swings of previous decades in Saudi Arabia, this time the reformers had "the vast majority of the population with them," especially the young.

JEDDAH, WHICH MEANS "GRANDMOTHER," is thousands of years old. It is said that Eve is buried here. The old part of town (*Al-Balad*), a hub of the spice trade, is a jigsaw of hundreds of coral stone buildings, overlaid with whitewashed plaster, and decorated with enclosed balconies made of teakwood from India. The balcony screens are cut into lattice formations and called *roshan*s, from the Persian word *rozen* meaning "window opening." Here ladies could sit and see out into the street without being seen themselves. The *roshan*s of Jeddah are similar to the *mashrabiya*s of Tunisia, Egypt, and the Levant. Their carved complexity in dark teak is layered against blinding white facades that are striking in their simplicity. The combination is a precious and sensuous balance. No two *roshan*s here are identical, yet the architectural pattern throughout the old port is uniform. "We say in Arabic that 'the houses talk to each other,'" said Abir Jameel Abusulayman, who in 2011 became the first female tour guide in Saudi Arabia. She took me to meet Ahmed Angawi, who runs a workshop that is reviving the craft of building *roshan*s. "Latticework in all its variations," Angawi told me, "represents a geometry that expresses both the unity and diversity of the Islamic world."

The *roshan*s are in natural dark-brown teak, when they are not painted green or sky blue. Green is the color of Islam and the kingdom, while the blue is inspired by the *mashrabiya*s of Sidi Bou Said, an urban masterpiece north of Tunis on the Mediterranean. The effect of the sky-blue *roshan*s against the white walls also conjures up the Greek islands, and there is one building here that is called the "Myconos house." Like the Greek islands, old Jeddah is delightfully populated with scrawny cats, the only cats I saw in Saudi Arabia.

There were also many other houses with peeling, leprous walls being refurbished. Construction teams were ubiquitous. In all, 650 buildings in old Jeddah, the maritime gateway of the holy mosques of Mecca and Medina, will be restored to form a UNESCO world heritage site. I felt privileged to be catching old Jeddah during a priceless moment in time. For with the social and economic reforms now sweeping Saudi Arabia, I could imagine a future of tourist armies holding selfie sticks, descending from cruise ships and overwhelming these still silent streets.

Like elsewhere in the kingdom, the smell of incense invigorates the interiors of old Jeddah. I went into a sweet shop, its hundreds of clear cases filled with Indonesian tamarind seeds, dried apricots from Syria, various dried fruits from Thailand, dozens of different kinds of dates from Saudi Arabia, and much more, making for a chromatic and rectilinear feast of color akin to a modern art canvas.

In the cool, dark interior of another building I walked up to the first floor, where Abdulaziz Ibn Saud lived between 1925 and 1927, when he was known as "King of Hejaz, Sultan of Nejd," before the two regions were officially combined to form Saudi Arabia in 1932. I sat by the window where Abdulaziz himself must have sat, trying to erase the passage of time. Without Abdulaziz and his galloping warrior charisma, the oil giant of Saudi Arabia would likely never have existed and the Middle East would be radically different. I next walked up to the roof, where there was a wood-framed enclosure with open windows called a *tairma,* a place for birds, according to Rawaa Baksh, an historical preservationist. I sat on a brocaded cushion on the floor, admiring a view, now cluttered with futuristic skyscrapers, that, literally until the 1950s, constituted only sea and desert beyond old Jeddah's cluster of houses. From here I also spotted a graceful four-hundred-year-old white mosque by the old port. T. E. Lawrence must have seen it, I thought, having begun his First World War Arabian adventures from this Red Sea port adjacent to Mecca in 1916.

Another name that old Jeddah brought to mind was "Abdullah" Philby. Harry St. John Bridger Philby, the brilliant Arabist, oriental linguist, and explorer, lived here in the early decades of the twentieth century. A British colonial agent, he would convert to Islam, adopt the name of Abdullah, and advise Abdulaziz Ibn Saud about how to maneuver against his own British compatriots and the Americans at the beginning of the oil age. Philby, besides being irascible and frustrated with the British colonial service, had evidently become attracted to the essential egalitarian nature of Arabian tribesmen, in which ordinary men addressed the king by his first name, a respite from the rigid class structure of English life that he was accustomed to.[28] Having been born in Sri Lanka and then spending many years abroad in the Indian subcontinent and the Arabian Peninsula, Philby's migration from a British agent to a Saudi one was less of an extreme conversion than one might assume. Philby's son Kim would also famously betray his country as a double agent for the Soviet Union during World War II and the early Cold War. The Philbys represented an extreme type of cosmopolitanism. They were loyal to feelings and ideals that rose above patriotism.

This was the opposite of the many Saudis—hundreds of thousands, actually—who over the decades were educated abroad, became sophisticated members of a globalized world, and yet unlike the Philbys returned home and retained their cultural values; the men still wearing ghutras and agals, the women wearing abayas and hijabs. Urban Saudis had become cosmopolitan without becoming rootless.

One Saudi diplomat, having spent many years abroad and now at home in traditional dress, told me: "According to the stereotypes, we have oil, we are the land of Osama bin Laden, we repress women, and we chop off heads. Vision 2030 has undermined those images. Now Vision 2030 [the transformation of Saudi Arabia and its society], of which the restoration of old Jeddah is a part, is itself being criticized for its problems and imperfections. But that's progress."

I thought about that for a moment. What he said was true. But progress as I knew was not clear-cut and linear. For that was the supreme lesson of the Loom of Time. While Saudis were experiencing more personal freedoms under MBS, the state was in key ways moving in a more repressive direction, as news reports made clear. MBS wanted it all: absolute control and a dynamic, idea-producing technocratic society at the same time. He may not be able to have both. As the scholar and former *Washington Post* correspondent David Ottaway warned: MBS was like Icarus, the young and hubristic character out of Greek mythology, who flew too close to the sun, so that his wax wings melted and he fell into the sea and drowned.[29] Only time will tell if the analogy is apt. But my own impressions indicated that MBS might well be able to avoid Icarus's fate.

CHAPTER

7

FERTILE CRESCENT

====

PART I

NO MAP CONJURES UP THE BIBLE AND THE STORY OF CIVI-
lization itself, with all its childhood familiarity and life lessons, like a
map of the Fertile Crescent. This ultimate geography constitutes a
wide belt of lush green space in the desert that starts near the mouth
of the Tigris and Euphrates close to the Persian Gulf, then proceeds
northwest between the two rivers through Iraq and southern Turkey
for many hundreds of miles, before arcing southwest down through
Syria and Lebanon to the Holy Land, or what has variously been
called Canaan, Israel, and Palestine. The age-old cities of Baghdad,
Damascus, and Jerusalem all fall within its domain, as do the great
place-names and archaeological sites of antiquity such as Babylon,
Nineveh, Mari, and Carchemish.* The wanderings of Abraham, the
biblical patriarch of the second millennium B.C., perfectly encompass
this entire picture, as Abraham was born in Ur in southern Iraq, migrated up through Mesopotamia† and Kurdistan to Haran in what is

---

* T. E. Lawrence worked as an archaeologist at the Hittite and Neo-Assyrian site of
Carchemish, northeast of Aleppo, on the Syrian-Turkish border, prior to the outbreak of
World War I.

† The Greek word for the land "between the rivers," the Tigris and Euphrates.

now the Turkish-Syrian border region, then south through Aleppo and Damascus to the West Bank. Abraham generally followed the path of cultivation, as the Fertile Crescent forms a very distinct geographical unity, though it now overlaps with practically half a dozen countries.*

And that is the problem in our own era.

Because empires are more natural and organic to world geography than modern states, the crumbling of the Ottoman Empire, which had comfortably embraced all of the wanderings of Abraham, led to the creation of an artificial gridwork of sovereign territories that turned the Fertile Crescent from a force of unity into one of chaos and violent conflict. Modern states divided what should have been kept whole, even as these states were themselves casually conceived by British and French imperialists, since just beyond this great arcing path of cultivation lay featureless desert terrain through which artificial borders had inevitably to be drawn.

Left alone, the Fertile Crescent is a natural and beautiful landscape that makes sense on a topographical map. But when laid across a modern political map, it begins to explain why Iraq and Syria, for instance, became the monstrosities that they did. For the compulsion required to forge unity over what was entirely contrived in the wake of the Ottoman imperial collapse led to some of the worst tyrannies in the second part of the twentieth century and to some of the bloodiest wars in the early part of the twenty-first.

The map of the Fertile Crescent entranced me as a boy in Hebrew School, yet it made for real-life nightmares in my adulthood as a journalist. For the radical, organized violence that would define the Ba'athist (Arab Socialist) regimes of Syria and Iraq, which I experienced close-up, had their roots in the dismemberment of Abraham's map.

---

* Iraq, Turkey, Syria, Lebanon, Israel, and the occupied Palestinian territories. See Yohanan Aharoni and Michael Avi-Yonah's *The Modern Bible Atlas,* particularly the maps on pages 5 and 26. Prepared by Carta, Ltd. (London: George Allen & Unwin, 1968).

———

IT IS THE LARGE, especially artificial states of Syria and Iraq that truly define the modern political geography of the Fertile Crescent. While together these two states form a thematic unit, there are enough differences between them to explore them one at a time, especially since their individual histories and characteristics are so complex and unique.

PHILIP K. HITTI, the late Princeton historian of the Middle East, writes, "The history of Syria, using the name in its geographic meaning, is in a sense the history of the civilized world in miniature." Because as Hitti suggests, historical Syria's geography includes not only Syria proper but the countries of Lebanon, Israel/Palestine, and Jordan, it "is perhaps the largest small country on the map." (In fact, as we shall later discover, it has always been the disparity between Syria's political borders and its yearning to legally incorporate its geographical borders that led to its fierceness, radicalism, and very focused sense of purpose during three crucial decades under the rule of the late Hafez al-Assad.) Indeed, historical and geographic Syria stands at the crossroads of three continents: Europe, Asia, and Africa, sprawling practically from the Nile to the Euphrates. As a geographical expression, Syria stretches from the Taurus Mountains in Turkey south to the Nefud desert of Saudi Arabia, and from the Mediterranean coast east to the Euphrates. As Hitti notes, Alexander, Pompey, Napoleon, and Allenby made all or part of their military reputations here, along a caravan and invasion route where trod Abraham, Moses, and the Holy Family. Moreover, Syria has been a stage set in its southern and eastern frontier zones for the perennial struggle between Arabian nomads and the already settled populations there, adding yet another layer of instability.*

---

* Philip K. Hitti, *History of Syria: Including Lebanon and Palestine* (New York: Macmillan, 1951), pp. vii, 3, and 59–61. This book, three-quarters of a century old, is one of those classic studies that virtually no one writes anymore, whose first fifty pages or so are dedicated to climate, topography, and prehistory. For that reason it is so appealing.

Syria was the homeland of the Semites, where both Judaism and Christianity emerged against the backdrop of pitiless deserts. Later the heartland of the Hellenic and Roman empires, Egyptians, Assyrians, and Babylonians all overran Syria, just as Iranians, Turks, and Russians have fought here in our own time, providing an ancient pattern to postmodern conflict.

Because it lies at the crossroads of continents, Syria has had different civilizational personalities in the course of its history. For a millennium after the fourth-century B.C. conquests of Alexander the Great, Syria was culturally oriented westward—across the Mediterranean Sea to Greece and Byzantium. As late as the fourth and fifth centuries A.D., Syria was still a Greek-speaking land along its coast, reflecting the values of Eastern, that is, Byzantine Christianity, its territory a hotbed of visionary monks and early Christian heresies. But with the rise of Islam and Islam's vast conquests of late antiquity, the last links with Rome and Byzantium were severed, while new ones with Mecca and Medina, to the south in Arabia, were formed. Hitti remarks that the seventh-century A.D. Muslim conquest returned Syria to its original Semitic orientation, in which the Hellenism of the long centuries following Alexander was but an interregnum.[1]

That is, Syria had turned away from the sea and back toward the desert: from West to East.

And there it would remain.

The first great Muslim empire following the death of Muhammad, that of the Umayyads, a leading clan in Mecca, had Damascus as its capital. The Umayyad Empire stretched from Morocco and southern Spain by the Atlantic, clear across North Africa and the Middle East, to the Indus and the shadowlands of China: an extent greater than the Roman Empire at its zenith. The very spiritual and architectural nucleus of this empire was the Umayyad Mosque in the heart of the Hamidiyah souk of old Damascus, commissioned in A.D. 706 by the sixth Umayyad caliph, Al-Walid ibn Abd al-Malik, on the site of a Byzantine cathedral. In my youthful diary, with its neat penmanship, dated June 8, 1976, during my first visit to Syria, I wrote obsessively that the mosque is 157 meters long and 100 meters wide, "with two square minarets of seemingly skyscraper proportions and a wide dome."

I went on:

"It is above all a monument to the classical era. Never before, except perhaps in the Minerva temple in Syracuse,* are so many historical and cultural styles blended so elegantly"—Aramaic, Roman, Byzantine, and early Islamic. "The courtyard columns are Roman Corinthian, with Greek [Hellenistic] geometric marble inlaid on some of the walls," with "Byzantine green and gold leaf mosaic" adjoining "Islamic arches." I was twenty-three years old. Yet I distinctly remember being struck for the first time by how early Islamic architecture, because Muslim artistic values were back then so new and undeveloped, freely borrowed from the pagan and Byzantine Christian cultures that had preceded it. An ancient church had been transformed into a magnificent mosque. The Umayyads were great, partly on account of how they had grafted previous civilizations onto their own. They, as Hitti points out, were the "successor state" to Eastern Rome, just as the Muslim Abbasids in Baghdad would later be the "successor state" to the Zoroastrianism of Sassanid Persia.[2] In other words, Syria's turn away from the West had been organic and gradual, and inside this great mosque in Damascus nearly fifty years ago, I beheld for the first time a scintillating and unstable equilibrium during a time of cultural transition.

For example, there is the personage of St. John of Damascus, through whom Greek thought found its way into Islam, as he argued with Muslims about free will and predestination. Surnamed *Chrysorrhas* ("golden stream"), because of his oratorical gifts, John wrote in Greek and knew Arabic and Aramaic. Those very intellectual riches combined with the vast territorial conquests of the Umayyads so that early medieval Syria constituted the very heartbeat of the Greater

---

* The Minerva Temple, the Duomo of Siracusa in Sicily, which I had visited several months earlier in 1976, had been a pagan site, mosque, and cathedral, combining elements of all.

Middle East: a position Syria would never know again. Though, in a somewhat reduced geopolitical sense, in the last third of the twentieth century under Hafez al-Assad, as we will soon see, Syria would once again achieve a sort of impressive centrality to the region.

This centrality was born out of disappointment and frustration. For as the klieg light of world history traveled far beyond Damascus—first to Abbasid Baghdad, later to Fatimid Cairo and Hafsid Tunis as other Arab empires succeeded the Umayyads, and finally to Europe—Syria would be forced after more than a thousand years to once again face the West in the nineteenth and twentieth centuries, even while it remained a politically and economically underdeveloped part of the East. Indeed, when the people of historic Syria finally rubbed their eyes after their four-hundred-year-long Ottoman sleep, they found themselves living in a new and crazily fragmented territory under quasi-colonial French rule. The primary identity that the Syrians possessed at this point in their history was a bond to the Arabic language, even as the Arab world was itself now so full of divisions. For opposition to the birth of a Jewish state in Palestine in 1948 would serve as the only beacon light of unity the postcolonial Arabs from Morocco to Iraq would know.

European colonialism, preceded by centuries of Ottoman imperialism, was believed by Syrians to have robbed them of their historical and political destiny, given the previous greatness of the Umayyads. And the Zionist state represented the last surviving remnant in Arab eyes of European colonialism in the Middle East. This situation gave the Palestinian Arabs iconic status within the anti-imperialist mindset of both Arabs and sympathetic Western journalists and intellectuals. Because the "Zionist entity" lay within the confines of historic and geographic Syria—stretching from the mountains of southern Turkey to the Nile and Arabia—the liberation of Palestine became the touchstone by which postcolonial Arab regimes in Damascus measured themselves. For after millennia of history, and a brief spell as the center of a great world empire, Syria remained but a vague geographical expression that could find single-mindedness only in a cause larger than itself: a cause that promised to unify the disparate parts of its own historic geography. "Greater Syria," as the Middle East expert Daniel Pipes put it, fatefully constituted "the history of an ambition."[3]

THE BRITISH TRAVELER AND Arabist Freya Stark wrote in 1928 from Syria that "I haven't yet come across one spark of national feeling: it is all sects and hatreds and religions." Years later, though, she would both reconsider and elaborate, saying, "Out of such diversity the idea of unity can grow."[4] Whichever quote more accurately represents the feelings of this romantic yet deeply studied area specialist, whose life was a testament to Clifford Geertz's "thick description," clearly Syria, as it had emerged as a multiethnic and multiconfessional region out of long-standing Ottoman neglect, was a challenging prospect for modern statehood.

What emerged following World War I, in the words of historian Ali A. Allawi, was an "uncertain and ramshackle" entity, with "numerous armed groups," little governance outside of Damascus, and provincial notables jealous of their power, too few of whom were competent and honest.[5]

Throughout most of history, Syria had belonged to empires ruled from elsewhere, and had never constituted a cohesive state of its own. Its two principal cities, Aleppo and Damascus, had served as centers of rival regions, with the merchants of Aleppo looking to business connections in Mosul and Baghdad (in today's Iraq) rather than to Damascus. Syria was sort of like Scandinavia or New England, or pre-nineteenth-century Germany and Italy before unification, a vague region rather than a specific country, Pipes observes. Though it was a truncated territory in one part of the Middle East, within its borders lived every warring Middle Eastern schism and heterodoxy: Sunnis, Shi'ites, Alawites, Isma'ilis, Druze, and literally every manner of Christian sect.[6] Precisely because internal unity was so impossible to achieve—and also because Syria occupied such a central geographical position in the struggle against Zionism and European colonialism— as Patrick Seale, perhaps the most knowledgeable twentieth-century observer of Syrian politics, puts it: Syria "can claim to have been both the head and the heart of the Arab national movement." That is, Syria required a grand project to hold its warring internal forces at bay. The fact that Syria suffered under French imperialism rather than the British variety as in Iraq, where the pace of constitutional reforms was quicker, only made the political frustrations and differences inside Syria more volatile.*

The French separated Greater Lebanon from Syria in 1920, so as to bring a large population of mainly Sunni Muslims under the domination of the Maronite Christians in Beirut, who were allied with France, spoke French, and had a concordat with the Vatican. Shorn also of the sanjak of Alexandretta in northwestern Syria in 1938 by the Turks (with the connivance of the French), Syrians seethed with political venom at the sight of their country's dismemberment. In any case, because the various sects and minorities were identified with specific regions, there was little fundamental basis for geographical unity. Rival paramilitary youth groups, one more extreme than the other, engaged in brawls and mass demonstrations in 1939–40. The organizational aspect of politics barely existed: it was all a matter of competing mafia-like bosses and strongmen, themselves identified with different ethnic and sectarian factions. The French departed in 1946, after having incited sectarian loyalties for the sake of a divide-and-conquer strategy, so that Syria was now, in the words of the Dutch area specialist Nikolaos van Dam, "a political entity without being a political community."[7] The first free elections were held in 1947, leading only to further confusion, nepotism, and gross mismanagement, as the new country's politicians were often encumbered by the twin beasts of illiteracy and corruption.

Of course, it is tempting to blame the French League of Nations mandate, that is, European imperialism, for the whole tragedy of modern Syria. As a Syrian envoy to Paris, Habib Lutfallah, warned in 1920,

---

* Patrick Seale, *The Struggle for Syria: A Study of Post-War Arab Politics 1945–1958*, with a Foreword by Albert Hourani (New Haven, CT: Yale University Press, [1965] 1986), pp. 1–3 and 5. The French and British did not properly colonize Syria and Iraq, but administered them as authorities mandated by the League of Nations.

"In Balkanizing Asia Minor, in multiplying small principalities, dust particles of states, [France] leaves the road open to anarchy that will create an endemic state of war." Nevertheless, it is by no means clear that a united Syria in the interwar period would not have been violently torn asunder by its communal contradictions. In fact, the French weren't all bad. They offered a measure of political freedom, allowing political parties and a relatively free media.[8] To blame the European imperialists entirely for today's Middle East, as some in the academy do, is too easy: it denies the Arabs of the Levant their own agency.

"It was not lines on a map that prevented unity," writes the Oxford-educated Arabist Tim Mackintosh-Smith. "Blame it as they might on other people's empires, Arabs have never been a happy family: not since the division of the spoils of Islam; not since the pre-Islamic War of al-Basus, that forty-year super-squabble over grazing rights. They had never really been a family at all, except in tribal fictions of shared descent. If empires were entirely to blame, it was as much as anything for inspiring, by reflex, the myths and mirages of unattainable union."[9]

EARLY 1949 SAW INDEPENDENT Syria's first coup d'état, and the first coup in the postcolonial Arab world in fact, led by Colonel Husni al-Za'im. It demonstrated, according to Patrick Seale, "the fragility of a western constitutional formula stretched like a new skin over the fissures of a traditional society." The coup solved nothing, however, as continued strikes and demonstrations led to further political fragmentation, with the army, meanwhile, busying itself with everything from smuggling to secret police work. Al-Za'im's regime "lay somewhere between political gangsterism and musical comedy," Seale observes. Before 1949 was out, there would be two further colonels' coups, led successively by Sami al-Hinnawi and Adib Al-Shishakli. Al-Shishakli proved to be postcolonial Syria's first serious ruler. He abolished multiparty democracy, consolidated military power, and instituted reforms. For a while, observers thought of him as the Syrian Atatürk.[10] Therefore, it is worth listening to Shishakli for a moment, whose words sum up the impossible nature of Syria's ethnic, sectarian, and regional divisions.

"My enemies are like a serpent: the head is the Jabal Druze, the stomach Homs, and the tail Aleppo. If I crush the head the serpent will die."[11] Al-Shishakli, while he was president, referred to Syria as "the current official name for that country which lies within the artificial frontiers drawn up by imperialism."[12] Alas, there was no denying, even by its leaders, the artificiality of a state that made better sense only as a vague geographical expression. As it happened, Nasserists, Communists, Ba'athists, Druze officers, and other religious and ideological interests made for another coup in 1954 that toppled Shishakli.

Seven months after Al-Shishakli's downfall, Syria held free, fair, and peaceful national elections. The results only exacerbated ideological tensions, did little to assuage ethnic, sectarian, and regional ones, and increased the power of men committed to rejecting all formal ties and compromises with the West.[13] What's more, it did not prevent future coups and upheavals, which continued unabated for the next sixteen years. By "the late summer of 1957 the country was on the verge of complete political disintegration," writes Oxford professor Eugene Rogan.[14] Whereas American and European liberals have seen democracy as a humanizing, progressive, and stabilizing force in the world that would ultimately enhance the power of the West itself, Syria was a country (and not the only one) where this was just not proving to be the case.

In the twenty-four years between 1946 and 1970, Syria experienced twenty-one changes of government, almost all of them extralegal, and ten military coups.[15] In November 1970, the forty-year-old Ba'athist Air Force general Hafez al-Assad, a member of the Shi'a-trending Alawites from the mountains of northwestern Syria, took control in a calm and bloodless coup, a "corrective movement," as he called it. Assad would govern until his natural death thirty years later in June 2000. He would prove to be among the most historic, if underrated, figures of the modern Middle East, turning a virtual banana republic— the most unstable country of the Arab world, no less—into a stable police state. Assad had taken power in Damascus after the twin fiascos of the June 1967 war against Israel and the Black September crisis of 1970 in Jordan, when Syrian officials displayed both strategic confusion and utter incompetence in reacting first to advancing Israeli forces on the Golan Heights and later to the botched Palestinian attempt to topple Jordan's King Hussein. Assad, who fiercely sympathized with the Palestinians but detested their impulsiveness and lack of judgment, brought something entirely new to independent Syria's politics: a combination of deliberate planning and policy discipline, aided by what was to him a necessary ruthlessness when the situation demanded it.

NO WESTERN OBSERVER SO minutely and perfectly understood Assad and the forces swirling around him as did the late Patrick Seale, an Oxford-educated foreign correspondent in the Middle East. Seale was born in Northern Ireland; his father, Morris Sigel Seale, had been a Jewish convert to Presbyterianism and a missionary in Syria, where Patrick spent much of his boyhood in the 1930s and early 1940s. Seale in the second half of the twentieth century emerged as a *type:* the classic British foreign correspondent and area specialist emotionally and intellectually committed to the Arab struggle against Israel, who had, as a consequence, gained repeated access to Syria, a place where obtaining entry visas for journalists was problematic. Seale's sympathy for Assad's regime was unabashed—a principal reason for his repeated visas. In 1985, he married the Syrian journalist Rana Kabbani, the daughter of a Syrian ambassador. Seale leveraged all of this unequaled access into unequaled knowledge, and was therefore constantly sought out as an expert on Syria, including by the Israelis. I met Seale once, in the office of President Jaafar Nimeiry of Sudan in 1985. I was in Khartoum to interview the Sudanese president, whereas Seale was there, it seemed, for a friendly visit with Nimeiry. Seale's contacts in the region were extraordinary and, in fact, I found him quite charming and friendly.

Seale may have been emotionally committed to the second most repressive regime in the Arab world after Saddam Hussein's Iraq (both regimes being, not coincidentally, Ba'athist, a deadly mixture of Arab nationalism and East Bloc–style socialism). But by no means was he deluded or even shallow: he had a penetrating analytical intelligence as much as a literary journalistic one. I have known quite a few journalists who had brilliant, cocktail-circuit minds. Seale had more depth than that. Perhaps it was his half-Jewish background in the midst of the most fundamentally anti-Israel state in the Arab world that gave him a useful complexity. He may have been both conflicted as well as a bit uncomfortable in his own skin, I mean to say. Whatever it was, he put it to good use.

Seale's biography *Asad of Syria: The Struggle for the Middle East,* is an essential classic, despite being published by academic presses and utilizing a rather unusual Latin alphabetic spelling for the Syrian ruler. It thoroughly explains an entire era in the Middle East from a viewpoint that Western observers rarely get—and still need to get. Analysis is impossible without comprehending the ground-level view of the far side of the moon. And as someone who lived for several years in Israel, and who served in its military shy of half a century ago, I am grateful for Seale's emotional attachment to Assad's Syria, since he turned it into something indispensable for me. I once heard a high-ranking Israeli security expert, referring to Syria, remark, "You have to be an animal to run that country." But an animal is governed solely by instinct, whereas Assad, as Seale voluminously demonstrates, was governed by objective analysis. Assad did not need to study the classic works of realism from Machiavelli to Hans Morgenthau to have realism embedded in his bones. The fact that his interests were diametrically opposed to those of Israel and the West during the Cold War and its aftermath—and the fact that he operated in a social and cultural context that the West barely understood—did not make his analysis any the less brilliant or accurate.

Oh, and by the way, Seale also reveals Henry Kissinger's goals in the post–1973 war Middle East far more insightfully than most people in Washington do. Seale strongly disapproves of Kissinger, but that is only because Kissinger's interests were absolutely opposed to Assad's, not because Seale misunderstood the American secretary of state. I say this as someone who has been a close friend of Kissinger's for the last decades of his life, and had many discussions with him about the Middle East. Reading Seale's pages, one realizes how little Washington really knows about Syria and Assad, a name that journalists in the American capital now identify with the far less substantial son, Bashar, rather than with the far more substantial father.

Hafez al-Assad was born in 1930 in a house of undressed stone in the Alawite mountains of northwestern Syria, one of his father's eleven children by two marriages. It was a family of peasants and minor village notables. He learned by rote in a rural school, and achieved the highest ambition by the standards of his environment: a career in military service, in an era when the recently departed French authorities had been promoting the Alawites and other minorities as a hedge against the dominant Sunnis. Seale writes of how this dreadfully narrow cultural and psychological universe in which Assad emerged led him in the early, violently unstable days of the Syrian republic to become a young coupist, negotiating tribal and ideological factionalism at its most brutal, and at its most intense and obscure within the armed forces.

Assad's innate caution and common sense manifested itself early in life. It is what separated him from all his more impulsive comrades and what ultimately would separate him from the barbaric nihilism of Iraq's Saddam Hussein decades later. Assad grasped politics early, unconsciously almost. He lacked any big ideas, the kind that allowed Anwar Sadat to captivate the Americans, but he did have a knack for espying other people's weaknesses and limitations, and at the same time seeing honestly his own constraints. That is, he quietly acquainted himself with a world of bitter truths and even worse options. In his thirties, he understood the pathetic disunity of the Arabs along with the complete strategic incoherence of the various Palestinian groups. As for Gamal Abdel Nasser, the romantic hero of Assad's youth, Assad quickly became aware of Nasser's tragic circumstances: despite Nasser's public bravado, stoked by the Arab masses demanding action of

him, the Egyptian leader knew that he lacked the military and technical means to defeat Israel. There was, too, Nasser's inability to deliver
any sort of victory to the Palestinians and his destructive war in Yemen,
battling tribesmen supported by Saudi Arabia. In fact, Nasser had
lived amid public adulation and private misery. All this, Assad intu-
ited. It was such realizations that gave Assad no illusions about himself
or his situation either. This would allow him to erect order where before there had only been chaos: the true mark of a Machiavellian
prince. Assad was remorselessly all business, and thus opaque and col-
orless to the outside world, a reason why the media dealt with him as
a fact of life, but no one to obsess about or become fascinated over.
Only Seale has succeeded in bringing him alive. Elie Kedourie, the
Iraqi Jewish analyst of the Middle East, with all of his bitterness
against the Arabs, and with all of his disdain for the worldview of
those like Seale, was known to have appreciated Assad's accomplishment.

A minority Alawite who kept Sunnis in powerful positions, Assad
had a personal distaste of ethnic politics, even as he was forced to practice it. He associated Syria's backward, amateurish political dealings
with bad Ottoman habits. His coup was preceded by a methodical
consolidation of power beforehand, so that no violence was necessary.
In Seale's meticulous telling, by Syria's chillingly bloody standard
Assad was rather a reluctant warrior, who in a better world and under
better circumstances might even have opted for the rule of law. As a
dictator, he was as moderate as the situation allowed for, while keeping
himself, his family, and his extended clan alive.

The truth was, Syria was a summation of dangerous parochial interests: of Sunni Arabs in the Damascus-Homs-Hama central corridor; heretical Shi'ite-trending Alawites in the mountains of the
northwest; of Druze in the south, with their close tribal links to Jordan; and of Kurds, Christian Arabs, Armenians, and Circassians in
Aleppo and beyond. In such a milieu, hatred of Israel offered an escape
from Syria's internal contradictions, allowing Syria a substitute for a
very weak national identity. For as Seale writes, Assad was "a man of

1967. The defeat inflicted by Israel made an indelible impression on him and in the agony of it was born his ambition to reach the top and to put things right."[16] But Assad's intransigence against the *Zionist entity*, his making of Syria the home of Arab "steadfastness" in the struggle with Israel—thus making Syria the *throbbing heart of Arabism*—never once made him trigger-happy.

Assad saw Israel as the impossible-to-swallow impediment preventing the restitution of Syria's rightful political influence within its natural geographical frontiers. Greater Syria, the story of an ambition, could live with a quasi-independent Lebanon and an implicitly subservient Jordan: Assad cared about real power more than he did about formalities. But Greater (or historic) Syria could not live with a non-Arab enemy state that was dominant rather than subservient. Israel would be tamed within Greater Syria or there could be no real peace, in his mind. Syria, though a Greek word, was after all the exalted *bilad al-Sham* in Arabic, "the nation of the Levant," the key Arab terrain after Mecca itself, which Allah had blessed above all nations, according to the Koran.[17] The Levant was synonymous with Syria more than with any other state in the eastern Mediterranean. Assad felt all of this in his bones.

But as a practical man who knew his own country's limitations, Assad forced himself into an alliance with Egypt's Sadat, a man he fundamentally distrusted. Assad's quiet, patient, and disciplined war planning paid off, though. This was not the Syrian banana republic of the 1967 war. The result was an impressively well executed surprise military attack by Syria and Egypt on Israel in October 1973. Yet, while Egypt's and Syria's immediate war aims were similar—to redeem Arab honor in the face of the 1967 humiliation—their political aims had always been different. For Egypt, the goal was simply to recover the Sinai Peninsula, taken by Israel in the 1967 war. Syria's goal, rather than limited like Egypt's, was all-encompassing. Syria needed to solve the Palestinian problem altogether. Not that Assad liked the Palestinian leadership; he despised it. But only by recovering Palestine in some legalistic manner could he make Greater (or historic) Syria whole again. It was also a matter of geography. Egypt was in North Africa; so

Palestine meant much less to Sadat than it did to Assad. Sadat understood that Nasser's tragedy—the reason his life ended in failure in the wake of the 1967 disaster—was not to execute a policy of limited aims.

It was Sadat's ability to recognize that Egypt had different interests than did the Arab world as a whole, and Kissinger's stark insight into what Sadat really wanted, that led to a political and emotional embrace between the two men. Excepting China's Zhou Enlai, I have never heard Henry Kissinger speak more tenderly of a foreign leader than he did of Anwar Sadat. Indeed, Kissinger always warmed up by a few degrees at the very mention of the Egyptian leader's name. The historical cliché—one adopted by Israel's friends in America—is that Kissinger had seen the 1973 war and Israel's initial battlefield losses as a useful turn of events, since it would force all parties to the conflict to require America's assistance to extricate themselves from it. There was a deeper truth, though. Kissinger saw an opportunity to decouple Egypt from the rest of the Arab struggle, thereby gaining a strategic victory for Israel while also forcing Syria to mend relations with the United States, for the sake of a disengagement of forces with Israel. Seale calls Kissinger the *"diabolus ex machina"* of the post-1973 war: the evil manipulator of events that robbed Syria and the Arab people of their rightful war victory. Of course, from Seale's pro-Syrian viewpoint Kissinger was just that. Still, Seale understands the essence of what Kissinger was able to accomplish for Israel and the United States perhaps better than did the pro-Israel community in Washington, which never felt altogether comfortable with Kissinger. (They always expected Kissinger to deliver a bit more for them.)*

Assad, according to Seale, saw most of this in a flash. And why shouldn't he have? Sadat had the luxury of his warmth and theatrics because Egypt was a more stable polity than Syria, and did not require the restitution of Palestine for its historical well-being. Assad, only three years into his rule in 1973, knew that he sat atop a political vol-

---

*   Martin Indyk's comprehensive study, *Master of the Game: Henry Kissinger and the Art of Middle East Diplomacy* (New York: Knopf, 2021), stands out as a deeply insightful elucidation of what Kissinger accomplished for all parties in the region.

cano in Syria, where one false move could mean the crumbling of his power base, even as he had no choice but to include Palestine in his war aims. Assad was made of hard, undressed stone—like the house he grew up in—because he had to be. He was the dry cynic whom journalists rarely find appealing and never make heroes of, but that didn't mean his analysis was flawed. To be sure, Assad proved to be right in the end: despite all the disadvantages of his situation, he survived to die a natural death; unlike Sadat, who despite all of his advantages and human qualities was assassinated.

Ever the self-disciplinarian, and also because he genuinely was fascinated with Kissinger, a Jew, Assad went out of his way to be polite in their meetings, even as he saw that Kissinger was threatening to turn his own strategic goals in Greater Syria upside down. The late Harold Saunders, a State Department official present at the meetings, remembers Assad telling Kissinger: "I profoundly disagree with your strategy. But I don't want it to affect our personal relations."[18]

Kissinger's shuttle diplomacy in 1974 resulted in a troop disengagement accord between Syria and Israel on the Golan Heights: an arrangement honored scrupulously by Assad, ever the realist, who understood his own limitations. Kissinger, in effect, had negotiated a de facto peace treaty between two sides that swore they were not at peace, a treaty that lasted until the Syrian civil war that began in 2011. Assad had been negotiating from a point of weakness, since Israeli columns were on the far side of the Golan Heights at the end of the 1973 war, threatening Damascus itself. He was nevertheless able to secure reasonable terms with his archenemy. Later, by diplomatically isolating Egypt following its 1979 peace treaty with Israel, and by making Syria the ally that the Palestinians were ultimately forced to rely on, Assad molded Syria into a pivotal regional power. In Seale's words, Assad made Syria "Israel's only remaining Arab opponent of any stature."[19] (Iraq, after all, the other Baʿathist rejectionist state, would be distracted throughout the 1980s in a war with Iran.)

In 1976, a year after the Lebanese civil war began, Assad (quietly encouraged behind the scenes by Kissinger and the Israelis) intervened on the side of the Christians against the Druze and Palestinians. It was a way for the Syrian leader, in vintage Machiavellian style, to exert dominance over a country that was part of Greater Syria, while also taming the Palestinians and Lebanese Sunni Arabs, who, left to their own devices, might very well have forced Syria into a war with Israel that it was not prepared to fight.

Assad truly defined an era in the Middle East, less because of all of the above than because of the way that he was able to keep a frightfully artificial and unstable country—at the region's very epicenter—relatively stable for decades. This would have been impossible had he any less emotional discipline, analytical rigor, and discriminating savagery than he did. The political geography of the Fertile Crescent is so illogical and tragic that it demands a ruler of absolute brilliance and (or) of absolute brutality as the admission price for stability.

For even Hafez al-Assad was barely able to keep Syria together.

In June 1979 at the artillery school in Aleppo, Sunni Muslim terrorists slaughtered thirty-two Alawite officer cadets and wounded another fifty-four.* A school staffer had assembled the cadets in the dining room and then let the gunmen inside. It was a declaration of war against Assad, an Alawite. For the next year, Sunni gunmen established themselves in the narrow alleyways of northern cities such as Aleppo and Hama, where they set fire to buildings, vehicles, and shops, and stirred up anti-regime demonstrations. They also staged strikes and assassinations in the name of erecting an Islamic state. By 1980, "Syria seemed close to an Islamic revolution," the Sunni equivalent of what had happened in Iran the year before, "as shops were closed to express support for the [Muslim] Brotherhood in all the major cities," writes Edward Mortimer, the British journalist and United Nations official.[20] At heart, the Sunnis felt that they had fared better under Ottoman imperial rather than under Ba'athist Alawite rule, as the Syrian Ba'ath, despite its pan-sectarian and pan-ethnic rhetoric, had basically evolved into a ruling party of minority groups.[21] Assad's intervention

---

* They may not have been all Alawis. A few might have been Christians and Sunni Muslims, according to Syrian government sources. Van Dam, *The Struggle for Power in Syria*, p. 106.

in Lebanon against the Sunnis and Palestinians only angered the Sunni Muslim Brotherhood in Syria all the more.

Initially, Assad found it difficult to face the truth: that all of his disciplined organizational skills over more than a decade had failed to preserve unity, and now the only way to stay alive and in power was to resort to abject barbarity—by now the effective language of Syrian political quarrels. To show that he meant business, the authorities ordered a military van to drive back and forth in front of Aleppo's best hotel dragging a knot of dusty bodies.[22] Assad's more ruthless and emotional younger brother, Rif'at, subsequently had risen to be the effective number two in the regime. Rif'at unleashed his own private praetorian guard, the infamous Brigades for the Defense of the Revolution. The violence spiraled upward. During the night of February 2–3, 1982, in the conservative Sunni city of Hama, Muslim Brothers crying *jihad* ("holy war") went on a looting and killing spree, murdering seventy men associated with Assad's Ba'athist regime. Hama had often been a hotbed of violent Sunni extremism going back to riots there in 1964, and now Assad had had enough. He and Rif'at ordered the city sealed off, and dispatched 12,000 government troops assisted by helicopters into the kill zone: for three weeks shelling and starving out insurgents and civilians alike, slaughtering as many as 20,000, perhaps even more. This heinous act, so out of proportion to what was required, left a deep moral stain on the elder Assad's legacy in the West.

Assad had smashed the Sunni Muslim Brotherhood once and for all, but in the process he had strengthened the grip of his homicidal younger brother, whose private army went on to challenge Assad himself, nearly bringing the country to another civil war by 1984. The Ba'ath party, the People's Assembly, and the other institutions of state proved useless in this power struggle. Alas, behind the curtain there was no state after all, just a mafia-style network of crime and patronage. Assad operated as an almost supernaturally gifted medieval prince in a world that he could manipulate for the relative good, but had little possibility of fundamentally improving.

Assad eventually exiled Rif'at and restored stability. But though Assad had proved brave beyond any measure in attacking Israel in

1973, in siding with the Christians against his own Muslims in Lebanon in 1976, and in breaking with Arab solidarity by establishing an alliance with Iran, despite all of his skills he simply could not make Syria into a modern polity. His people had remained subjects, and never became citizens. As a minority Alawite in a country that had little identity except as a vague geographical expression, and was a hornet's nest of tribes and sectarian and ethnic groups, he had all he could do merely to retain control.

Assad's life is critical to an understanding of how the Greater Middle East has oscillated between empire and anarchy, with issues of democracy and authoritarianism of distinctly secondary significance. With the French empire in Syria extinguished in 1946, Syria teetered on the brink of anarchy until 1970. It was only Assad's extraordinary and unequaled talents as a leader that staved off the next bout of anarchy, which would erupt under his son, Bashar, in 2011. In fact, the elder Assad's life and struggles, and the failed elections and other futile attempts at stability that preceded his nonviolent coup of 1970, constitute the ugly facts on the ground that those in the West who blithely believed that democracy was the answer to Syria's problems utterly and willfully ignored.

Bashar al-Assad was never meant to be the ruler of Syria. Educated at home and abroad as a medical doctor, he was placed in the line of succession only after the death of his older brother, Bassel, in a car accident. Bassel was the hard and somewhat reckless military man who was supposed to have succeeded his father. To be sure, Bassel was strong in ways that Bashar was weak. Bashar came to power because, being Assad's son, he in his very person formed the only point of solidarity for Syria's competing factions of military and intelligence chiefs. Bashar's first impulse upon the death of his father was to liberalize the system, allowing more freedom of expression in society. But because changing such a system entails more risks than preserving the status quo, and because his military and security advisers—as well as a thoroughly corrupt business establishment tied to the Assads by marriage—were opposed to liberalization in any case, Bashar quickly retreated into his authoritarian shell. As for the Arab Spring, it quickly opened the door to anarchy in Syria, with dozens of competing armed guerrilla groups forming within a matter of weeks and months after the first anti-regime demonstrations. I suspect the utter brutality of the regime's response to this internal challenge was driven less by Bashar's personal evil than by his own weakness—his inability to control the behavior of the byzantine security structure just below him—and the fact that Syria, under the carapace of tyranny, was really a writhing nest of anarchy all along: it was only the elder Assad's brilliance that for decades had kept the place relatively peaceful.

No doubt, the father when grooming the son for power stressed the need to be strong (read *violent*) when the situation demanded it. And very likely the son at many junctures during the civil war believed that he was merely living up to the example set by his father in Hama. Bashar's mother, Anisa Makhlouf, who died in 2016 and had been married to the elder Assad for forty-three years, reportedly encouraged Bashar to demonstrate an extremely tough response to his enemies. The elder Assad had mastered the art of survival, and had given his country relative peace for three decades. "[The elder] Assad staves off the future," I wrote in *The Atlantic* in 1993. "It is Assad, not Saddam Hussein or any other ruler, who defines the era in which the Middle East now lives. And [the elder] Assad's passing may herald more chaos than a chaotic region has seen in decades."[23] Indeed, to what ultimate purpose was always the question about his rule, given the manifold increase in abject cruelty required by his son merely to keep the father's creation together.

THE WASHINGTON FOREIGN POLICY establishment generally believed that had the Obama administration intervened quickly in the early years of the Syrian civil war it might have reestablished order, erected a more liberal regime, and wrested Syria from an Iranian grip. I am skeptical that this was ever a possibility.* The descent from a se-

---

* Former White House coordinator for the Middle East Philip Gordon makes the same point. Philip H. Gordon, *Losing the Long Game: The False Promise of Regime Change in the Middle East* (New York: St. Martin's Press, 2020), p. 205.

ries of peaceful demonstrations to a violent and complex sectarian conflict happened in a matter of weeks and months, not years.[24] America's monumental failure to rebuild Iraq in its own image, even as Iraq is next door to Syria and also Ba'athist, should have served as a lesson about American military intervention in complex Islamic societies. Nevertheless, significant elements of America's post–Cold War foreign policy establishment saw the rest of the world, especially the Middle East, as a mere extension of their own personal experience systems: as though the American history of freedom were more relevant to Syria and Iraq than Syria's and Iraq's own histories. Many in the Washington elite were obsessed with abstract ideals about democracy and human rights and therefore discounted the actual record of the past in specific places. In any case, one-man-one-vote in the context of an intense Sunni-Shi'ite regional rivalry was often about entrenching one group over another through the tyranny of the majority. Tellingly, in the whole Washington foreign policy debate over Syria—a place where elections would merely have legalized Sunni domination—the history that I have recounted in these pages went virtually unmentioned and remained relatively unkown.

The great mid-twentieth-century Spanish philosopher José Ortega y Gasset wrote, "Breaking the continuity with the past, wanting to begin again, is a lowering of man and a plagiarism of the orangutan."[25] Precisely because a long memory is given to man, to reject that godsend means to reduce man to the level of the beasts. Never was this truer than in some of the arguments put forward about remaking Syria, as well as remaking Iraq and Libya.

SYRIA'S TRAGEDY IS THAT its people yearned to have no borders at all between the Taurus Mountains, the Nefud desert, and the Euphrates; and to be ethnic and sectarian communities under some distant and benign sovereign, sort of a postmodern version of the Ottoman Empire, for which collapse they and others throughout the Middle East have never found an adequate solution. Given this reality, various futures now remain open. For example, were Bashar al-Assad's Alawite regime in Damascus ever to collapse, as many Western elites doubtlessly hope, the Syria-Lebanon border could be effectively erased as Sunnis from both sides of the border united and Syria's Alawites gathered in the northwest to form pockets of resistance. None of this would be peaceful, of course. The only recourse would be the equivalent of imperial rule from the outside, which would require a measure of toughness that American officialdom is naturally unwilling to countenance—though the Turks, Iranians, and until recently the Russians certainly are willing. Given our own limitations, we have no solution for Syria. We never had.

I'LL NEVER FORGET MY first visit to Greater Syria in 1976. I was young and of course did not conceive of it as such at the time, thinking of it as Syria, Jordan, Israel, and so on. But I do remember the effect that its borderlands had on me. Syria's southern border with Jordan was a crude highway toll station in the midst of a featureless plateau on both sides: an artificial creation of man. The border with the Israeli-occupied West Bank was merely a narrow stream with a grand biblical name, the Jordan River: another rather artificial border. But I do remember being awestruck by the dramatic sight of the Euphrates River at Raqqah in eastern Syria, after a long bus ride across a desert wilderness from Aleppo. That was a border! For the opposite bank marked the end of Greater Syria and the beginning of Mesopotamia, though I was still deep within Syria's legal borders. Finally, nothing in that months-long odyssey in the spring and summer of 1976 affected me as much as the first sight of the Arabian desert deep inside Jordan. I had been hitchhiking from Amman south to Aqaba. The flat, gravelly plateau continued monotonously for hours. Then the plateau suddenly ended. Hundreds of meters below as I peered over a ledge, extending to the horizon, was a howling sandy wilderness punctuated by steeply rising mountains of red and coppery-black rock, with a heat film veiling the vista like a thin curtain. This was Ras al Naqab, the beginning of the true Arabian desert. It was where Greater Syria in a strict geographical sense ended; just as it had ended on the Euphrates, and just as it had ended in the southern foothills of Turkey's Taurus Mountains. Jordan and Israel, as brilliant as they were as political and modern historical creations, be damned: the geography told another story. The problem was that the Syrians of the postcolonial era took that Abrahamic geography quite literally: as their own patrimony. And that was always the master key to the bloody politics of Damascus.

IRAQ, COMPARED TO SYRIA, was always the harder political riddle to solve. Iraq was even more artificial than Syria, and therefore its politics were even more brutal. Because anarchy was always closer to the surface in Iraq, the tyranny was always worse there than in Syria. The Fertile Crescent grants no respite.

In March 1984, when I first visited Iraq, Saddam International Airport, built by a French-led consortium, was only two years old. The gleaming and futuristic new terminal featured what was then state-of-the-art Islamic semi-domes, constructed with various metals. Everywhere there were monstrously sized photographs of the dictator, Saddam Hussein, peering down on you, larger and more ubiquitous than in any other Arab dictatorship with which I was acquainted first-hand. You knew instinctively not to be caught staring at these watchful, monolithic photographs, as men whose eyes were like icy black voids, wearing dark bulging suits, holding half-concealed weapons, were all over the arrivals hall, observing the passengers. By 1984, I had been back and forth to Hafez al-Assad's Syria several times. Yet I was unprepared for the paranoia and repression that I felt in my throat and in my stomach my first moments in Iraq, and which never left me there. The Dutch-Lebanese journalist Kim Ghattas has likened Saddam's rule to "a block of concrete" upon people's chests.[26]

Syria of the mid-1970s, with its fresh plateau breezes, glittering bazaars, panoramic archaeological sites drenched in primary colors, new Mercedes buses connecting the towns, and welcoming inquisitiveness toward strangers—an atmospheric equivalent to Israel, crazy as it sounds—was now a distant memory. Syria's ambience lived up to its historical billing as a broad vista of sects and trade routes and civilizations. Now I pushed open the window of my luxury hotel-prison room in Baghdad: the air was dense, suffocating, with the smell of dung and dried mud from the nearby Tigris. Mud is always thick in the air here, refined by the breezes generated by the river, and breathed into your nostrils as dust. Because there were no hills or mountains as in Syria, there was no landscape. Morning revealed clusters of cinderblock storefronts with crude sheet-metal signs in Arabic, connected by new modern highways. Oil booms propagate ugliness. The city was packed with contract workers from Pakistan, Egypt, the Philippines, and so on, wearing blank expressions in the hotels and on construction sites. Alienating monumental architecture like dragon's teeth breaking into the sky celebrated the greatness of the dictator. There was no humanity, or even history, in any of it. The sense of impending violence was everywhere. And this was to say nothing of the long, machine-gun-guarded walls of the presidential palace. I remember what a Saudi who had lived all over the Fertile Crescent told me: "Iraqis are from rough Bedouin stock; whereas Syrians were often Lebanese-style merchants."

I was one of about two or three dozen Western journalists granted visas to Iraq at that moment, and one of only a handful of Americans, in order to observe the battle front of the ongoing Iran-Iraq War. Oil and war defined the country, driving out other realities. Because both Iran and Iraq had toppled their monarchies and created revolutionary states within twenty years of each other, the war was that much more bitter.[27] Saddam's Iraq was not Assad's Syria, where I had always journeyed around the country myself, filed my stories by telex at local post offices, and met and talked with people wherever I found them. Here regime *minders* escorted us nearly everywhere, and my articles were read and typed up by an official utilizing a telex machine, behind a plate-glass window.

The elite media and Washington establishment, then as now, have often been guilty of creating simplistic, black-and-white categories: dictatorships and democracies, moderates and radicals, pro-American and pro-Soviet regimes. Iraq and Syria were then—and through the turn of the twenty-first century—lumped together as radical Ba'athist dictatorships, each equally repressive. This was a narrow version of the truth. As a journalist, I usually saw regimes in various shades of gray, covering the spectrum from Western democracies at one end and to-talitarian dictatorships at the other end. Autocracy was never an enemy for me: merely a broad category in an incredibly varied world, with liberal autocrats like in Oman and evil ones like in North Korea. And in that spirit, I found Saddam's Iraq crucially different from the elder Assad's Syria.

It was first a matter of geography, and then a matter of personality.

Whereas Syria bordered the Mediterranean, and thus harbored a cosmopolitan thread throughout much of its history, softening its des-ert aspect, Iraq was decisively inland. It was always a harder, less-forgiving country. All of this is relative, of course. I am only talking about these countries in relation to each other: for to travel from Sad-dam Hussein's Baghdad to Hafez al-Assad's Damascus in the 1980s, as I did, was always to experience a much greater degree of freedom, as pathetic as this may seem.

ADAM AND EVE, IT turns out, did not live in a garden paradise, but in a turgid mud swamp. The Tigris and the Euphrates "flow with such a low gradient that they meander considerably and throw numerous side-branches," creating many "lakes and swamps," interspersed with "dreary wastes strewn with dry wadis and salt lakes," writes Georges Roux, the twentieth-century French historian of the Near East. The ancient Mesopotamian settlements "were built of nothing but mud."[28] Then there is the British travel writer Robert Byron's description of Iraq from 1933: "It is a mud plain ... From this plain rise villages of mud and cities of mud. The rivers flow with liquid mud."[29] But keep in mind that this swamp has the bone-dry climate of a desert that is constantly cracking the mud and turning it into fine dust, with blisters of salt deposits. Roux notes that temperatures in Mesopotamia, from prehistory onward, reach 120 degrees in summer, and the average annual rainfall is under ten inches, most of which comes all at once in the early spring, causing devastating floods.[30]

However, since all of the land for hundreds of miles to the west, until the Mediterranean Sea, and all of the land for over 1,500 miles to the east, until the Indian subcontinent, is essentially riverless, rainless desert and mountains, this dreary artery of mud was where ancient civilization could at least develop; and thus it formed the backbone of the Fertile Crescent.

But the valley of the Tigris and Euphrates, contrary to what is taught in Sunday school classes, did not exactly prosper, despite being the assumed mother of civilization. The two rivers and the land between them, *Mesopotamia*, were never unified in the way of the Nile Valley in Egypt. Roux explains that since antiquity the Nile had an "annual flood of almost constant volume," with "the great lakes of East Africa acting as regulators." Because the Nile "freely inundates the valley for a time and then withdraws," it required only the "cheap and easy 'basin type' of irrigation," where canal slits were dug and men simply waited for them to fill up with Nile water. But the Tigris and Euphrates have no great lakes at their source to regulate their floods. They are two rivers instead of one, with the Tigris born in the snows of Kurdistan and the Euphrates flowing down from the mountains of Armenia. Moreover, their flooding occurs too late for the winter crops and too soon for the summer ones. Alas, irrigation in Mesopotamia has always been a drudgery involving reservoirs, dikes, and regulator sluices. And unlike Egypt, nothing is guaranteed. Drought, famine, and high waters sweeping away the mud-brick houses have been the regular stuff of history here. Roux writes that these unfortunate natural conditions have bred a "fundamental pessimism" among Iraq's inhabitants.[31]

This pessimism grew not only out of the perennial struggle of men against nature, but also out of the struggle of men against other men— another thing that existed less in Egypt. Freya Stark writes, "While Egypt lies parallel and peaceful to the routes of human traffic, Iraq is from earliest times a frontier province, right-angled and obnoxious to the predestined paths of man."[32] That is because the Nile has always been a natural migration route, with the invasions it suffered relatively few and therefore well remembered—those of the Hyksos, Alexander, and Napoleon. But Iraq was rarely left alone. From the west came Amorites, Hittites, and medieval Umayyad armies; from the east came Aryan Kassites, Achaemenid and Sassanid Persians, Mongols, and so forth, culminating in the forces of Iran's Ayatollah Khomeini at the time of my first visit there. And all this is to say nothing of the nomadic pastoralists who perennially migrated north from Nejd in Arabia to infiltrate Mesopotamia, which offered no natural barriers of defense.[33]

Iraq was not only more prone to invasion than Egypt, it was also less demographically and culturally cohesive. In ancient Egypt, all power lay with a single king, whereas Mesopotamia was a land of city-states.[34] Though it has been sometimes assumed that Iraq is an organic outgrowth of ancient civilizations—Sumer, Akkad, Assyria, Babylonia—each of these civilizations that encompassed part of present-day Iraq was often at war with the other parts: Sumerians of southern Mesopotamia fought Akkadians of central Mesopotamia, Assyrians fought Babylonians, and so forth. Throughout antiquity three basic splits predominated: between the mountain people in the north, usually Kurds; the people of central Mesopotamia, around Baghdad; and those of southern Mesopotamia near the Persian Gulf. The birth of Islam in the seventh century A.D. only hardened these divisions.

Islam, with its subsequent fissures, transformed the divide between central and southern Mesopotamia from a vaguely historical and regional one into a specific sectarian one, since the region around Baghdad is overwhelmingly Sunni, while the south is overwhelmingly Shi'ite. The difference here between the histories of Syria and Iraq is suggestive. Just as the golden age of Damascus is associated with the seventh- and eighth-century Umayyad caliphate, the golden age of Baghdad is associated with the succeeding Abbasid caliphate of the eighth through thirteenth centuries. As the first Arab dynasty, the Umayyads, who borrowed artistically from the Hellenistic and Byzantine epochs, governed mainly at a time when the Sunni-Shi'ite split was still not quite the structural and formal one it later became, whereas the later Abbasids, owing to the proximity of Iran, were heavily Persianized (though the Abbasid dynasty itself was officially Sunni). Thus, Iraq, located at the geographical frontier of the Sunni world, hard up against the plateau and mountains of Iran with its strong Shi'ite influence, since the Middle Ages has experienced a level of sectarian tensions unknown to Syria, whose Shi'a-trending Alawites were usually bottled up in the mountainous northwest of the country.

The Mongols under Hulagu, a grandson of Genghis Khan, overran Baghdad in February 1258, reducing the Abbasid capital to ashes and exterminating much of the population. The Mongols destroyed the irrigation system, leaving a malarial swamp. Later, Mesopotamia became a battleground of Sunni Ottoman Turkey and Shi'ite Safavid Persia. When the Persian Shi'ites captured Baghdad and its surroundings in 1623–24, thousands of Sunnis were killed and the Sunni mosques destroyed. Fifteen years later, the Ottoman sultan, Murad IV, captured the city and slaughtered thousands of Shi'ites. After a 280-year uneasy Ottoman sleep, the British wrested away Mesopotamia in another sideshow of World War I. The British found a place that, even more than Syria, was a region rather than a country: one with sharp and binary divisions even worse than Syria's. And by attaching the oil-rich Kurdish mountains in the north to this divided land of Mesopotamia, the British had created a truly tense and combustible polity in an historically grim and brutal setting. The fact that *Iraq* is an Arabic term for "well-rooted" was especially ironic.

Britain poured money, schoolteachers, and technical know-how into Iraq in the early and mid twentieth century, which, by making it more economically and politically dynamic, only made it more volatile, as the dynamism created ethnic and sectarian elites that were always pulling in different directions. Because of its artificiality as a state, even more artificial than Syria, Baghdad was perennially more antagonistic to Israel than even Damascus, since anti-Zionism served as a unifying cause: the ultimate rejectionist state, in other words, even if Iraq's lack of proximity to Israel made it less relevant than Syria. A British spy once described Egyptian president Gamal Abdel Nasser's hatred of

Iraq as "almost pathological," for you couldn't find two Arab peoples as different from each other as Egyptians and Iraqis.[35] Whereas Egypt was always a unitary state and civilization that was more easily governed, the American political scientist Michael C. Hudson, on the eve of Saddam Hussein formally coming to power in Baghdad in the late 1970s, would prophetically call Iraq "the archetypical overloaded political system."[36]

The relentlessly chaotic decades of the mid and late twentieth century that set the stage for Saddam's rule provided further demonstration that there was never really any stable middle ground for Iraq. That part of Iraq's history will be dealt with in the next chapter, for it forms a story all its own. While Hafez al-Assad wrought a respite of thirty years for Syria's sustained crisis of governability, Saddam Hussein Abd al-Majid al-Tikriti—to give him his full tribal and regional name—offered, instead, a thermonuclear-style summation of all Mesopotamia's violent tendencies reaching deep into the Mesopotamian past.

IT WAS LENIN ACTUALLY, before Stalin, who pioneered the notion of the totalitarian state, in which there was no private space for the individual. Lenin also understood, again before Stalin, that it was necessary to murder and incarcerate the innocent. For how else could a dictator inculcate total fear in the population? To punish only the guilty would provide the innocent, who constitute most of the population, with peace of mind. And that, of course, would undermine the sort of control that Lenin believed was necessary.[37]

Saddam Hussein was no different.

Of peasant background, he had risen as a young coupist through the murderous labyrinth of Iraqi politics. But unlike Assad, rather than demonstrate a watchful restraint, Saddam was an outright thug, with a direct role in violence and assassination attempts. He also had a gift for organization: that is, he could intimidate large groups of people to do things for him. And he was a Ba'ath party leader in a country where such nationalist socialist ideology was both a platform for modernization and a veneer for coercion and criminality. In 1968, he helped engineer a coup that brought his Tikriti cousin, Ahmed Hassan al-Bakr, to power. Saddam became al-Bakr's unofficial number two, and was effective in two broad areas: modernizing the country through, among other things, the seizure of foreign oil revenues; and the expansion of the security services in order to eliminate regime rivals. By 1976, with al-Bakr ailing, Saddam became the unofficial ruler of Iraq. In 1979, his dictatorship became formal. At this point, he might have become the equivalent of Assad in Syria: a Ba'ath socialist ruler who could solve the country's chronic instability by a mixture of methodical planning, the exercise of extreme caution, and the discriminate use of violence at key moments. But Iraq wasn't Syria and Saddam wasn't Assad. (Indeed, the Ba'ath parties of Syria and Iraq were continually at odds and plotting against each other.) Saddam, actually, was more like Lenin.

On July 22, 1979, six days after officially replacing al-Bakr as president of Iraq, Saddam convened a meeting of Ba'ath party leaders, which he ordered videotaped and which is available on YouTube. Seated onstage, calmly smoking a Cuban cigar given to him by Fidel Castro, Saddam announced that much to his sadness, sixty-six party leaders had been uncovered as traitors and constituted a fifth column. As each name was read out, guards grabbed a baffled and shocked man from his seat and forced him out of the auditorium. At the end of this seemingly endless process, those still seated, white with both fear and relief, spontaneously leapt to their feet shouting undying loyalty to Saddam. Of the sixty-six named, twenty-two were quickly ordered executed by firing squads composed of other Ba'ath party leaders, thus implicating the whole senior Ba'ath officialdom in the bloodshed, even though the evidence against the accused ranged from the flimsy to the nonexistent. By August, hundreds more Ba'ath officials, guilty or innocent, were executed. Wider purges followed that autumn.[38] The country now was literally Saddam's. He had achieved total fear.

It is estimated that in the twenty-four years of Saddam's official rule, 250,000 Iraqis were murdered: a result of execution, torture, poison gas, ethnic cleansing, and so forth.[39] In other Middle Eastern countries, torture and executions take place. In Iraq, they were systemic and practiced on an industrial scale. All of this violence does not include the Iran-Iraq War, which Saddam started with an invasion of the oil-rich Iranian province of Khuzestan in September 1980, and which took the lives of many hundreds of thousands of soldiers on both sides. This war was no abstraction to me. On one visit to the front, two hours north of Basrah in the Howizeh Marshes straddling the Iraq-Iran border, I saw hundreds of bodies of dead Iranian teenage soldiers, floating like dolls in the water, without wounds, the victims of Iraqi poison gas attacks. Finches, wagtails, and a few water buffaloes were the only living things.[40]

When Saddam invaded Kuwait in August 1990 exactly two years after the conclusion of the Iran-Iraq War, Assad was said to have quipped about Saddam: he is like a chain smoker, as soon as he ends one war he has to start another one.* Assad, of course, during the decades of his rule, studiously avoided war with Israel, except when in 1973 he had made a deliberate plan of attack coordinated with the Egyptians.

Notable though not unusual among Saddam's depredations, given the Iraqi Arab hatred of the disruptive Kurds, was the 1988 Anfal genocide, which included the use of sarin, mustard gas, and nerve agents against tens of thousands of Kurdish women, children, and elderly persons.[41] In a related incident that year, Iraqi authorities returned fifty-seven boxes to the Kurdish city of Sulaymaniyah. Each box contained a dead child, with its eyes gouged out and blood drained from its body. The families were forced to accept a communal grave and pay individually for their child's burial.[42]

Taha Yassin Ramadan, one of Iraq's vice presidents, was typical of the men whom Saddam handpicked to surround him. When Ramadan was appointed the minister of industry in the 1970s, he reportedly said: "I don't know anything about industry. All I know is that anyone

---

* There was no love lost between the two rival Ba'athist regimes. As Iraqi defense minister Adnan Khairullah, Saddam's brother-in-law, told me and other reporters in Baghdad, "We are not sorry we have our differences with Hafez Assad. If he sends us a bomb in a box, we do the same." Robert D. Kaplan, "Only the Names Change in Long Iraqi-Syrian Feud," *Atlanta Journal-Constitution*, March 11, 1984.

who doesn't work hard will be executed." In January 1991, five months after Iraq invaded and occupied Kuwait, Ramadan threatened to mutilate anyone investigating Iraqi human rights abuses there. Ramadan, an ethnic Kurd loyal to Saddam, was instrumental in the gassing of five thousand Kurdish civilians in Halabja in 1988.[43]

Then there was Saddam's half brother, Barzan Ibrahim al-Tikriti, who ran the intelligence service. Barzan had gotten it into his head that an American, Robert Spurling, a technician for the luxury Novotel in Baghdad, was a spy. While boarding a flight to Paris with his Belgian wife and three daughters in June 1983, Spurling was seized by the secret police. Over the next 110 days, Spurling later testified to Amnesty International, "electric shocks were applied to my hands, feet, kidney region, genitals and above all, to my ears." He was beaten with rubber truncheons and threatened with mutilation. But he considered himself lucky, since he had regularly to listen to the cries and screams of those in other cells undergoing torture. He was released in the months prior to the resumption of diplomatic relations between Iraq and the United States. (Iraq was fighting Iran, America's archenemy at the time, and so policy was necessarily cynical.) I first heard the story about Spurling from a Canadian diplomat during my visit to Baghdad in March 1984. A few days later I had it confirmed by the late William Eagleton, then the chief U.S. diplomat in Iraq. Spurling had recuperated in Eagleton's residence after his release from prison the previous October. Eagleton told me that the idea of Spurling being a spy was utter nonsense.[44]

Spurling's was only one case among literally more than a million, but it was illustrative. It was the kind of thing that simply never happened to Americans in the elder Assad's Syria. The differences between the two Ba'athist regimes were undeniably extreme for those like me peering deep into the weeds of both countries. Remember that there was a time in the 1980s and 1990s when liberals and neoconservatives alike were employing terms like *appeasement* and *never again* in their livid reactions to America's decision to reestablish and then maintain formal diplomatic relations with Saddam's regime. I had published a book in 1993 about the State Department's Arabists who I suggested were "cowering in a dark alley" when it came to their dealings with Saddam.[45]

But this only reveals an especially unappealing truth: crying "appeasement" was actually naïve when dealing with Saddam's regime, since Iraqis later experienced bloodcurdling atrocities on a scale that only Saddam himself could have contemplated—as hundreds of thousands more died as a consequence of the 2003 American and British invasion. Perhaps, given Mesopotamia's geography and history, it literally took Saddam's "procrustean totalitarianism," in the words of one analyst, to keep order, however hideous that order was, for decades in Iraq.[46] Otherwise, anarchy reigned. Truly, Iraq, even more so than Syria, provided the ultimate stage set for the seventeenth-century English philosopher Thomas Hobbes, who believed that without a *Leviathan* to monopolize power, there was no one to keep order—and to keep all men from killing all other men. It was a realization, however imperfect, that would destroy my peace of mind in the years following Saddam's overthrow. For the Arabists whom I had criticized turned out to be far wiser than myself and many others.

FERTILE CRESCENT

═══

PART II

─

"Ever since the nineteenth century, when so-called reforms
were initiated in the Ottoman Empire, there have not been
wanting western ministers and diplomats to look on middle
eastern politics with hope and expectancy. It is quite common
knowledge that in the last hundred years the middle east has
seen no quiet, that disturbance has succeeded disturbance . . . It
might therefore seem more prudent to assume that the distem-
per of the modern east is not a passing one, that its political
instability is rather the outcome of a deep social . . . crisis which
the schemes of the reformer . . . can scarcely assuage or mollify.
And yet . . . the prevalent fashion has been to proclaim the latest revolution as the herald of a new day . . ."[1]

This polemic goes on like that for almost four hundred pages, in
which virtually every detail of political turmoil in Egypt, Syria, and
Iraq and every Western failure there since the late Ottoman Empire to
the middle Cold War years is excruciatingly recounted, with virtually
every large-scale cruelty established, with little respite, so that all the
violence and turbulence achieves a thick, undeniable reality that no
idealism or social science theory can ameliorate; with the only solution

to anarchy appearing to be strong, no-nonsense rule: whether by a local dictator or by an imperial power. The writer, Elie Kedourie, who passed away in 1992, published *The Chatham House Version and Other Middle-Eastern Studies*—perhaps the most challenging, dissident work of area studies in the twentieth century—well over half a century ago. Chatham House or the Royal Institute of International Affairs and its director of studies for three decades, Arnold Toynbee, become in Kedourie's book illustrative of an elitist British sentimentality toward the cultures of the Middle East (and to Arab nationalism in particular) that hid from, rather than faced up to, the impure, realist requirements of politics and necessary force.

But Elie Kedourie's merciless precision as a slayer of cant and formulaic thinking constitutes much more than a switchblade attack on polite, conventional wisdom about the Middle East. Kedourie, who spoke English, French, and Arabic, was an area specialist as significant as the greatest Arabists and foreign correspondents. But unlike most area specialists, he wrote without sympathy for his subjects, and deliberately so, and at the same time intuitively grasped the subtleties and abstractions of intellectual argument that his writing ignited. Kedourie was an intellectual with a deep historical memory. He forgot nothing. He was equipped with the knowledge base of a reporter, that is, he revered facts on the ground going back decades as a way to refute all theory. This combination of skills, as we shall see, gave him the clairvoyance of a Samuel Huntington or a John Mearsheimer.* Most significantly, he had an old world integrity that is awe-inspiring in this age of rampant credentialism. At twenty-eight, in 1954, he turned down a doctorate from St. Antony's College, Oxford, because he would not make changes to a passage in his thesis about a Mesopotamian revolt to appease one of his examiners, the great orientalist Sir Hamilton Gibb.

Therefore, at this juncture I want to pause and consider Elie Ke-

---

* Huntington's *Political Order in Changing Societies* (1968) foresaw many of the problems in the developing world, just as his essay "The Clash of Civilizations?" (1993) foresaw the era beginning with 9/11. Mearsheimer's *The Tragedy of Great Power Politics* (2001) foresaw China in the starkest terms as the future great power rival of the United States.

dourie, whose lifework both explores and sums up the extreme difficulty of moderate governance in the Fertile Crescent. Kedourie may
have been cynical and even condescending regarding the Arab world.
Again, the fact that he wrote without sympathy is problematic, since
as we know from the anthropologist Clifford Geertz and so many others, each culture makes sense within its own domain and therefore has
to be taken seriously. Nevertheless, because Kedourie's work constitutes such a bracing challenge to received expert opinion, we ignore
him at our peril.

Kedourie was a shy, retiring man with backbone. "A short, wintry
smile from him was the equivalent of a warm embrace or a slap on the
back from many others," recalls Martin Sieff, former chief news analyst for United Press International.[2] "Austere . . . in manner," and with
a smile that had "finality about it," was how the British author David
Pryce-Jones described him.[3] Kedourie didn't even socialize with his
students at the London School of Economics. In our current age of sly
operators with media strategies, who appear on television and master
the art of soundbites and TED talks, Kedourie by contrast communi-
cated almost exclusively through text. Only by reading him at length
could one know how he has politely decimated, with a "potent and
lucid" style, all manner of "leftist theory" and social science belief about
the Middle East, writes Martin Kramer, founding president of the
Shalem College in Jerusalem.[4]

Elie Kedourie grew up in a prominent Jewish family in Baghdad,
and as a fifteen-year-old schoolboy witnessed close-up the June 1941
pogrom known as the *Farhud* ("Looting"), in which the Iraqi army and
police murdered over 180 Jewish men, women, and children, and raped
countless Jewish women. The Farhud came after the British Army had
put down a local military coup that sought to align Iraq with Nazi
Germany. The British, in order to appease the Arab population afterwards, let the Iraqi army and police vent their frustration by going wild
for several days. Kedourie, in *The Chatham House Version*, blames the
British authorities for failing to protect the Jews, despite having taken
over responsibility for Mesopotamia from the Ottoman Empire in the
aftermath of World War I. He writes that the Jews could "cheerfully

acknowledge" the "right of conquest," whether exercised by the Otto-mans or by the British, because "their history had taught them that there lay safety."⁵ But the British failure to enforce the law and provide imperial order was the kind of transgression that religious and ethnic minorities could ill afford, he goes on. After all, the multiethnic Otto-man and Habsburg empires, with their deeply rooted cosmopolitan-ism, had protected minorities much better than the uniethnic states and democracies that replaced them. Kedourie thus (in this particular case, that is) argued for more imperialism, not less.

Kedourie's essential diagnosis of Great Britain's Arab policy in his lifetime was that the British Foreign Office's awe of an exotic culture, combined with the "snare"⁶ of a misunderstood familiarity toward English-speaking Arabs—who used the same words, but meant very different things when discussing such issues as rule of law and constitutions—led to a profound lapse of policy judgment. To this one must add guilt regarding the post–World War I border arrangements that allowed for, among other things, a Jewish national home in Pales-tine. In the minds of this naïve generation of British officials, once Zionism and imperialism could be done away with, the Arabs would enjoy peaceful and stable institutions.

More than half a century ago Kedourie countered with what has in recent decades become a commonplace, that neither imperialism nor Zionism was especially the problem. As he put it, it is only a "fashion-able western sentimentality which holds that Great Powers are nasty and small Powers virtuous."⁷ In any case, he continues, even without imperialism and Zionism, other outside powers would naturally work to involve themselves in this vast, energy-rich region as part of the normal course of history. The West was a problem, certainly, but in a different way than late British colonial officialdom and some of their American Cold War successor-acolytes had imagined it. As it turns out, Westernization and modernization, by introducing a measure of bureaucratic efficiency, were only amplifying the coercive, illiberal power of newly independent Arab regimes themselves. Consequently, the nascent Arab middle classes were even more dependent on the goodwill of those vicious new regimes than they had been on the colonial powers. Indeed, everything from import licenses to securing jobs to school admissions required a silent pact with the authorities. A quiet bargain was struck. And when oil wealth was suddenly added to the sociological fire of a pseudo-Westernizing Arab world, as Fouad Ajami (echoing V. S. Naipaul) explained: inhabitants of the great cities of the Middle East began experiencing the West only as "things" and not as "process"; importing the "fruits of science" without as societies producing them themselves.[8] The result were sophisticated milieus, West Beirut being one for a time, of "Western airs and anti-Western politics."[9]

The Arab youth were especially dangerous, Kedourie unsentimentally observes: full of "passion and presumption," they possessed the techniques of Europe without intuiting the centuries-long cultural processes that had made Europe what it was. They hated their fathers' world, and envisioned utopia rather than civil society with all of its messy backtracking, compromises, and checks and balances. Thus, they paved the way for replacing Arab nationalism with Islamic fundamentalism—a phenomenon of a rapidly urbanizing Middle East, where the traditions of the village have been weakened and must be fortified anew, amid anonymous crowds of strangers, in more abstract and ideological form.

Of course, though Kedourie won't admit it, something similar might be said about many Jews in mandatory Palestine, who favored violent, terrorist militias—it seems that every group and sect and ethnicity became inflamed and radicalized as new artificial boundaries arose from the dust of the Ottoman Empire.

FOLLOWING THE COLLAPSES OF several major Arab states, the despair with which the class of Middle East experts in Washington has viewed the region in recent years is one that Kedourie arrived at long ago, and not cynically: rather, through painstaking historical research. In *The Chatham House Version* and a companion volume, *Democracy and Arab Political Culture*, Kedourie narrates the intricate daily political maneuvering over the course of a century in several Arab regions, exposing a politics unsurpassed in its unceasing and often violent disorder, in which once the Ottoman Empire with its caliphate crumbled, leaving an Islamic world without a recognized religious authority, various groups and factions and ideologies competed for which one could be the most pure: that is, the most extreme. Today's problems are old problems, going back to the decades of Ottoman decline, with the realization that the Middle East from Algeria to Iraq has still not found a solution to the final collapse of the Turkish sultanate in 1922.

Constitutionalism was variously and continuously attempted in nineteenth- and twentieth-century Egypt, as we know. The de facto British rulers welcomed this, wanting to lessen the burden of daily governance for themselves. For decades they tried. But they could rarely make it work. The modernizing Khedive Ismail in 1868 had set up a parliamentary assembly in Cairo. But such stillborn attempts at Westernization ultimately ran up against a blunt fact that still persists, albeit in far more subtle form, almost 150 years later during the Arab Spring of 2011: the vast gap between a peasantry and barely literate downtrodden underclass at the edge of the cities and a Westernized class of enlightened would-be reformers. The mass demonstrations in Tahrir Square against the regime of Hosni Mubarak were 1848 all over again: that year of hope-filled liberal risings in Europe that ultimately failed because the educated classes demanding change were just not quite large enough and not quite secure enough to carry the day.

All of this is implied in Kedourie's book *Democracy and Arab Political Culture*, published in 1992 by the Washington Institute for Near East Policy (one of the rare occasions when a think tank produces an enduring work of not merely policy, but intellectual merit). This small, densely argued, and deeply researched book presents a debilitating saga of regional, sectarian, and ethnic divisions that combine with feudalism, tribal conflicts, and illiteracy to make orderly constitutional progress in Egypt and the artificial states of the Fertile Crescent impossible—all of them being rough equivalents of Cold War Lebanon with its on-again, off-again violence, in which democracy for too long has reflected, rather than alleviated, the region's bloody communal divides.

THE PAN-ISLAMISM OF THE Ottoman Empire would in part give way to the pan-Arabism of the twentieth century, both being attempts at regional unity. Arnold Toynbee, in a book that Kedourie actually praised somewhat, *The Western Question in Greece and Turkey*, notes in a very controversial passage the fact that the Ottoman Empire "keeps a celebrated Christian cathedral as her principal mosque and a famous European city [Istanbul] as her capital, lends an appearance of dominion which is gratifying to Middle Eastern populations."[10] Because the Arab world was largely united under the Ottomans, and then divided under the Europeans, this lent a hazy and superficial logic to anti-European Arab nationalism and concomitant attempts at Arab unity; even as Arab disenchantment with and revolts against the late Ottoman Empire had been incessant. The problem, though, is that while the history of the Middle East has occurred largely under the melding force of great empires—Greek Hellenes, Romans, Byzantines, Achaemenid and Sassanid Persians, Ottomans, British, French, Soviets, and Americans—the Arabs are a people that, for reasons including sect and geography, left to their own devices have usually exhibited more disunity than unity. Even the Oxford orientalist Gibb announced: "The Arab nation . . . like all other nations, is not an entity of geographical or historical association, but the function of an act of will."[11]

This "will" had originally been the creature of disaffected Ottoman officers and others, of Arab extraction, who, once the empire crumbled, suddenly found themselves able to pursue what had previously been only a dream. As Kedourie sardonically explains, "They came to politics not through consideration of concrete difficulties or the grind of pressing affairs or daily responsibility, but by way of a doctrine. Their doctrine," he goes on, "was compounded of certain European principles which made language and nationality synonymous, of a faith in sedition and violence, and of contempt for moderation."[12]

This is mean language, but follow his point:

"When, therefore, the miraculous circumstances [of British and French victories in World War I, and the establishment of League of Nations–mandated territories] gave them suddenly a country to govern, it was not gratitude to fate and their patrons that they felt, but rather that they were cheated of their dream. They had desired an Arab country and an Arab state, and they got Iraq," with its wholly invented, Frankenstein monster of a geography: forcing together as it did, mutually hostile Sunnis, Shi'ites, and Kurds. The new gridwork of states cleaved the Arab nation at the same time that the end of the caliphate had done likewise. Subsequently, these newly minted Arab nationalists denounced the imperialist dismemberment of the Arab nation and the creation of such "arbitrary and artificial" boundaries. "This was indeed true," Kedourie wryly states, "for what otherwise can boundaries be when they spring up where none had existed before?"[13]

Because the borderless Arab polity that these Arab nationalists aspired to was simply impossible to establish owing to the very variety of cultures and situations across several time zones, any attempt at borders to carve up the vast desert tracts of the now-defunct Ottoman Empire was bound to be flawed and artificial. This was famously manifested by the Sykes-Picot Agreement of 1916, in which Great Britain and France secretly arranged to divide the Levant—between Anatolia in the north and the Arabian desert in the south—into arbitrary spheres drawn with a ruler.* Thus, the whole Arab nationalist enterprise was compromised from the start (even as there is little indication that a united Greater Syria and Mesopotamia, had it ever come into being, could have governed itself well). In both *The Chatham House Version* and *Democracy and Arab Political Culture,* Kedourie details the

---

* In the end, at a meeting on December 1, 1918, in London, before the start of the Paris Peace Conference following World War I, British prime minister David Lloyd George and French prime minister Georges Clemenceau kept the spirit of the Sykes-Picot Agreement while adjusting some of its features. They agreed that the Mosul region would go over to British control, allowing for the formation of British Iraq with Baghdad as its capital. The whole of Palestine and Transjordan would also be controlled by the British, rather than under international administration. Meanwhile, the whole of Syria north of Palestine, including Lebanon, would fall under French rule. Allawi, *Faisal I of Iraq,* p. 179.

dysfunction of Iraq politics lasting almost four decades from 1921 to 1958, with its British-backed monarch imported from the Hejaz, ministerial intrigues, and tribal rebellions, further undermined by ethnic and sectarian differences, featuring massacres of Assyrians, Yazidis, and others.* Indeed, Iraqi king Faisal I was forced to return to Baghdad from a visit to Switzerland in 1933, because, as he put it: "I fear that the Iraqi people might attack the Assyrians, whom they accuse of being ingrates. The Assyrians might start murdering Iraqi military personnel and mutilating their bodies. The Kurds might also take matters into their own hand and slaughter the Assyrians in their villages."[14]

In all, there had been fifty-seven cabinets installed in Baghdad during this period. However, Kedourie's is not the only point of view. Miami University professor Adeed Dawisha, also born in Baghdad, in his 2009 book, *Iraq: A Political History from Independence to Occupation*, presents an equally detailed picture of those four decades in Iraq as sustaining a feisty, if tumultuous democracy and a freewheeling press. The fact that Dawisha was born in 1944, eighteen years after Kedourie, and is Christian rather than Jewish, may partially explain his more benign view of Iraq in those decades. But we can all agree that Iraq's experiment with democracy was for a long period of the twentieth century a close-run affair. It was chronically plagued by sectarian upheavals and crises, managed for a time by the strong-willed rule of Faisal I and his supremely talented prime minister, Nuri Pasha al-Sa'id.[†] This legacy should have sobered rather than inspired those call-

---

* The tribes in the 1920s and 1930s owned several times more rifles than the government. Dawisha, *Iraq*, p. 33.

† Nuri Pasha al-Sa'id is well worth a biography in his own right. Born in 1888 in Baghdad, he got his start in Ottoman Tripolitania resisting the Italian occupation of Libya. A prisoner in Egypt, he fought alongside Faisal and T. E. Lawrence throughout the Arab Revolt against the Ottomans in the desert of the Hejaz. As the Ottomans retreated from Damascus in 1918, Nuri led Faisal's Arab forces into the city. He also played a role in Faisal's discussions with the Zionist leader Chaim Weizmann. (There is a famous photo of Nuri, Faisal, and Lawrence together at the Paris Peace Conference.) Helping Faisal I rule Syria under the early French mandate, he went with Faisal to British Iraq following Faisal's ouster from Damascus by the French. Thereafter Nuri was a permanent fixture in Iraqi governments for three and a half decades, helping to lead the police and the army, and serving countless times as prime minister. In 1958, when an Arab nationalist coup toppled Faisal II and killed members of the royal

ing for immediate elections in the aftermath of the U.S. invasion of 2003.

Freya Stark, the great British travel writer who knew Iraq during this period, commented on "the age-long disparities of Mosul, Baghdad and Basrah that cut the country into three; the still more ancient cleft of Shia and Sunni which cut it into two; [and] the ever-running sore of the minorities," which all had to be held in check.[15] Though I regrettably supported the invasion, I did warn in print beforehand that "the removal of Saddam [Hussein] would threaten to disintegrate the entire ethnically riven country if we weren't to act fast and pragmatically install people who could actually govern."*

This long-running and tenuous experiment with limited democracy in Iraq, lauded for years in the middle of the twentieth century by respectable journalists and enthusiastic international statesmen, came crashing down at dawn, July 14, 1958, when Sunni Arab nationalists, inspired by the pan-Arab coup in Egypt six years before, and led by Iraqi army colonels Abdel Karim Kassem and Abdul Salam Arif, murdered the prime minister Nuri Pasha Al-Sa'id and practically the entire Hashemite royal family—a young king, his aged grandmother, aunt, servants, and so on—and handed some of the bodies over to the mob for public mutilation. "Regicide," Kedourie says, is "peculiarly heinous and impious," since kingship, "a storehouse of devotion and loyalty," is a "dyke against bestiality."[16] More than that, the murder of the royal family in Iraq was one of the great seminal crimes of the twentieth century, like the murder of the Romanov royal family in

---

family, Nuri escaped dressed as a woman. The next day he was captured, executed, buried, and dug up; his body was then dragged through the streets of Baghdad, burned, and mutilated by a mob. Nuri was the ultimate and capable intriguer and administrator, an early Arab nationalist who later was sympathetic to the British. His was not a life of great and abstract ideals, but of the real and the possible under increasingly difficult and brutal circumstances. Rather than a visionary, he was a pragmatist and master of technique. Iraq could have done much worse than to have his like in power in the monstrous decades following his death.

* Robert D. Kaplan, "A Post-Saddam Scenario," *The Atlantic,* November 2002. In many other essays over the years prior to the Iraq War, I was openly skeptical about installing democracy anywhere, especially in the Middle East. For example, see this essay, published in the aftermath of 9/11: Robert D. Kaplan, "Don't Try to Impose Our Values," *Wall Street Journal,* October 10, 2001.

Russia, exactly forty years earlier in July 1918. Just as that earlier crime presaged seven horrific decades of Bolshevik rule, the 1958 coup in Baghdad presaged a series of military regimes, as one coup followed another—seven coup attempts in all—in the course of which Ba'athism was adopted.[17] This culminated in the coming to power in 1968 of the Tikriti Hassan al-Bakr and his cousin and powerful internal security chief, Saddam Hussein—who would prove to be Iraq's ultimate Hobbesian nemesis. Saddam's 1990 invasion of Kuwait revealed Arab nationalism for what it had always been: a matter of blood and iron rather than unity.

Marching on Kuwait and persecuting the Shi'ites, policies alive in the minds of the interwar Iraqi politicians, and rooted far back in Ottoman realities and inclinations, took on an added urgency under the Sunni army officers who ruled as Arab nationalists after 1958. In Kedourie's telling, this was all an old Iraqi story. The Baghdad regime of Saddam Hussein as well as the Ba'athist one next door in Damascus, ruled by Hafez al-Assad, pursued a virulent pan-Arabism as a salve to their own internal contradictions. Their borders being artificial, they obtained legitimacy only from the dream of unity across all Arab borders. And it naturally followed that the more artificial the state, the more anti-Zionist it was. Sunni Arabs in Iraq, especially, writes Kedourie, dreamed of being "the Prussia or Piedmont of a new Arab empire."[18] The scholar Vali Nasr writes, "The Sunnis compensated for their minority status in Iraq by merging the country's identity with that of the larger Sunni Arab world."[19] Indeed, whenever I traveled to Baghdad and Damascus in the 1980s, I was told that I was inside "the throbbing heart of Arabism."

Syria, too, as we know, in the early and middle decades of the twentieth century proved, in terms of ethnicity, sect, and geography, irreconcilable to constitutional development, with frequent clashes and National Assembly chaos. There was a "lack of any traditional political bonds between Damascus and Aleppo," Kedourie writes. "The three *coups d'état* of 1949 were the prelude to successive . . . interventions by army officers which put paid . . . to any possibility of Syria being governed through parliamentary and representative institutions."[20] Between 1947 and 1954, Syria had three national elections that all broke down according to regional, sectarian, and other differences. In February 1993, I laid this out in an argument in *The Atlantic* predicting that the elder Assad's passing could eventually return Syria to its post-imperial ungovernable roots.[21] It was precisely because Syria was ungovernable except by the most brutal means that army officers, terrified for the country's future, bonded with Egypt to form the United Arab Republic between 1958 and 1961. But that desperate attempt at Arab unity proved short-lived because neither the Egyptians nor the Syrians could decide who should really be in charge. Syria, rather than enjoy the history of a state or empire like Iran, had always been a mere vague geographical expression between the rugged plateau of Anatolia in the north and the scorching sands of Arabia to the south. Its inhabitants had always thought of themselves as either Sunnis, Shi'ites, Druze, Greek Orthodox, Maronites, or Jews. Though they all spoke Arabic, this was of little political significance until after the breakup of the Ottoman Empire. The post–World War I borders drawn by the British and French, though denounced for a hundred years now by historians, journalists, and other experts, are treated with much more detachment by Kedourie. The new borders "would of necessity be in the nature of a compromise. It is inappropriate to demand that political settlements should be 'natural' or 'logical.' Politics is neither like a geometrical theorem, nor like the mating instinct."[22]

Kedourie is clearly without sympathy. But this does not make him wrong.

In fact, Faisal I, in an echo of his observations about the near impossibility of governing Syria, had this to say in a private memorandum about his experience in governing Iraq: "With sadness, I have to say that it is my belief there is no Iraqi people inside Iraq. There are only diverse groups with no patriotic sentiments."[23] The solution, he said, was to erect a strong centralized state, neutral regarding the different sects and ethnic groups, that was, nevertheless, able to restrain itself in the exercise of power. In other words, in Syria and even more so in Iraq, the terrain that existed for good governance between anarchy and tyranny was forbiddingly narrow. No wonder that post-1958, the road led to abject tyranny. Faisal, with all of his frustrations that helped drive him to an early death, had actually come closest to inhabiting that narrow terrain.

THE UNITED STATES INVADED Iraq in 2003 and the result was chaos; the United States did not intervene in Syria in 2011 and the result was also chaos. While the media blames U.S. policy for what transpired, the deeper reason is the legacy of Ba'athism, a toxic mix of Arab nationalism and East Bloc–style socialism, hammered out in the Europe of the fascist-trending 1930s by two members of the Damascene middle class, one Christian and the other Muslim: Michel Aflaq and Salah al-Din Bitar.[24] Because Saddam's aging Ba'athist regime in Iraq either would not have survived the Arab Spring or would have ignited mass killing in an attempt at survival, the result there, even if George W. Bush had not invaded in 2003, might well have been chaos. Saddam's very bestiality and ideology of Ba'athist resistance, mixed with the absolute hatred of him by Kurds and Shi'ites, might well have ensured immense bloodshed. Indeed, it was only the empty shell of Ba'athism that lay between the richly developed civilization of Iran and the Mediterranean Sea, making Iran's empire of proxy militias inevitable. Smarter American policy might well have ameliorated the result, but that would have required a distinctly pessimistic worldview similar to Kedourie's.

Ba'athism, writes Kedourie, was built on "annihilation."[25] Because it was a rickety edifice of unworkable utopian principles, in practice it was all about whatever tribe and clan happened to wield power. In Syria, the ruling, Shi'a-trending Alawites oppressed the Sunnis, and in Iraq, the Sunnis oppressed the Shi'ites. In the 1970s and 1980s, it made, in Fouad Ajami's words, Syria and Iraq "prisons," even as Lebanon writhed in "anarchy."[26] Whenever I was in Iraq under Saddam, I compared it in my mind to Nicolae Ceauşescu's Romania, where I also went repeatedly in the 1980s, and which was the most pulverizing tyranny in the East Bloc. Syria, as I have argued, was actually less extreme. But in both Iraq and to a lesser extent even in Syria, I always sense a terrifying emptiness and extremity: anarchy hidden under the carapace of tyranny. Ba'athism, like Nasserism in Egypt, was a dead end. Such was the sum total of Britain's and France's colonial experiment in the Fertile Crescent. Bitter, no doubt, at his own childhood memory of the Farhud, Kedourie writes, "it is the British themselves who cheerfully led the way into these wastes."[27]

The British in Iraq in the early and middle decades of the twentieth century had championed the Sunnis, "tamed the Shi'ites and Kurds and made it clear to the Jews, the Assyrians and the other groups that they had to look to Faisal [the Hashemite monarch] and his men for their protection and welfare." The new constitution, meanwhile, denied any safeguards for these communities. Kedourie rails against "the hysterical mendacity of Colonel [T. E.] Lawrence" and "the brittle cleverness and sentimental enthusiasm of Miss [Gertrude] Bell," both of whom Hollywood has made into such heroes. He accuses Lawrence of, among other things, lying about the capture of Damascus in 1918 and afterwards becoming obsessed with finding a country in the Fertile Crescent for his beloved Sharifian dynasty to rule. Unsurprisingly, he considers Lawrence's epic, *Seven Pillars of Wisdom* (1926), bad history, "full of advocacy and rhetoric." As for Miss Bell, she demonstrates little more than a "fond foolishness . . . thinking to stand godmother to a new Abbasid empire."[28] This is all vanished history now, part of a lost world. But Kedourie brings it alive with his biting, sustained, and righteous passion. I disagree with him, finding *Seven Pillars of Wisdom* a landmark literary work of military history, travel writing, and ethnographic thick description. I also disagree with him regarding Gertrude Bell, one of the most extraordinary Arabists of all time, a brilliant linguist and fearless explorer of Middle Eastern deserts, who while she bears responsibility along with Lawrence, Winston Churchill, and others for midwifing Iraq into existence, openly acknowledged how difficult governance itself in the new state would be, because of the vast differences among the various Arab groups themselves.*

---

* See for example two of the biographies of her: *Gertrude Bell* by H.V.F. Winstone (1978) and *Desert Queen* by Janet Wallach (1996).

Of course, what burns in Kedourie's memory is the Farhud, whose antecedents included the perceived naivete and dishonesty of British policy in the Middle East since the end of World War I. Because *The Chatham House Version* depends so much on a singular human rights atrocity for its emotional ballast, it constitutes moral history.

It is important to underline again why Kedourie hates the British in the Middle East so much. It is not because of imperialism or illogical borders or the other fashionable things historians, academics, and journalists now chirp about. It is because he demands a Leviathan to protect men from other men. He understands a hard, sometimes unpalatable truth: that Thomas Hobbes was a moral philosopher, who, I repeat, wrote that without the coercive power of some authority monopolizing the use of violence, the weak cannot be protected from the strong. The Jews of Baghdad required a Leviathan to protect them, and the British failed in their responsibility to do so. Under the Ottoman Empire, the Jews at least enjoyed "communal standing and self-government."[29] Kedourie, with his defense of imperialism, is a reactionary with decades of evidence to back him up, and is therefore hard to dismiss. He is certainly driven by ethnic grievance, given his own Iraqi Jewish background. But so have been many writers on the Middle East when you examine their private motives. And he is among the most brilliant of this category.

To be fair to the British, the illogic of their policy was driven by the realization that they were determined to leave Iraq, and therefore told themselves that the situation there was improving even if it was not. Their rush to leave robbed them of "the illusion of permanence," which is the essence of successful imperialism.*

Moreover, while Kedourie insists on direct, imperial rule by Great Britain, this was simply not possible under the circumstances. Remember that following a tribal rebellion along the Euphrates in 1920 that had led to nearly 2,500 British imperial soldiers killed, wounded, and missing in action, the British, in light of that episode—and in

---

* I borrow the phrase from Frances G. Hutchins's *The Illusion of Permanence: British Imperialism in India* (Princeton, NJ: Princeton University Press, 1967).

light of a war in Europe that had just killed almost a million of their men—were both unwilling and unprepared for such a burden. "The [Euphrates] uprising was the final nail in the coffin of the policy that sought to turn Iraq into a protectorate directly ruled by Britain," the Iraqi historian Ali Allawi observes.[30] Because the British defeat of the Ottomans in the Great War had saddled it with the ruins of the latter's empire, for Britain to desert Mesopotamia altogether would have been irresponsible. The only option then was indirect rule through Faisal I, who despite all his limitations had more legitimacy, given his royal Hejazi lineage going back to the Prophet, than any other prospect at the moment. On account of the tribal, sectarian, and ethnic divisions of the new state with their intimations of chaos, an independent and democratic Iraq was being supported in the 1920s by only a few urban intellectuals and the eccentric British Arabist Harry St. John Bridger Philby.[31]

Thus, the British chose the middle path of indirect rule, and the middle path would have its victims at times, notably the Jews of Baghdad in the Farhud.

THIS ALL ENDS UP at Chatham House, intellectually presided over for so many years by Arnold Toynbee, the author of the formidable twelve-volume *Study of History,* recording twenty-six world civilizations, and published between 1946 and 1957. *The Chatham House Version* is the term used by Kedourie to encompass "assumptions, attitudes, and a whole intellectual style" that roughly justified and ran parallel to the worldview of the likes of Colonel Lawrence and Miss Bell. I have always found Toynbee's great lifework, as unwieldy as it is, to be quite useful and entertaining. His very emphasis on geography, history, and civilizations is a remedy to the way that policy studies have been sterilized by too much political science. Toynbee is just so creatively illuminating on so many topics: for example, his understanding of how in the Middle East there has been a vague historical alliance between the Arabs, Greek Orthodox, and Armenians against the Jews, Turks, and Persians (something that the ayatollahs have obviously upset); how overly militarized empires like Assyria have virtually disappeared from history; how history is a repetition of hubris and downfall; and so much else. Nevertheless, Kedourie is of a different view. He doesn't merely deliver one of literature's most brilliant hatchet jobs on Toynbee—a genre that can often be cruel more to the purpose of perverse entertainment rather than to elucidation. Rather, he patiently explains how Toynbee's interpretation of the Middle East—and of the Arab world in particular—does not hold up to the record of what has actually happened there since the nineteenth century.

Toynbee's entire worldview is wanting, according to Kedourie. Toynbee places too little emphasis on economics and institution-building, or the lack thereof, in a region. Toynbee extols culture and despises politics, even as it is politics that must be engaged in to make the world livable. Toynbee's "dogmatic and insistent moralism ... refuses to concede what common experience teaches, namely that the wicked do quite often flourish like the green bay tree, that in human affairs force and violence are occasionally decisive." And, as you might expect, there is the issue of the Jews. Running throughout Toynbee's voluminous work is a profound note of hostility, laced with an indeterminate lack of sympathy and context, for them. Toynbee contrasts the "gentle ethos" of Christianity and Manichaeism with the "violent ethos" of Maccabean Judaism and Sassanid Zoroastrianism. Toynbee was a tried-and-true appeaser who met with Alfred Rosenberg and Adolf Hitler in 1934 and again in 1936 in Germany. He believed that Gandhi's and Tolstoy's effect on human history would, in any case, be greater than that of Hitler and Stalin, since all politics is "tainted with cynicism."[32] And crucially, he persisted throughout his lifetime in believing that Palestine had been promised wholly and unambiguously to the Arabs.

Whereas Kedourie lives in the world of life and death of real people on the ground, Toynbee seems to inhabit a more beautiful, ethereal world of ideas and aesthetics. Kedourie respects the Ottoman Empire because it was cosmopolitan and afforded relative safety to minorities like the Jews. Toynbee has little use for the Ottoman Empire for about the same reason: it was a universal state that sought dominion over several cultures and civilizations, undermining their purity. Toynbee sees universal states as the mechanism for global decline, robbing as they do indigenous groups of their richness and distinctiveness. It is an interesting argument, since it would have made Toynbee, who died in 1975, a powerful intellectual opponent of American-style globalization.

As for the Arabs, in Toynbee's view they are the victims of the living death of Ottoman rule. He thus defends Arab nationalism as representative of a pure civilization, and accepts at face value the pan-Arab ideal for political unity. Early in his career, Toynbee nurtured the attitude that the Arabs had been the victims of Britain's and France's double-dealing with them. This puts Toynbee somewhat at odds with the likes of Lawrence and Miss Bell, who were variously complicit, however guiltily, in all of this—though, they, like Toynbee, are far more similar than different because of their general sympathy and—Kedourie would allege—naivete toward the Arabs.

Behind the psychology of such Britons was the assumption, in Kedourie's words, "that the world and its ways—the existence of unequal relations 'resting ultimately on force'—may be conjured away with high-minded covenants and pious, elevated declarations."[33] But, again, to be fair to the likes of Lawrence and Miss Bell, they labored under the severe limitation that complete withdrawal from Mesopotamia was irresponsible and total and direct imperial rule impossible. They could only make the best of the narrow space of political action afforded them. And they did this by partially engaging in illusions.

As for Kedourie, he remains the Jew on the ground in a murderous, unstable Arab region, undermining the lofty and guilt-ridden judgment of a British luminary, Arnold Toynbee, who sees the same region through a redemptive moralism. Kedourie's realism, even with its blind spots, not only puts him in a category with such great thinkers of the genre as Hans Morgenthau, Robert Strausz-Hupé, and Henry Kissinger, but he actually adds a vital layer to their worldview by, again, anchoring his extended argument in a human rights tragedy interwoven with obscure events that he personally witnessed as an impressionable youth.

THE FACT THAT PAN-ARABISM was in recent decades replaced by Islamism is not a contradiction but, once more, part of the same old story, according to Kedourie. Pan-Islamism was employed by the Ottomans to justify their empire in the Middle East. And given that the Arab world is the cradle of Islam, Islamism was conceived by the Arabs as a force of unity, just as Arab nationalism formerly was. The fact that one movement is religious and the other secular is of secondary importance, especially since secularism is a Western construct, even as religion has always infused the Arab world to a degree that the West has not known since the days when it was called Christendom.

This brings us to another unpleasant realization of Kedourie's: the fact that whereas Western liberal thought is more at home defining conflicts abroad as between heroes and villains, the Middle East features contests where it is often villains versus other villains. As Kissinger quipped about the 1980s Iran-Iraq War, "it's a pity both sides can't lose." Whereas the elder Assad's killing of 20,000 people in the Syrian city of Hama in February 1982 was a great tragedy, had the secular Arab nationalist Assad been defeated there, with the Sunni Muslim Brothers emerging victorious, "they would have wreaked as great a destruction" on Syria as Assad's Ba'ath party had done. "Here," writes Kedourie, "were two absolutist ideologies in confrontation, and between them no space was left at all for constitutional government even to breathe."[34]

Alas, the Arab world in the Fertile Crescent since independence following World War II has journeyed from pan-Arab nationalism to an interlude of revolutionary Marxism in the late 1960s (when in thrall to certain radical Palestinian groups) and finally to fundamentalism (which now itself might be passing). It all broke down in the streets of civil-war-torn Lebanon in the 1970s and 1980s, and more recently in the genocidal terror and communalism of Iraq and Syria in the early twenty-first century—which the essence of Kedourie's scholarship saw coming. The Americans not only created the havoc in Iraq after 2003, they also exposed what was lurking there all along. The very extremity of Saddam's methodical murder machine, though it cannot be excused, was partially a function of the society he had to keep under control. Had Kedourie lived a decade longer he might have given the younger Bush better counsel than he got before invading Iraq. True, Kedourie might have championed the urge of imperialism on the part of the Americans, but more to the point, he would have delivered pitiless, unvarnished advice on the nature of Iraqi politics and society through-out the twentieth century, warning the president that to invade was to govern, and to govern such a place required no illusions about the na-ture of human perversity. Of course, this was something successful empires knew only too well. *Good luck, and expect the worst,* Kedourie might have said to Bush.

But will Kedourie always be proved right? That is the question. At the end of *Democracy and Arab Political Culture,* he notes that democ-racy had been tried for decades in Arab countries and "uniformly failed."[35] Arab regimes may have been despotic, but their methods "were understood and accepted" by the populations themselves. Yet the spread of Western ideas into the Middle East has complicated that thesis, he admitted just before his death. How far have such ideas gone? Even the Arab Spring, as I've said, came along too early. Yet, the spread of ideas through technology is inexorable in a more urbanized and claustrophobic world. The mass eruptions of hope for a more lib-eral society in Cairo's Tahrir Square, beautifully evoked in Egyptian novelist Ahdaf Soueif's memoir, *Cairo: My City, Our Revolution,* con-stituted a veritable festival of ideas and inspiration, based on the belief that young Egyptians could, in fact, "change the world."[36] But now in 2023, we know that all that happened was the resumption of the dy-nasty of despotic, Nasserite pharaohs, with President Abdel Fattah al-Sisi proving to be more bloody and ruthless than Mubarak even. Others will try though, and in the end may yet prove Kedourie wrong. That is the hope.

But it could well be a long process, in which protesters will have to adhere to that tough measurement set by Albert Camus, who, in *The Rebel* (1951), declared that those who rise up against central authority must lay out a better regime with which to replace it, or else they, too, are morally inadequate. Kedourie in his lifetime never saw Camus's standard met in the Middle East. Though one could argue that Saudi Arabia, a major regional power, has found a way toward replacing a closed, taboo-laden society with a more open and tolerant one, without undergoing an experiment with democracy. Kedourie did not disparage Arabs so much as he disparaged their experiments with democracy. Thus, the experience of Saudi Arabia and the Gulf sheikhdoms in recent years has somewhat proved his point.

Of course, in 1979, in Iran, a regime was toppled and an equally developed framework of authority quickly put in its place. The Iranian Revolution, as repugnant as it has been, was the product of an age-old state and civilization harking back to Persian empires of antiquity, with a penchant for philosophy and abstractions. Relatively few places in the Arab world have evinced the organizational sophistication of Iran. The Iranian Revolution was a true world-historical event, unlike the coups in the Arab world. And so the Middle East as it still exists, with some notable exceptions, is the same one that Kedourie describes in his historical writings. It was Kedourie, remember, the Zionist Jew, who had appreciated the rule of Hafez al-Assad, comprehending more than a third of a century ago that the alternative to the elder Assad would have been sheer chaos. Uncomfortable, unappealing to many as Kedourie's work may be, the searing quality of his analysis is such that we can only label it as timeless. And therefore his wisdom, as flawed as it is in parts, is a thread that I must never let go of.

WHEN IT COMES TO Hobbesian tyrants, the United States under the administration of George W. Bush achieved the near impossible. It replaced the blood-soaked totalitarianism of Saddam Hussein with a situation in Iraq that was equally bloody—perhaps more so, depending upon which statistics you believe. Saddam, as we know, murdered a quarter of a million people not counting the near-million deaths in the Iran-Iraq War, which he did much more than the Ayatollah Khomeini to initiate. But the U.S. invasion of Iraq ignited a war that killed between 150,000 and 600,000 Iraqis, again, depending upon the survey you choose.* This was not counting nearly 4,500 American military deaths. War planners could clearly have benefited from Kedourie's absolute pessimism about Iraq, had he still been alive. It might well have saved innumerable lives.

The wounds of the Iraq War will never heal, not only for individual Iraqis and American military families, but for myself as well, as I have often recounted.

I was traumatized by my own experiences in Iraq under Saddam and at the incomparable suffocating air of repression I felt during two visits there in the 1980s, when I had my passport confiscated by Iraqi security agents on one occasion and not returned for ten days until the morning I left the country. I was in any case never successful in getting any Iraqis to talk to me outside of staged official interviews. I came to the conclusion that it was impossible to imagine a situation worse for the country than Saddam's rule. Nobody genuinely smiled or seemed to genuinely smile, ever. Behind everyone's face in any indoor setting were photographs of Saddam hanging from the walls. The country was like a vast prison yard lit by high-wattage lamps. Thus, in the immediate aftermath of 9/11, I helped draft a report, assisted by about a dozen others, recommending among other things that the younger Bush administration topple Saddam's regime.[37] I had never believed that Saddam was implicated in 9/11. I also never believed that Iraq was prepared for democracy.† Rather, I felt that the United States could use the opportunity afforded by 9/11 to install a better dictatorship in Iraq, something along the lines of the Egyptian and Pakistani varieties (under the military men Hosni Mubarak and Pervez Musharraf), which by providing both stability and a more enlightened authoritarianism, could have immeasurably improved both the human rights situation inside Iraq and America's strategic position in the region. I certainly knew this wouldn't be easy, as I had myself warned of anarchy in Iraq in a post-Saddam era in *The New York Times* some years earlier.[38]

---

* The Iraq Family Health survey has the lower number; the *Lancet* survey the higher one. See "Casualties of the Iraq War" in Wikipedia.

† See the note on page 253 in this chapter.

I was wrong. I failed my own test as a realist. Because in the immediate aftermath of 9/11, I had rationalized to myself that regime change might actually be possible without the country falling apart, I failed to sufficiently calculate the advantage to Iran should Iraq begin to crumble, a distinct possibility if we were to start to play god with the country. My reasoning was doubly flawed because I was basing my judgment on my experience inside Iraq in the 1980s, before the economic sanctions of the 1990s had pivotally weakened and impoverished institutions and the society, making Iraq even more susceptible to implosion. I simply did not at the time think through the issue of military intervention properly, overwhelmed as I was by my own dark memories of Iraq. Iraq had been such a radical experience for me: a place where one Western diplomat warned me soon after I arrived, "If the security services here become suspicious of you, there is nothing any of us in any of the embassies can do." It was as though the foreign diplomats, too, along with the Iraqi population, were hostages of the regime. I never experienced fear like I did in Saddam's Iraq. In short, I was a journalist who had gotten too close to my story.

I returned to Iraq in the spring of 2004, embedded as a reporter with 1/5, the 1st Battalion of the 5th Marines, which put me in the thick of street fighting for several days during the First Battle of Fallujah that April.* That, in addition to other harrowing experiences in post-Saddam Iraq in 2004 and again in 2005, when I experienced fighting and security operations around Mosul, completely devastated me. It wasn't fear for my life—like anyone who has experienced war and is truthful about it, I was continually terrified in the pit of my stomach—rather, I was devastated by the sickening knowledge that I had been wrong to support the war, again, especially as a realist.

As overpowering as the experience of totalitarianism is firsthand, the experience of anarchy firsthand is more intense still. Totalitarianism at least has rules to follow for the average person; anarchy has no rules. Roving armed gangs and abductions at street corners, mixed

---

* The Second Battle of Fallujah, which was even bloodier, took place in November and December 2004.

with wayward rocket attacks, are worse than even a dictator's grim visage and the long arm of the security services. Alas, any kind of a state is almost always better than no state at all. The great philosophers have dealt with this dismal issue for millennia, but to learn about it through vivid, actual experience is life-changing.* Though I played merely a bit part in the buildup to the Iraq War, as the American-led invasion dissolved into anarchy in 2006, I fell into a depression that lasted several years and required medical help.

I plowed through my depression. You deal with such a thing, you rarely cure it, whatever the doctors may claim. I decided in 2006 to begin researching a book about what I labeled the "Greater Indian Ocean" (now called the Indo-Pacific) that required deep reporting for years on end in several Muslim countries from Oman to Bangladesh to Indonesia, where I daily experienced anger at the U.S. invasion of Iraq close-up. I didn't avoid such voices. I wanted to hear them all. I certainly didn't hide within a solidarity group like some in Washington, rationalizing to one another the rightness of their cause. The result of my purgatory in the Muslim world of the Greater Indian Ocean was not to gravitate to extremes, self-serving or otherwise. I did not become an apologist for the Iraq War, justifying my mistake and blaming the Bush administration and its Defense Department for poor execution of what was in theory a good idea; nor did I become an isolationist opposed to wars and military involvement overseas altogether. Instead, I vowed to remain in the philosophical center and be a better realist. I vowed to double down on believing in granular, ground-level knowledge from the field in place of lofty concepts and *causes* that have often been the curse of Washington. I would not give up on reporting just because I had gotten too close to a story. I vowed to be both more empathetic and at the same time more distant regarding my subject matter—to consider both heartrending situations in far-off countries and American national interests—if that were at all possible: and to continue exploring the most difficult and unappealing of truths.

---

* As a journalist in 1993, in Sierra Leone, Liberia, and Côte d'Ivoire, I experienced incipient anarchy. But it wasn't on the scale of post-Saddam Iraq.

There would be no easy way out for my worst error; no solution, no epiphany afforded me. I would have to live with it, that's all. Wisdom, in any case, even a little bit of it, must be painfully acquired. As the great philosopher José Ortega y Gasset said, "Man's real treasure is the treasure of his mistakes."[39] That is my solace.

I sometimes think that had the United States not invaded Iraq, Iraq would have fallen apart anyway in the course of the Arab Spring eight years later, as Syria did, with a similar loss of life. In that case the younger Bush would have been blamed by the Washington elite for not toppling Saddam when he had the chance. It is an interesting counterfactual. But at the end of the day I realize I am stuck with history as it has actually happened.

Washington went through relatively little soul-searching. Those who were far more identified than me with the decision to invade Iraq blamed what happened on bad officials and some bad generals, as if their abstract conceptions of remaking the Middle East had little to do with it. America, being so rich, powerful, and geographically blessed, can simply shrug off failed wars like Iraq and Afghanistan, so that the consequences for the country are mitigated. Following the Iraq debacle, people who supported invading Iraq henceforth advocated different forms of military intervention in Libya and Syria: two other states nearly as internally divided by tribe, ethnic, and sectarian group as Iraq—and just as artificially created—where the only unifying glue was also a severe form of authoritarianism. It was as if Iraq had never happened. At the root of it all was a breathtaking lack of curiosity and imagination regarding the history and ground-level reality of all those distant places. They had little interest in Libyan tribes or Syrian sects or the other factors that made those states barely states at all. Again, it was as though America's own historical experience mattered much more to them than the historical and cultural experiences of those countries themselves. Thus, in an intellectual sense, they suffered from a form of isolationism, even as it went by the name of interventionism.

But I am talking here of only one part of the East Coast foreign policy elite. As regards the Middle East, there was another part. These were the people who had clairvoyantly predicted exactly what would happen in Iraq, and who were consequently opposed to the war from the beginning. The Middle East was a mystery to many of them, too. But at least they admitted as much, and consequently they knew enough to want to exercise restraint in dealing with the region. Unfortunately, these people did not channel their clairvoyance into any sort of a positive vision for the region: a vision that held out hope for the countries themselves and a sustainable policy direction for America, without the need of large-scale military intervention. Rather, they simply rested on their laurels of getting the Iraq War right and, in the wake of that disaster, merely projected a form of restraint worldwide for the United States to follow.

Former secretary of defense Chuck Hagel, a veteran of the Vietnam War who had opposed the Iraq War, once told me that whereas Vietnam changed America, Iraq changed only the Washington elite. Iraq, he went on, which engaged an all-volunteer army rather than a mass conscription one, did not unleash mass demonstrations across the country and a counterculture the way that Vietnam did. But the Iraq debacle did establish for many years two opposing camps within the policy elite in the American capital and its intellectual hinterlands. The lines of debate changed from Democrats versus Republicans to interventionists versus restrainers; or to put it another way, Wilsonians versus neo-isolationists. The Wilsonians believed that because the United States had had such an historically transformative experience with mass democracy, its system—or a variation of it—was destined for every country in the world to enjoy, whereas the neo-isolationists believed that America should be a light unto the nations but no more, and persuade by example rather than by force or active engagement in other countries' affairs. The Republican Party was split between interventionists and restrainers, just as the Democratic Party was. Thus, talk of bipartisanship and party divides was irrelevant in the post–Iraq War years when this debate raged.

In particular, the Iraq War forever shattered the tenuous Reaganite alliance within the Republican Party that existed between old-fashioned moderate realists such as Colin Powell, Brent Scowcroft,

and James Baker III and muscular interventionists such as Dick
Cheney and Paul Wolfowitz. To see photos of all five of these men
chummily collaborating in 1990 and 1991 during the First Gulf War in
the administration of George H. W. Bush is to experience a wave of
nostalgia for a well-functioning bygone age, compared to the hatreds
between them as a result of the Second Gulf War twelve years later,
when the younger Bush's invasion of Iraq put a veritable Berlin Wall
between the two groups and helped rupture Washington in the process.

States and empires weaken or collapse when their elites fall into
division, and the Iraq War, by splitting the elite and fraying the tissue
of intangibles that held together a soft imperial-like aura for America
in the Middle East, ended the American empire there. It was not an
economic burden that undermined the United States in the Middle
East—a typical cause of imperial decline—but the intellectual failure
of important sections of the American policy elite, detached as they
were from the intractable realities of Middle Eastern countries themselves.

IRAQ WAS AN ORIGINAL mistake, meaning that intervening in a large
and complicated Islamic country with the aim of remaking society had
never actually been tried previously by the United States and therefore,
at least in a theoretical sense, nobody could be sure the effort would
fail. But the toppling in 2011 of Muammar Gaddafi in Libya was an
unoriginal and therefore, in a sense, an even less forgivable mistake,
since the recent example of Iraq should have warned off the interventionists, whose actions created chaos in a strategically located oil-
producing state on the Mediterranean, leading to the deaths of
thousands and the destruction of hundreds of thousands of livelihoods
at a minimum, in addition to sowing more chaos throughout the countries of the Sahara and Sahelian Africa. Gaddafi, whose bizarre behavior and even more bizarre costumes, reminiscent as they were of the
ancient Carthaginians in Gustave Flaubert's 1862 novel *Salammbô*, had
been steadily evolving into a pro-Western tyrant who held together a

country that was not really a country, but rather an amorphous carto-graphic blank space whose western region, Tripolitania, had tradition-ally been oriented toward Greater Carthage and Tunisia, and whose eastern region, Cyrenaica, had traditionally been oriented toward Al-exandria in Egypt. There was absolutely no tactical or strategic ratio-nale to remove him. National interest dictated that we leave him in place.

Then there was Syria, another abject, unoriginal failure of imagina-tion, where the lessons of what had just happened in neighboring, fel-low Ba'athist and fellow Arab Iraq made little impact upon many in Washington. Arguably the most knowledgeable area specialist on Syria in the United States is Joshua Landis, head of the Center for Middle East Studies at the University of Oklahoma and the author of the influential blog *Syria Comment*. Landis, educated at Harvard and Princeton, speaks Arabic and lived for years in Syria. When most Washington policymakers, as well as the U.S. intelligence commu-nity,[40] were predicting Bashar al-Assad's imminent demise early in the civil war, Landis warned that the younger Assad would survive—and in fact, he did.

When the Washington policy nomenklatura was demanding mili-tary intervention to erect a better Syria, Landis reflected that "the lib-eral, pro-Western class in Syria was small. It would be quickly destroyed between the hammer of Islamist groups and the anvil of Assad's secu-rity apparatus." Furthermore, there was "no 'Syrian people,'" he said. In an echo of Freya Stark, "Syrians are deeply divided along religious, ethnic, class and regional lines." The number of militias was in the "thousands." The notion of Washington think-tankers that the Obama administration should have funded the moderate militias "is bunkum." The "radicals got money because they were successful. They fought better, had better strategic vision and were more popular," Landis pa-tiently explained. "The so-called moderates were simply local strong-men who gathered around themselves cousins, clan members, and fighters from their village and the village next to theirs. But go two or three villages away, and they were viewed as foreigners and trouble-makers, who were venal and predatory."[41]

Given that in Syria different armed groups began to form soon after the first demonstrations of the Arab Spring in early 2011, and given that, as Landis noted, "thousands" of such militias would eventually form, there was never a possibility of putting Syria at peace except by occupying the country with armed forces, and that was something the United States was simply never going to do, or even to take the lead in doing. Remember that this was a regional war, with the Iranians, Saudis, Turks, Qataris, and others all backing various armed elements inside Syria. Thus, to solve Syria meant essentially assuaging the various fault lines of the Muslim Middle East.

There is more.

Witness the fact that from the very beginning the Syrian uprising suffered from an acute lack of central control or any coherent leadership whatsoever. It quickly devolved into a conservative Sunni revolt, which is what drew the Muslim Brotherhood, the Saudis, Qataris, and Turks into the conflict in the first place. As Landis reports, primordial loyalties to clan and religion quickly took over, since it was only such loyalties that could deal with the suffering. Indeed, once the regime began to falter, what remained was less a hope than "the state of nature," observes Jonathan Spyer, an Israel-based journalist with much experience on the ground in war-torn Syria and Iraq.[42]

Thousands of miles away from the actual fighting, humanitarian and imperial-sounding voices would not be deterred, however. The most articulate and arguably most prominent of them was Leon Wieseltier, who was at the time the literary editor of *The New Republic*. Referring to the incoherent Syrian opposition, he said that "we can help them to cohere." After all, "moral responsibility" requires that a great power be "bold." And given that "the overwhelming majority of Americans have not experienced the effects" of the Iraq and Afghanistan wars (around 50,000 American dead and wounded out of an American population of 330 million), "I am of the party of American energy, which believes that America can never be tired, because the stakes for the world are too high."[43] Wieseltier, who had supported the Iraq War with similar arguments, made a direct appeal to historical responsibility. Facts, according to this worldview, were things to be overcome rather than practically absorbed and considered. Whereas someone like Wieseltier had the luxury of beautiful intellectual formulas, policymakers were stuck with the bureaucratic consequences and blame—as someone like former deputy secretary of defense Paul Wolfowitz, whose worldview was close to Wieseltier's, knows only too well.

Yet, all the arguments supporting military intervention in Syria—establishing no-fly zones, setting up civilian protection corridors and safe zones, cratering runways, arming friendly militias, removing Assad outright, and so forth—left President Barack Obama cold.* (I was not convinced by these arguments either.) Though in the conventional wisdom of Washington elites, Obama's failure to intervene in Syria is a blight on his record, in fact, as Landis observes, it was a "success"; since Obama "kept his foot on the brakes" and resisted what, in effect, was a replay of the run-up to the Iraq War, even if Iraq was not falling apart prior to our intervention as Syria was.[44] While no one was asking Obama to send in hundreds of thousands of troops to liberate Syria and make it a democracy, the effect of the various measures being recommended to him, whether establishing safe zones or cratering runways, or such, would have certainly risked drawing the United States deep into what was already a quagmire beyond its means to ultimately resolve. This would have been especially true if some of those recommended actions—undermined, as one might expect, by the fog and confusion of a complex, internecine war—failed to achieve their purpose, in which case the United States would either have had to escalate further or suffer a humiliating failure.

The irony is that while the Washington conventional wisdom maintains the Iraq War was to blame for making Obama gun-shy about saving a large number of lives in Syria, the truth may be the opposite: that the failure of the Iraq War did serve one useful purpose. It kept the United State largely out of Syria.

---

* Goldberg, "The Obama Doctrine." Another excellent analysis on the problems of intervention was provided by George Washington University professor Marc Lynch in "What's Really at Stake in the Syria Debate," *WarOnTheRocks*, October 10, 2016.

———

IN THE POST-IMPERIAL HISTORY of the Fertile Crescent, only one ruler kept order for decades while at least trying to obey certain limits: Hafez al-Assad. Admittedly, the standards here are extremely low. Saddam Hussein killed hundreds of thousands of people, not counting those killed in the Iran-Iraq War that he began. Bashar al-Assad killed hundreds of thousands in the course of a civil war that he did not begin. By contrast, the elder Assad is guilty of killing tens of thousands in the midst of a sectarian insurrection launched against him. The fact that we can label the elder Assad the Syria-and-Iraq region's least bloody and most stable ruler demonstrates just how utterly impossible to rule, on account of such artificial borders and weak state identities, the principal geographic entities of the Fertile Crescent really are. Alas, it is still better than anarchy. Syria and Iraq were always happier as loci of far-flung empires, or as imperial possessions of other empires, than as modern states themselves.

In the first two decades of the twenty-first century there was no real sense of civilization as we understand it in the principal political geographies of the Fertile Crescent: Iraq and Syria. Secular totalitarianism, best typified by Saddam Hussein, had "bulldozed" the past, freeing young men of traditional constraints and exposing them to radical religious forces. The collective memories of kindness and tolerance that came naturally to cosmopolitan cultures such as the Ottoman Empire had been wiped away by Ba'athist rule.[45] Rather, there was a concoction of postmodern technology such as the internet and videotapes, intermingled with barbarity—torture and decapitations— exemplified by the Islamic State in Iraq and Sham (the Levant or Greater Syria). And yet while ISIS spiritually existed outside of geography, its formation and rule depended on the anarchic void that was created by decades of Ba'athism and an American invasion. Ba'athism had led inexorably to ISIS, in other words. Under Saddam, the Sunnis had dominated. Now that the state had fallen away, too many Sunnis continued to run riot as Salafists. Unlike the Iranian Revolution, which had *tiers-mondiste* and even some Western philosophical elements to enrich it, making the birth of a Shiʻite clerical state a truly world-historical event, ISIS offered no ideology or useful interpretation of the past. Thus, it was sterile in a way that not even the essentially blue-collar Iranian Revolution was. ISIS, which featured beheadings, sex slaves, and the utter subjugation of women, registered the end of the line for Syria and Iraq.

Beyond ISIS lay no great vision or ideology, no salvation, merely the wreckage of all dreams and grand schemes. And the end of the line for Syria and Iraq now meant not annihilation, but the tedious requirement of reinventing basic governance—and building from scratch some sort of social contract. *How can we exist without killing each other, and how can we do so in the face of lower prices for our oil and gas in an age of renewables?* Only such an attitude could stave off the territorial appetites of outside powers like those of the postmodern Iranians, Turks, and Russians, ready with their own imperial dreams to carve up the carcass of two failed and artificial states. As I write, Syria is barely a state and Iraq faces perhaps a new era of violent internal explosions due to the failure of democratic governance. In the third decade of the twenty-first century, the Fertile Crescent was at the beginning of time.

FERTILE CRESCENT

PART III

"FOR MAPMAKERS—IF NOT FOR INTERNATIONAL LAWYERS—there *is* such a place as Kurdistan," wrote the CIA area specialist Stephen C. Pelletiere in 1984.[1] Kurdistan is an ellipse of mountainous territory, rich in oil and water, that constitutes the northern rim of the Fertile Crescent, overlapping as it does Iraq, Syria, Turkey, and Iran. The Kurds now number between 30 and 45 million: counting them is hard due to remote terrain and intermarriage with other groups. In political terms they were a relatively stable element in an age of cosmopolitan empires, notably the Ottoman Turkish and Safavid Persian. But with the collapse of the imperial world following World War I came the suppression of minority peoples under the straitjacket of new nation-states, in which one group often sought to eliminate the rights of others. The stateless Kurds, who were natural to the Ottoman world, henceforth, by virtue of their very existence and demand for equal rights, became a principal disrupting force in the politics of Iraq, Syria, Turkey, and Iran. This struggle was quickened in the cases of Iraq and Iran, which, having nationalized their oil industries in the mid-twentieth century, suddenly had the financial wherewithal to militarily confront their own Kurdish populations. If any group holds the key to the anarchy of the Fertile Crescent in the modern and postmodern eras, it is the Kurds. In 1999, I wrote in *The New York Times:* "As states

in the Middle East become weaker, the stateless Kurds become comparatively more important. This is especially true of Iraq. Saddam
Hussein's demise could break Iraq into Kurdish and Arab parts, tempting Turkey's military into an occupation of oil-rich Iraqi Kurdistan."²
The Kurds are a tribal people, and as Gertrude Bell wrote in 1920 in
reference to the new state of Iraq, which comprised both Arabs *and*
Kurds: "The tribes don't want to form part of a unified state; the towns
can't do without it."³ Because the Kurds were generally in the mountains and the Arabs lived in the towns, the state advanced the latter.

THE STORY MIGHT AS well begin in the winter of 401 B.C., when a
tired and defeated army of Greek mercenaries was slowly making its
way home from Mesopotamia, after failing to topple the Persian king
Artaxerxes II. Crossing the Taurus Mountains in what is today southeastern Turkey, the mercenaries were set upon by bands of Carduchi, a
fierce group of bowmen, who caused more harm to the Greeks in seven
days of hit-and-run raids than had the Persians during the entire Mesopotamian campaign. An account of the harrowing retreat was provided by Xenophon, one of the Greek commanding officers. Xenophon
wrote that the Carduchi lived in the mountains and were not subject
to outside authority: "Indeed, a royal army of a hundred and twenty
thousand had once invaded their country, and not a man of them had
got back."⁴

Xenophon's account remains relevant today. The Carduchi may
well have been Kurds, an Indo-European people speaking a language
akin to Persian, who first occupied the Zagros and Taurus ranges in
the second millennium B.C. The Kurds are among history's greatest
warriors. Saladin, the Muslim general who repossessed Jerusalem
and much of the Holy Land from the Crusaders, was a Kurd. Their
bows and slings have long since been replaced by the likes of Soviet-
made AK-47 assault rifles and rocket-propelled grenades. Perched
on isolated slopes, amid oak and mountain ash, as I saw during my
first visit with them in the late 1980s in northern Iraq and northwestern Iran, Kurdish guerrillas known as *peshmerga* ("those who are pre-

pared to die") have wiped out whole units of Turkish, Iraqi, and Syrian forces.

Kurds occupy one of the most tantalizing bits of real estate on earth. The deserts of the Middle East and the plateaus of Central Asia and Anatolia all ram up against the 10,000-foot massifs of Kurdistan. Kurdish areas of Iraq are home to some of the Middle East's biggest oil fields, while a Kurdish region of southeastern Turkey is home to one of the world's biggest hydroelectric projects, since the mountains of Kurdistan sit astride the headwaters of both the Tigris and Euphrates rivers.

Nevertheless, despite this geographical bounty, modern statehood eluded the Kurds. Worse, the Kurds as a tribal people have been divided among themselves, so that they have always been hostage to the strategies of others, with one Kurdish guerrilla group often fighting at cross-purposes with another. For decades, the Kurdistan Workers' Party or PKK (*Partiya Karkeren Kurdistane*), armed by regimes over the border in Syria and Iraq, constituted Turkey's chief internal security problem. Even under Saddam Hussein's totalitarianism, Kurdish guerrilla groups, supported at times by Syria and Iran, occupied parts of northern Iraq; while other Kurdish fighters supported by Saddam were among the most potent irregular forces deployed against Iran during the Iran-Iraq War. This, of course, was all prologue to the explosion of Kurdish military and diplomatic power across the region following the U.S. invasion of Iraq and the Syrian civil war. Lacking a state of their own, the Kurds thrive when existing states are in turmoil.

To be sure, although Kurdistan never officially existed as a state, a lesson in geopolitics could easily begin with the Kurds. For decades, even before the cataclysms of the early twenty-first century in the Fertile Crescent, Kurdish fortunes have served as a barometer of the strength or weakness of every state in the region.

Perhaps because Kurds were a distinct people, with their own language and culture, for at least 1,500 years before converting to Islam in the seventh century A.D., their religious affinity with Turks, Arabs, and Persians has counted for relatively little. If anything, religion has helped to estrange the predominantly Sunni Kurds from their neighbors. Kurds from Iran flaunt their secular values as a way of demonstrating their opposition to the Shi'ite theocracy in Tehran. In Turkey, however, a state founded on Atatürk's fiercely secular principles, Kurdish revolts—even prior to Recep Tayyip Erdoğan's Islamic counterrevolution—combined fundamentalism with nationalism.

Religion, race, and language aside, what seems to make a Kurd a Kurd is an almost spiritual affinity with the beloved moors and snow-streaked mountains of Kurdistan. As the first row of domed, yellowy hills appeared on the horizon, rippling upwards from the desert floor in northeastern Iraq, my Kurdish driver in 1986 glanced back at the desert, sucked his tongue in disdain, and said, "Arabistan." Then, looking toward the hills, he murmured, "Kurdistan," and his eyes lit up. But if geography helps to define the Kurds, it also helps to divide them. The ranks of jagged peaks, with their walled-in valleys and forbidding chasms, seal the Kurds off from one another as much as from the outside world. Kurdish tribalism, which makes the Kurds an assemblage of clans and competing families and political movements, is in significant measure a function of geography.

In the aftermath of the First World War the Kurds actually came close to winning a state of their own. The 1920 Treaty of Sèvres, whose purpose was to carve up and distribute the Ottoman Empire, provided for a Kurdish homeland in eastern Turkey. The following year, however, Kemal Atatürk defeated an invading Greek army and, by laying the groundwork for a new, cohesive Turkish state in Anatolia, was able to demand the treaty's revision. His new state brutally repressed the Kurds in the 1920s and 1930s. But after the Second World War the Soviets, who had occupied northern Iran, allowed for the establishment of a small pro-Moscow Kurdish republic around the city of Mahabad. Yet as a result of Anglo-American pressure and an increasing preoccupation with Eastern Europe and the Balkans, Stalin abandoned his Iranian holdings at the end of 1946, leaving the Kurds at the mercy of the Iranian shah, who crushed the fledgling regime and executed its leader, Ghazi Mohammed. For decades afterwards, as I personally witnessed, photos of Ghazi Mohammed occupied a prominent place in Kurdish redoubts in Iraq and Iran.

Another influential figure in Mahabad was Mulla Mustafa Barzani, who afterwards fled to the Soviet Union, where he lived for a decade in exile. He later returned to lead several rebellions in northern Iraq—supported this time covertly by the United States, Israel, and Iran, all of which wanted to undermine the Ba'athist regime that had replaced the Hashemite king in Baghdad. It was an old Kurdish story: without a state of their own, Kurdish leaders had to periodically switch paymasters, according to the politics of the moment. The most serious of these Barzani-led rebellions broke out in March 1974, when the Iraqi regime of Ahmed Hassan al-Bakr and Saddam Hussein had to use tanks and planes to repel Barzani's forces. But after an agreement between Iraq and Iran in 1975, the shah withdrew his support from the Kurds and the revolt collapsed. The peshmerga retreated to their caves in the mountains and Barzani went into exile in the United States, where he died in 1979.

The outbreak of the Iran-Iraq War in September 1980 provided the Kurds with another opportunity. As Iraqi troops were diverted to the war front in the center and south of the country, fewer were available to confront resurgent peshmerga. Northern Iraq henceforth became a cauldron of Kurdish separatism. Heading north into the mountains from the city of Sulaymaniyah in 1986, I came to a point where the hitherto ubiquitous billboard pictures of President Saddam Hussein suddenly vanished. So did Iraqi soldiers. Replacing them were peshmerga with bandoliers, wearing turbans, baggy trousers, vests, and cummerbunds. According to the world map I was still in Iraq. But Baghdad's writ was now hardly law.

I found northern Iraq at the time home to no fewer than five Kurdish guerrilla armies. In the Turkish border area Mustafa Barzani's son, Masoud Barzani, led the Kurdistan Democratic Party (KDP). The Ayatollah Khomeini was backing the Barzani clan, as the shah had done for a time in the early 1970s. Thus, Barzani's KDP, which had been supported by the United States and Israel, as well as by the shah, was in the following decade a tool of anti-American forces. Barzani's troops were at the time threatening Iraq's international highway and oil pipeline to Turkey. Over to the east, near Iraq's border with Iran, I came across Jalal Talabani's Patriotic Union of Kurdistan (PUK), also backed by Iran and Syria. The Barzani and Talabani clans alternated over the years and decades between estrangement and reconciliation. To complicate matters further, at the time of my visit Talabani was hosting on his territory another peshmerga force, Abdel Rahman Qassemlu's Kurdistan Democratic Party of Iran (KDPI), which was cooperating with Saddam against Khomeini's regime. There were also other, smaller peshmerga forces with their own cross-cutting alliances. At one point, five miles from the Iranian border, I actually looked out over a deforested valley and beheld several different Kurdish armies.

This interlude of Kurdish power would be followed by another, but with great tragedy in the interim. In the final stages of the Iran-Iraq War in 1988, as Saddam began to recover his freedom of military maneuver, he launched the infamous Anfal campaign, a full-scale assault on Iraqi Kurdistan in which 100,000 civilians, including many women and children, were murdered by Iraqi forces, sometimes employing poison gas. Then in 1990, following the end of the Cold War and only two years after the conclusion of the stalemated Iran-Iraq War, Saddam invaded Kuwait. The aftermath of the American-led liberation of Kuwait in 1991 saw Saddam's forces take revenge on the Iraqi Kurds in the north as well as the Iraqi Shi'ites in the south. This, in turn, led to Provide Comfort, a massive American-run military operation that protected almost 2.5 million Kurdish refugees on both sides of the Iraqi-Turkish border, and which culminated in a no-fly zone over northern Iraq, thereby preventing Saddam's forces from attacking the Kurds by air.[5] The no-fly zone was the principal factor in the emergence of an autonomous Kurdish region in northern Iraq. Thus, after mass suffering, the Kurds had received a measure of real freedom.

The Cold War's conclusion had unlocked a Pandora's box: unleashing the Kurds, with American help, as a geopolitical force in the Fertile Crescent and beyond. That is to say, the end of the Cold War had created America's unipolar moment, which in turn led to the invasion of Iraq, followed some years later by the Arab Spring in Syria: thus undoing the post–World War I peace agreements that had created the artificial states of Syria and Iraq in the first place, as well as creating Atatürk's uniethnic Turkish Republic. Put another way, both world wars and the Cold War that followed constituted one singular period in European history: the Long European War of 1914–1989. And its expiration has had momentous consequences for the Middle East.

The Kurdish story continued in all its tumultuousness. America's ill-fated invasion of Iraq, followed by its equally abrupt and ill-thought-out withdrawal, created a vacuum filled in 2014 by ISIS, the Islamic State. The peshmerga subsequently emerged as the most potent indigenous military force against those extremists. In fact, the peshmerga's war against ISIS, supported by the United States and a global coalition, permitted the Kurds to consolidate de facto control over northern Iraq, including for a time the oil-rich region of Kirkuk, located between Mesopotamia and the Kurdish mountains. Consequently, the Kurdish Regional Government under President Masoud Barzani (Mulla Mustafa's son) believed that now the time was finally ripe for an independent Kurdistan, given that the Iraqi state was on the verge of collapse. The referendum conducted in Kurdistan in 2017 by the regional government resulted in 93 percent of votes cast in favor of independence. Alas, the regional government had miscalculated what the international effect would be. Baghdad and Tehran immediately imposed a flight ban on all points inside Kurdistan and sealed the borders against trade as well. The Barzanis of the KDP and the Talabanis of the PUK traded accusations for the debacle. Subsequently, the Kurds backed down, withdrawing their threats to declare independence, and entered into a confused dialogue with Baghdad and its own various factions instead.[6]

Kurdistan now exists inside a murky realm of virtual independence and organic links to the Baghdad government. It is stable and prosperous only by comparison with the abysmal political and economic conditions that prevail in Arab Iraq to the south. Meanwhile, its young population, which has no living memory of the armed struggle against Saddam's Ba'athist regime, demands reform, an end to massive corruption, and improved governance.[7]

———

MEANWHILE, IN NORTHERN SYRIA, the principal Kurdish group is the Democratic Union Party or PYD (*Partiya Yekitiya Demokrat*), whose military arm is the People's Protection Units or YPG (*Yekineyen Parastina Gel*). The PYD and its People's Protection Units grew out of Abdullah Öcalan's Marxist Kurdistan Workers Party, or PKK. Öcalan, a Turkish Kurd, had built up the PKK when he was based in northern Syria in the 1980s and 1990s, causing the Turkish government to field well over 100,000 troops in southeastern Turkey to fight there against Öcalan's northern-Syria-based insurgency. Soon after the start of the Syrian civil war in 2011–12, the YPG and its People's Protection Units quickly filled the vacuum left by the withdrawal of Syrian government troops and administrative staff. The Kurdish majority centers of northern Syria—Afrin, Kobani, and the Jazirah—were now all self-governing. Truly, it was the cataclysms of the early twenty-first century in Syria and Iraq that let the Kurdish genie out of the bottle—the one big group that was left stateless following the First World War was getting its revenge across the northern Fertile Crescent.

Crucially, it was the multiyear struggle of Öcalan's PKK inside the Turkish border in the last decades of the twentieth century that had intensified Kurdish identity on the other side of the border in both Syria and Iraq. Northern Syria proved to be a hub of this phenomenon, as the withdrawal of the Syrian government from the region coincided with a migration of ethnic Kurds from central and southern Syria northward into the PYD zone, just as Kurds from southern Turkey and northern Iraq were also drifting into northern Syria to assist in the struggle against both the Islamic State (ISIS) and Bashar al-Assad.[8]

That struggle was particularly bloody. Between September 2014 and March 2015, the Islamic State laid siege to the Kurdish-majority town of Kobani, just inside Syria, close to the Turkish border. Seventy percent of the town was destroyed and Kobani and its environs lost two-thirds of their population, many of whom became refugees and displaced persons.[9] In the end, U.S. airpower and Kurdish ground forces drove out ISIS. This collaboration led to the creation of the

American-supported Syrian Democratic Forces, a combined land army of Kurds and Sunni Arabs, numbering in the tens of thousands.[10]

The geopolitics of it all were complicated in the extreme. Though Russia was supporting Assad against the Kurds, it was also using the Kurds and particularly the People's Protection Units as a means to soften Erdoğan's Turkey, even as Russia was cooperating with Erdoğan in other spheres. The United States, as we know, was backing the Kurds against ISIS, to the chagrin of Turkey.[11]

Again, on account of the sheer complexity of it all, we must regard the post–Cold War history of Kurdistan—or the northern part of the Fertile Crescent in Syria and Iraq—as a species of anarchy. Therefore, the struggle to forge coherent and responsive governance is particularly acute here.

I ARRIVED IN THE middle of the night in Sulaymaniyah, the main city of the eastern part of Iraqi Kurdistan, controlled by the Talabani clan. (The western part with the capital of Erbil is controlled by the Barzani clan.) The airport was a small and cramped shed-like structure that recalled to me airports in Africa in the 1980s and 1990s. There was a grim makeshift quality to the place. Because flights to Sulaymaniyah often arrived in the middle of the night, the line at passport control was long and snaking. There was a separate line for changing money, needed in order to purchase visas at $70 in yet another line. I sensed an atmosphere of haggling and negotiation. But I reminded myself that except for places that unexpectedly descend into war or economic collapse, airport buildings and procedures tend to improve over time. Someone reading these words in a few years may well laugh and say, "That was then, before the nice airport was built." Dawn was not far off by the time I located my luggage, escaped the scrum, and left the airport. I found a driver to take me to my hotel. The city had grown immensely since my last visit in 1986, more than a third of a century ago, when it was an overgrown and hilly village, a jumping-off point for visiting with Kurdish guerrillas fighting both Iraq and Iran. It was now raining lightly, and the roads were marked by puddles and potholes. The few sidewalks I saw were broken. Development was ever-present but ramshackle, except for the odd hotel, luxury goods store, and steak house, which were all spanking new and brilliantly lit like stars in the vacant black heavens. The obsessive urban planning that defined a place like Saudi Arabia was altogether absent. The hotel was a gleaming space-age tower, but the construction and interior decorating already betrayed the mark of coming decay. It was the only skyscraper in the city. The cash machine provided U.S. dollars rather than local Iraqi dinars, which, as I learned, were used interchangeably with dollars. You paid in dollars and got change in dinars, or vice versa. Credit cards were rarely accepted outside of a few hotels. This was a cash economy where your pockets bulged. What all these immediate first impressions suggested is that I was in a place in a very fragile phase of development: legally part of Iraq, functionally independent; legally a democracy, functionally divided between two clans.

I was also conscious of being in a rather remote, isolated place, notwithstanding the crosscurrents of dynamic change happening in so many other parts of the world. Kurdistan was not only landlocked among somewhat hostile neighbors all around, but also "sky-locked," as one expert had put it to me before my arrival, since those same neighbors controlled the air access to Kurdistan that limited the number of flights here to a few, often arriving in the middle of the night.

Morning came and with it a dramatic view of domed mountains in all directions, naked and yellowy-gray in the early spring. Driving around town Sulaymaniyah suddenly appeared more normal and less intimidating than in the predawn hours, with some nicer storefronts and signage, and a more even pattern of development. I chided myself for my nighttime gloom. The signs were in English and Arabic script, though Kurdish, as I've said, is an Indo-European language closer to Persian than to Arabic.

The first place I visited was the national museum housed on the site of what had been an Iraqi torture center during Saddam Hussein's rule. The nondescript building, divided into a seemingly endless jigsaw of damp gray prison cells, had once been packed with inmates, with no heat and very few toilet facilities. It was claustrophobic in the extreme.

One's imagination ran riot here, contemplating what exactly had happened in the long decades of the 1980s and 1990s, especially after the failed 1991 Kurdish uprising and massively violent Iraqi reaction, which led to a no-fly zone imposed by the United States against Saddam's regime. One room had been inhabited by fifteen-year-old boys declared by the Iraqi authorities to be eighteen, so they could be legally executed. A boy had scrawled on a cement wall: "I am about to be executed by Ba'athism." There were also a series of rooms lined with thousands of mirrors and points of light, each one symbolizing one of the hundreds of thousands of Kurds massacred by "the Ba'athist occupiers." Kurdish schoolchildren silently crowded the museum during my visit, streams of them, looking intently at photos of the torture victims. This place was a real shrine to a certain tragic period in Kurdish history. In 1999, I had experienced the same level of communal memory, built on devotion to the dead, at the museum in Yerevan dedicated to the victims of the Turkish genocide against the Armenians. Outside on the museum grounds, Soviet-era tanks and artillery pieces, employed by Saddam against the Kurds, stood like rotting dinosaurs, as if they were centuries rather than decades old.

In the nearby parks of Sulaymaniyah, there were numerous statues of Kurdish poets from the past. Poets were revered here, another sign of collective memory. Modernity and the nationalism that accompanied it were ever-present in Sulaymaniyah. Traditional dress featuring hijabs, men's scarves worn in the *jamana* style, and baggy trousers was generally confined to old people in the local bazaar with its teahouses and Persian-style mosque. Nevertheless, it became clear to me that I was in the midst of a very well defined nation without an identity crisis. The problem here, as I was about to learn, wasn't identity or borders even. It was basic governance. After all, the cash economy coupled with the absence of credit cards meant that vast amounts of money could not be adequately traced.

I WAS IN A HIP, elegant café in Sulaymaniyah, with soft jazz playing in the background. Men and women dressed in dark colors and wearing designer glasses were at tables alone, working with their computers. Here I conducted an interview with the president of the Middle East Research Institute, Dlawer Ala'Aldeen. Since he was based in Erbil, it was the first and only interview by Zoom that I conducted in all my journeys. He wore a jacket and tie and spoke with a British-trained accent: a learned academic who spoke with authority.

"The Kurdish region has fared well only when compared to the rest of Iraq," he told me. "Ours is a different, lesser scale of failure. The rule of law is weak here but at least there are no armed non-state actors." Iraq proper was a failed state, he and everyone else in Kurdistan would go on to tell me, consumed by an ethnic and sectarian spoils system in which meritocracy had little place. In Baghdad the prime minister was always a Shi'ite, the speaker of the parliament a Sunni, and the president a Kurd, who each brought along convoys of ethnic compatriots into the government.

But Ala'Aldeen took no solace from this fact. "We in Kurdistan could have been at such a higher level of development, like Malaysia, for example, and ahead of Tunisia," he said. "Instead we are like Lebanon," an exceedingly brittle and immeasurably corrupt state. "The Kurds are experts at survival," he went on. "But survival leaves little room for creativity and institution-building. The Talabani and Barzani clans for decades were state-destroyers, again, in order to survive against hostile surrounding forces. But now we have to build a state. We have no one to blame but ourselves for wasting much of the past twenty years since the American invasion of Iraq. We now have the legal protection provided by the Iraqi constitution. None of our neighbors, however bad their intentions, would stop us from separating the judiciary from the executive branch of government, for example. Instead, governmental structures in Kurdistan have evolved naturally, and that is a bad thing. There is a great danger in leaving the growth of a state to the law of nature," he explained. "Building institutions and a separation of powers is the way out of nature. And institution-building does not necessarily equate with democracy. Institutions have to come first. Look at the success of Singapore and the United Arab Emirates. They are not democratic but they work and there is the rule of law."

Indeed, to repeat, you could not escape from Lee Kuan Yew's Singapore anywhere in the Middle East. So many aspired to that model of development in which rule of law, dignity, and justice took precedence over elections.

But then Ala'Aldeen turned positive.

"We now have a civil society that never existed before. It started twenty years ago [after the American invasion], whereas in the rest of Iraq civil society is much more recent. Just look where you're sitting now," referring to the café that he saw in the background on his computer screen, which could not have existed without a measure of freedom and globalization. "Because of the spread of civil society the leaders and politicians have to play by new rules. They have to present themselves differently, and that leads them to adjust in other ways. The private sector is also expanding, and will eventually be less corrupt than it is now. There is no going backward here, given that security is not really an issue."

His voice was not alone. As others would tell me, despite the apparent failures here, despite the unpaid salaries and the dead-broke refugees who had fled Iraqi Kurdistan, despite insufficient press freedom, and despite the squandered oil wealth, an emerging global civilization expressed through social media and the internet meant that the Loom of Time was perhaps slowly at work here, too.

NEVERTHELESS, KURDISTAN'S PROBLEMS COULD not be minimized.

Sarwar Abdulrahman was both an historian and a parliamentarian. His office offered a view of the dreary and cruddy sprawl that is Sulaymaniyah, so far from the pulsing neon and Plexiglass dynamism of even troubled East Asian societies like Malaysia, which Dlawer Ala'Aldeen had specifically mentioned as marking a level of development that Kurdistan should already have achieved. Abdulrahman was different in style than Ala'Aldeen, less sophisticated in dress and language, less international, but bearing a similar message.

"In a recent election only 30 percent of the people voted. Boycotting elections is the only means of protest, since both ruling families, the Barzanis and Talabanis, are deeply unpopular. After the American invasion, we learned that while one dictator went away, other smaller dictators came to take his place." Here he mentioned not only the two ruling clans but also the brilliant and sophisticated Kurdish president of Iraq and former prime minister of Kurdistan, Barham Salih, whom foreigners were especially enamored of. Abdulrahman was not impressed, however, as Salih despite his international connections had made too little difference when he had been in power here, despite bringing an American university to Sulaymaniyah.

"We are just surviving, not developing," Abdulrahman went on. "How can we develop when those in power are filling their pockets?" Then he spoke passionately about the many schools that badly needed renovation and the malls that had been built through cash payoffs. As for the new civil society, he said that even that requires better functioning institutions in order to make a difference. Nevertheless, unlike the disastrous Arab Spring in artificial territories like Syria and Libya, he said that "our people will not destroy order" because despite the different clans, there was still a real ethnic state here, even if it wasn't going anywhere.

Was ethnicity enough to maintain order? I wondered. Egypt with its overwhelming Sunni Arab population still required a police state. So did Saudi Arabia, which also had relatively few broad-based ethnic or sectarian divisions, despite the various tribes and the Shi'ites in the Eastern Province. Turkey might teeter following the end of Erdoğan's rule, I thought, and yet its Turkish-Kurdish divide might be only a small factor in its future instability. As for Kurdistan itself, it was surrounded by historical enemies, and the mountainous terrain did indeed help provide its people with a unique identity. But the further removed the persecutions of the Saddam era became, and the more plugged into a global culture its young people became, the less of a defense against disorder a singular ethnicity might provide its people. The state would have to deliver more in terms of honesty, efficiency, and development or there could be an explosion here, I thought. For Kurdistan clearly lacked the social contract between ruler and ruled that was so impressive to witness in Saudi Arabia and the smaller Gulf Arab states. I thought of the basic theme in the late Samuel Huntington's classic work, *Political Order in Changing Societies* (1968), which was that modernity produces tumult. As soon as one level of political and social development was reached, populations, which were always ungrateful, craved more privileges. Revolutions and uprisings were thus never-ending and woven into the fabric of history. A few years down the road, after the novelty of new personal freedoms wears off, the Saudi population might then demand political freedoms and less oppression. That's why I felt, early in my visit, that I was surely seeing Kurdistan at a transitory moment. Since it was obvious to me, if history was any guide, that people here would not forever accept the status quo. And that was the key to the Loom of Time. It was another way of stating Huntington's assertion about the permanence of change and upheavals, peaceful and otherwise. To suggest that the Arab Spring failed and that was that, well, this misjudged the meaning of history, which was that other risings would surely come, in different forms, subtle and not, and may already be under way. Meanwhile, all I could do was listen to people here. And if I heard the same thing repeatedly, it might mean that I was on the right track.

ZMKAN ALI SALEEM WAS the program director of the Institute of Regional and International Studies at the American University in Sulaymaniyah. He had been studying Iraq firsthand for decades. When I told him that I was searching for middle grounds of governance in the Greater Middle East, between anarchy and tyranny, he interrupted:

"In Iraq there is still no middle ground, particularly in Baghdad. Various political groups, militias, patronage networks buy off the government in a very unstable, violent system which fails to provide even security and basic services to the population. That, in turn, has led to resentment and never-ending protests. As for Kurdistan, it is a duopoly composed of the Barzani-run Kurdistan Democratic Party [KDP] and the Talabani-run Patriotic Union of Kurdistan [PUK]. The level of corruption is extreme, as oil and other business revenues are used to buy patronage networks. The KDP is stronger and less fragmented than the PUK, since its power is concentrated in the hands of fewer people. When you get to Erbil, run by the KDP, you will see how wealthier, more developed, and organized it is, compared to Sulaymaniyah, run by the PUK, which gets fewer services and less of the oil revenue."

He explained that this bleak situation had gone on for over three decades—not since the American invasion of 2003, but ever since the First Gulf War of 1991. The aftermath of the 1991 war had led to the no-fly zone over northern Iraq, resulting in Saddam withdrawing his forces from the region. That led to the infusion of international NGOs and massive Turkish aid, as Turkey decided to work with the Barzanis and Talabanis against Abdullah Öcalan's PKK.

"It is fascinating to watch," he went on, "how a restricted circle of clan leaders, who have failed to build a real state, can restrain an entire population for three decades. In Kurdistan the duopoly acts with impunity."

"THIS PLACE IS LIKE DISNEYLAND: strange, funny, ironic," said Hiwa Osman in a playful but at the same time serious tone. I was in another café that might have been in Paris or Manhattan, with young people in small groups or alone with their computers. The only thing that might have identified it as Kurdistan was that everyone was smoking. Osman was a journalist and intellectual. He also made the point that Kurdistan should be at a much higher level of development, instead of being a sleepy "kleptocracy" with desultory protests by teachers and civil servants achieving little, as though they were carrying out obligatory exercise in a prison yard. You couldn't open a small business without making payoffs. Even though $10 billion in oil revenue came in annually as part of an agreement with Iraq, and the United States and the countries of the European Union paid for the military and a plethora of donor projects, it was still hard to say where all the money ended up.

"Look," he said, "Sulaymaniyah is a place where practically every family has shed blood over the decades for the country's independence. Everyone feels like they have paid a price for freedom. Yet there is still no social contract like in the states of the Arabian Gulf where no one has paid a price for their prosperity. Kurdistan," he continued, "is a place of general apathy. Voter turnouts aren't 30 percent. They're actually below 20 percent. Yes, there are free elections, but no accountability, while the men with guns rule. Is democracy the best system for everyone? It is an interesting question."

He then spoke about the PUK region of eastern Kurdistan, reinforcing what others had told me. Even when the grand old man of local politics and former Iraqi president Jalal Talabani was alive, the PUK was a nest of powerful little men and various factions surrounding the leader, who governed "PLO-like" in the corrupt manner of Yasser Arafat. It was just so hard to get anything administrative done here, the reason why Sulaymaniyah languished. When I told him my impressions of the airport, he nodded his head in agreement. Even allowing for the mass killings of the Saddam regime, Osman said that "in terms of services—schools, hospitals, public transportation— Saddam was better." Saddam, he told me, would make an unannounced visit to a hospital, select a patient arbitrarily, and if that patient was not being properly attended to, "Saddam would just execute the hospital administrator." It was altogether brutal. Such a regime might have collapsed in mass bloodshed during the Arab Spring much like Syria's, had George W. Bush not toppled it in 2003. But it had its benefits compared to the current situation. As for the future here, Osman did not think that liberalism was necessarily the reigning aspiration of the majority of young people. "The mosques on Fridays are packed with poor youth, the ones you don't see in these cafés, who are susceptible to ideology. Political Islam is one possible future for Kurdistan. Don't count it out."

Or there was another alternative. As the head of an independent media organization, who was a survivor of Saddam's genocidal Anfal campaign, told me, repeating the words of others I spoke with: "It is better to have one dictator rather than many, like now." Alas, the "many" little dictators of the moment were not even self-made men, but the sons and other descendants of the likes of Mulla Mustafa Bar-zani and Jalal Talabani, who had lived in the mountains and had real charisma and capabilities. Kurdistan, among so many other things, was a story of family decline.

"A SMOOTH, GRADUAL TRANSITION away from the two clans is be-coming harder to imagine. Instead you could have a rough transition, such as violence, a coup d'état, what have you," said Stam Saeed, a tall and sophisticated young man with an Apple watch who aspired to write about Kurdistan for publications like *Foreign Affairs* and *Foreign Policy,* and who spoke knowingly about Machiavelli and Thucydides. Saeed was the chief of political research for the Change Movement, a small party in the parliament that had been around a long time and had its own problems. His reasoning for a "rough transition" was sim-ple: "if nothing is happening, then something awful may happen." The explosive elements, he explained, were there to see. There was a Salafist movement in the mosques. The young and connected generation wanted a better life and had little interest in stories about heroic strug-gles in the mountains told by their grandfathers. Trust beyond the family barely existed. "You can bribe a judge and get anything you want done. There is no rule of law, no transparency. The half of the population that is middle class is slipping deeper into debt. The PUK," he continued, "is so internally divided that violent clashes between the factions are possible, as is a conflict between the PUK and KDP." Saeed did say that a possible alternative to a rough transition was a new political movement led by a populist or charismatic leader, some-one who could rise above the clans and capture the imagination of the public and wipe the slate clean.

In this vein Saeed mentioned Barham Salih. If Salih left the presi-dency of Iraq in Baghdad and returned to Kurdistan, he might qualify as such a messianic figure. Salih was one of those blessed men, a tech-nocrat, like Ashraf Ghani, the former president of Afghanistan, who had innumerable international contacts and was deeply Westernized, oozing erudition. Thus, outsiders were in awe of him. The question was, however, not whether he could hold a seminar at an Ivy League college, but could he work within a deeply corrupt and thuggish system to force change. Ashraf Ghani wound up fleeing Afghanistan rather than fighting the Taliban. Salih, on the other hand, had spent years in both the PUK and the Iraqi government following the 2003 invasion. He had real bureaucratic skills and was adroit at infighting. He had also tried his hand at running Kurdistan before as prime minister and thus had learned useful lessons. Therefore, the comparison with Ghani was not altogether fair.

Though the future was ultimately unknowable, it seemed hard to believe that the current stasis was permanent. I kept in mind that Sulaymaniyah and eastern Kurdistan were poorer and more dissatisfied than Erbil and western Kurdistan, where the real money and development were, and where I would also get the Kurdish government point of view.

It was time to leave Sulaymaniyah and listen to others in Erbil.

THE DRIVE NORTHWEST FROM Sulaymaniyah to Erbil took three hours. Mountains rose like sawtooth granite cathedrals flecked with snow, overlooking dark green pastures. A towering ridgeline extended to the horizon, as though a curtain were drawn against the sky. Flanks of smaller mountains tumbled down into folded valleys, with cows and sheep munching on grass in a riot of steep-angled hillsides. In some places the curvature of the terrain looked as smooth as marble. Here and there on stony outcrops were villages constructed of undressed cinder blocks, with the men in *jamana*s and baggy trousers and the women covered in hijabs. Rivers and streams were mirror-like in their cold clarity. The road wasn't bad, despite the half-a-dozen checkpoints manned by men in full kit and assault rifles. The scenery could not have been more dramatic. At the point marking the division between the PUK- and KDP-controlled areas, men scanned my passport, as though I were traveling from one country to another. As soon as I passed the checkpoint into KDP-controlled territory, billboard pictures of Masoud Barzani replaced those of Jalal Talabani.

In KDP territory there was much more construction, with brightly painted bulldozers at work, along with better built houses and many slick roadside advertisements. Finally the car descended into an utterly flat plain where the city of Erbil sprawls in a grid pattern.

Erbil, a city of 1.5 million people, is twice the size of Sulaymaniyah. This was a real global city, compared to the sandpaper, archaeological mien of Sulaymaniyah. I saw a vast panorama of tall and well-built apartment houses, landscaped boulevards with new overhead road lamps, and well-engineered overpasses and underpasses. In some cases the glittering domes signified shopping malls rather than mosques. There were international chain hotels, gated communities, and cafés like those in Silicon Valley and Abu Dhabi. The dynamism was almost Asian. In Erbil at least one could compare Kurdistan to Malaysia. Prices, as I was to learn, were exorbitant. This was where all the oil money was, and where the Kurdish government was, and consequently where all the foreign diplomats and other officials came to live and do business. It was clear from the lack of development in Sulaymaniyah and the rest of the PUK area that *Kurdistan* was a misnomer. There were really two Kurdistans in northern Iraq, one better run and richer and the other worse run and poorer. Billboard pictures of Masoud Barzani lined Erbil's roads. He was the de facto ruler, even as his son, Masrour, was officially the prime minister. Again, one dictator seemed better than many.

Erbil was two cities, though: the so-called gold zone where all the development was, and an older part centered around the seven-thousand-year-old Citadel, a steep glacis originally occupied by the Sumerians and Assyrians from early antiquity, and stormed by the Mongols in A.D. 1258. Here was the bazaar that took you back decades in dress and manners. Not only were there Kurds and Turkmen, but many Arabs who had fled Iraq proper for the relative safety and opportunities of Erbil. I noticed no Westerners besides myself in the old part of town. Erbil had been discovered by the oil and international development communities, which kept to themselves. But it still lacked the security required for global tourism. The night before I arrived, a barrage of Iranian missiles had hit the area near the new U.S.

consulate here. Thus, as in Jeddah, I felt privileged to be visiting an old city still off the holiday map, as it were: in this case buildings and fortress walls that were a delicious confection of Turkish, Persian, Byzantine, and Kurdish styles.

And yet despite its ancient treasures adjacent to topflight hotels, cafés, and restaurants, this place was still *Kurdistan*. Better governance in Erbil compared to Sulaymaniyah only went so far. At the city's fanciest hotel, receptionists asked me if I could pay for my incidentals in cash rather than with a credit card. Everywhere in Erbil it was still a cash economy.

"MOST KURDS DON'T TRUST banks. They don't know what a bank is or what it does. They have no idea about credit cards. They and their ancestors grew up fighting one or another of the surrounding states, so their circle of trust is narrow. They are suspicious of government in general. It's a generational thing. Only the young and connected even know what plastic is." The speaker was an official in the Kurdish regional government in Erbil who preferred not to be named. That way he could talk more freely about corruption.

"Both sides, the KDP and PUK, misuse budgets. Corruption within the government is hard to deal with. Actually the least corrupt branch of government is the ministry that deals with the peshmerga, because the peshmerga are supported by the Pentagon and other foreign defense ministries, so their finances are regulated somewhat by international militaries. Otherwise, the Kurdish Regional Government has made some progress in ending double salaries and other abuses, but there is a long way to go. Also digitalization is ending some of the corruption and leading to reform. But it is a long-term process after years and decades of massive corruption that goes along with a weak or nonexistent history as a modern state."

The official pointed out that the Barzani and Talabani clans had fought a bloody civil war between 1992 and 1996, in the wake of Kurdistan's obtaining de facto independence from Iraq when the Americans instituted a no-fly zone against Saddam. The civil war has led to suspicion ever since. He told me that the Kurdistan Regional Government could do little about the comparative lack of development in Sulaymaniyah "because of PUK chaos," mentioning the coup in July 2021, when Jalal Talabani's son, Bafel, took tenuous control of the party. In sum, "you need institutions. It is only with strong institutions that give you the option to decentralize decision-making, which is the mark of modern governance. The KDP," he went on, "was still in the stage of a strong individual leader, Massoud Barzani, because institutions in Erbil are weak. The PUK is decentralized, but with weak or nonexistent institutions, so there is chaos in Sulaymaniyah."

MOHAMMED SHAREEF TAUGHT POLITICS at the University of Kurdistan in Erbil. Because he had grown up partly in the United Kingdom and made trips back and forth between there and Kurdistan, he was able to see changes over the years and decades. "I do see progress here. I do see maturation toward a liberal system. However landlocked Kurdistan may be, and however dependent we are on ruthless enemies like Turkey and Iran, people in Kurdistan are basically free to live their lives as long as they stay away from criticizing certain individuals."

"The bureaucracy is more polite," he went on, "more efficient; visiting a government office is less of an ordeal than it used to be. You quietly take a ticket and wait your turn. Years back people would crowd around a bureaucrat pleading for attention. Because of increased travel abroad, the culture is slowly evolving along Western lines. People are more demanding of government. Given the oil wealth, they want more of something akin to a 'nanny' state. Government is a mirror of the culture of a population, and the culture here is little by little improving. Women's rights in Kurdistan" have been undergoing a slow revolution, he said. Though, as others told me, even as there were still strict taboos concerning sexual relations, the taboos against dishonesty, laziness, inconsistency, and other such things were much weaker.

But Shareef told me that with all of Kurdistan's problems, "absolutely" you could not compare Kurdistan today to the sufferings of the

Saddam era. People with memories remain grateful to the Americans for the no-fly zone and for removing Saddam. The Iraq War is not so unpopular here, he insisted, an amazing thing for an American to hear. Only those who are relatively young and lack usable memories, he explained, complain that the Saddam era was better, especially whenever their salaries are not paid or they suffer economic deprivations. Of course, the issue was the old one of the simple passage of time coupled with demands for a better life that accounted for the occasional nostalgia for the Ba'athist regime, a regime that fewer and fewer Kurds had actually experienced. Meanwhile, I happened to be in Kurdistan on March 16, 2022, thirty-four years to the day after Saddam's March 16, 1988, poison gas attack on thousands of Kurdish civilians in the town of Halabja. At 11 A.M., all the traffic in Erbil stopped and all pedestrians stood still, observing a few moments of silence to commemorate the event. The memory of the Ba'athist terror state was still strong.

"Iraq," Shareef summed up, "only exists in the mind of the State Department. Too much water has flowed under the bridge since the no-fly zone in 1991. Whatever Kurdistan's problems, Baghdad and the other cities in Arab Iraq are far more unstable and insecure. The younger generation of Kurds in the schools and in the universities are studying English and not Arabic. Nobody wants to visit Iraq."

NIYAZ BARZANI, THE HEAD of foreign relations for his relative, Kurdish president Nechirvan Barzani, doubled down on everything that Shareef said.* "Iraq is a very sad story," Barzani began. Even during the decades before the 1958 coup and certainly afterwards, "there was never an extended period of stability and prosperity except at the expense of one ethnic or sectarian group or another. The biggest problem with Iraq is that no one has ever been loyal to the institutions of state. The loyalty has always been to one group or another. As of now

---

* The presidency in Kurdistan was largely ceremonial. Much more power resided with the prime minister, Masrour Barzani. And Masrour's father, Massoud Barzani, had to approve all big decisions.

we don't have an Iraqi government except in name only: we have a Shi'ite regime, that's it. In Iraq proper, the real elements of power and intimidation lie outside government." And government, he might have said, is all about monopolizing the use of force.

Barzani added: "The U.S. decision to remove Saddam was the right decision. You gave the Iraqi people the chance to live a different story, to break from their past. Unfortunately, they did not take the opportunity."

I wish I could have believed him. The problem is that it is very difficult for any nation or large group of people to break from its past. And foreign policy should be about a nation's interest, not a political science experiment.

EVEN IF THE SITUATION in Iraq was much worse, Kurdistan was still badly governed. Two clans-cum-gangs and weak institutions essentially defined it. Yet it wasn't particularly repressive. And minorities were well treated. Life was normal and predictable. Meanwhile, Kurdistan's much bigger neighbors—Iraq proper, Syria, Turkey, and Iran—were either lawless, as we know in the case of Iraq; at war in the case of Syria; suffering vast economic mismanagement in the case of Turkey; or both terrifically repressive and also mismanaged in the case of Iran. Whereas Kurds incessantly complained, people on the other side of the border in any direction were often altogether miserable. Life here was normal, just disappointing. Life nearby was often intolerably unsafe. The Kurds, given their history, were not doing too badly. But no one with whom I spoke was at all satisfied with the current domestic situation. In their universal demands for better government there were grounds for hope.

SAFAVID IRAN

═══

UNLIKE THE STATES OF THE FERTILE CRESCENT, WHICH are all artificial creations of the twentieth century, Iran is synonymous with a significant geographical feature, the high-altitude Iranian plateau, protected by seas and mountains. Like Egypt's Nile Valley, Iran is heir to a singular language and civilization in a variety of forms going back millennia. Iran's distinctiveness is further enhanced by being virtually surrounded by non-Persian peoples.[1] Age-old Iran was the archrival and political-cultural opposite of the Greek city-states and Alexander the Great, much as it was the archrival of the West, the Arab Gulf states, and Israel. Ever since Herodotus, for reasons of geography and civilization, Iran has been at the center of world history, and has been the seat of great empires—Achaemenid, Sassanid, and Safavid—stretching from the Mediterranean to the borderlands of India and China. Indeed, the Achaemenid Empire of Cyrus and Darius in early antiquity can be considered the first true empire and universal government in recorded history. Under both the shah and the ayatollahs, Iran, in the twentieth and twenty-first centuries, believed it had the historical, cultural, and moral authority to shape the Greater Middle East in all the areas where Persian empires once held mastery.[2]

Though Iran may have constituted an imperium reaching back to antiquity, it was the early modern Safavids at the beginning of the sixteenth century, with their introduction of Shi'ism as a quasi–state religion, who bequeathed to Iran "an uninterrupted political identity" and the beginning of a standardized state long before the age of modern nationalism, notes Yale professor Abbas Amanat. The Safavids accomplished this, in part, by forgoing claims to eastern Anatolia, southern Mesopotamia, and swaths of Central Asia, thus giving Iran sustainable borders, based largely on the Sunni-Shi'ite split.³ In other words, Shi'ism got to define Iranian nationhood more than did the concept of ancient Persia. Of course, that is now in the process of being flipped on its side, as a postrevolutionary upheaval in the Iran of the 2020s will have the effect of reasserting a secular Persian identity to go along with this era of global cosmopolitanism. Therefore, think of what I henceforth have to say as a postmortem on clerical Shi'ite Iran.

IN THE BEGINNING, the religion-based state-building spirit of Safavid-cum-Shi'ite Iran was somewhat similar to what the two other so-called gunpowder empires of the early modern age, the Ottomans and the Mughals, were doing for Turkey and India. The Safavids themselves constituted a Sufi order of Kurds, Turkomans, and other minorities in the northwestern, Azeri Turkish part of Iran near the Caspian Sea, who went on to extend their rule throughout the Iranian plateau and its environs at the turn of the sixteenth century. Thus began the long march to the modern era of Shi'ite revolution.

The Safavid-inspired Shi'ite clergy that came to power in 1979, with its elaborate bureaucracy and hierarchy formed over the course of the past five centuries, and profiting from an imperial and cultural tradition going back to antiquity, had no comparison in the Sunni Arab world. That is mainly why the 1978–79 Iranian Revolution, rather than a mere coup or popular rebellion or spate of anarchy as is common throughout the Middle East, saw one intricate power structure, that of the shah, quickly replaced by another, that of the ayatollahs, with their tradition of deep learning and Jesuit and Dominican flair.⁴ Shah Mohammed Reza Pahlavi had represented a Westernized state harking back to ancient and implicitly secular Persian traditions, whereas Ayatollah Seyyed Ruhollah Musavi Khomeini, to give him his full name and title, represented a Shi'ite state based on Iran's early modern Safavid roots.[5] In either case, basic stability and the question of wielding enough coercive power to govern were never the problem. "The Persians have understood the machinery of government longer than Arabs, Berbers, or Turks," observes Carleton Coon.[6]

In addition to historical and cultural advantages over the Arabs, revolutionary Iran had demographic and economic ones as well.

Iran, along with Egypt and Turkey, is one of the most populous states in the Middle East. But unlike many Arab states, Iran over the years has gotten its rate of population growth down to 1.3 percent in 2020, with only 10 percent of its people under the age of fifteen, so that its population is not dramatically increasing and is therefore not a burden upon it, as it is a burden on Iran's rival Saudi Arabia, where a quarter of the population is under fifteen.[7] Iran, moreover, one of the world's leading oil and gas producers, is located astride not one but two hydrocarbon-rich zones, the Persian Gulf *and* the Caspian Sea. Iran, thus, is the geopolitical organizing principle for both the Middle East and Central Asia.

And yet Iran would not have fallen into the depths that it did, with such a bleak, radical, utterly despised, and dysfunctional regime that virtually destroyed the middle class, without serious weaknesses that also hark back to history and culture.

For example, as well-defined as Persia is as a polity, almost 40 percent of the population is Azeri Turk, Turkmen, Kurd, Arab, or some other non-Persian ethnic group.[8] And given the far-flung geographical mosaic of these communities, distributed as they are around the vast Iranian plateau, stability and sufficient governmental control could never be taken for granted. Iran is full of contradictions, even geographical ones.

The twentieth century actually began hopefully for Iran, with a constitution and separation of powers promulgated under the severely weakened Turkic Qajar dynasty in 1907. At this juncture, the rest of the Middle East was far behind Iran in political development. Yet the advancement was short-lived, and was followed within two years by civil war, before a restoration of the constitution in 1909: this tumultuous march of events demonstrated just how fragile the society, political system, and Qajar dynasty were. Following the even greater turmoil of World War I, with the Russian Revolution literally right on Iran's doorstep, an atmosphere of institutional feebleness and decline enabled the rise to power of Reza Khan, an officer in the Persian Cossack Brigade, who toppled the Qajars and founded his own Pahlavi dynasty in 1925.*

Reza Khan Shah, as he came to be known, was inspired by Atatürk, who had taken power in Turkey in the same period. But Reza Khan proved to be only a lesser Atatürk, without the latter's sophistication and cosmopolitan upbringing at the western edge of the Ottoman Empire. Reza Shah's Westernization of the country was highly superficial and eccentric—nomads were ordered to stop wandering; pictures of the camel, judged a "backward" beast, were forbidden—while the new shah amassed vast personal wealth. Modernization and institution-building were concentrated in the capital, creating "two cultures" in Iran, writes the UCLA professor Nikki R. Keddie: the Westernized culture of the cities and the increasingly embittered peasant culture of the countryside.[9] Then, over time, as oil wealth accumulated and urbanization accelerated, the contradictions between a glittering Westernized class around Reza Shah's son, Mohammed Reza Pahlavi, and a profoundly backward peasantry also accelerated, and in the 1970s the village essentially migrated en masse to the city and vanquished it, with the faction of ayatollahs led by Khomeini as the vanguard.[10] Whereas in the 1950s, 30 percent of Iranians lived in cities, by the 1970s half of Iranians did.[11] I noted the same phenomenon elsewhere in my travels, but in Iran it had been more extreme and had its own peculiar characteristics.

Iran isn't Turkey, in other words. The Anatolian plateau, because it is less arid than its Iranian counterpart, holds enough interconnected areas of settlement so that the difference between villages and large towns and cities, as marked as it is, is still less pronounced than in Iran. More important, Anatolia has a thousand miles of frontage on the

---

* Pahlavi refers to a Persian script of late antiquity, and is redolent of a pre-Islamic past.

Mediterranean, besides a long Black Sea coast that has linked it throughout history to the Balkans and European Russia.[12] The Iranian plateau was a geographical bridge too far: just too far away and cut off from Europe for a Westernization strategy—a badly conceived one at that, and one distorted by the economics of oil—to take hold without a violent revolutionary reversal. This revolutionary reversal, it should be said, was not supported by all of the ayatollahs, since many of them believed that political power would only corrupt their ranks, and would eventually cause them to be hated. Even within clerical ranks, Khomeini was a radical.

Culturally brilliant and geographically vital to both the Middle East and Central Asia, revolutionary Iran was a mass of ironies, as I discovered during a visit of several weeks there in the mid-1990s, when I was able to obtain a visa to travel throughout the country, thanks to an Iranian official I had met at an international conference. This resulted in two long chapters on Iran that I published in earlier books, *The Ends of the Earth* (1996) and *The Revenge of Geography* (2012). But now, in the age of Google, I could not go back to Iran since the Iranian security services could easily learn that I had served in the Israeli military.

In 1994, when I traveled throughout Iran, I saw that the Islamic Revolution had already begun disintegrating. In Tehran back then, the mullahs in parliament were railing against declining morals, while the facades of apartment buildings were cluttered with satellite dishes, with the most popular television show *Baywatch* and the most popular channel MTV. Following the 1980–89 Iran-Iraq War and the death of Ayatollah Khomeini, the communications revolution had started to make inroads on the geography of the Iranian plateau, so that the battle between East and West was being fought anew inside Iran itself. I discovered that the economy had been placed in the hands of opaque and informal mobster-traders, with links to the working-class bazaars, who mixed the trade in consumer goods with illegal arms shipments. (I even did a profile of one such *bazaari* for *The Atlantic*.[13]) I visited the holy city of Qom, with its spectacular faience shrines framed against dun-drab volcanic mountains, and interviewed Islamic seminary students engaged in the abstractions of medieval thought while tyranny and corruption filled the void around them. But I also found Qom a major center for the study of law, languages, and philosophy, another example of Iran's high level of culture. The students asked about my Judaism, in a curious and respectful way. In Isfahan, I took a late night walk along the Zayande Rud, the river that runs through the town, where families camped out, sitting on carpets around little fires that they had made to celebrate the Zoroastrian holiday of No Ruz. It was a sign of Iran's robust pre-Islamic identity, which, combined with its unique Persian language, made it an authentic age-old cluster of civilization and not an artificial state like Syria and Iraq. And on that late night walk, despite the remonstrations of the clergy, I noticed a lot of hand-holding between young men and women, and a lot of makeup and fingernail polish on the women. In Shiraz, I visited the tomb of the fourteenth-century Persian poet Hafiz, a place where large numbers of Iranians gather at dusk, bearing roses in their hands to celebrate Hafiz's life-giving sensuality. Hafiz wrote metaphorically of wine and the pleasures of the flesh, and is denounced by Islamic conservatives as quasi-blasphemous. Yet I saw groups of Iranians having their pictures taken by his tomb.[14]

I sensed a culture of layers, rich with paradoxes as well as with ideas and philosophy, where people had discovered private spaces of freedom within an elaborate revolutionary system. Whereas Saudi Arabia and the Arab Gulf states were venues of raw, transparent, and empirical power politics, emanating from a tradition of tribal disputes in the desert, interpreting Iran had always been more difficult, since it emanated from a rich tapestry of empires, in which Khomeini, to quote the late intellectual and Middle East scholar Fouad Ajami, was but a "turbaned shah."[15]

The past is everywhere in Iranian politics. Indeed, there has always been this stylistic extravagance and tendency for rhetorical overreach. When Khomeini spoke of "Great and Lesser Satans" and of the "world-devouring arrogance" of the United States, former CIA area specialist Graham Fuller observed that Khomeini was echoing the theatrical manner of the Safavid Empire.[16]

———

YET TO UNDERSTAND THE nature and the mechanics of the clerical regime—so necessary in order to glimpse Iran's future beyond the Islamic Revolution—one must first explore the Safavid imperial inheritance in terms of the Shi'ite religion.

Shi'ism lends itself to being a state religion, not only because it was spread throughout Iran by the Safavid Empire, but because of its particular religious ideology. Shi'ism literally means *Shi'at Ali*, or "the party of Ali," the nephew and son-in-law of the Prophet Muhammad, and according to Shi'ites the Prophet's rightful successor. Ali ruled as caliph from A.D. 656 to 661, when he was assassinated. Since then Shi'ites were essentially in opposition against the traditional line of succession of the Sunni caliphs, becoming a faction or "party," as their name suggests. Iranians, moreover, are Twelver Shi'ites. They believe in both the political and spiritual rule of the twelve successive and rightful imams following Muhammad, the last of whom, the Mahdi, is hidden and lives in "occultation" and will reveal himself at the end of days. Shi'ite tradition, in other words, significantly more so than Sunni tradition, is obsessed with power and *who rules* the faithful. This is because of a great perceived wrong done to them in Islam's early days, when not only was Ali assassinated, but his son Husayn and Husayn's army were massacred at Karbala in southern Iraq by the forces of the Caliph Yazid of the Umayyad Empire. A strong degree of pessimism and resentment, as well as of martyrdom, is thus baked into Shi'ite psychology, making Shi'ites generally suspicious of political authority except for their own. Indeed, as Vali Nasr explains, while the Sunnis have a "preoccupation with order," the Shi'ites have a preoccupation with "values," and therefore put less stock in what the ruling majority believes. They are true oppositionists.[17]

The British journalist Edward Mortimer, in his pathbreaking book *Faith and Power: The Politics of Islam*, points out that in the case of Twelver Shi'ites, such skepticism about those in authority has a firm doctrinal basis. "The fact that government tends to be bad or un-Islamic is not just an observable and regrettable fact: it is in the nature of things so long as the rightful Imam has not taken matters in hand, which is now not going to happen until the end of time." Because of this debasement of the state, it renders a separate *"religious organization* ... not dependent on the state, *absolutely necessary."* Thus, the Iranian Shi'ite clergy were able to develop a "distinct *corporate* identity" that eventually made them a highly organized, alternative political force to that of the shah.[18]

Yet it was Khomeini who, opposed to other Shi'ite clerics, took this corporate identity one step further in the struggle against a fiercely secular, repressive, and bombastic shah. Islam, Khomeini insisted, is political or it is nothing. Driving home the point: "Was not the Prophet, God's prayers be upon him, a politician?"* Thus, Khomeini in his writings has circled back to Muhammad as the first true revolutionary, who created a faith that bred a chain of unending political upheavals. But whereas Sunni Islam in recent decades has had difficulty in creating stable political entities, on account of its weaker bureaucratic tendency, Khomeini was personally leading his Twelver Shi'ites precisely in the direction of state control.

And this direction in which he led them was also decidedly undemocratic, though with a twist. Khomeini stated that Islamic government for Shi'ite Iran must be "the representative of [the martyred] Ali." Therefore it must be legitimate, unlike Ali's usurpers, and that meant in Khomeini's view "constitutional." But as Mortimer explains, Khomeini did not mean constitutional in the usual—or at least in the Western—sense of the term. For above the government there must be a "supreme leader," a *faqih* or jurist, "an expert in divine law which the government exists to enforce."[19] This *Wilayat al-Faqih* ("rule of the jurist") meant guardianship on the basis of theological knowledge that gives the *faqih* or jurist a semi-divine mandate.[20] Khomeini here quotes a proverb that "the jurists are rulers over the sultans," since the former are wiser in the ways of Islamic law and therefore wiser in the ways of the political world.[21]

---

* Mortimer, p. 326. The words "is political or it is nothing" are the author's summation of Khomeini's thought.

The nineteenth-century Egyptian Sunni modernist Mohammed Abduh also wrote about a jurist ruling according to his knowledge of the law, and in constant consultation with popular leaders.[22] But in Khomeini's formulation there is something dangerously utopian about this construct and imitation of the Platonic notion of a philosopher-king: that of an infallible wise man to whom elected leaders must submit.[23] For example, the key difference between a supreme leader, a *faqih*, and a pope is that the Catholic pope rules not a defined geography but a community of the faithful who all live under their own elected or nonelected governments in their own sovereign territories, to which the pope himself can always appeal but cannot order in a secular sense to do anything, whereas Khomeini's *faqih* holds supreme power over a specific government and a specific geography. This makes Khomeini's ideal jurist, who rules in the name of religion but whose rulings must be unequivocally political—because they involve human beings within concrete physical borders—the most dangerous sort of dictator, since his rulings, however cruel or unjust, are given in the name of a higher religious and moral virtue.

There is a name for this phenomenon: Leninism. Vladimir Lenin minted the modern technique and justification for mass, organized cruelty and thought-control in the name of a higher virtue and purity. For Communism and the dictatorship of the proletariat might as well have been a religion, in which all forms and manner of human activity were judged according to a single ideological standard, just as most everything in revolutionary Iran was seen and judged in religious terms. Whether it was the Communist Party or the theocratic rulebook, it was forced upon everyone's mind, was in every school, in every private company, in every military unit, and so forth. In the early years at least, before the Islamic Revolution began to calcify, the Shi'ite clergy practically sucked the oxygen out of the air of politics.

In a way what had happened was almost inevitable. Because the Pahlavi state's own absolutism, coupled with its failure to build a political constituency, had demolished all forms of political infrastructure, little other than a revolutionary Shi'ite regime could have emerged back then. The fact that one stable political system led to another was a mark of both Iran's modernity and the abiding influence of the early modern Safavids.[24]

In fact, while the images and symbolism were Islamic, the methods of the Islamic Revolution in Iran, in which Khomeini was installed as the supreme leader or *faqih*, were European. The show trials and executions of the ideological enemies of the new regime (usually officials of the former Pahlavi monarchy), the large-scale confiscation of private property, the theatrical indoctrination sessions and shaming, the forcing into exile of hundreds of thousands of men and women—"all this owes far more to the examples of Robespierre and Stalin than to those of Muhammed and Ali," writes Bernard Lewis.[25]

Tragically, though the Islamic Revolution claimed to have given Iran a new and more egalitarian start, all links to Iran's late Qajar-era constitutional past, which had seemed so promising and democratic at the time, were rejected and barely even thought of.[26] The tyranny of the Pahlavis was simply replaced by that of the ayatollahs; just as the tyranny of the tsars was replaced by that of the Bolsheviks in Russia. And in each case, the result was worse than before, owing to the radical, utopian element—and assumption of perfect virtue—which traditional monarchy often thankfully lacks. Had it not been for the Russian and Iranian revolutions, both Russia and Iran might have evolved in the course of the twentieth century into highly imperfect constitutional monarchies and half-hearted friends of the West, rather than into the moral and political monstrosities that they became.

One might add that the new Islamic Republic, especially under the pseudo-French influence of Abolhasan Bani-Sadr, who served as its first president directly under the Supreme Leader, bore a hazy Marxist *tiers-mondisme* (third-worldist element), as the revolution reached out especially to the ruralized urban poor in the spirit of class warfare, and owing to the revolution's support for liberation movements across the globe.[27] In fact, the first foreign visitor to the Islamic Republic was Palestine Liberation Organization chairman Yasser Arafat, the very icon of third world revolution at the time. Moreover, Egypt's late leader Gamal Abdel Nasser was championed in revolutionary Tehran for his anti-Westernism, and for humiliating the United States and the European powers a generation before Khomeini did.

For the Islamic Revolution was very much about revenge and *empowerment*. After all, fresh in Iranian minds was the 1953 coup against the prime minister Mohammed Mosaddeq, which in the popular mind at least was orchestrated by the CIA and British intelligence, followed by the reinstatement to full power of Shah Mohammed Reza Pahlavi. There was, too, the memory of Iran—though never formally colonized like the Arab world—having suffered territorial violation by the Russians and the British in the nineteenth and early twentieth centuries. All this came to a boil in the streets of the Iranian capital in the late 1970s, and especially in the taking of fifty-two hostages from the U.S. embassy in Tehran. Yet as historically justified as this resentment arguably was, it obviously had gone too far. For there was the dangerous air of utopia hovering about the mass anti-shah demonstrations, and the rejection altogether of the international order. As in Jean-Jacques Rousseau's own utopian work, *The Social Contract*, the Iranian Revolution was about beginning anew from scratch, as if the trials and tribulations of the secular world throughout history were of little consequence.[28] Only the ideal, in this case that of the Shi'ite *Wilayat al-Faqih*, mattered.

Iran in the late 1970s, as the journalist and area specialist Robin Wright observes, constituted the twentieth century's "last great revolution." As she puts it, the Iranian Revolution constituted "one of the century's seminal turning points," which in the Middle East can only be compared to the establishment of the state of Israel and the collapse of the Ottoman Empire.[29] The Iranian Revolution spurred sectarian violence from the Middle East to the Indian subcontinent. It made Shi'ite Iran and Wahhabi Saudi Arabia doctrinal and strategic rivals after having been uneasy allies in an American-led order, and took the Lebanese civil war on an even more tortuous and violent path.* Truly,

---

* This is the subject of Kim Ghattas's 2020 book *Black Wave: Saudi Arabia, Iran, and the Forty-Year Rivalry That Unraveled Culture, Religion, and Collective Memory in the Middle East.*

Khomeini's worldwide impact as a revolutionary leader can be likened to that of Lenin, Mao Zedong, and Ho Chi Minh. No Muslim thinker in the early modern or modern eras—not Mohammed Abduh, not Hassan al-Banna, nor any other—has had Khomeini's regional and global effect.[30]

The effect was global because the Islamic Revolution was the first world-class revolution to be televised. Technology had all along played a key role in the shah's overthrow. For years tapes and videocassettes of the exiled Khomeini's sermons had been circulating inside Iran. Then in October 1978, then–vice president of Iraq Saddam Hussein, partly under misguided pressure from the shah, expelled Khomeini from the Shi'ite holy city of Najaf in southern Iraq, where he had been living in exile since 1965, forcing Khomeini into a new place of exile, much farther removed from Iran, in the Paris suburb of Neauphle-le-Château. But there, in the freer and therefore more accessible atmosphere of the French capital, Khomeini sat cross-legged beneath an apple tree, rallied his followers, and methodically seduced a sympathetic world media with his turban, white beard, austere gaze, and uncompromising responses to questions that were prepared in advance.

And why shouldn't a liberal media have been intrigued? Just as the French revolutionaries had promised war on the crowned heads of Europe, and just as the Bolsheviks had promised a war on all forms of imperialism, beginning with the tsar's, Khomeini, this exotic and aged holy man, was promising a war on the shah's tyranny and the imperialism of the West. The test of all great revolutions is that their goals are not restricted to their countries of origin.

BUT IT IS PRECISELY the uncompromising and sweeping goals that make a revolution great which also turn it into a catastrophe, since successful policy is almost always a matter of moderation and compromise rather than of extremes. Revolutions embody a tyranny of virtue. They render the old order and those who support it not just wrong but immoral, and thereby deserving of destruction. This is an intellectual world of romance and intolerance, whereas enlightened governance has always been about finding a practical middle ground. It rarely oc-curs to revolutionaries that the order they are rebelling against can always be made worse: that the heaven they aspire to can always turn into a deeper hell. This is exactly what happened in Russia and Iran, and for a time in late-eighteenth-century revolutionary France.

In the years immediately following the 1978–79 revolution, Iran be-came a place of fear and suffocating repression. Music was banned; the sexes separated. Coeducation was eliminated. Women were forced to cover all of their bodies in black except for their faces. "Morals police" patrolling the streets enforced such discipline. There were stonings and firing squads. Alcohol was forbidden. The poor remained poor and the middle class was economically decimated. The sprawling capital of Tehran wore the backdrop of a bleak and dreary modernism, as people were forced to repress their natural instincts. Human life, with all of its joy, had been crushed by a doctrine. The sum result of the Islamic Revolution in Iran was for several decades a cynical generation. The decade-long Iran-Iraq War, by enforcing a grim and bloody discipline on the country—and both continuing and intensifying the psychology of martyrdom—was actually, according to one expert, the revolution's "only golden age."[31] As for religion itself, the revolution that was made in the name of it marked the end of true devotion, as worship became inseparable from politics. Iran remained for many years in a calcified late-Soviet phase: meaning the collapse of the mullahs' rule was just as likely to lead to a form of chaos, ethnic separatism, or a new tyranny, rather than to a liberal order, despite the liberal birth pangs of revolt in 2022, centered around removing the hijab.

And yet, "no other country in the Muslim world is so rife with in-tellectual fervor and cultural experimentation at all levels of society" as Iran, writes Vali Nasr, who for many years was the dean of Johns Hop-kins University's School of Advanced International Studies, "and in no place in the Muslim world is modernity . . . examined as seriously and thoroughly."[32]

Iran harbors more human potential than perhaps any civilization on earth, yet it inhabited a political hell that is, in fact, the price exacted by many a revolution. The Islamic Republic was partially born of unforeseen contingencies in 1978–79: the exile of Khomeini from Najaf to Paris, which brought him to the attention of the world media; the shah's cancer, which made him politically weak and indecisive; the generally vacillating response of President Jimmy Carter to the mass anti-regime uprising and takeover of the U.S. embassy. The current Iranian upheaval—perhaps even a social-media-driven counterrevolution—could also be a matter of unforeseen contingencies: that is, Shakespearean interactions among key actors that by shifting Iran on its axis move the entire Near East into a new cycle of history. Remember that the popular revolt against wearing the hijab, ignited by the murder of twenty-two-year-old Mahsa Amini, an ethnic-Kurdish woman, at the hands of the morals police in September 2022, was only the first chapter in an unpredictable chain of events.

The Council on Foreign Relations scholar Ray Takeyh writes, "The Islamic Republic stands today as a regime without a real constituency [much like the shah's], covering itself in an ideology that few believe in. Its security forces look formidable, but so did the shah's army and secret police."[33]

Iran's future, therefore, will be just as tumultuous, surprising, and dramatic as its recent past, changing the Greater Middle East in the process. For the struggle to find a system of order in Iran that is at once stable and legitimate as well as humane now seriously commences.

NOW, AFTER A HALF century of darkness, we could be at the beginning of the end. Just as the Islamic Revolution saw power transfer relatively seamlessly from the shah to the mullahs, Iran could see another transfer of power just as dramatic. Iran may be geopolitically coherent enough to avoid the chaos that accompanied the yearnings for democracy in such an artificially drawn state as Iraq next door. Don't be cynical about the prospects for Iranian democracy.

A postrevolutionary regime, or especially a counterrevolutionary one that repudiates the ayatollahs, could change the Middle East as much as the collapse of the Berlin Wall changed Europe.

For decades, Washington has supported the conservative Gulf

Arab autocracies against a fiercely anti-American and anti-Israel Iran. These monarchies may not be democracies, but they are venerable emirates and kingdoms that were not artificially conceived and are relatively well governed. Saudi Arabia may understandably offend Western humanitarians, but as I have written, the Saudis have employed technology to streamline governance, and have allowed women to dress less modestly and live more normal lives.

Nevertheless, the future could see the U.S. moving closer to a newly democratic Iran, while helping to broker peace accords between it and Israel, and also with the Gulf Arabs. Of course, competition between Iran and the Arab states would not end even should the mullahs fall, but it could very well be mitigated by a new Tehran that turns away from regional adventurism and concentrates on internal development.

Indeed, the Gulf monarchs would welcome a more liberal Iran— and see no contradiction with doing so—if Tehran ended its hostile intentions in Yemen and elsewhere, and curbed its weapons programs, nuclear and otherwise. Get rid of the radical faction of mullahs and the Middle East could enter a period of relative peace. Iraq, Syria, and Lebanon could all gradually stabilize without the presence of Iranian-backed militias.

And while Iran is not Arab, a dramatic demonstration of democracy there could have a positive influence on the emerging politics of Arab North Africa, including Egypt, where regimes are less enlightened than in the Gulf.

There is, of course, a new wild card in this, China, and how a new Middle East would chain-react with Beijing's increasing influence. As Saudis were at pains to tell me, China comes to the table with lots of business, a devouring need for Gulf oil, and no moral lectures about human rights or democracy. China's hunger for hydrocarbons will partly offset the global trend toward renewables in the coming years.

But the Saudis and other Gulf Arabs will still require a substantial security relationship with the U.S., as it may be decades before China's military presence in the region equals that of America. At the end of the day, only the U.S. can protect the Gulf Arabs.

A democratic Iran would add a twist to all this. Not only would it be—by several magnitudes—more economically dynamic than the current Iranian state, but because of geography and geopolitics it would be a critical junction for China's Belt and Road Initiative. The Chinese won't mind if Iran is democratic, and the new Iranian regime would likewise want the further development of overland transport links—rails, roads, and pipelines—to China.

A post-clerical Iran would initially be very pro-Western, because of its experience with the mullahs. But over time, as it became a large puzzle piece of Eurasian integration, it might develop even stronger ties with authoritarian China than, for instance, Germany now has.

That is to say, a more peaceful and more integrated Middle East could actually present a new challenge to the U.S., because of competition with Beijing. Some 85 million people from a highly strategic territory will suddenly be integrated into the global economy; Iran will become a gold mine for international business and integral to the next phase of globalization. A democratic Iran won't enhance a post-American world as much as complicate and diversify it.

WAY OF THE
PATHANS

═══

MY FIRST VISIT TO AFGHANISTAN WAS IN NOVEMBER 1973. I traveled by bus from the Iran border in the west and visited the three main cities of Herat, Kandahar, and Kabul on my way east to the Pakistan border. As I crossed the border from the shah's Iran, a tall Australian in long hair, beads, and high leather boots, who was coming from the other direction, pointed behind him at the Afghan frontier post and exclaimed in a loud and self-dramatizing tone, "Back there is the *east.*"

Truly, whereas the Iranian side of the border was neat and almost antiseptic, the Afghan border post was utter chaos. As for the cities I visited, there was a backbreakingly poor, fly-blown, and frontier aspect to all of them, filled with bearded men in turbans and other forms of tribal dress. I was twenty-one and felt that I had gone back in time to another century.

I was completely ignorant, of course.

The Afghanistan I saw then was crucially at peace. The narrow ring road that made passenger bus service among the major cities relatively safe and easy was a marvel of development and engineering. The post offices worked, as I sent letters home that arrived. There was still a clear way forward for the country. Rather than anarchic, Afghanistan was then more orderly than at any moment in my subsequent experience over the past half century.

In fact, 1973 was the year when storm clouds had begun gathering over the country's politics. Only four months prior to my trip, in July

1973, King Mohammed Zahir Shah, whose four decades in power had delivered relative stability and modest development, was toppled by his first cousin and former prime minister, Mohammed Daoud. Daoud was close to the Soviets, and was backed by the less extreme Parcham ("Banner") branch of the Afghan Communist Party. His intention was to extend the arm of the regime beyond the major cities into the tribal hinterlands for the sake of compulsory modern development. But the male-dominated tribes didn't want any part of modern development, since it was a threat to their way of life, however backward their way of life may have seemed to others. The tribes demanded to be left alone so that *government* was something that would continue to exist only in the cities and along the narrow road between them. Afghanistan may have been underdeveloped, but the former king's tyranny had been an easygoing and non-ideological one; unlike Daoud's. Now the knock on the door in the middle of the night became common.

Five years later, in 1978, Daoud was assassinated by the more extreme Khalq ("Masses") branch of Afghan Communists, loyal to the poet and self-declared Marxist idealist Nur Mohammed Taraki, who had become impatient with Daoud's lack of results and the slow pace of change. Many political prisoners began to be executed at Kabul's Pul-i-Charkhi prison. A year after that, Taraki himself was toppled and strangled to death by his fellow Communist conspirator Hafizullah Amin, described by foreign diplomats as a "brutal psychopath." It was at that moment that the mujahidin rebellion across the country gathered strength, as a reaction to Amin's crescendo of purges, mass executions, and rural land confiscations. In an attempt to restore domestic order inside their new Afghan satellite, the Soviet military invaded at the end of the year, killing Amin and installing a more moderate Parchami, Babrak Karmal, as the new Afghan leader. Little by little, by seeking increasing control over Afghan affairs, the Soviets had gotten themselves deeply enmeshed in Afghan politics, so that their invasion was a logical endpoint to years of failed quiet interventions starting with King Zahir Shah's overthrow. The subsequent Soviet war against the mujahidin pitted a modernizing urban elite of Communists against hundreds of thousands of deeply religious and tribal backwoodsmen, whom the United States and Saudi Arabia would eventually sustain from bases inside Pakistan. Almost a half century of continuous warfare had now commenced.

The next time I visited Afghanistan was in 1987, from Pakistan, traveling by foot and mule and wearing a traditional *shalwar kameez* and a flat woolen hat from the Hindu Kush region. I was embedded with one of the mujahidin groups fighting the Soviets. Traveling by bus up the Khyber Pass to get to the Afghan border area, I watched the landscape lose its watery, terra-cotta glow and be replaced by a mass of corrugated, pie-crust hills, whose scarred, cindery gradients warned of both heat and cold and other means of physical discomfort. The earth heaved upwards, away from the lush, tropical floor of the Indian subcontinent and into the cool, empty wastes of Central Asia.[1]

In weeks of deprivation, on this and other journeys with the mujahidin, in order to witness their war against the Soviets during a two-year period in the late 1980s, the division between Afghanistan and its Pakistani borderlands became lost to me, and a new, hard division had emerged in the course of both my experiences and my continuous reading about Afghanistan. This new division that I had discerned was a political and historical one. It was between empire and anarchy, which in the case of Afghanistan and the Pakistani border provinces of the North-West Frontier and Baluchistan was more distilled and sharply defined than in any place I knew of between the Mediterranean and China.* For this vast and desolate region of sandpaper-like plains and limestone cliffs that separated the Iranian plateau from the Indian subcontinent was in political terms a struggle of outside imperial powers against indigenous, barely organized tribal confederations.

And it could take on a deadly modern aspect.

My last foray into war-torn Afghanistan of the 1980s was to the southern city of Kandahar, named after Alexander the Great, whose Arabic name was Iskandar. In fact, much of what I saw there summoned up antiquity. Soviet carpet bombing had reduced the city to a sprawling quilt of ruins etched on the barren sand, like Palmyra in the

---

*   The North-West Frontier Province has since been renamed Khyber Pakhtunkhwa.

Syrian desert. Holed up in this new-age archaeological site was a Soviet-backed regular army taking fire from mujahidin guerrillas on all sides. It was the autumn of 1988, an historic moment. The Soviet forces that remained in the city and at the nearby airport were further south than any of their comrades had ever been, and their imminent withdrawal would signal the first northward redrawing of the Kremlin's imperial map since the later seventeenth century. Never before or since had the Soviets been this close to the ultrastrategic warm waters of the Indian Ocean: a geopolitical prize that had helped kindle the Kremlin's interest in Afghanistan in the first place.

But Kandahar airport had now become the Soviet Khe Sanh.[2]

The Afghan tribes had thus laid waste to another empire, just as centuries before their very identity had been created by an imperial struggle. Afghanistan had always been a fragile webwork of tribes and ethnicities located between the tsarist Russian Empire to the north and northwest and the British Empire in the Indian subcontinent to the south and southeast.

THE MODERN AFGHAN STORY begins in Kandahar with one man on horseback. That man was Ahmad Khan, leader of the ethnic Pashtun or "Pathan" contingent in the army of Nadir Shah the Great, the Persian king whose forces had sacked and looted Delhi in the mid-eighteenth century. Even though Nadir Shah had defeated the forces of Ahmad Khan in battle, the Persian king henceforth incorporated Ahmad Khan's forces into his own army, gaining Ahmad Khan's loyalty.

One night in 1747, sensing a plot against the king, Ahmad Khan and his tribal Pathans rode into the royal camp at Quchan, in eastern Iran, to protect him. At dawn, the sight of Nadir Shah's headless body greeted the Pathan force. Ahmad Shah and his four thousand horsemen fled the camp as the king's erstwhile followers looted it. Pursued by these hostile troops, Ahmad Khan sent a diversionary force to Herat and led the bulk of his cavalry southeast toward Kandahar.

"On his ride to Kandahar, Ahmad Khan thought quickly," Sir Olaf Caroe, the British soldier and diplomat, writes in *The Pathans:*

550 B.C.–A.D. 1957.[3] Kandahar was in a frontier zone between the Persian homeland to the west and the Mughal territories to the east, which the Persians under Nadir Shah had recently conquered. In this immense desert tract of blood and turmoil, Ahmad Khan conceived of an oasis of order: a native Afghan kingdom that would be sanctioned by whoever would now rule Persia, in exchange for which he would aggressively patrol Persia's new territories to the east. *Afghan* is the Persian word for "Pathan." Pathan legend has it that just at that moment Ahmad Khan fell upon a caravan spiriting to Persia the very Indian treasures that had tempted Nadir Shah some years earlier. This treasure included the Koh-i-noor diamond, which was to finance Ahmad Khan's new Afghan empire.

Ahmad Khan was only twenty-four when he became King Ahmad Shah. In a camp outside Kandahar, as Caroe tells it, the other Pathan tribesmen "took pieces of grass in their mouths as a token that they were his cattle and beasts of burden."[4] Because Ahmad Shah liked to wear an earring fashioned of pearls, he became known by the title *Durr-i-Durran* ("Pearl of Pearls"). Henceforth, he and his Pathan kinsmen from southern Afghanistan and its eastern borderlands would be known as the Durranis.[5] The Durrani Empire would eventually become modern Afghanistan, a weak tribal domain following Ahmad Shah's death located between stronger empires in several directions. The last king of this cycle was Zahir Shah, deposed in 1973.

BUT THROUGH ALL OF that history, though the timeline corresponds with the early modern era—from the Renaissance to the Industrial Revolution—Afghanistan never really became modern. Modernism is about ideologies, mass movements, and state-building as accompaniments to technological development, whereas the principal basis of Afghan politics has always been the tribes, which resist such organizational categories. Tribes connote a partially organized and egalitarian grouping, existing as vast extended families with numerous subdivisions. They are, in the evocative phrase of the late French ethnologist Germaine Tillion, "republics of cousins."[6]

Yet tribes are severely underestimated, especially by liberals and Marxists, who are obsessed with *progress,* which they equate with the modernizing power of a strong state that can heal social wrongs. Tribes, on the other hand, represent a social force below the level of the state.[7] Tribes are associated with anarchy only because of their interaction with modernity, that is, with our own world and the disruption it has caused to their societies. Afghanistan, along with Yemen, are currently the most violent versions of this tragic phenomenon. But on their own, armed with only the tradition and religion so disparaged by Western liberals, tribes function quite well, as Saint Augustine himself intimated in his thoughts about North Africa.[8] Indeed, anarchy came to Afghanistan not with Ahmad Khan in the 1700s, but with the local Soviet-supported Communists in the 1970s, who attempted to forcibly inflict a modern European ideology onto age-old tribal patterns that they viewed as corrupt and "backward," just as anarchy came to Iraq when Americans tried to impose Western democratic principles onto a society that despite the horrors of Ba'athism—another modern ideology rooted in Europe—remained to an impressive degree tribal.[9]

This was all brought home to me during a visit I made nearly a quarter century ago to the Pakistani province of Baluchistan on the border with Afghanistan, with 9/11 still in the future. I was speaking to the head of the 20,000-strong Raisani tribe, Nawabzada Mir Lashkari Raisani, inside his walled compound protected by white-turbaned bodyguards armed with Kalashnikov assault rifles. The Raisanis, who are ethnic Baluch and speak a language of south Indian origin, are traditional enemies of the Bugtis, another ethnic-Baluch tribe, and are part of the mosaic of cultures that form the rugged frontier joining the subcontinent with southern Central Asia. "The government wants to destroy the tribal system," Mir Lashkari Raisani told me. "But there are no institutions to replace it. Much of my time is spent deciding cases that in another country would be handled by family courts." As we devoured mounds of rice and spicy grilled meats laid out on a carpet in his residence, he went on: "The tribes are large social-welfare networks. They don't need Pakistan. Only the army needs Pakistan." The tribes and the various ethnic groups could defend themselves well without the state, that is. They—not the state—monopolized the use of violence. And because there were many competing tribes, it was a Hobbesian situation, in which no one group monopolized the use of violence: anarchy, in other words. Indeed, the international arms bazaar and the unrestricted flow of drugs and electronic goods actually increased the tribes' autonomy, he explained.[10]

Such circumstances have only intensified in the aftermath of 9/11 and in the decades following, which saw more weapons flow into the region, even as the Afghan and Pakistani states have struggled to maintain coherency. In the Pakistani borderlands of Afghanistan, the Pakistani army, as Raisani indicated, remains the only existing institutional force beyond the tribes themselves. And the Raisani tribal leader's dismissive reference to it demonstrates how ineffectual in his eyes that army has been in the territories adjoining Afghanistan.

Truly, Afghanistan and to a lesser extent Pakistan are weak states hovering between empire and anarchy, as we will increasingly discover. But inside these weak, albeit formalized political constructions are, as the British scholar Anatol Lieven observes, very strong and well-functioning groups, especially tribal and feudal ones.[11]

Moreover, these strong and well-functioning groups form a distinct spatial pattern on the map, one that does not at all cohere with legal borders. In this way, being a journalist covering the mujahidin war against the Soviet occupation force in the 1980s was very instructive in a geopolitical sense. It taught me the real divisions of the relief map in this part of the world, which make a mockery of the somewhat false divisions registered by legal borders.

Covering the war meant traveling great distances with the mujahidin. And the mujahidin reflected all the ethnic and tribal divisions of Afghanistan, which in turn mirrored geographical ones. Although the formal political map registered a border separating Afghanistan from Pakistan that runs from north to south, there was really no border at all since the tribal Pathans lived on both sides of it; nor did the Pathans respect this border since the Pakistani army was ineffectual hereabouts and the Afghan army barely existed. Even the legal aspect of the border, drawn by the British envoy Sir Mortimer Durand in

1893, was never accepted by Afghanistan, since it stranded millions of Pathans, the dominant Afghan ethnic group, in so-called tribal agencies on the other side of the frontier in British India, later to become Pakistan. Nevertheless, there was a real border—the Hindu Kush mountain range dividing northern Afghanistan from eastern and southern Afghanistan. The Pathans lived south and east of the Hindu Kush on both sides of the legal-cum-fictitious Afghanistan-Pakistan border, while the ethnic Tajiks lived north of the mountain range.

The Tajiks, who spoke a provincial form of old Persian called Dari, were as a rule better educated than the Pathans, and unlike the Pathans they were less marked by tribalism. This gave them an advantage in fighting the Soviets. In fact, the Tajiks produced the most effective and charismatic mujahidin leader, Ahmad Shah Massoud. Massoud, who was born around 1950, studied engineering in Kabul before the war and spoke fluent French. The relative absence of tribalism among Tajiks and their penchant for modern-style organization allowed Massoud to mobilize thousands of mujahidin regulars. By the time the Soviets withdrew in failure from Afghanistan at the end of the 1980s, Massoud's guerrilla army numbered 50,000.[12]

It took three weeks of trekking over some of the most rugged terrain in the world to get from the Pakistan border to the Panjshir valley, on the northern side of the Hindu Kush, which constituted Massoud's area of operations. Only the hardiest journalists could manage it and I was not one of them. In any case, Massoud and his better organized Tajiks were the exception to the general reason why the Soviets lost the war: the Soviets lost because of their inability to deal with the force of nature that was the tribal Pathans of the Afghan and Pakistani borderlands, whose very internecine divisions, lack of coordination, and quixotic, brutal, and black-and-white mentality in regard to fighting made the guerrilla threat they posed impossible to address. The Pathans, in a word, were an extension of an altogether rugged and impossible landscape.

HERE WE ARE AT the core issue regarding the whole challenge of governance and political stability in Afghanistan and Pakistan: a region which U.S. policymakers, in their flair for ugly and hackneyed phraseology, called "AfPak." In a word, it is all about the Pushtuns (in the softer tone of the southern dialect), or Pukhtuns (in the guttural sounds of the northern one), or in an old Hindustani variant favored by the British, Pathans. Whatever you choose to call them, they have been an undeniable element of energy, explosiveness, and instability afflicting this region.

In fact, looking at a relief map, one could easily construct a country called Pukhtunistan—home to the world's more than 50 million Pukhtuns, or Pathans—lying between the Hindu Kush mountains and the Indus River, and overlapping with the Afghan-Pakistani frontier. The Afghanistan-Pakistan border, as we have seen, is in reality no border at all but, in the words of Sugata Bose, a Harvard historian, "the heart . . . of an expansive Indo-Persian and Indo-Islamic economic, cultural, and political domain that [has] straddled Afghanistan and Punjab for two millennia."[13]

To understand the people of this world, whose tribal configurations preceded Ahmed Shah and the concept of Afghanistan by thousands of years, we should begin, to repeat, with the impossibly dry and intimidating landscape, specifically that of the Pakistani tribal agencies that abut present-day Afghanistan. "One secret of the hold of the North-West Frontier is to be sought in the tremendous scenic canvas against which the Pathan plays out his life, a canvas brought into vivid relief by sharp, cruel changes of climate . . . appalling heat, a dust storm across the Peshawar plain," writes Sir Olaf Caroe, the ultimate British colonial area specialist who dealt with the Pathans from World War I through the latter years of the Cold War. "The weft and warp of this tapestry is woven into the souls and bodies of the men who move before it. Much is harsh, but all is drawn in strong tones that catch the breath, and at times bring tears, almost of pain."[14] Caroe was clearly a sentimentalist, as *New York Times* foreign correspondent Declan Walsh suggests.[15] But given Caroe's extended service in the region, he had earned his opinions, which, when I first encountered them in a bookstore in Peshawar in 1988, had a certain ring of truth, given the deprivations I had experienced trekking for dozens of miles with the mujahidin.

Truly, it is a landscape that helps breed both violence and stoicism, according to the anthropologist Charles Lindholm, who spent years doing fieldwork among the Pathans.[16]

The Pathans are the largest existing tribal society in the world, divided into hundreds of tribes in turn subdivided into clans or *khels,* which then break down into smaller, extended family systems. We are talking about a deep, albeit informal, level of organization, however opaque and premodern it might actually be. Their expertise at war was first observed by Herodotus 2,500 years ago.[17] In the course of the millennia, the Pathans have ground up one foreign invader after another: Mongols, Sikhs, British, Soviets, and Americans. To the British, the Pathans were "the most admirable foes they ever faced in battle," writes the late English journalist Geoffrey Moorhouse.[18]

The Pathan mindset is popularly expressed through *Pukhtunwali,* "the way of the Pathan," essentially the somewhat mythical Pathan code of behavior. The first and most important commandment of Pukhtunwali is *badal,* "revenge." Not merely the man who has been wronged, but his family and *khel,* even his tribe, must seek revenge as an obligation. Another commandment is *melmastia,* "hospitality," especially to the stranger, with offerings of food and lodging.[19] Female honor, loyalty, and chivalry represent other commandments in this harsh, pre-Islamic canon of conduct. There is also *jerga,* "arbitration," used for governance and settling disputes: an illustration of how the Pathans need no lectures from the West concerning democracy. To be sure, Western leaders have had an obsession with formalizing political behavior in distant societies that they barely understand and do not appreciate.

Of course, too much talk of Pukhtunwali tempts stereotyping, given there have been "Pathan pilots and pop stars, generals and ambassadors," as Walsh points out.[20] Nevertheless, Pukhtunwali captures a decisive element of Pathan culture that I experienced firsthand with the mujahidin in the 1980s; with the Taliban representing the other end of the spectrum from the pilots and pop stars.

The Soviets in 1979 had begun driving millions of these Pathans across the Durand Line into Pakistan, which the Pathans then used as a rear base to launch attacks back across the border into Soviet-occupied Afghanistan. The Pathans had the advantage of still being among their supportive kinsmen on the Pakistani side of the border, as well as receiving massive aid from the Americans, Saudis, and Pakistani military dictator Muhammad Zia-ul-Haq. This was both for ideological and geopolitical reasons: indeed, the Soviet empire could not be allowed to advance into the Indian subcontinent and toward the Indian Ocean and had to be rolled back. Meanwhile, Massoud's Tajiks were assaulting the Soviets north of the Hindu Kush. The mujahidin, Pathan and Tajik both, as well as less numerous ethnic groups such as Uzbek forces under warlord Rashid Dostum, did not have to defeat the Soviets, but only make their occupation too costly to sustain.

After a decade of fighting, the Soviets had had it. Upon the Soviet withdrawal in 1989, the mujahidin rushed in and took power. Anarchy followed, since the mujahidin were never a united movement but an assemblage of disparate groups. The Tajiks were divided from the Pathans, and the Pathan groups were divided among themselves by *khel,* tribe, region, and varying approaches to Islam. The foreign occupation of the 1980s quickly morphed into a Hobbesian nightmare of all against all, with cities bombed and destroyed so that one faction could gain a temporary advantage over another. To call it a civil war was too kind, since that implied a neat, bifurcated reality of one organized side fighting another. It was made worse by the fact that during the Soviet occupation the Pakistanis and the Americans had given much of their aid to the most extreme and bloody Pathan groups, notably Gulbuddin Hekmatyar's Hezb-e-Islami ("Islamic Party"), led significantly by urban-educated Pathans. Again, it was urbanization and the encounter with modernism, particularly at university in Kabul, that had led to more extreme ideology.

The chaos was such that Pakistani journalist Ahmed Rashid, traveling in 1993 from the Pakistani border to Kandahar in southern Afghanistan, encountered twenty roadblocks, each manned by a different armed group.[21] Afghanistan was in such a state of disintegration—with rapes of young boys and girls, kidnappings, and armed robberies common and going unpunished—that the Taliban emerged in the southern and eastern part of the country to fill the vacuum in the mid-1990s. The greater the disorder, the more extreme is the order that follows, as the population becomes sufficiently desperate for any kind of antidote.

The Taliban would become the face of ethnic-Pathan nationalism for years to come, even as the group identified itself as purely Islamic. The punishments the Taliban meted out such as stoning and beheading were spiritually informed not only by Islamic shari'a law but by Pukhtunwali. This was not extremism born of urbanization and modern ideology, like that of the Afghan Communists in the 1970s, but neither was it altogether primitive as so many have alleged. The Taliban, by ultimately favoring ideology over kinship patterns, has been in its own twisted way a force of modernization. With its weaponry invented in the West and the Soviet Union, and backed as Taliban forces are by Pakistan's Inter-Services Intelligence (ISI) agency, which also assisted in the Taliban's formation, the Taliban represent the Greater Middle East's interaction with Westernization, and in this case a conscious rejection of it.

The Taliban's utter rejection of the West, whose backing of the mujahidin in the 1980s was a factor in the anarchy of the early 1990s, played a role in its decision to allow Osama bin Laden's Al-Qaeda to establish bases in Afghanistan. Bin Laden had a history in Afghanistan. He had supported the mujahidin against the Soviets with arms and money from the Pakistani borderlands in the 1980s, and was naturally tied to several mujahidin groups. The point is that the Taliban did not emerge out of a vacuum. The group had roots in the mujahidin movement itself, that is, in its more conservative and tribal elements. And to the mujahidin, to the Taliban, and to Osama bin Laden, the Communist assault on their way of life that had begun in the 1970s and continued through the Soviet invasion represented just one form of godless Western penetration of their lands; just as the Americans who would invade Afghanistan in 2001—following the al-Qaeda attacks on the Pentagon and World Trade Center—represented another. Whereas Americans understood the concept of the West as including the United States and Europe, for the Afghans it also included the

Soviet Union, since Communism was a philosophy of the modern outside world born of Western intellectuals. Thus, the struggle went on after the United States invaded. Instead of the Soviets being besieged by Pathans, strengthened by bases over the legal border in Pakistan, American soldiers and marines were, beginning in the 2000s, besieged by Pathans, also helped to an extent by bases inside Pakistan. The same Pathan leaders that the Americans had specifically supported as part of the mujahidin movement against the Soviets, such as Hekmatyar and the altogether ruthless warlord Jalaluddin Haqqani, were now prominent in the struggle against the American invaders themselves. Haqqani, who had taken considerable money and arms from the Americans in the 1980s, aligned his fighters in the Pakistani borderland of Waziristan with al-Qaeda in the 1990s and beyond.*

The Americans had exchanged places with the Soviets.

The light and lethal footprint that the Americans adopted upon their October 2001 invasion of Afghanistan, in which Green Berets and other special operations forces bonded with the Northern Alliance (the organizational descendant of the Tajik fighters aligned with Massoud), succeeded in toppling the Taliban regime. But soon afterwards, the Americans began to build massive bases and pour more and more troops into Afghanistan, unwittingly imitating what the Soviets had done: indeed, the principal Soviet fortification of Bagram, north of Kabul, became the principal American fortification. America's longest war, which would last two decades, had begun; and Afghanistan, which in 2001 was already in its third decade of war, began to experience violent military conflict as a permanent multigenerational condition.

The American military was now dealing with a country that ranked near the bottom of the United Nations' Human Development Index. Whereas Iraq on the eve of the 2003 U.S. invasion ranked 126th out of 189 countries, its literacy rate hovered around 70 percent. Afghanistan's

---

* I met Jalaluddin Haqqani in his house in Peshawar in February 1988. In the semi-darkness leaning against a wall was a tall and regal Saudi, who may have been Osama bin Laden.

literacy rate by contrast was 28 percent. And Afghanistan encompassed 30 percent more territory than Iraq. Consider also that 77 percent of Iraqis lived in urban areas at the time of the heaviest U.S. military involvement, concentrated heavily in greater Baghdad, so reducing violence in the Iraqi capital had a calming effect on the entire country. In mountainous Afghanistan, urbanization stood at only 30 percent, thus counterinsurgency efforts in one village or region would likely have no effect on another.[22]

The American military tried nearly everything in Afghanistan. It applied counterinsurgency, in which relatively small numbers of troops lived among communities of Afghan civilians, protecting them from Taliban assaults while focusing on their humanitarian needs. Such small bases were spread throughout significant regions of the country. I was embedded as a reporter in two of them for weeks at a time in 2003 in eastern and southern Afghanistan. Because it was still early in the war, morale was reasonable at these bases and there was the expectation that the war would somehow be triumphant. But the years wore on. The American military frequently changed commanders, who each brought in his own new or improved strategy. The Americans surged more and more troops into the country. Periodically over the twenty-year period, a "new beginning" or some such was announced. We were always said to be making progress, even if we weren't. We were always on the cusp of building democracy, even as the Afghan regimes we supported were brought to power in flawed and at times chaotic elections. These regimes were mired in corruption and infighting, and controlled relatively little of the countryside, where the Taliban roamed and ruled. Meanwhile, tensions over policy ebbed and flowed between the American military and the American embassy in Kabul, as well as with the contingents of coalition troops from other countries. Finally, after many years, it was privately admitted though never publicly stated that we remained in Afghanistan not because of any democratic ideals we believed would take root there, but because of fear of a humiliating repeat of Saigon in 1975, when the Vietnamese capital was overrun by Communist troops, with the last Americans and their Vietnamese dependents clinging to helicopters on the way out.

No other country in the world at the time symbolized the decline of the American empire as much as Afghanistan, especially immediately after the final, bloody, and chaotic withdrawal in the late summer of 2021. In the beginning, there was an idealistic sense of mission. Following that, once it became obvious that we couldn't remake the country into a stable democracy, we felt we had, like the nineteenth-century British, to work with the tribes in order to avoid another 9/11 from being launched on Afghan soil. But that strategy, too, which represented imperialism in its highest and most mundane form, became politically impossible to sustain in Washington and on the home front.

In fact, while the Chinese, Pakistanis, Indians, and Iranians are all developing energy and mining projects in and next door to Afghanistan, the United States has no commercial future in the country. It spent hundreds of billions of dollars there to create what could never be created: a self-sustaining democracy vaguely along Western lines. Only contiguous powers, especially China, through a combination of energy and commercial deals that bring some order and development, can help stabilize Afghanistan. The United States, obsessed as it was with Western-style democracy, could not.

Indeed, Afghanistan represents the triumph of the deterministic forces of geography, history, culture, and ethnic and sectarian awareness, with Pathans, Tajiks, Uzbeks, Hazaras, and others violently competing for patches of ground.[23] The American military interventions in Afghanistan, Iraq, and Libya were all about the idea that we could remake societies, and that our historical experience was somehow more important to these countries than their own historical experiences and ideals.

China, which has been essentially uninterested in how its trading partners governed themselves, has had the advantage at least in this part of the world. For China is consciously realist, embracing stability over anarchy.

THE DETERMINISTIC FORCES OF geography also have quite a lot to say about twentieth- and twenty-first-century history in Pakistan.

Pakistan covers the northwestern desert frontier of the Indian subcontinent. British civil administration extended only to Lahore, in the fertile Punjab, near Pakistan's eastern border with India; its Mughal architecture, gardens, and rich bazaars give Lahore a closer resemblance to cities in India than to any other place in Pakistan. But the rest of Pakistan—the tribal agencies and the alkaline wasteland of Sind—has never really been subdued by the British or anyone else—certainly not by civilians. This area was grossly underdeveloped compared with British India. Even Karachi, a city of 27 million riddled by sectarian violence, was only an isolated settlement on the Arabian Sea when the British departed, thus it lacks the civilizing urbanity of Lahore. Islamabad, Pakistan's sterile capital, with its avenues lined with Mughal-cum-Stalinist structures, was not built until the 1960s. Thus, when 7 million Muslim refugees, fleeing India at Partition, created Pakistan, the military naturally took control of this sprawling frontier land, beset by tribal and ethnic rivalries, where politics quickly became a bureaucratic forum for revenge and unsavory trade-offs, involving water wells, flour mills, electricity grids, and the like.[24] To repeat, Pakistan is a weak state, barely able to contain a plethora of strong, restive, and deeply committed groups. Likewise, whether officially under military or civilian government, Pakistan has always been essentially a military-run state that sets parameters for what the civilian politicians can and cannot do.

This is not to say that Pakistan is an artificial creation, as much of the conventional wisdom has it. Rather than a simulated modern entity, Pakistan is the very geographical and national embodiment of all the Muslim invasions that have swept down into India throughout its history, while Pakistan's southwest is the subcontinental region first occupied by Muslim Arabs invading from the Middle East. The Indus River, much more than the Ganges, has always had an organic relationship with the Arab, Persian, and Turkic worlds. It is historically and geographically appropriate that the Indus Valley civilization, long ago a satrapy of Achaemenid Persia and the forward bastion of Alexander the Great's Near Eastern empire, today is deeply enmeshed with political currents swirling through the Middle East, of which Islamic extremism forms an element. This is not determinism but merely the recognition of an obvious pattern.

But being historically and geographically well rooted does not in itself guarantee stability. Although a Muslim frontier state between mountains and plains has often existed in the subcontinent's history, that past belonged to a world not of fixed borders, but rather of perpetually moving spheres of control as determined by the deployments of armies—such was the medieval world. The Ghaznavids, the Delhi sultanate, and the Mughal dynasty all controlled the subcontinent's northwestern frontier, but their boundaries were vague and somewhat different from one another. Thus, Pakistan cannot claim its borders are legitimated by history alone. Legitimacy can only come from good governance and strong institutions. Without that, we are back to the medieval map, what in Washington's eyes is "AfPak."[25]

The fact that Pakistan's political personality is seen as perverse (prone to religious extremism and conspiracy theories) is usually blamed on its dictatorial and military character. But as I have said, quoting Anatol Lieven, Pakistan's perversity emerges not from the absolutist power of its regime but from its very institutional weakness. Pakistan's weakness is responsible for its corruption, its atrocities, human rights violations, and so forth. Rather than drill power down from elected parliamentary institutions to the public space, Pakistan's so-called democratic institutions are merely a forum for crooked deal-making, as gangs, bosses, feudals, and all sorts of unsavory elements subvert a system that works only in the abstract. Democratic institutions in the West are by definition impersonal—that is, one's *connections* are not supposed to ultimately matter that much. But in Pakistan the situation is the opposite, since institutions only work on the basis of various patronage and kinship patterns. Politics at the geographical point where the Near Eastern Muslim world meets the Sanskrit civilization of India is in the final analysis not modern but feudal, because with the exception of the Taliban it is based not on ideas or ideologies, but on family dynasties and other personal relationships. Pakistan is a "negotiated state," where the heavily armed Pathans are co-opted by being given a substantial role in the military and bureaucracy, and the

far more numerous Punjabis get to run things.²⁶ And because the Pathans live on both sides of a weak and porous border, Pakistan has
been undermined for almost half a century by war in Afghanistan.

Western lectures about democracy will not fix Pakistan. Democracy is merely a bureaucratic formula whose intrinsic value depends on
the culture in which it operates. Pakistan already has democracy, more
or less, and it has not resolved its fundamental problems of governance. What can shake Pakistan going forward is not the West or
democracy, but the larger forces of the natural environment and China's emergence as a great power. Floods on a biblical scale, like in 2022,
and China's energy and transport corridor have become pivot points of
Pakistan's destiny.

PAKISTAN'S DIMINISHING UNDERGROUND WATER table and over-
used soils have been in a critical state for decades actually, and the
situation is only getting worse. At some point these environmental
background noises can aggravate already tense intercommunal relations, and tempt anarchy in the process. Or the reverse might happen.
An environmentally driven "hard regime" might emerge, in the phrase
coined by Canadian political scientist and environmental expert
Thomas Homer-Dixon: a regime more authoritarian than any Pakistan has known in the past.²⁷ But given Pakistan's institutional weakness and the many armed groups in the tribal agencies and elsewhere,
this seems like less of a viable alternative than the semi-anarchy mentioned above. It is possible to get a combination of both.

China's increasing influence in Pakistan may indicate a more hopeful scenario. Pakistan is key to China's Belt and Road Initiative (BRI),
since only the Silk Road through Pakistan can join China's land Silk
Road across Eurasia with its maritime Silk Road across the Greater
Indian Ocean. China is investing $46 billion to build an 1,800-mile
superhighway and high-speed railway from China's western Xinjiang
Province south all the way through Pakistan to the Arabian Sea port
of Gwadar, near the entrance of the Persian Gulf. Nothing since independence in 1947 carries the potential to help stabilize Pakistan's un-

ruly badlands more than the successful completion of this project, because the very process of building this energy and transportation corridor could create jobs, spur development, and therefore calm regional insurgencies, making Pakistan in effect more governable. Ideally, it could be a virtuous cycle, as Pakistan is swept into a Eurasian system of trade and finance, which, while certainly not clean or absent of corruption, would nevertheless be more efficient, cleaner, and less corrupt than the type of governance Pakistan has experienced over the past seventy-five years.

But it could also turn out very differently. This leads to a discussion of "AfPak" and Central Asia in the early and mid twenty-first century, which means introducing geopolitical theory. And that starts with Halford Mackinder.

HALFORD MACKINDER, THE GREAT British geographer of the early twentieth century, vaguely foresaw both world wars when he proposed that, as the European imperial powers had staked out the habitable part of the earth by the end of the nineteenth century, they would henceforth have no further outlet for their energies except to fight each other. Mackinder also announced that with the development of railways crisscrossing the Eurasian landmass, control of the "Heartland" of Eurasia would ultimately lead one of the great powers to dominate the Afro-Eurasian "World-Island," that is, the Eastern Hemisphere. Mackinder's idea was somewhat vague; the Heartland might have been interpreted to lie anywhere from Eastern Europe to Iran to Central Asia itself. His great insight was not so much identifying the interior of Eurasia as the geographical "pivot" of history, but observing that the fight between Russia and Germany for control over the Eurasian interior had not been settled by World War I, and that their titanic struggle would go on—which it did, culminating in a second world war. Because both Russia and Germany had different regimes in the Second World War than in the First, Mackinder's clairvoyance suggested that geography, indeed, could be a determining factor above and beyond the world of men.

To assess twenty-first-century Central Asia, which of course is part of the Greater Middle East, we need to put Mackinder's worldview together with the "Rimland" thesis of the early- and mid-twentieth-century Dutch-American geopolitician Nicholas J. Spykman. The two are usually seen in opposition to each other: Mackinder identified the key to world power as the Eurasian interior; Spykman identified it as Eurasia's navigable Rimland. The forty-four-year-long Cold War had both Mackinderesque and Spykmanesque qualities: the contested spaces—the Korean Peninsula, Vietnam, South Asia, Iran, Turkey, Greece, and so on—all were located more or less on the southern Rimland of Eurasia, from the western Pacific to the Indian Ocean to the Mediterranean (as opposed to the northern coastline in Russia, which is ice-blocked much of the year). America's containment strategy was about keeping the Soviet Union, the great Heartland power, from advancing into the southern Rimland. The Soviets saw this as encirclement, and their 1979 invasion of Afghanistan, which began more than four decades of war there, was partly motivated by a desire to advance south toward the Indian Ocean, in order to break this encirclement. To be sure, Afghanistan constitutes a Heartland territory only three hundred miles from the Indian Ocean Rimland. Still, the Soviet invasion of Afghanistan notwithstanding, much of this remained in the realm of abstract theorizing throughout the Cold War. But as we shall see, because of the advancement of transportation technology, Afghanistan's geopolitical potential is about to mature and become increasingly obvious. Indeed, Afghanistan's very ungovernability does not detract from its being a crossroads of trade and empire.

Much of this was lost on recent American administrations. In fact, the last consciously geopolitically minded American presidency was that of George H. W. Bush, since the Cold War, as an extension of World War II—as well as a worldwide competition between great military powers—concentrated the minds of many presidents of the era. In the post–Cold War period, ideals, values, and "global" issues have distracted attention from the geopolitical chessboard. But, consciously or not, and however incompetent its withdrawal was in 2021, the Biden administration was in fact operating geopolitically when it came to Afghanistan, after a fashion at least. And its playbook was that of Nicholas Spykman. Let me explain.

America's Indo-Pacific strategy, designed to counter China, has been very Spykmanesque, as it concentrates on the southern, navigable Rimland of Eurasia. That is, it concentrates on building up forces and relationships along the Eurasian coastline from Japan south to Australia and then westward across the Indian Ocean to the Persian Gulf—the grand southern sweep of Eurasia's maritime border. By withdrawing from Afghanistan without sufficiently enunciating a diplomatic and security strategy for the heartland region of Central Asia, the Biden team chose the Rimland over the Heartland. However, the Rimland and the Heartland are about to fuse in the coming years. And much may depend on what happens in Afghanistan.

With the American withdrawal, Afghanistan's possibilities and its problems began to increasingly affect the rest of Central Asia, whether through refugees or terrorists streaming across its northern borders into the former Soviet republics of Kyrgyzstan, Uzbekistan, and Turkmenistan, or the pipelines that may be constructed to transport gas from Turkmenistan south through Afghanistan to the cities and Indian Ocean ports in Pakistan. At the same time, Central Asia was about to begin the process of becoming an organic whole, with Afghanistan, the former Soviet republics, and China's Xinjiang province (actually East Turkestan) increasingly influencing each other. Afghanistan may have been at war these past four decades, but the former Soviet Muslim republics, despite their artificiality in terms of borders and ethnic maps, have been, by and large, slowly congealing into credible states able to increasingly withstand a Russia weakened by the Ukraine war.

This greater Central Asia now forms the heart of China's Belt and Road Initiative (BRI). For many centuries, with some exceptions, China was unable to go to sea in a substantial way because of the distraction caused by insecure land borders. But now that those borders are secure, China has the luxury to build a great navy. Seeking domination over the South China Sea and brutally repressing the Turkic Muslim Uighurs in Xinjiang are thus very much related, since by pitilessly locking down Xinjiang and reaching out over its borders to the rest of Central Asia through BRI, China may finally have some serenity in its most historically turbulent borderland.

In addition to striking west from Xinjiang across Central Asia to Iran and beyond, the BRI, as I've said, will proceed south from Xinjiang through Pakistan, to the Chinese-built port of Gwadar on the Indian Ocean (providing the Pakistani Taliban don't disrupt it). This route may include spur lines into a postwar Afghanistan. Meanwhile, the Indians and Iranians may build an energy and transport route from Iran's Chabahar port on the Indian Ocean north through western Afghanistan to gas-rich Turkmenistan.

The more the Heartland and the Rimland are interconnected, and the more China's BRI becomes regionally dominant, the greater the potential for China to dominate Mackinder's World-Island, including Spykman's Rimland. This is imperialism indeed, very mercantilist, and cartographically reminiscent of the seventh- to tenth-century Tang dynasty. Significantly, the Chinese have been increasing their security relationship with the Central Asian republics, in the form of military bases and the dispatch of war planes and drones, as well as bringing Central Asians to China for security-related training.

Of course, Russia, weakened though it may be, will have a say in all of this. Courtesy of the tsarist and Soviet empires, Russian is still a lingua franca throughout much of Islamic Central Asia, where Russia's military and security services are still prevalent. Russia and China are officially strategic allies, but they obviously compete in Central Asia (even if Russia's war in Ukraine will weaken its capacity elsewhere). But it should be American policy that no single power dominate Central Asia. For that to happen, the United States will have to remain active in Central Asia beyond simply monitoring Afghanistan-based terrorism from perches over the horizon. By active, I don't mean via the insertion of troops, but through a robust and well-defined diplomatic and economic strategy. In effect, the United States needs to convey to the countries of Central Asia what Secretary of State James Baker III conveyed to Mongolia in 1990: think of us as your third neighbor, far away only geographically.

Indeed, as landlocked Central Asia becomes more connected to the Indian Ocean through transport routes and pipelines, American soft power will be necessary to shore up the Indo-Pacific. Otherwise—unless Russia can check the Belt and Road Initiative, which is doubtful—China could be on its way to commanding the World-Island. Remember that the United States won World War II and the Cold War because no one power dominated Eurasia, so that the geopolitical and economic heft provided by the resource-rich temperate zone of North America was enough to tip the balance first against Nazi Germany and later against the Soviet Union. China must never dominate the World-Island the way the United States has geopolitically dominated the Western Hemisphere.

PREVENTING THE CHINESE FROM dominating the World-Island will not be easy, barring a future upheaval inside China itself. For the Chinese are everywhere between the Mediterranean and their own borderlands in Xinjiang. Besides their hub at Djibouti, they envision military bases at Port Sudan on the Red Sea and at Jiwani on the Pakistan-Iran border. They will administer an Israeli port in Haifa. China is the largest trading partner for both Saudi Arabia and the United Arab Emirates; it is also investing billions in Egypt and many more billions in Iran. Unlike many in Washington, who separate regions in order of perceived importance, Chinese strategists think organically about geography. They recognize that in a smaller, more interconnected world, regions and continents work together and flow into each other. And they are right. The story of the Greater Middle East is now that of the world itself, and how every part of that world reacts with every other part. From Afghanistan to Kurdistan to Ethiopia and beyond, local realities are complex and often intractable. Nevertheless, no place is beyond the reach of geopolitical, economic, and cultural forces that operate at a global level. Such complexity should make us more humble.

EPILOGUE

———

A FAILURE OF
IMAGINATION

*I*n War and Peace, *Tolstoy writes that Count Rastopchin, a general and statesman, "had known for a long time that Moscow would be abandoned, but had known it only with his reason, while with all his soul he had not believed it, and he was not transported in imagination into that new situation."¹ Rastopchin had a prescient intellect. But because he could not vividly picture in his mind the fall of Moscow to Napoleon and the subsequent abandonment of the city by its inhabitants, he was helpless when it actually happened. Reason and analysis are not enough, as I learned in Ethiopia and other places. True clairvoyance is really about a powerful imagination.*

Pearl Harbor, 9/11, the rapid fall of Kabul, and the Russian invasion of Ukraine were all, at least in a theoretical and analytical sense, somewhat predictable by experts. But they were unimaginable, so we were all surprised. The best example I know concerning this category of mistake happens to be my own. In 1996, in the London Observer, *I wrote: "Sooner or later, Saddam Hussein will fall; nothing, not even he, lasts forever. When he goes we are likely to witness more chaos than ever before in the modern history of Iraq."² Nevertheless, my problem was that while Iraq's tyranny was something I had vividly experienced firsthand in the 1980s, Iraq's chaos was something I could only know theoretically until I returned to Iraq in 2004 embedded with the U.S. military. Thus, in the aftermath of September 11, 2001, burdened by my awful memories of Iraq under Saddam, but unable to actually imagine the Iraqi anarchy that I had speculated about, I supported the Iraq War, and, in the manner of Tolstoy's Count Rastopchin, I would soon find myself in my own eyes "ridiculous, with no ground under his [my] feet."*[3]

One of the many things I learned from Iraq was that simply because you cannot imagine an occurrence or situation doesn't mean it cannot happen. For example, many liberals dismissed worries that Donald Trump could be elected president in 2016 because he was so tawdry and inappropriate as a person that they could simply not imagine him as president. Few could have imagined a virtual end to air travel for well over a year, on account of a pandemic, though experts had studied just such a circumstance. The list goes on. Knowing something and actually believing it can be two different things.

The Greater Middle East, from the Mediterranean to China, will similarly test our imaginations in the years to come. There are things that we know are possible but we simply cannot palpably imagine how exactly they would come about, and therefore in our minds we largely discount them. Remember that the 1978–79 Iranian Revolution was entirely unimaginable until it actually happened, despite years of warnings from experts about the vulnerabilities of the shah. What about a counterrevolution in Iran that would change the Middle East much as the revolution did? Once more, the fact that it was nearly impossible to imagine didn't mean it wouldn't happen. And, in fact, such a counterrevolution actually started to happen while I was in the midst of finishing this book.

The only way to grapple with the mysteries of the future is to use one's imagination—something that is essentially literary—as much as one uses history and political science. As to how we should judge what eventually unfolds, we should remember the words of the young Henry Kissinger in his first book, A World Restored: *"Every statesman must attempt to reconcile what is considered just with what is considered possible."*[4] *And because what is possible often falls short of what is just, those in power, when reacting to events, will often have only bad choices available to them.*

Accepting that, certain precepts bear repeating.

Rather than pine exclusively for democracy in the Greater Middle East, we should desire instead consultative regimes in place of arbitrary ones: that is, regimes that canvass public opinion even if they do not hold elections.

Monarchies, including the Gulf sheikhdoms, tend to consult more with various tribes, factions, and interest groups than do secular modernizing regimes, which have too often been arbitrary dictatorships, Ba'athist or otherwise. In other words, aim for what is possible rather than what is merely just. Elie Kedourie believed that "settled society" constitutes a value so important that it might be worth "paying the price of tyranny" to have it.[5] Still, we should also heed Dostoevsky, who believed that in the face of extreme cruelty, "too high a price is asked for harmony."[6] Thus, it is the middle path that should be sought. The middle path offers the only hope for a better world. Idealistic raptures in the service of change must be avoided. Camus, for example, wrote that it is the rebel's own responsibility to build a more just version of order than the order he seeks to topple, otherwise there will be anarchy, and anarchy is a "form of servitude,"[7] since without order there is no way an individual can benefit through hard work.

Rebellions will be unceasing and there will be much to be anxious about. The disruptions of the Greater Middle East, as I said at the beginning of this book, have had as a principal cause the interaction of traditional societies with Westernization. Gertrude Bell once hoped that "the East will be strong again and develop its own civilization, not imitate ours, and then perhaps it will teach us a few things."[8] That was a fond hope, but completely impossible in a world immeasurably more interconnected than was Bell's early-twentieth-century one, making pure civilizations no longer possible, if they ever were. The future disruptions in the region will inevitably be tied in some way or other to the rigors of intense globalization acting upon Middle Eastern societies.

The most overpowering image I have of this vast region between the Mediterranean and China is one not from my own experience but from that of the great early-twentieth-century traveler and China hand Owen Lattimore. In Inner Mongolia, he saw a line of camels that had crossed Turkestan standing "two paces, perhaps four paces" away from a line of railway cars. "Two paces, perhaps four," separating two thousand years, he thought. Thus was united for a brief moment in time the age of caravans that had "padded back and forth" in the great distance between the Han Empire and the Roman Empire and "the age of steam, destroying the past and opening the future."[9] In our lifetime and in the next this vast expanse *and age-old caravan route will be further united by high-speed trains, highways, energy pipelines, and fiber-optic cables, all having their effect on regional geopolitics, as antiquity continues to merge with the present. Empires break up into states, in turn influenced by transoceanic trade and cultural influences, adding new layers of complexity, even as new forces of empire and anarchy populate the canvas. Thus, the story continues . . .*

ACKNOWLEDGMENTS

This book could not have been researched and written without the support of the Foreign Policy Research Institute (FPRI) and the Smith Richardson Foundation. At FPRI, I thank its president Carol "Rollie" Flynn for understanding the challenges I faced and encouraging me throughout the process. Colly Burgwin, Eli Gilman, and Olivia Martinez were also indispensable. And at FPRI a very special thanks goes to Robert Freedman. At Smith Richardson, Marin Strmecki was particularly helpful in not only supporting this project but in helping me better think through my ideas.

My literary agent, Henry Thayer, was of critical importance in shaping the proposal for this project. Henry is an agent in the old-fashioned sense: a reader, life companion, and adviser. More support came, as always, from the whole team at Brandt and Hochman Literary Agents. My editor at Random House, Molly Turpin, was a deeply perceptive reader and critic, and an altogether delightful person to work with.

In Turkey, Asli Aydintaşbaş was generous with her ideas and suggestions. So were Ali Aslan and former ambassador Eric Edelman. In Egypt, Rasha Serry was a resourceful, efficient, and altogether charming assistant. Shafik Gabr and former American University in Cairo president Francis Ricciardone opened their Rolodexes for me, and in so many other ways provided logistical and personal support. I also thank Scott Macleod and Parag Khanna for getting me started in Egypt. In Ethiopia, American diplomat Sean Jones hosted me at his home in Addis Ababa and was generous with his friendship and insights. Umberto Tavolato, Alex Rondos, and Gerard Prunier provided practical help and intellectual analysis. Hallelujah Lulie was a very smart and efficient guide and adviser.

In Saudi Arabia, ambassadors Frank Wisner and Douglas Silliman got me under way with contacts. Saud Kabli, Fahad Nazer, and Mutrik Alajmi expertly organized a schedule and the other logistics involved with my trip, for which I am very grateful. Saud Kabli, in particular, proved a great companion who understood my method and what I was after. Thanks also go to Karen Elliott House for advice and support.

In northern Iraq, Dov Zakheim introduced me to J. Mac Skelton and Shvan Najm at the American University in Sulaymaniyah, who henceforth arranged my visit and went far out of their way to help me. I am also grateful to Michael Rubin of the American Enterprise Institute for his advice, and in particular to Zhyar Baqi Fareeq for his organizational and logistical help.

Shayan Rauf, a young multilingual area specialist, was a particularly close reader whose philosophical advice and factual corrections improved the manuscript.

Small parts of this manuscript appeared as works-in-progress in *National Geographic, Foreign Policy, Bloomberg, The Spectator,* and *The National Interest,* for which I thank the editors of those publications.

NOTES

═══

PROLOGUE: CHINA IN THE AFTERLIFE OF EMPIRE

1. Josh Chin and Liza Chin, "The Two Faces of China's Surveillance State," *Wall Street Journal*, September 2, 2022.

CHAPTER I. TIME AND TERRAIN

1. Bernard Lewis, *The Middle East: A Brief History of the Last 2,000 Years* (New York: Simon & Schuster, 1995), pp. 244–45.

2. Marshall G. S. Hodgson, *The Venture of Islam: Conscience and History in a World Civilization*, vol. 1, *The Classical Age of Islam* (Chicago: University of Chicago Press, 1961), pp. 123, 133, and 158.

3. Carleton S. Coon, *Caravan: The Story of the Middle East* (New York: Henry Holt and Company, 1954), p. 349.

4. Olivier Roy, *The Failure of Political Islam,* trans. Carol Volk (Cambridge, MA: Harvard University Press, [1992] 1996), pp. 12–13.

5. Maxime Rodinson, *Muhammad* (New York: New York Review Books, [1960 and 1980], 2020), p. xvi.

6. Edward Mortimer, *Faith and Power: The Politics of Islam* (London: Faber and Faber, 1982), pp. 34, 40, and 288.

7. Marshall G. S. Hodgson, *The Venture of Islam: Conscience and History in a World Civilization*, vol. 3, *The Gunpowder Empires and Modern Times* (University of Chicago Press, 1974), p. 3.

8. Paul Bowles, *The Sheltering Sky* (New York: Library of America, 1949), p. 8.

9. Arnold J. Toynbee, *A Study of History,* abridgment of vols. 1–6 by D. C. Somervell (London: Oxford University Press, 1946), pp. 555–56.

10. Toynbee, *A Study of History,* p. 556.

11. Toynbee, *A Study of History,* p. 556. Johann Wolfgang von Goethe, *Faust II,* 1831, pp. 501–09 (R. Anstell's translation).

12. Barry Cunliffe, *By Steppe, Desert, and Ocean: The Birth of Eurasia* (United Kingdom: Oxford University Press, 2015), pp. 201, 255, 273, 392, and 420.

13. Ibn Khaldun, *The Muqaddimah: An Introduction to History,* trans. from the Arabic by Franz Rosenthal, ed. and abridged by N. J. Dawood (Princeton, NJ: Princeton University Press, 1967), p. 12.

14. Ibn Khaldun, *The Muqaddimah,* pp. 93, 109, 119, 133, 136, and 140.

15. Albert Hourani, *A History of the Arab Peoples,* with a new afterword by Malise Ruthven (Cambridge, MA: Harvard University Press, 1991), pp. 461–62.

16. Hodgson, *The Venture of Islam,* vol. 1, p. 125.

17. Luo Guanzhong (A.D. 1330–1400), *The Romance of the Three Kingdoms,* trans. Martin Palmer (New York: Penguin, 2018), p. 1.

18.   John Darwin, *After Tamerlane: The Rise and Fall of Global Empires, 1400–2000* (New York: Bloomsbury Press, 2008), p. 22.

19.   Darwin, *After Tamerlane,* p. 469.

20.   Tim Mackintosh-Smith, *Arabs: A 3,000-Year History of Peoples, Tribes, and Empires* (New Haven, CT: Yale University Press, 2019), p. 96.

21.   Hourani, *A History of the Arab Peoples,* p. 144.

22.   Hourani, p. 95.

23.   Hodgson, *The Venture of Islam,* vol. 1, pp. 281–82.

24.   Barnett R. Rubin, *The Fragmentation of Afghanistan: State Formation and Collapse in the International System* (New Haven, CT: Yale University Press, 1995), p. 4.

25.   See Robert F. Worth's "Mohammed bin Zayed's Dark Vision of the Middle East's Future," *New York Times,* January 9, 2020.

26.   Mackintosh-Smith, *Arabs,* p. 520.

27.   Walter Russell Mead, "The West and Middle East Dictators," *Wall Street Journal,* April 15, 2019.

28.   Charles Hill, *Trial of a Thousand Years: World Order and Islamism* (Stanford, CA: Hoover Institution Press, 2011), pp. 153–54.

29.   Michael C. Hudson, *Arab Politics: The Search for Legitimacy* (New Haven, CT: Yale University Press, 1977), p. 91.

30.   Rubin, *The Fragmentation of Afghanistan,* p. 5.

31.   Marshall G. S. Hodgson, *The Venture of Islam: Conscience and History in a World Civilization,* vol. 2, *The Expansion of Islam in the Middle Periods* (University of Chicago Press, 1974), pp. 570–74. Hodgson, *The Venture of Islam,* vol. 3, pp. 165–66.

32.   Arnold Toynbee, *The Western Question: In Greece and Turkey; A Study in the Contact of Civilisations* (London: Constable and Company, 1922), p. 1.

33.   Toynbee, *The Western Question,* pp. 17–18 and 108.

34.   Ussama Makdisi, *Age of Coexistence: The Ecumenical Frame and the Making of the Modern Arab World* (Oakland: University of California Press, 2019), p. 24.

35.   Bowles, *The Sheltering Sky,* p. 145.

36.   Francis Fukuyama, *The Origins of Political Order: From Prehuman Times to the French Revolution* (New York: Farrar, Straus and Giroux, 2011), pp. 278 and 286.

37.   Steven A. Cook, *False Dawn: Protest, Democracy, and Violence in the New Middle East* (New York: Oxford University Press, 2017), p. 246.

38.   Roderick Beaton, *George Seferis: Waiting for the Angel; A Biography* (New Haven, CT: Yale University Press, 2003), p. 302.

CHAPTER 2. AEGEAN

1.   Constantine Cavarnos, *Orthodox Iconography* (Belmont, MA: Institute for Byzantine and Modern Greek Studies, 1977), p. 37.

2.   Claude Lévi-Strauss, *Tristes Tropiques,* trans. John Weightman and Doreen Weightman (New York: Penguin Books, [1955] 2012), p. 38.

3.   George Santayana, *The Life of Reason: Or the Phases of Human Progress* (New York: Charles Scribner's Sons, 1905), pp. 6, 33, and 84–85. Timothy Ware, *The Orthodox Church* (Middlesex, England: Penguin Books, [1963] 1975), p. 9. Philip Sherrard, *The Wounds of Greece: Studies in Neo-Hellenism* (London: Rex Collings, 1978), p. 61.

4.   Arnold Toynbee, *A Study of History,* abridgment of vols. 7–10 by D. C. Somervell (New York: Oxford University Press, [1957] 1987), p. 193.

5.   Hourani, *A History of the Arab Peoples,* pp. 341–42.

6.   Robert D. Kaplan, *Balkan Ghosts: A Journey Through History* (New York: St. Martin's Press, 1993), p. 241.

7.   J. G. A. Pocock, "An Overview of *The Decline and Fall of the Roman Empire,*" in Karen O'Brien and Brian Young, eds., *The Cambridge Companion to Edward Gibbon* (New York: Cambridge University Press, 2018), p. 24.

8.   Toynbee, *A Study of History,* abridgment of vols. 7–10, p. 195.

9. Hugh Trevor-Roper, Introduction to *The Decline and Fall of the Roman Empire* (New York: Everyman's Library, 1994), p. lxii.

10. Lord Kinross, *The Ottoman Centuries: The Rise and Fall of the Turkish Empire* (New York: William Morrow, 1977), pp. 41 and 47.

11. Elie Kedourie, *The Chatham House Version and Other Middle Eastern Studies* (Boston: University Press of New England, [1970] 1984), pp. 317–18 and 336.

12. Fouad Ajami, *The Dream Palace of the Arabs: A Generation's Odyssey* (New York: Pantheon Books, 1998), pp. 32–34 and 66.

13. Patrick Seale, *Asad: The Struggle for the Middle East* (London: I.B. Tauris and Co., 1988; Berkeley: University of California Press, 1989), p. 29. Citations refer to the University of California Press edition.

14. Toynbee, *A Study of History,* abridgment of vols. 1–6, p. 16.

15. Ryszard Kapuscinski, *Travels with Herodotus,* trans. Klara Glowczewska (New York: Vintage International, 2008), p. 80.

16. Freya Stark, *Alexander's Path* (Woodstock, NY: Overlook Press, [1958] 1988), p. xvii.

17. Paul Theroux, *On the Plain of Snakes: A Mexican Journey* (Boston: Houghton Mifflin Harcourt, 2019), p. 5.

18. "Sailing to Byzantium," 1926.

19. Edward W. Said, *Orientalism* (New York: Vintage, [1978] 1979), pp. 1, 12, 41, and 73–74.

20. Said, *Orientalism,* pp. 57, 96, 104, 196–97, 295, 301, and 322.

21. Said, pp. 314–16.

22. Bernard Lewis, "The Question of Orientalism," *New York Review of Books,* June 24, 1982.

23. Edward Said, "Orientalism: An Exchange," *New York Review of Books,* August 12, 1982.

24. Samuel P. Huntington, "If Not Civilizations, What?," *Foreign Affairs,* November/December 1993.

25. Joseph Brodsky, "Flight from Byzantium," *New Yorker,* October 28, 1985.

CHAPTER 3. CONSTANTINOPLE

1. Ernest Hemingway, "Old Constan," *Toronto Daily Star,* October 28, 1922.

2. George Ostrogorsky, *History of the Byzantine State,* trans. from the German by Joan Hussey (Oxford: Basil Blackwell, 1956), pp. 377, 380, and 549.

3. John Ash, *A Byzantine Journey* (New York: Random House, 1995), p. 287.

4. Robert Mayhew, "Gibbon's Geographies," in O'Brien and Young, eds., *The Cambridge Companion to Edward Gibbon,* pp. 43–45.

5. Edward Gibbon, *The Decline and Fall of the Roman Empire,* vol. 4 (New York: Everyman's Library, [1910] 1994), p. 119.

6. Pocock, "An Overview of *The Decline and Fall,*" p. 24.

7. Fred Parker, "Gibbon's Style in *The Decline and Fall,*" in O'Brien and Young, eds., *The Cambridge Companion,* pp. 167–68. Charlotte Roberts, "The *Memoirs* and Character of the Historian," also in *The Cambridge Companion,* p. 206.

8. Edward Gibbon, *The Decline and Fall of the Roman Empire,* vol. 1, p. 196.

9. Gibbon, *The Decline and Fall of the Roman Empire,* vol. 4, pp. 5–6, 9, and 11.

10. Edward N. Luttwak, *The Grand Strategy of the Byzantine Empire* (Cambridge, MA: Harvard University Press, [2009] 2011), p. 410.

11. Edward Gibbon, *The Decline and Fall of the Roman Empire,* vol. 5, p. 40.

12. Gibbon, vol. 4, pp. 204, 212, and 331.

13. Luttwak, *The Grand Strategy of the Byzantine Empire,* p. 112.

14. Gibbon, vol. 4, p. 595.

15. Gibbon, vol. 5, p. 221.

16. Gibbon, vol. 5, pp. 230–32 and 239.

17. Gibbon, vol. 5, p. 325.

18. Gibbon, vol. 5, pp. 424 and 426.

19. Edward Gibbon, *The Decline and Fall of the Roman Empire,* vol. 6, p. 333.

20. Gibbon, vol. 6, p. 311.

21. Mary Lee Settle, *Turkish Reflections: A Biography of a Place* (New York: Simon & Schuster, 1991), pp. 75–77.

22. Carl Max Kortepeter, *The Ottoman Turks: Nomad Kingdom to World Empire* (Istanbul: Isis Press, 1991), pp. 25–28 and 39.

23. Hill, *Trial of a Thousand Years*, pp. 17–18.

24. Gibbon, vol. 6, p. 391.

25. Mortimer, *Faith and Power*, pp. 141–42 and 145–46.

26. Tarek Osman, *Islamism: What It Means for the Middle East and the World* (New Haven, CT: Yale University Press, 2016), p. 163.

27. Soner Cagaptay, *Erdogan's Empire: Turkey and the Politics of the Middle East* (London: I.B. Tauris, 2020), pp. 5–6 and 71.

28. Simon A. Waldman and Emre Caliskan, *The New Turkey and Its Discontents* (New York: Oxford University Press, 2017), p. 50.

29. Ragıp Soylu @ragipsoyl, Twitter, https://twitter.com/ragipsoylu/status/1281657592117366785.

30. Tuvan Gumrukcu, "Turkey Gave Hamas Members Passports, Israel Says," Reuters, August 26, 2020.

31. Yossi Kuperwasser and Lenny Ben-David, "Turkish Hyper-Activity Reverberates Throughout the Middle East," Jerusalem Center for Public Affairs, September 10, 2020.

32. Cagaptay, *Erdogan's Empire*, pp. xv and 55.

33. Cagaptay, pp. 137–38.

34. Cagaptay, pp. 64 and 70.

35. M. Hakan Yavuz and Nihat Ali Ozcan, "The Kurdish Question and Turkey's Justice and Development Party," *Middle East Policy*, Spring 2006.

36. Michael Rubin, "One Way the Kurdish Insurgency Could Lead to the Collapse of Turkey," *The National Interest*, September 9, 2020.

37. Mortimer, *Faith and Power*, pp. 138–39.

38. Waldman and Caliskan, *The New Turkey and Its Discontents*, pp. 168 and 171.

39. Malik Mufti, *Daring and Caution in Turkish Strategic Culture: Republic at Sea* (New York: Palgrave Macmillan, 2009), p. 4.

40. Simran Khosla, "How Other Famous Landmarks Compare to Erdogan's Huge New Palace," Agence France-Presse, November 6, 2014.

41. Nikos Kazantzakis, *Journeying: Travels in Italy, Egypt, Sinai, Jerusalem and Cyprus*, trans. Themi Vasils and Theodora Vasils (Boston: Little, Brown and Company, [1961] 1975), p. 21.

42. Nicholas Danforth, "Why a Turkish Dictator Let Himself Lose an Election," Al-Monitor (website), August 6, 2021.

CHAPTER 4. LOWER NILE

1. Mortimer, *Faith and Power*, p. 19.

2. Clifford Geertz, *The Interpretation of Cultures: Selected Essays* (New York: Basic Books, 1973), pp. 10, 35, 36, 40, 49, 51, and 87.

3. Geertz, *The Interpretation of Cultures*, p. 6.

4. Charles King, *Gods of the Upper Air: How a Circle of Renegade Anthropologists Reinvented Race, Sex, and Gender in the Twentieth Century* (New York: Doubleday, 2019), pp. 9 and 341.

5. Geertz, p. 11, 14, 28, 30, 53, 408, and 442.

6. Geertz, pp. 259–62, 269–70, and 276–77.

7. Geertz, p. 308.

8. Samuel P. Huntington, "The Clash of Civilizations?," *Foreign Affairs*, Summer 1993. Samuel P. Huntington, *The Clash of Civilizations and the Remaking of World Order* (New York: Simon & Schuster, 1996).

9. Geertz, p. 311.

10. Barrington Moore, Jr., *Social Origins of Dictatorship and Democracy: Lord and Peasant in the Making of the Modern World* (Boston: Beacon Press, [1966] 1993), pp. 19–20, 28–30, and 38.

11. Moore, *Social Origins of Dictatorship and Democracy*, pp. 70–73, 105, and 109.

12. Moore, pp. 111 and 153.

13. Moore, pp. 295, 304–05, 313, and 413.

14. Moore, p. 485.

15. Max Rodenbeck, *Cairo: The City Victorious* (New York: Knopf, 1999), p. 14.

16. Robert D. Kaplan, "Egypt's Zabaleen Build Their Lives on Garbage," *Atlanta Journal and Constitution,* February 17, 1985.

17. Kazantzakis, *Journeying,* p. 29.

18. Rodenbeck, *Cairo,* pp. 17–18.

19. Kazantzakis, pp. 33–34.

20. "Egypt's Literacy Rate 1976–2020," Macrotrends.net/countries/EGY/Egypt/literacy-rate.

21. Kazantzakis, pp. 63–64.

22. Afaf Lutfi Al-Sayyid Marsot, *A Short History of Modern Egypt* (New York: Cambridge University Press, 1985), p. 82.

23. M. Cherif Bassiouni, *Chronicles of the Egyptian Revolution and Its Aftermath: 2011–2016* (New York: Cambridge University Press, 2017), p. 621.

24. Mackintosh-Smith, *Arabs,* pp. 447 and 490. Eugene Rogan, *The Arabs: A History* (New York: Basic Books, 2009), p. 192.

25. Herbert Kitchener letter to Edward Grey, March 7, 1912. Elie Kedourie, *The Chatham House Version and Other Middle-Eastern Studies* (Boston: University Press of New England, [1970] 1984), p. 85. Al-Sayyid Marsot, *A Short History of Modern Egypt,* p. 82.

26. Rogan, *The Arabs,* p. 165.

27. Elie Kedourie, *Democracy and Arab Political Culture* (Washington, DC: Washington Institute for Near East Policy, 1992), pp. 74–75.

28. Kedourie, *The Chatham House Version and Other Middle-Eastern Studies,* p. 132.

29. Kedourie, *Chatham House Version,* p. 159.

30. Kedourie, *Democracy and Arab Political Culture,* p. 81.

31. Peter Hessler, *The Buried: An Archaeology of the Egyptian Revolution* (New York: Penguin Press, 2019), p. 165.

32. Bassiouni, *Chronicles of the Egyptian Revolution and Its Aftermath,* p. 6.

33. Robert D. Kaplan, "Mubarak's Opening: Egypt After Controlled Elections," *The New Republic,* July 2, 1984.

34. Mortimer, *Faith and Power,* pp. 251–55. Hessler, *The Buried,* pp. 74–75. Robert P. Mitchell, *The Society of the Muslim Brothers* (New York: Oxford University Press, 1993), p. 327.

35. Hessler, pp. 166, 178, 194, 203–04, 228, and 230.

36. Kenneth N. Waltz, *Realism and International Politics* (New York: Routledge, 2008), p. 53.

37. Robert F. Worth, *A Rage for Order: The Middle East in Turmoil, from Tahrir Square to ISIS* (New York: Farrar, Straus and Giroux, 2016), pp. 233–34. See, too, Steven A. Cook's *False Dawn,* p. 89.

38. Bernard Lewis, *What Went Wrong? The Clash Between Islam and Modernity in the Middle East* (New York: Oxford University Press, 2002), p. 55.

39. Francis Fukuyama, *Political Order and Political Decay: From the Industrial Revolution to the Globalization of Democracy* (New York: Farrar, Straus and Giroux, 2014 and 2015), pp. 7, 23, 50, 416–17, 431, and 550.

40. Gilles Kepel, *Away from Chaos: The Middle East and the Challenge to the West,* trans. from the French by Henry Randolph (New York: Columbia University Press, 2020), pp. 138–39.

41. John Waterbury, *Hydropolitics of the Nile Valley* (Syracuse, NY: Syracuse University Press, 1979), p. 23.

42. See Samuel P. Huntington, *Political Order in Changing Societies* (New Haven, CT: Yale University Press, 1968), p. 7.

43. C. P. Cavafy, "In Church" (1912), in *The Greek Poems of C. P. Cavafy as Translated by Memas Kolaitis,* vol. 1, *The Canon* (New Rochelle, NY: Aristide D. Caratzas, Publisher, 1989), p. 45.

44. Mohammed Soliman, "There Is No Indo-Pacific Without Egypt and the Suez Canal," *The National Interest,* April 19, 2021.

45. Sean Mathews, "The Competition for Egypt: China, the West, and Megaprojects," *Al Jazeera,* March 15, 2021.

CHAPTER 5. UPPER NILE

1. Donald N. Levine, *Wax and Gold: Tradition and Innovation in Ethiopian Culture* (Chicago: University of Chicago Press, [1965] 1986), pp. ix, 5–7, 17, and 284.

2. Donald N. Levine, *Greater Ethiopia: The Evolution of a Multiethnic Society* (Chicago: University of Chicago Press, [1974] 2000), pp. xv–xvi.

3. See especially Anthony Mockler's *Haile Selassie's War: The Italian-Ethiopian Campaign, 1935–1941* (New York: Random House, 1984).

4. Levine, *Greater Ethiopia*, pp. 40 and 56–59.

5. Levine, *Greater Ethiopia*, pp. 85 and 128.

6. Levine, *Greater Ethiopia*, p. 150.

7. Levine, *Wax and Gold*, pp. 82 and 93–94.

8. Levine, *Wax and Gold*, pp. 174, 242–43, and 250–52.

9. Levine, *Wax and Gold*, p. 245.

10. See Donald N. Levine's *The Flight from Ambiguity: Essays in Social and Cultural Theory* (Chicago: University of Chicago Press, 1985).

11. Walter Russell Mead, "Tribalism Isn't Going Anywhere," *Wall Street Journal*, November 16, 2020.

12. Mead, "Tribalism Isn't Going Anywhere." See, too, Steven A. Cook's treatment of the ideas of economist Mancur Olson, Jr., and political scientist Samuel Huntington in Cook's *False Dawn*, p. 83.

13. The above three paragraphs borrow from Tavolato's reports in 2020 and 2021 for the European Council on Foreign Relations. See, too, Aidan Hartley's "Ethiopia Is Slipping into Civil War," *The Spectator*, November 23, 2020.

14. Rodinson, *Muhammad*, p. 29.

15. Robert D. Kaplan, "A Tale of Two Colonies," *The Atlantic*, April 2003. Robert D. Kaplan, *Surrender or Starve: Travels in Ethiopia, Sudan, Somalia, and Eritrea* (New York: Vintage Books, 1988 and 2003), chapter on Eritrea.

CHAPTER 6. ARABIA DESERTA

1. This and the succeeding paragraphs about Doughty are extracted with additions and changes from my book *The Arabists: The Romance of an American Elite* (New York: The Free Press, 1993), pp. 45 and 48–51.

2. Charles M. Doughty, *Travels in Arabia Deserta*, vol. 1 (Cambridge: Cambridge University Press, 1888 [Dover reprint, 1979]), pp. 91, 172, and 553.

3. Doughty, *Travels in Arabia Deserta*, vol. 1, pp. 112 and 244, *Travels in Arabia Deserta*, vol. 2, p. 205.

4. Doughty, vol. 2, pp. 539–40.

5. Edward W. Said, *Orientalism* (New York: Pantheon Books, 1978), p. 237 of the Vintage paperback edition.

6. Doughty, vol. 1, p. 95.

7. T. E. Lawrence, *Seven Pillars of Wisdom: A Triumph* (New York: Penguin Books, [1926] 1977), p. 36.

8. Geertz, *The Interpretation of Cultures*, p. 6.

9. Lawrence, *Seven Pillars*, p. 41.

10. David Rundell, *Vision or Mirage: Saudi Arabia at the Crossroads* (London: I.B. Tauris, 2021), pp. 5, 8, and 27.

11. Rodinson, *Muhammad*, pp. 298–99.

12. Mortimer, *Faith and Power*, pp. 159 and 176.

13. Robert Lacey, *Inside the Kingdom: Kings, Clerics, Modernists, Terrorists, and the Struggle for Saudi Arabia* (New York: Penguin Books, 2009), p. 4.

14. Lacey, *Inside the Kingdom*, p. 48.

15. Karen Elliott House, *On Saudi Arabia: Its People, Past, Religion, Fault Lines—and Future* (New York: Knopf, 2012), pp. 10 and 68–69.

16. Rundell, *Vision or Mirage*, p. 255.

17. Edward Shirley, *Know Thine Enemy: A Spy's Journey into Revolutionary Iran* (New York: Farrar, Straus and Giroux, 1997), p. 195. See, too, J. B. Kelly's *Arabia, the Gulf and the West* (New York: Basic Books, 1980).

18. Thomas W. Lippman, *Saudi Arabia on the Edge: The Uncertain Future of an American Ally* (Lincoln, NE: Potomac Books, 2012), pp. 15, 17, and 20.

19. Oswald Spengler, *The Decline of the West*, trans. from the German by Charles Francis Atkinson (New York: Vintage Books, [1918 and 1922] 2006), p. 345.

20. Donna Abdulaziz, "Saudi Arabia Revs Up the Party," *Wall Street Journal*, December 28, 2021.

21. Barbara Bray and Michael Darlow, *Ibn Saud: The Desert Warrior Who Created the Kingdom of Saudi Arabia* (London: Quartet, 2010), pp. 507–08 (Skyhorse edition).

22. Isaiah Berlin, *Four Essays on Liberty* (New York: Oxford University Press, 1969), p. xlii.

23. Megan K. Stack, "The West Is Kidding Itself About Women's Freedom in Saudi Arabia," *New York Times*, August 19, 2022.

24. Ilan Berman, "Joe Biden's Pressure on Saudi Arabia Has High Stakes," *The National Interest*, March 1, 2021.

25. "Many Saudis Are Seething at Muhammad bin Salman's Reforms," *The Economist*, January 6, 2022.

26. David Ignatius, "A Saudi Official's Harrowing Account of Torture Reveals the Regime's Brutality," *Washington Post*, July 28, 2021.

27. Bray and Darlow, *Ibn Saud*, p. 70.

28. Anthony Cave Brown, *H. St. John Philby, Kim Philby, and the Spy Case of the Century* (Boston: Houghton Mifflin, 1994), p. 114. Robert Lacey, *The Kingdom* (London: Fontana Paperbacks, [1981] 1982), p. 3.

29. David B. Ottaway, *Mohammed bin Salman: The Icarus of Saudi Arabia?* (Boulder, CO: Lynne Rienner Publishers, 2021), p. 8.

CHAPTER 7. FERTILE CRESCENT: PART I

1. Philip K. Hitti, *History of Syria: Including Lebanon and Palestine* (New York: Macmillan, 1951), p. 420.

2. Hitti, *History of Syria*, p. 535.

3. See Daniel Pipes, *Greater Syria: The History of an Ambition* (New York: Oxford University Press, 1990).

4. *Freya Stark Letters*, vol. 1 (1914–1930), ed. Lucy Moorehead. Privately printed. (Compton Chamberlayne, Salisbury, Wiltshire: Compton Russell, 1974). Freya Stark, *East Is West* (London: John Murray, 1945), p. 122 of 1986 Century paperback edition.

5. Ali A. Allawi, *Faisal I of Iraq* (New Haven, CT: Yale University Press, 2014), pp. 231 and 259.

6. Pipes, *Greater Syria*, pp. 15–18.

7. Nikolaos van Dam, *The Struggle for Power in Syria: Sectarianism, Regionalism and Tribalism in Politics, 1961–1980* (London: Croom Helm, [1979] 1981), pp. 18–19.

8. Robert F. Worth, "Syria's Lost Chance," review of Elizabeth F. Thompson's *How the West Stole Democracy from the Arabs: The Syrian Arab Congress of 1920 and the Destruction of Its Historic Liberal-Islamic Alliance*, *New York Review of Books*, October 6, 2020.

9. Mackintosh-Smith, *Arabs*, pp. 445–46.

10. Patrick Seale, *The Struggle for Syria: A Study of Post-War Arab Politics, 1945–1958*, with a foreword by Albert Hourani (New Haven, CT: Yale University Press, [1965] 1986), pp. 31–32, 44–45, 118, and 122.

11. Seale, *The Struggle for Syria*, p. 132.

12. Pipes, p. 152.

13. Seale, *The Struggle for Syria*, p. 185.

14. Rogan, *The Arabs*, p. 305.

15. Pipes, pp. 152 and 172.

16. Patrick Seale, *Asad of Syria: The Struggle for the Middle East* (Berkeley: University of California Press, [1988] 1989), p. 492.

17. Graeme Wood, *The Way of the Strangers: Encounters with the Islamic State* (New York: Random House, 2017), p. 98.

18. Seale, *Asad of Syria*, p. 257.

19. Seale, *Asad of Syria*, p. 267.

20. Mortimer, *Faith and Power*, p. 267.

21. Van Dam, pp. 16–17 and 31–32.

22. Stanley Reed III, "Little Brother and the Brotherhood," *The Nation*, May 16, 1981.

23. Robert D. Kaplan, "Syria: Identity Crisis; Hafez al-Assad Has So Far Prevented the Balkanization of His Country. But He Can't Last Forever," *The Atlantic*, February 1993.

24. Osman, *Islamism*, p. 188. Faisal Mohammad Rather, Balal Ali, and Shahnawaz Abbas, "From Civil Uprising to Sectarian Conflict in Syria," *Quarterly Journal of Chinese Studies*, Summer 2015. David S. Sorenson, *Syria in Ruins: The Dynamics of the Syrian Civil War* (Santa Barbara, CA: Praeger, 2016), p. 5. Lucy Rodgers, David Gritten, James Offer, and Patrick Asare, "Syria: The Story of the Conflict," BBC News, March 11, 2016.

25. José Ortega y Gasset, *History as a System: and Other Essays Toward a Philosophy of History* (New York: W. W. Norton, [1941] 1962), p. 81.

26. Kim Ghattas, *Black Wave: Saudi Arabia, Iran, and the Forty-Year Rivalry That Unraveled Culture, Religion, and Collective Memory in the Middle East* (New York: Henry Holt and Company, 2020), p. 219.

27. Graham E. Fuller, *The Center of the Universe: The Geopolitics of Iran* (Boulder, CO: Westview Press, 1991), p. 34. A RAND Corporation Research Study.

28. Georges Roux, *Ancient Iraq* (New York: Penguin Books, [1964] 1982), pp. 23–27. See, too, Kaplan, *The Arabists*, pp. 246–49, from which the succeeding paragraphs are reprinted and adapted.

29. Robert Byron, *The Road to Oxiana* (London: Pan Books, [1937] 1981), p. 46.

30. Roux, *Ancient Iraq*, p. 24.

31. Roux, pp. 24–25.

32. Stark, *East Is West*, appendix, p. 198.

33. Hourani, *A History of the Arab Peoples*, p. 92.

34. Peter Hessler, *The Buried: An Archaeology of the Egyptian Revolution* (New York: Penguin Press, 2019), p. 40.

35. James Barr, *Lords of the Desert: The Battle Between the United States and Great Britain for Supremacy in the Modern Middle East* (New York: Basic Books, 2018), p. 226.

36. Michael C. Hudson, *Arab Politics: The Search for Legitimacy* (New Haven, CT: Yale University Press, 1977), p. 274.

37. Gary Saul Morson, "Leninthink: On the Pernicious Legacy of Vladimir Lenin," *The New Criterion*, October 2019.

38. Adeed Dawisha, *Iraq: A Political History from Independence to Occupation* (Princeton, NJ: Princeton University Press, 2009), p. 214.

39. "War in Iraq: Not a Humanitarian Intervention," *Human Rights Watch*, January 25, 2004.

40. Robert D. Kaplan, "War in the Marshes: Iranians Make Little Headway in Drive into Iraq," *Atlanta Constitution*, March 6, 1984.

41. "Kurdistan in the Time of Saddam Hussein" and "Civil War in Iraq." Staff Report to the Committee on Foreign Relations of the U.S. Senate, May 1991.

42. David Pryce-Jones, "Self-Determination, Arab-Style," *Commentary*, January 1989.

43. Lawrence Joffe, "Taha Yassin Ramadan: Long-serving Saddam Enforcer Notorious for His Violence and Mafia-style Trade Links," *The Guardian*, March 20, 2007.

44. Robert D. Kaplan, "Tales from the Bazaar," *The Atlantic*, August 1992. Robin Wright, "White House Ignored Iraq Rights Abuses for Years . . . Critics Say Washington Made a 'Grotesque' Mistake in Restoring Ties to Baghdad in 1984," *Los Angeles Times*, August 30, 1990.

45. Kaplan, *The Arabists*, p. 263.

46. Dawisha, *Iraq*, p. 240.

CHAPTER 8. FERTILE CRESCENT: PART II

1. Elie Kedourie, *The Chatham House Version and Other Middle-Eastern Studies* (Boston: University Press of New England, [1970] 1984), p. 1.

2. Martin Sieff, "Isaiah Berlin and Elie Kedourie: Recollections of Two Giants," *Covenant: Global Jewish Magazine*, November 2006.

3. David Pryce-Jones, *Signatures: Literary Encounters of a Lifetime* (New York: Encounter Books, 2020), p. 149.

4. Martin Kramer, "Elie Kedourie," in *Encyclopedia of Historians and Historical Writing*, vol. 1 (London: Fitzroy Dearborn, 1999), pp. 637–38.

5. Kedourie, *Chatham House Version*, p. 301. Robert D. Kaplan, "In Defense of Empire," *The Atlantic*, April 2014.

6. Kedourie, p. 3.

7. Kedourie, p. 6.

8. Fouad Ajami, *The Arab Predicament: Arab Political Thought and Practice Since 1967* (New York: Cambridge University Press, 1981 [1982]), pp. 7 and 44. V. S. Naipaul, *Among the Believers: An Islamic Journey* (New York: Penguin Books, [1981] 1982), p. 19.

9. Fouad Ajami, *The Dream Palace of the Arabs: A Generation's Odyssey* (New York: Pantheon, 1998), p. 140.

10. Arnold J. Toynbee, *The Western Question in Greece and Turkey: A Study in the Contact of Civilisations* (London: Constable and Company, 1922), p. 30.

11. P. W. Ireland, ed., *The Near East: Problems and Prospects* (Chicago: University of Chicago Press, 1942), p. 70.

12. Kedourie, pp. 213–14.

13. Kedourie, p. 214.

14. Allawi, *Faisal I of Iraq*, p. xxi.

15. Freya Stark, *East Is West*, p. 208 of 1986 Century edition.

16. Kedourie, pp. 236–37.

17. Dawisha, p. 209.

18. Kedourie, p. 258.

19. Vali Nasr, *The Shia Revival: How Conflicts Within Islam Will Shape the Future* (New York: Norton, 2006), p. 91.

20. Elie Kedourie, *Democracy and Arab Political Culture* (Washington, DC: Washington Institute for Near East Policy, 1992), pp. 44–45.

21. Kaplan, "Syria," *The Atlantic*, February 1993.

22. Kedourie, *Chatham House Version*, pp. 387–88.

23. Allawi, p. 538.

24. Robert D. Kaplan, "Baathism Caused the Chaos in Iraq and Syria," *Foreign Policy*, March 7, 2018.

25. Kedourie, *Arab Democracy and Political Culture*, pp. 89–90.

26. Ajami, *The Arab Predicament*, pp. 27 and 53.

27. Kedourie, *Chatham House Version*, p. 229.

28. Kedourie, pp. 33, 259, 262, and 301.

29. Kedourie, p. 306.

30. Allawi, pp. 314, 324, 356, and 359.

31. Allawi, p. 376.

32. Kedourie, pp. 358–60. Elie Kedourie, "Arnold Toynbee & His 'Nonsense Book,'" *The New Criterion*, March 1990.

33. Kedourie, *Chatham House Version*, p. 377.

34. Kedourie, *Democracy and Arab Political Culture*, p. 98.

35. Kedourie, p. 105.

36. Ahdaf Soueif, *Cairo: My City, Our Revolution* (New York: Bloomsbury, 2012), p. 25.

37. Bob Woodward, *State of Denial: Bush at War, Part III* (New York: Simon & Schuster, 2006), pp. 84–85.

38. Robert D. Kaplan, "Iraq, After Saddam," *New York Times*, December 21, 1998.

39. Ortega y Gasset, *History as a System*, p. 81.

40. Jeffrey Goldberg, "The Obama Doctrine," *The Atlantic,* April 2016.

41. John Judis, "America's Failure—and Russia and Iran's Success—in Syria's Cataclysmic Civil War," interview with Joshua Landis, *TalkingPointsMemo,* January 10, 2017.

42. Jonathan Spyer, *Days of the Fall: A Reporter's Journey in the Syria and Iraq Wars* (New York: Routledge), 2018, pp. 10, 29, and 32–33.

43. Leon Wieseltier, "Specks of War" and "Close to Zero," *The New Republic,* April 5, 2012, and June 7, 2012, respectively.

44. Judis, "America's Failure."

45. Reuel Marc Gerecht, "Violent Young Men, Here and Abroad," *Wall Street Journal,* August 13, 2019.

CHAPTER 9. FERTILE CRESCENT: PART III

1. Stephen C. Pelletiere, *The Kurds: An Unstable Element in the Gulf* (Boulder, CO: Westview Press, 1984), p. 14.

2. Robert D. Kaplan, "Redrawing the Mideast Map," *New York Times,* February 21, 1999.

3. Gertrude Bell in a letter to her father, Sir Hugh Bell, in *Lady Bell: The Letters of Gertrude Bell,* 1927. Susan Meiseles, *Kurdistan: In the Shadow of History,* with chapter commentaries by Martin van Bruinessen (New York: Random House, 1997), p. 79.

4. Xenophon (430–354 B.C.), *The Persian Expedition,* trans. Rex Warner, with an introduction and notes by George Cawkwell (New York: Penguin Books, [1972] 1984), p. 173. Robert D. Kaplan, "Sons of Devils: In a Turbulent Region the Stateless Kurds Play the Role of Spoiler," *The Atlantic,* November 1987. The following paragraphs borrow from this article.

5. Meiseles, *Kurdistan,* p. 330.

6. Pishko Shamsi, "The Future of the Kurdistan Region After the Defeat of ISIS and the Failure of the 2017 Independence Referendum," Foreign Policy Research Institute, Philadelphia, April 1, 2020.

7. Shamsi, "The Future of the Kurdistan Region."

8. Harriet Allsopp and Wladimir van Wilgenburg, *The Kurds of Northern Syria: Governance, Diversity and Conflicts* (London: I.B. Tauris, 2019), pp. 13–16, 20–21, 36, and 61.

9. Allsopp and Wilgenburg, *The Kurds of Northern Syria,* pp. 18–20.

10. Robert E. Hamilton, Chris Miller, and Aaron Stein, *Russia's War in Syria: Assessing Russian Military Capabilities and Lessons Learned* (Philadelphia: Foreign Policy Research Institute, 2020), p. 2.

11. Allsopp and Wilgenburg, pp. 194 and 196.

CHAPTER 10. SAFAVID IRAN

1. Fuller, *The Center of the Universe,* p. 16.

2. Fuller, pp. 241 and 244.

3. Abbas Amanat, *Iran: A Modern History* (New Haven, CT: Yale University Press, 2017), pp. 1, 19–21, and 75. Edward Shirley, *Know Thine Enemy: A Spy's Journey into Revolutionary Iran* (New York: Farrar, Straus and Giroux, 1997), p. 118.

4. Roy, *The Failure of Political Islam,* p. 172.

5. Shirley, *Know Thine Enemy,* p. 118.

6. Coon, *Caravan,* p. 292.

7. Macrotrends.net and indexmundi.com.

8. Fuller, p. 17. Wikipedia.org.

9. Nikki R. Keddie, *Roots of Revolution: An Interpretive History of Modern Iran* (New Haven, CT: Yale University Press, 1981), p. 111.

10. Robert D. Kaplan, *The Ends of the Earth: A Journey to the Frontiers of Anarchy* (New York: Random House, 1996), p. 194.

11. Ray Takeyh, *The Last Shah: America, Iran, and the Fall of the Pahlavi Dynasty* (New Haven, CT: Yale University Press, 2021), p. 205.

12. Kaplan, *The Ends of the Earth,* pp. 194–95.

13. Robert D. Kaplan, "A Bazaari's World: To Understand Iran—and Perhaps Even the

Future of Other Parts of the Islamic World—One Must Understand a Man like Mohsen Rafiqdoost," *The Atlantic*, March 1996.

14. Kaplan, *The Ends of the Earth*, pp. 227 and 233–34. Osman, *Islamism*, p. 211.
15. Ajami, *The Dream Palace of the Arabs*, pp. 148 and 150.
16. Fuller, pp. 13–14.
17. Nasr, *The Shia Revival*, pp. 39 and 51.
18. Mortimer, *Faith and Power*, pp. 300–01 and 303.
19. Mortimer, pp. 327–28.
20. Osman, *Islamism*, pp. 191–92.
21. Mortimer, p. 328.
22. Mortimer, p. 239.
23. Nasr, p. 126.
24. Amanat, pp. 741 and 897–98.
25. Lewis, *The Middle East*, p. 378.
26. Amanat, p. 728.
27. Mortimer, p. 346.
28. Hill, *Trial of a Thousand Years*, p. 90.
29. Robin Wright, *The Last Great Revolution: Turmoil and Transformation in Iran* (New York: Knopf, 2000), p. xvii.
30. Amanat, p. 866.
31. Shirley, pp. 24 and 59.
32. Nasr, p. 213.
33. Takeyh, *The Last Shah*, p. 264.

CHAPTER 11. WAY OF THE PATHANS

1. Robert D. Kaplan, *Soldiers of God: With Islamic Warriors in Afghanistan and Pakistan* (Boston: Houghton Mifflin, 1990), pp. 23–24 and 79–81.
2. Kaplan, *Soldiers of God*, pp. 219–20.
3. Olaf Caroe, *The Pathans: 550 B.C.–A.D. 1957* (Karachi, Pakistan: Oxford University Press, 1958), p. 254.
4. Caroe, *The Pathans*, p. 255.
5. Kaplan, *Soldiers of God*, pp. 192–94.
6. Ernest Gellner, *Muslim Society* (New York: Cambridge University Press, 1981), pp. 24–26, 29, and 33. Germaine Tillion, *Le Harem et les cousins* (Paris: Editions du Seuil, 1966).
7. Faleh A. Jabar and Hosham Dawod, *Tribes and Power: Nationalism and Ethnicity in the Middle East* (London: Saqi, 2003), p. 8.
8. Garry Wills, *Saint Augustine* (New York: Viking, 1999), p. 119.
9. Rubin, *The Fragmentation of Afghanistan*, p. 84.
10. Robert D. Kaplan, "The Lawless Frontier: The Tribal Lands of the Afghanistan-Pakistan Border Reveal the Future of Conflict in the Subcontinent, Along with the Dark Side of Globalization," *The Atlantic*, September 2000.
11. Anatol Lieven, *Pakistan: A Hard Country* (New York: PublicAffairs, 2011), p. 12.
12. Kaplan, pp. 38–41.
13. Sugata Bose, *A Hundred Horizons: The Indian Ocean in the Age of Global Empire* (Cambridge, MA: Harvard University Press, 2006), p. 56.
14. Caroe, p. xv.
15. Declan Walsh, *The Nine Lives of Pakistan: Dispatches from a Divided Nation* (London: Bloomsbury Publishing, 2020), p. 81.
16. Charles Lindholm, *Generosity and Jealousy: The Swat Pukhtun of Northern Pakistan* (New York: Columbia University Press, 1982), p. 204.
17. James W. Spain, *The Way of the Pathans* (Karachi, Pakistan: Oxford University Press, 1962), p. 29.
18. Geoffrey Moorhouse, *To the Frontier* (London: Hodder and Stoughton, 1984), p. 185.
19. Spain, *The Way of the Pathans*, pp. 46–47.
20. Walsh, *The Nine Lives of Pakistan*, p. 86.

21. Ahmed Rashid, *Taliban: Islam, Oil and the New Great Game in Central Asia* (London: I.B. Tauris, 2000), p. 22.

22. Robert D. Kaplan, "Man Versus Afghanistan," *The Atlantic*, April 2010.

23. Robert D. Kaplan, "Time to Get Out of Afghanistan: The United States Is Spending Beyond Its Means on a Mission That Might Only Be Helping Its Strategic Rivals," *New York Times*, January 1, 2019.

24. Kaplan, "The Lawless Frontier."

25. Robert D. Kaplan, "What's Wrong with Pakistan?" *Foreign Policy*, July/August 2012.

26. Lieven, *Pakistan*, pp. 23–29, 204, 235, and 260.

27. Thomas Homer-Dixon, "Environmental Scarcities and Violent Conflict: Evidence from Cases," *International Security*, Summer 1994.

EPILOGUE: A FAILURE OF IMAGINATION

1. Leo Tolstoy, *War and Peace*, trans. from the Russian by Richard Pevear and Larissa Volokhonsky (New York: Vintage Classics, 2008), p. 885.

2. Robert D. Kaplan, "Kurds Draw a Blueprint for a New, Borderless Order," *The Observer*, September 8, 1996.

3. Tolstoy, *War and Peace*, p. 885.

4. Henry A. Kissinger, *A World Restored: Metternich, Castlereagh and the Problems of Peace 1812–22* (Boston: Houghton Mifflin, 1957), p. 5 of paperback edition.

5. David Pryce-Jones, *Signatures: Literary Encounters of a Lifetime* (New York: Encounter Books, 2020), p. 150.

6. Fyodor Dostoevsky, *The Brothers Karamazov*, trans. from the Russian by Constance Garnett (New York: Modern Library, [1879–80] 1996), p. 272.

7. Albert Camus, *The Rebel: An Essay on Man in Revolt*, translated from the French by Anthony Bower (New York: Vintage International, [1951] 1991), pp. 25 and 70–71.

8. Meiseles, *Kurdistan*, p. 31.

9. Owen Lattimore, *The Desert Road to Turkestan*, with a new Introduction by David Lattimore (New York: Kodansha America, [1929] 1995), p. xv. See also Lattimore's *Studies in Frontier History* (London: Oxford University Press, 1962), p. 12.

INDEX

ABOUT THE AUTHOR

———

Robert D. Kaplan is the bestselling author of twenty-two books on foreign affairs and travel translated into many languages, including *The Tragic Mind, Adriatic, The Good American, The Revenge of Geography, Asia's Cauldron, Monsoon, The Coming Anarchy,* and *Balkan Ghosts.* He holds the Robert Strausz-Hupé Chair in Geopolitics at the Foreign Policy Research Institute. For three decades he reported on foreign affairs for *The Atlantic.* He was a member of the Pentagon's Defense Policy Board and the Chief of Naval Operations Executive Panel. *Foreign Policy* magazine twice named him one of the world's Top 100 Global Thinkers.

robertdkaplan.com